SPEAKER'S BOOK OF ILLUSTRATIVE STORIES

•

Edited by
MAXWELL DROKE
and the Editors of QUOTE

DROKE HOUSE
INDIANAPOLIS

Library of Congress Catalogue Card Number: 56-13152
Printed in the United States of America

ABILITY

Near Abingdon, Va., there is a wood carver whose artistic output runs heavily to bears. He carves them swiftly and unerringly from almost any sort of wood, and "primitives" though they are, each one has a remarkably individual bearishness. "I don't see how you do it so easily," I said to him one day, watching his quick knife.

"Well, ma'am," explained the wood carver, "I just look at a little block of wood till I see the b'ar; then I cut away the wood and thar's the b'ar."

—BEULAH PENNELL, in *Reader's Digest*.

✤ ✤ ✤

At a dinner in Hollywood to celebrate his birthday, Charlie Chaplin entertained guests throughout the evening by imitating people they knew: men women and children, his chauffeur, his Jap servants, his secretaries. Finally he sang at the top of his voice an aria from an Italian opera—sang it superbly.

"Why, Charlie, I never knew you could sing so beautifully," my daughter exclaimed.

"I can't sing at all," Chaplin rejoined. "I was only imitating Caruso."

—KONRAD BERCOVICI, in *Good Housekeeping*.

✤ ✤ ✤

Salvador Dali, asked by a visitor about painting technique, said, "To be a great painter, an angel must be touching your wrist when you apply brush to canvas." "But how do you summon this angel?" the visitor asked. "It's difficult to domesticate an angel," replied the artist. "That's a secret known only to a few great painters."

—LEONARD LYONS.

ACCIDENT—Prevention

A chauffeur in an Eastern city was being honored. For a long period of time he had achieved a record unmarred by accident.

Someone asked for his secret.

"Oh," he said, "just stay away from places where accidents are likely to happen!"

✣ ✣ ✣

ACCURACY

When I was a high school student, I was asked to give the Gettysburg Address at a Lincoln's Birthday ceremony. Afterward an old gentleman came up to me. "Son," he said, "I liked the way you gave that speech, but you made the same mistake as everyone else. I heard Mr. Lincoln at Gettysburg so I know what I'm talking about. Everyone says, '*of* the people, *by* the people and *for* the people,' but Mr. Lincoln said, 'of the *people*, by the *people* and for the *people*.' It makes a big difference."

—TED HATLEN, in *Reader's Digest*.

✣ ✣ ✣

For years an old gentleman living in a farmhouse outside St. Louis invited his St. Louis doctor to visit him and enjoy the wonderful hunting. After three vacation trips to the farm, during which he hunted without ever finding his quarry, the tanned, healthy doctor asked his host: "Why do you keep saying the hunting is wonderful out here? How can the hunting be good when I never find anything?"

"Doc," was the reply, "it's the huntin' that's good—not the findin'!"

—LEONARD LYONS.

✣ ✣ ✣

She was a college graduate trained in thoroughness, accuracy and efficiency. When she applied for a job to a wholesale grocer, he was impressed and engaged her. As her first task, she was told to make a complete inventory of his stock, beginning with the goods in the cellar.

Three days passed. The merchant saw her come and go each

day, and finally, wondering what she was doing all that time down in the cellar, he went to find out. She was working at his stock of peanuts, pretty, flushed, and energetic. Asked how she was getting along, she wiped her dewy forehead and said, "I've had time to count only a few sacks, but I'm sure my figures are exact. So far, there are precisely 26,657,871 peanuts."

—Gelett Burgess.

✣ ✣ ✣

A surveyor, working around an Army post on the edge of a western town, became acquainted with the soldier who fired the cannon for retreat each evening. The surveyor questioned the soldier: "Do you fire this cannon at the same time each evening?"

"Yes," the soldier replied. "At six o'clock on the dot, and I time it carefully with this watch. I check it every day by the jeweler's clock, about two blocks from here."

Several days later the surveyor entered the jeweler's shop and began talking to him. "That's a mighty fine clock you have there," he said, indicating the prominent time-piece in the window.

"It keeps perfect time," answered the jeweler. "In fact, that clock hasn't varied a second for two years."

"That's really a wonderful record."

"Yes, and we have a perfect check on it, too. Every evening at exactly six o'clock, they fire a cannon over at the Fort, and this clock is always right on the dot."

—*Continental News.*

✣ ✣ ✣

"Bomber" Harris who softened up German resistance, and helped smash German war industry, could drop a blockbuster—verbal variety—very neatly on his own. A statistical report of the forecasts prepared by the meteorological department was handed Harris.

The officer displaying it remarked proudly, "You will see, sir, that we are dead right on forty-six per cent of occasions."

"And have you realized," inquired Harris drily, "that if you had forecast exactly the opposite throughout, you would have been correct on fifty-four per cent?"

—Irving Hoffman, *Hollywood Reporter.*

✣ ✣ ✣

The editor of a weekly paper was the bitter enemy of abbreviations that constantly showed up in news releases. So when he got a story telling that a concert featured Mozart's Twelfth Mass, he edited it to read, "Twelfth, Massachusetts."

—*Louisville Courier-Journal Magazine.*

✣ ✣ ✣

In a restaurant at Columbia University, a refugee professor, speaking English with that acquired precision which so often shames the native-born, ordered "figs and cream." The waitress brought a dish of figs covered with cream. "I ordered figs *and* cream," the professor protested.

"There they are," she retorted.

"But this is figs *with* cream," he persisted.

"But I don't see . . ." she began, bewildered.

"Madam," said the professor, icily, "would you say a woman and child were the same as a woman with child?"

—*Reader's Digest.*

✣ ✣ ✣

Abraham Lincoln won many arguments through sheer force of logic. On one occasion, having failed to make a stubborn opponent see the error of his reasoning, Lincoln said, "Well, let's see. How many legs has a cow?"

"Four, of course," came the ready answer.

"That's right," said Lincoln. "Now suppose we call the cow's tail a leg, how many legs would the cow have?"

"Why, five, of course."

"Now that's where you're wrong," said Lincoln. "Simply calling a cow's tail a leg doesn't make it a leg."

✣ ✣ ✣

A guide in Yosemite National Park was conducting a group of travellers through the valley. As they rode through the big trees, one of the tourists asked the guide if he knew how old the trees were.

"Yes, indeed," he replied with a touch of pride. "Them giant trees is three thousand and six years old, goin' on three thousand and seven."

Amazed at the accurate knowledge the old fellow displayed, the persistent tourist asked, "But how do you know the number exactly?"

"Wal, you see, it's this way," the old guide explained. "There was a smart young lady out here from the East, and she told me them big trees was three thousand years old. And that was just a little over six years ago, so I figger they must be goin' on three thousand and seven by now."

✤ ✤ ✤

A retired admiral looked from a window of his country place and saw his two young sons happily munching green apples. He shouted to the older boy, "How many apples have you eaten?"

There was a silence that smacked of mutiny. He bellowed again, "How many of those apples have you eaten?"

The younger son slowly turned and said with all the dignity of his seven years, "Please don't roar at him, father—he's counting."

—*English Digest,* London.

✤ ✤ ✤

A small boy sitting in the rear of a classroom appeared to be daydreaming. The teacher was curious.

"Do you have trouble hearing, Johnny?" she asked.

"No, ma'am," the boy replied politely. "I have trouble listening."

—*Wisconsin Journal of Education.*

✤ ✤ ✤

ACHIEVEMENT

There was a dignity in Mrs. Allen's gaunt, weathered New England face that you never forgot. Ever since her husband's death left her with two boys to raise, she had run Allen's General Store on Main Street. With the help of her older son, a conscientious, hardworking boy, she built up such a good business that the younger one was able to go through college. He became a famous Chicago surgeon.

A few years ago a summer visitor arrived who "had no idea that the mother of the great Dr. Allen, was right here in *town*." The moment she found out she hurried down to the General Store, where Mrs. Allen was waiting on customers. After purchasing some sun glasses and chatting with Mrs. Allen for several minutes, the customer, assuming her most ingratiating smile, said, "And of course you must be so proud of your son."

"Which one?" asked Mrs. Allen.

—SALLY LORIMER.

✤ ✤ ✤

Don't think that you're either too young or too old to do great things: Jefferson was 33 when he drafted the Declaration of Independence. Benjamin Franklin was 26 when he wrote *Poor Richard's Almanac*. Charles Dickens was 24 when he began his *Pickwick Papers* and 25 when he wrote *Oliver Twist*. McCormick was 23 when he invented the reaper; and Newton 24 when he formulated the law of gravitation.

But—Emanuel Kant at 74 wrote his finest philosophical works. Verdi at 80 produced *Falstaff* and at 85 *Ave Maria*. Goethe at 80 completed *Faust*. Tennyson at 80 wrote *Crossing the Bar*. Michelangelo completed his greatest work at 87. Titian at 98 painted the historic picture *Battle of Lepanto*. Justice Holmes at 90 was still writing brilliant opinions.

—LOUIS NIZER, in *Pageant*.

✤ ✤ ✤

A man who had a cello with a single string used to bow on it for hours at a time, always holding his finger in the same place. His wife endured this for months. Finally in desperation she said, "I have observed that when others play that instrument there are four strings, and the players move their fingers about continuously."

The man stopped for a moment, looked at his wife wisely, and told her, "Of course the others have four strings and move their fingers about constantly. They are looking for the place. I've found it!"

—WILLIAM SAROYAN, *Fables* (Harcourt Brace).

ACTION

To prove his point that action may be more important than analysis, Albert Einstein used to tell the parable of the toad and the centipede.

One day when the centipede was proudly displaying his hundred legs, the mischievous four-legged frog ventured to ask him a question:

"When you wish to get from Here to There," he queried, "which of your one hundred legs do you move first?"

The centipede began to think. He tried first one leg, then the other. To his consternation he discovered that he was unable to move a single leg. He could no longer walk at all!

✤ ✤ ✤

During the Festival of Britain, Sir Winston Churchill visited the Dome of Discovery, and was taken up in a lift to a telescope where he was told he could view the outer spaces. He viewed them briefly and then said, "Take me down. I am more interested in what is happening on the earth."

—VIRGINIA COWLES.

✤ ✤ ✤

An old Connecticut farmer, as rough and rugged as his stony acres, was asked if he hoped for the best. With eyes flashing, he replied shortly, "No; I don't hope for it—I hop for it!"

—JEROME CLEVELAND.

✤ ✤ ✤

An old man was asked how he managed to overcome the obstacles in his path to success.

"There's no trick to it," he smiled. "You know, when trouble is so high you can't climb over it, so wide you can't walk around it, so deep you can't dig under it, the only way to beat it is to duck your head and wade right through it."

—S. MARTINO.

✤ ✤ ✤

Dr. Samuel Johnson, English poet and man of letters, hated to hear others complain. He once said, "I hate a fellow whom pride, or cowardice, or laziness drives into a corner, and who does nothing, when he is there, but sit and *growl;* let him come out as I do and *bark.*"

✣ ✣ ✣

When Orson Welles, after several centuries of preparation for pictures that were never made, finally decided on *Citizen Kane,* he tested dozens of Hollywood stars and finally reached Dorothy Comingore.

"The job is yours," said Welles simply.

"But listen . . ." she began defensively.

"The job is yours," repeated Welles.

"Now, Mr. Welles," insisted the actress. "I think I ought to tell you something. I'm going to have a baby."

"When?"

"About seven months," said the expectant mother, timidly.

"All the better!" Welles yelled ecstatically. "If you start in the picture it'll really prove to those bums that I'm going to finish it on time."

—Kyle Crichton, in *Collier's.*

✣ ✣ ✣

Last summer, hoping to inspire his workers with promptness and energy, a New York executive hung a number of signs reading "DO IT NOW" around his factory and office. When he was asked some weeks later how his staff had reacted, he shook his head sadly.

"I don't even like to talk about it," he said. "The cashier skipped with $4000, the head bookkeeper eloped with the best secretary I ever had, three typists asked for an increase, the factory workers voted to go out on strike, and the office boy joined the Navy."

—Sid Ascher, in *Caravan.*

✣ ✣ ✣

A young doctor chose to make Japan his field of work. His friends tried to dissuade him from going there.

"Look," they said, "you are absolutely helpless against the suffering of that giant nation. You disappear in that vast mass of humanity. What can you do about their epidemics? What can you accomplish against war, famine, flood?"

As he started up the gangplank, the young man gave them his confident answer: "When it is dark about me, I do not curse at the darkness; I just light my candle."

—THOMAS DREIER.

✣ ✣ ✣

Walter S. Knudsen was famous for getting things done without flapping. One day a worried assistant rushed in. A certain important report was missing. What would he do?

"There are two kinds of reports," said Knudsen quietly. "One says you can't do it. The other kind says it has been done. The first is no good. The second you don't need. So let's hear no more about it."

—*Tit-Bits,* London.

✣ ✣ ✣

Professor David L. Thompson, of McGill University, has dug up a distressing bit of philosophy. "Did it ever occur to you," he says, "that our language is full of suggestions that it is a privilege to work sitting down?

"We respect our chairman; we honor the throne; we speak of a professor's chair, a seat in parliament. The lawyer looks to the judge's bench; and the Turks speak of their divan, and the Hebrews of the sanhedrin, all in the same sense. Even the word president means the man in the best seat. All this betokens a habit of mind, respecting the man who does his work sitting down."

But actually the man who gets off his royal cushion and goes out into the field, pounds the highways and byways and sees what is going on—he is the success. Why not devise a new title of merit—Stander, Pavement-Pounder, Get-Arounder, or some such to elevate to the pinnacle where he belongs—the out*standing* guy that stands up, goes out and gets ideas?

—*Printers' Ink.*

✣ ✣ ✣

ADVERSITY

My kindly and frugal father taught me to entertain myself with simple things. One of my childhood hobbies was to collect the cocoons of the Cecropia moth, and in the spring to watch the moths emerge as things of night beauty. Their struggle to escape from confinement always excited my pity, but one day, with a fine pair of scissors, Father cut the imprisoning silk away from one such creature, helping it to emerge. In no time the moth was dead.

"Roy," my father said, "the struggle the moth makes to come out of the cocoon drives the poison from its body. If that poison is not driven out, the moth will die. When people struggle for what they want they become stronger and better, but if things come too easily they become weak, and something in them seems to die."

I know I have been able to bear adversity better because my father so vividly taught me this profound truth.

—LeRoy V. Brant

✤ ✤ ✤

One day a naturalist observed a beautiful butterfly fluttering as though in distress. It seemed to be caught, and could not release itself. The naturalist, thinking to release the beautiful thing, took hold of its wings and set it free. It flew a few feet, and fell dead.

The man picked it up. Then he discovered the cause of its death—the life blood was flowing from the tiny arteries of its wings. Nature had fastened it to its chrysalis, and was allowing it to flutter so that its wings might become strong. It was the muscle-developing process that nature was giving it, so that it might have an unusual range among the flowers.

✤ ✤ ✤

ADVERTISING

Little Charles had never been outside of the large city where he was born. Then one day he was invited to go for an auto ride into the country with his uncle and aunt. A sudden shower came up, then stopped. Charlie spotted a rainbow, the first one he had ever seen in his young life.

His aunt urged him always to remember the beautiful sight.

"Sure," he said, "it's beautiful. But what is it supposed to advertise?"

—*Camillus.*

✣ ✣ ✣

A British industrialist and a newspaperman were discussing advertising, pro and con.

Said the industrialist: "I simply don't believe in it. It may be all right for firms starting up with something new. But you see, my firm is more than 100 years old. Everybody knows all about us. Why do we need to spend money on advertising?"

Just then the church bells began to ring. The newspaperman said: "That church has existed for thousands of years. But it still rings a bell every Sunday to remind people of its existence."

✣ ✣ ✣

A lion met a tiger as they drank beside a pool. Said the tiger, "Tell me why you're roaring like a fool."

"That's not foolish," said the lion with a twinkle in his eyes. "They call me king of all the beasts because I advertise."

A rabbit heard them talking and ran home like a streak. He thought he'd try the lion's plan, but his roar was a squeak. A fox came to investigate—had luncheon in the woods. So when you advertise, my friends—

Be sure you've got the goods!

✣ ✣ ✣

At a luncheon table two executives were discussing advertising. One said to the other, "Well, do you find your advertising is getting results?"

The other replied, "I sure do. The other day we advertised for a night watchman, and the next night we were robbed."

✣ ✣ ✣

"I'll say your ads bring results," a woman wrote to the *Alabama Beacon*. "My lost dog has been returned—with six pups."

✣ ✣ ✣

AGE

One time when the late Harvey W. Wiley—noted pure food authority—was in his 90's, the Metropolitan Life Insurance Co.

had him as its main speaker at a big dinner in Washington for its representatives and friends.

The chairman introduced the high brass of the company who were present and explained the absence of this vice president and that vice president by saying that they were 70 and that travel and evening activities were too much of a strain for them. When Dr. Wiley was introduced he remarked: "All this talk about vice presidents being too old at 70! Why at 70 I was expecting additions to my family!" And he was.

—*Senior Citizen.*

✣ ✣ ✣

When Oliver Wendell Holmes was in his 80s, regularly each year the newspapers announced that he was planning to retire. It annoyed him vastly.

"The old gentleman," Taft called Holmes. Strange, how the old gentleman's words struck home to the nation, how deeply they had begun to bite! Even men who would not have dreamed of reading a legal opinion had become somehow aware of him.

One day a newspaperman, seeking copy, decided to walk around Capitol Square and ask passers-by if they had heard of Justice Holmes.

A mechanic in overalls was sitting on a bench reading the sports page. The reporter strolled up. "Holmes?" the mechanic said. "Oh, sure! He's the young judge on the Supreme Court that's always disagreeing with the old guys."

—CATHERINE DRINKER BOWEN, in *Yankee From Olympus* (Little, Brown and Co.).

✣ ✣ ✣

AGGRESSIVENESS

Darryl Zanuck is one Hollywood producer who doesn't like to be agreed with too easily. One day in Caliente he was refreshing himself after producing *Noah's Ark,* an Old Testament hodge podge which was doing badly at the box office, when suddenly a kick bounced him against the bar.

"What was that for?" he demanded, glaring at the kicker, a writer named Arthur Caesar.

"For taking a book that's been a smash hit for 5000 years and making a flop out of it," said Caesar. Zanuck, who admires aggressive people, gave Caesar a contract on the spot.

—*Life.*

✤ ✤ ✤

AGRICULTURE

Asked if fertilizer would stimulate a certain plant's growth, a farmer replied: "I can't rightly say for sure. I've never been able to understand whether the stuff actually stimulates the plants or whether it is just so downright repulsive that they try to grow away from it."

✤ ✤ ✤

ALTRUISM

While in New York recently, I saw a small truck loaded with glassware back out of a factory driveway into the path of a large truck. Most of the glass was broken in the crash and the driver seemed on the verge of tears. A big crowd gathered and one benevolent old gentleman said compassionately, "I suppose you will have to make this good out of your own pocket?"

"I'm afraid so," lamented the driver.

"Well, well," said the old gentleman. "Here's a dollar for you. Let me pass your hat and I dare say some of these kind people will help you out too."

Over a hundred people dropped bills into the outstretched hat. The driver, stowing the money away as the crowd dispersed, nodded toward the retreating back of the benevolent old gentleman. "That's what I call a real smart man. He's my boss."

—James P. Hodges, in "Life in These United States."

✤ ✤ ✤

AMBITION

In the railroad terminal of an eastern city, an old lady and a small girl sat knitting side by side. The needles ran swiftly and surely between the old lady's worn fingers, while the little girl, biting her tongue in concentration, was trying to pick up a dropped stitch. Finally, with tears in her eyes, she handed her knitting to the old lady. "I'm in a mess again, Grandma. Please fix it for me."

In no time the knitting was returned to her, all damage repaired. The little girl sighed in admiration. "You know, Grandma," she said, "sometimes I wish I was blind too."

—Christine Nelson

✤ ✤ ✤

Upon graduation from college, Roy Chapman Andrews, the explorer, had his heart set on getting a job in a museum. He approached the director of the American Museum of Natural History in New York. "I'll even wash floors if I have to," he pleaded.

"With your training you wouldn't really wash floors, would you?" asked the director.

"Not any kind of floors," admitted Andrews, "but museum floors are different."

—*Rotecho.*

✤ ✤ ✤

AMERICA

Approaching Pella, Iowa—an enterprising community founded by Dutch immigrants in the middle of the last century—I passed a large farmhouse with a shady avenue leading to it. Over the gate were these Dutch words: WIE HAD HET GEDACHT?

Later I asked what the sign meant and was told that the prosperous farm belonged to a Dutch immigrant who had arrived penniless in the United States. He started as a farmhand, and America had so exceeded his hopes as a land of opportunity that he could think of no more suitable name for his farm than: WHO COULD HAVE THOUGHT IT?

—Cornelius Nicholas Bakker

✤ ✤ ✤

An American labor delegation visited the Russian Skoda works. The American visitors asked their guides: "To whom does this factory belong?" The answer was: "We, the people, own it."

They asked: "Who owns the machinery?" and the guides answered: "We, the people, do."

The Americans asked: "Who gets the profits?" and were assured: "We, the people, do."

They saw three large cars in the courtyard and asked: "Who owns those three cars?" The guides informed them: "One is owned by the Commissar for Defense, the second is owned by the Chairman of the Workers Committee, and the third belongs to the representative from Moscow, who is visiting here now."

Then a Skoda delegation arrived in America on a tour of the industrial plants, and the American labor leader showed them through the Ford factory.

"Who owns this factory?" asked the Skoda men. The American told them: "Mr. Ford does."

"Who owns the machinery?" they asked, and were told, "Mr. Ford does."

"Who gets the profits?" they continued, and were told, "Mr. Ford does."

Then, in the adjoining parking lot, they saw 30,000 cars parked and asked: "Who owns all those cars?" The American told them: "We, the people."

—BURNETT HERSHEY.

✣ ✣ ✣

The greatness of America was the subject of an essay contest won by Blythe Ann Johnson, a Litchfield, Minnesota, high school freshman. She wrote:

"America is great because we drag our faults into the open for all to see and criticize and help to correct—we do not hush-hush and pretend all is well, to look beautiful outwardly while rotting from the inside—this makes America noisy and our faults public, but it is clean and healthy."

This explanation of America's greatness isn't based on wealth and possessions. A 15-year-old girl could see that the value of America lies, not in our material wealth, but in the capacity of our people to build from within; to unashamedly analyze ourselves and make corrections on the basis of that analysis; to subordinate false prides and build a kind of strength that no amount of foreign interference can weaken.

—*Highways of Happiness.*

✤ ✤ ✤

ANGER

The cook, fresh from the Ozarks, was discussing her daughter's behavior: "I found out she ain't sick at all. It's just a case of the pokin' grits. That no-count man she wanted to marry left town with another woman, and my daughter's madder than mad, pokin' her chin out and grittin' her teeth. Ain't nothing the matter with her but the pokin' grits."

—Dr. Ruth Salmon.

✤ ✤ ✤

A Quaker farmer did not believe in violence of any sort. But he found his temper severely tested when the old cow not only knocked him down but spilled the full pail of milk as well.

After struggling to his feet and brushing himself off, working all the while to control his anger, he said through taut lips, "I'll not strike thee, dumb beast, I'll not kick thee—but I'll twist thy blankety-blank-blank tail!"

✤ ✤ ✤

ANIMALS

A noted scientist, whose research dealt with the careful measurement of animal intelligence, set to work to devise a series of four learning problems to test the intelligence of chimpanzees by noting which ones could solve the progressively more difficult problems and thus secure a reward for their efforts.

The chimps were duly put through the four learning tasks, and most of them succeeded but at different rates of speed, which would have been the case with human learners. However, much to the surprise and consternation of the scientists, one extra bright chimp actually showed them how to solve the problem series by still a fifth method!

—John A. Blake, *Nature Magazine.*

APOLOGY

In the good old days, a king and queen were so fond of their court jester they often had him as their sole dinner guest. On one such occasion, the jester asserted: "An apology can be worse than an insult."

"Either you prove that," remarked the royal host, "or I'll have you beheaded."

After dinner, his Royal Highness leaned over to pet his spaniel. Wham! The jester landed a lusty kick on the royal pants, then quickly cried: "Pardon me, Sire, I thought you were the Queen."

—Alex F. Osborn.

✤ ✤ ✤

APPRECIATION

As a simple, unpretentious admirer of fine art, Elbert Hubbard derived much pleasure from visiting the great art galleries. One day he was admiring a certain priceless painting when a friend chidingly remarked, "Why do you allow yourself to become so enthused over things you can never afford to own?"

"I would rather be able to appreciate things I cannot have," replied the sage, "than to have things I am not able to appreciate."

—*Christian Science Monitor*.

✤ ✤ ✤

ARGUMENT

It is told that two Chinese got into an argument, words were bandied about and finally blows were struck. The fighters were immediately taken to the clubrooms, where the affair was aired in the open.

For fighting in public, both men were fined. But the man who struck the first blow was fined more heavily. He was the real offender.

"What was the matter with your father?" it was asked him. "Was he so lacking in scholarship that he did not teach you the proper use of words? Are you so lacking in arguments, so poor in the knowledge of poetic phrases, that you must strike a blow to win your point?"

—CARL GLICK, *Shake Hands with the Dragon* (Whittlesey House, McGraw-Hill).

✤ ✤ ✤

ART

An old artist, in Italy, called one of his pupils aside. "I have long been working on what I hoped would be my masterpiece, but I am both old and ill. Thou must finish it. Do thy best."

The young man, appalled by the task, breathed a fervent prayer for help, and then began to paint. After several weeks, the picture was finished. With ecstasy the old man gazed upon it. "Thou hast verily done well, my son. I paint no more." And Leonardo da Vinci had begun to climb the ladder of fame.

✤ ✤ ✤

Dante Gabriel Rossetti, the English painter and poet, used as much imagination in selling his pictures as in making them. One day, after he had completed a canvas, he asked a friend to accompany him to the zoo.

"Why the zoo?"

"I want to borrow an elephant to wash my windows," explained Rossetti.

"To wash your windows!" said the surprised friend; "that's ridiculous!"

"Of course it is," agreed Rossetti, "but it sells pictures. You see, when people observe such a spectacle in front of my house, they gather in great numbers, and many come into my house and buy my pictures."

—*Sunshine*.

✤ ✤ ✤

Anyone who says artists aren't practical people has not heard of a well-known Massachusetts painter who was solicited by his church for a sizable donation.

"I haven't any money," said the artist, "but I will give you a $200 picture."

But when all the contributions were tallied, there was still a budget deficit. The minister made a strong appeal to the congregation to increase the donations if they possibly could.

"All right," said the artist willingly. "I will do my share. I'll raise the price of the picture to $300."

✤ ✤ ✤

The composer, Maurice Ravel, was an enthusiastic collector of rare books and prints, fine porcelains, and other *objets d'art*. In his study, occupying a place of honor on a pedestal, stood his most treasured possession—a ball of smoked crystal, which he pointed to with great pride.

"Maurice," his guests would whisper in awe, "where did you get it? It's exquisite!"

"You really think so?" he would answer modestly. "Well, it's just a burned-out electric bulb."

—*Titmus Tidings.*

✤ ✤ ✤

ATHEISM

An atheist, in a dining car, sat next to a clergyman. Deliberately he started a conversation calculated to embarrass the man of God.

"Are you a clergyman, sir?"

"I am."

"Preach out of the Bible, do you?"

"I do."

"I suppose you find a great many things in the Bible you cannot understand?"

"Some things, yes."

"Well, what do you do with them?"

"I do what I am doing with the bones from this steak. When I come to a piece of bone I just lay it aside and go on eating the meat, and let some fool insist on choking himself with the bones."

—*Tarbell's Teachers' Guide* (Revell).

AUTOMATION

A Ford company executive was showing union-leader Walter Reuther around one of the Ford units that had been newly "automated."

"How're you going to collect union dues from those machines, Walter?" the Ford man asked.

By way of answer, Reuther asked, "And how're *you* going to sell them cars?"

✤ ✤ ✤

BALANCE

"Talking about dories," the Old Salt said, "fellers do the craziest things—'tickly if they don't know surf." He chuckled. "I 'member—forty years ago 'twas, I guess—the Gloucestermen used to come in here every once in a while durin' an easterly. They'd anchor off shore and row in for the mail or a paper.

"T'any rate this one time—'twas in the winter—two fellers made to come ashore in a dory, rowin' the bow and center thwarts. Did all right, too, till they came to the breakers. She rode the first roller pretty good. Then she started up the second one. Goin' up was all right. But when she passed the crest with all that weight forrard, her nose dug in. It dug right in, and over she went, stern after stem like a windmill. There was a couple of pretty wet fishermen crawled up on the beach that day. Cold, too. Ice all over their oilskins." He chuckled again, though not without sympathy.

"And all because there was nobody aft?" I asked.

"Yessir. All because there was nobody aft for balance."

—Lockhart Amerman, *Presbyterian Life.*

✤ ✤ ✤

BEAUTY

One evening long ago in Amherst, Massachusetts, Edward Dickinson, father of poetess Emily Dickinson, rang the town fire bell. As the excited townspeople poured from their houses shouting, "Where's the fire?" he calmly pointed to a gorgeous pink and gold sunset coloring the western sky. He had summoned his neighbors to share his pleasure.

—HALFORD E. LUCCOCK, *Like a Mighty* (Oxford University Press).

✣ ✣ ✣

Jean Francois Millet, the famous artist, declared that beauty does not lie in the face. "It lies," he said, "in the harmony between man and his industry. Beauty is expression. When I paint a mother I try to render her beautiful by the mere look she gives her child."

✣ ✣ ✣

BEHAVIOR

All day long the weary elevator operator had been patiently answering questions the department store shoppers had thrust upon him. Just before closing time a voice from the rear of the crowded car asked, "Suppose the elevator cables broke, would we go up or down?"

Unable to compose himself any longer, the operator snapped, "That, my dear lady, depends entirely on the kind of life you have led."

—*O'Bannon's Between Calls.*

✣ ✣ ✣

"Daddy," said little Jimmy, "please read to me!"

But daddy was busy with his own book. To divert his son, he took a map of the world from his desk and cut it up into a jig-saw puzzle. He carefully mixed up the pieces before giving the puzzle to his son. "There," he said, "that will keep you busy most of the evening."

In less than thirty minutes, the boy came back saying he had finished. The father could scarcely believe his ears. But the boy took him to the table and showed him the map, with every piece in place.

"Jimmy, how did you do this so quickly and so well?"

"Well, Daddy," answered the boy, "on the other side of the

map was the picture of a man. I put the man together, and when I made the man right, the world was right."

✤ ✤ ✤

BELIEF

In April, 1904, the Wrights began to carry on practice flights in a cow pasture on a farm near their Dayton home. Though these experiments were the big scientific news of the century, almost nothing was ever said about them by the newspapers, not even by those in Dayton. This was not because the Wrights were secretive. They could hardly have kept secret what they were doing in that open field, for there was an interurban car line and a public highway on one side of it and a railroad on another.

Dan Kumler was city editor of James M. Cox's *Daily News* in Dayton during those years. "People who had passed the pasture on interurban cars used to come to our office," Kumler recalled, "to inquire why there was nothing in the paper about the flights. Such callers got to be a nuisance."

"Why wasn't there anything in the paper?" I asked.

"We just didn't believe it," confessed Kumler, grinning.

—FRED C. KELLY, *Harper's Magazine.*

✤ ✤ ✤

A clergyman was once asked by a doctor if he preached the salvation of souls. Upon receiving an affirmative reply, the doctor persisted:

"Did you ever see a soul? Did you ever hear a soul? Did you ever taste a soul? Did you ever smell a soul?" To all of these he received negative responses. But when the doctor asked, "Did you ever feel a soul?" the clergyman replied that he had done so.

"Well," summarized the doctor, "there are four of the five senses against you. So I must cling to my doubts."

Then it was the clergyman's turn. "You are a doctor of medicine," he said. "It is your business to treat pains. Did you ever see, hear, taste or smell a pain? No; of course you haven't. You have only felt pain. There are four senses to one against you. Yet you know, and I know, that there is pain. By the same evidence, I know that the soul exists."

BIBLE

Some time ago, a man took his worn New Testament to a bookbinder to have it bound with a fine Morocco leather cover, and to have "The New Testament" printed on the edge in gold-leaf letters.

At the appointed time, he returned to the shop to find his New Testament beautifully bound. The bookbinder had one apology.

"I did not have small enough type in my shop to print out fully the words on the edge, so I abbreviated them."

The man wondered how such an abbreviation could be made. He turned the book over and looked on the edge. There, standing out dynamically, were the letters—T. N. T.!

—*Evangel.*

✤ ✤ ✤

George Adam Smith, when lecturing before a group of ministers, read a passage from the Bible so effectively that his hearers broke into applause. Angrily Smith paused and said, "Gentlemen, we accept God's word. We do not approve it."

✤ ✤ ✤

"What would you think," asked a skeptic of a friend, "if I should tell you that in ten minutes I could produce arguments that would utterly annihilate the Bible?"

Replied his friend: "About the same thing I would think if I saw a gnat crawling up the side of Mount Washington, threatening to smash the whole thing with his weight."

—*Tarbell's Teachers' Guide* (*Revell*).

✤ ✤ ✤

Voltaire said that in 100 years the Bible would be a forgotten book, found only in the museums. When the 100 years were up, Voltaire's home was occupied by the Geneva Bible Society.

—*Friendly Chats.*

✤ ✤ ✤

An African embassy, bearing costly presents to Queen Victoria, was rec'd with royal honors. In response to the question they brought from their Prince as to the secret of England's greatness, Victoria produced a richly bound copy of the Bible and sent it back with this message: "Tell your Prince that this book is the secret of England's greatness."

—DAVID O. MEARS, *Signs of the Times*.

✣ ✣ ✣

BOASTFULNESS

In the woods of the Far West there once lived a bear who could take it or let it alone. He would go into a bar and have just two drinks. But finally he took to drinking by himself most of the day. He would reel home at night, kick over the umbrella stand, knock down the lamps and ram his elbows through the windows. Then he would collapse on the floor. His wife was greatly distressed and his children were very frightened.

At length the bear saw the error of his ways and began to reform. In the end he became a famous teetotaler. He would tell everybody about the awful effects of drink and would boast about how strong and well he had become since he gave up the stuff. To demonstrate this, he would turn cartwheels in the house, kicking over the umbrella stand, knocking down the lamps, and ramming his elbows through the windows. Then he would lie down on the floor, tired by this healthful exercise, and go to sleep. His wife was greatly distressed and his children were very frightened.

Moral: You might as well fall flat on your face as lean over too far backward.

—JAMES THURBER, *Fables for Our Time* (Harper).

✣ ✣ ✣

BOOKS

"I want to buy that book in the front window called *How to Captivate Men,*" said the little girl to the book salesman. The salesman looked dubiously at the child.

"Really," he said, "that's not the sort of book for you at all. What do you want it for?"

The child was insistent. "I want to give it to my daddy for a birthday present."

The salesman was determined to alter her request. "Surely,"

he said, "there are hundreds of other books that your daddy would rather have than that."

"No," said the child firmly, "I know he'd like that particular one. You see, he's a private detective."

✣ ✣ ✣

BOOKS—Reading

The people of Franklin, Massachusetts, once wrote to Benjamin Franklin: "We have named our town after you and would like a donation of a sum of money, in order that we may put a bell in the church steeple."

Franklin replied: "I am very much honored, very glad indeed to send you a sum of money, only don't buy a bell with it. Buy a public library, because I have always preferred sense to sound."

A hundred and fifty years later, William Lyon Phelps, then a professor at Yale, became curious about that gift. He wrote to the librarian at Franklin, Massachusetts. She replied that the donation had been received in 1786. With the money the town bought 116 books. Of that group, she said, 86 volumes still remained in the library!

✣ ✣ ✣

BOY SCOUTS

A young lad had joined the Boy Scouts and his family was delighted by the way the youngster took hold of his new duties, like doing his good turn each day and behaving much better around home. And his very bad habit of procrastination became a thing of the past. One day his father said to him:

"Son, I see you have finally broken that habit of procrastinating."

"That's right," said the small tenderfoot, "and that's why I always do my good deed the first thing in the morning and get the darned thing over with."

✣ ✣ ✣

BREVITY

Called on for an impromptu speech at a dinner one night, a Yale graduate bethought himself of his alma mater, and lauded her by showing that the "Y" stood for "Youth," when all might enjoy the benefits of college. "A" stood for the "Appreciation" of fine things which the college makes possible. "L" for "Loyalty," the stem for all endeavor.

After about thirty minutes of that sort of thing, he arrived at and ended with the "E," which he said stood for "Efficiency" of a Yale graduate.

Three seats down, a drowsing listener aroused himself sufficiently to murmur to his neighbor, "Thank goodness, he didn't attend the Massachusetts Institute of Technology!"

✣ ✣ ✣

A British fledgling reporter had been reprimanded for his overlong accounts and told to be brief. His next story was turned in as follows:

"A shocking incident occurred last night. Sir Reggy Blank, a guest at Lady Briny's ball, complained of feeling ill, took his hat, his coat, his departure, no notice of his friends, a taxi, a pistol from his pocket and finally, his life. Nice chap. Regrets and all that."

—JOHN CANNING, JR., quoted in *The Quill.*

✣ ✣ ✣

There is too much speaking in the world, and almost all of it is too long. The Lord's Prayer, the Twenty-third Psalm, Lincoln's Gettysburg Address, are three great literary treasures that will last forever; no one of them is as long as 300 words. With such striking illustrations of the power of brevity it is amazing that speakers never learn to be brief.

—BRUCE BARTON, in *Collier's.*

✣ ✣ ✣

Clarence Budington Kelland's antipathy to florid introductions applied to introductions of himself. Once on a big radio hookup, the program director soared to heights of hyperbole, taking five of the 15 minutes to give Bud a build-up. Comparing Kelland to the great writers since Shakespeare, he wound up with a panegyric of Bud's books for boys. "And now, Mr. Kelland," he concluded, "will you step to the microphone and tell the world exactly what you think of the young people of America."

Bud stood up. "They're swell," he said—and sat down. And not all the director's sweating could cue him back on again. The public loved it.

—Oren Arnold, in *The Baltimore Sunday Sun.*

✣ ✣ ✣

In my youth I read with admiration the reply of an editor to this question: "What is the longest word in the English language?" Answer: Pro-antidisestablishmentarianism. But alas and alack, I am now a sadder and wiser man. My favorite editor missed the mark by a thousand and one syllables.

Yes, let us face it—the longest word in any language is the "One More Word" of public speakers in general and of preachers in particular.

—Glenn H. Asquith, in *Christian Herald.*

✣ ✣ ✣

Dr. Hu Shih, Chinese ambassador to the U. S. at one time, is not only a scholar and a diplomat, but a wit, and he enjoys using American slang. A lady once cabled him an invitation to her home in Hawaii, beginning in her best oriental manner, "O sage and honorable sir, deign to honor our humble board," etc. for 300 words.

Dr. Hu Shih promptly cabled: "Can do. Hu Shih."

—*World Digest.*

✣ ✣ ✣

BROTHERHOOD

A famine was on in the land and a beggar on a street corner reached out to Tolstoy, who was passing by. Russia's great man stopped, searched for a coin but found none. With genuine sorrow, he said: "Don't be angry with me, my brother. I have nothing with me."

The beggar's face lighted up as he replied, "But you called me brother—that is a great gift."

—*Northwestern Christian Advocate.*

Two small boys were fighting on the playground. By the time the principal arrived, an older girl had separated them. "They're all right now," she said. "I don't know what made them act like this. They're cousins but they fought as if they were brothers."

—HELEN HEARN, *Instructor*.

✤ ✤ ✤

There is a legend in the Talmud of a traveler coming at twilight to a camping-place. As he looked off in the distance he saw a strange object. Through the gathering dusk it seemed to take the shape of a terrible monster. He resolved to go closer and see, if possible, what it was. Drawing nearer, he saw that it was a man. Much of his fear vanished then. Thereupon he ventured still closer and found that the object was not only a man like himself, but that it was his own brother!

—GEORGE LE ROY WILLETS.

✤ ✤ ✤

It was sleeting, and slushy underfoot. Pedestrians were hurrying along 42nd Street in New York with their coat collars up about their ears, scarcely glancing at passersby. A young Negro, carrying a heavy valise in one hand and a huge suitcase in the other, was hurrying toward the Grand Central Station, slipping and skidding as he went. Suddenly, a hand reached out and took the valise and at the same time a pleasant but positive voice said to him;

"Let me take one, brother! This is bad weather to have to carry things."

The Negro was reluctant, but the young white man insisted, with the remark, "I'm going your way."

All the way to the station the two chatted like two old friends.

Years later, Booker T. Washington, who told the story, said, "That was my introduction to Theodore Roosevelt."

—*Chaplain*.

✤ ✤ ✤

Cicero warned his hearers not to obtain slaves from the Britons: "They're so stupid and dull." A Moor wrote in the fourteenth century: "These Germans are tall of stature and light of skin, but I have heard it rumored that they do not take baths."

When the Ohio territory applied for statehood, a member of the U. S. Congress said, "They are so rude and unlettered they will never make good citizens." But the British developed empire; the Germans have been outstanding in science, philosophy, music, art; Ohio had given the country seven presidents. Who are we to draw sharp lines between groups, to shut ourselves out from fuller fellowship when the world's new trend must now be toward brotherhood?

—*International Journal of Religious Education.*

✤ ✤ ✤

A somewhat disheveled member of an audience at a church discussion meeting on brotherhood angrily interrupted the speaker, shouting, "Brotherhood has been preached for the last two thousand years, and look at the state of the world!" The speaker promptly replied: "Yes, and water has been in the world a good deal longer than that, and look at the state of your face!"

—REV. REX H. KNOWLES.

✤ ✤ ✤

At a junior high school in New York City, the Youthbuilders, a student organization, were discussing racial and religious discrimination. "Is there any of that in this school?" the leader asked. "Yes, there is!" cried one child. "In the lunchroom, we all sit separate." It was true. Jewish children sat by themselves, and so did Catholics, Negroes, and other special groups.

That, the Youthbuilders decided, was wrong. They asked the principal's permission to start an Honor Table, at which a student would sit by invitation. There were 35 different national backgrounds represented in the school and half a dozen religions, and the club invited a rotation of races and religions to the Honor Table. Many friendships formed across racial and religious lines. That was last year. This year no Honor Table is necessary.

—WEBB WALDRON, in *Future.*

✤ ✤ ✤

CAUTION

Jones was waiting for a bus when a stranger approached and asked the time. Jones ignored him. The stranger repeated the request. Jones continued to ignore him. When the stranger finally walked away, another waiting passenger said curiously:

"That was a perfectly reasonable question. Why didn't you tell him what time it was?"

"Why?" said Jones. "Listen. I'm standing here minding my own business and this guy wants to know what time it is. So maybe I tell him what time it is. Then what? We get to talking, and this guy says, 'How about a drink?' So we have a drink. Then we have some more drinks. So after a while I say, 'How about coming up to my house for a bite to eat?' So we go up to my house, and we're eating ham and cheese in the kitchen when my daughter comes in, and my daughter's a very good-looking girl. So she falls for this guy and he falls for her. Then they get married, and any guy that can't afford a watch I don't want him in my family."

—HERBERT ASBURY.

✤ ✤ ✤

CHALLENGE

Garibaldi, the Italian patriot, warned his men: "I do not promise you ease. I do not promise you comfort. But I do promise you these: hardship, weariness and suffering. And with them I promise you victory."

✤ ✤ ✤

In one of our southern towns there is a public monument to the boll weevil, that pest which nearly destroyed the cotton-raising industry of this country before ways of controlling it were discovered. In view of the boll weevil's evil repute, it seems strange that a monument should be erected to it. This is the story: When the boll weevil first appeared, its depredations were so extensive and alarming many southern agriculturists despaired of ever again being able to raise cotton successfully. In desperation they turned to the development of other crops, and so, in the end, found themselves grateful for the thing that had driven them out of their rut. To them, the boll weevil was a blessing in disguise.

—*Pick-Up.*

CHANCE

I met a lumberjack named Rocky on the street one day and remarked, "You're out of camp early this year."

"I quit," he replied.

"How did you come to do that?"

"Well, I had a hard time deciding what to do. I was tired of working and wanted to go on a binge. Still, I felt I should finish the season in the woods. After bothering about it quite a while I decided to leave it to chance."

"Chance?"

"Yeah. I threw my axe into the air. If the axe came back down I was to quit."

—LON WOODRUM, *Reader's Digest.*

✣ ✣ ✣

CHARACTER

During the days of the First World War Enrico Caruso was asked if he would sing at a concert for the benefit of servicemen. The chairman who extended the invitation said, "Of course, Mr. Caruso, as this is a charity affair, we would not expect you to do your best. Your name will draw the crowd. I would suggest that you merely sing some selection requiring little strength or skill."

With some vehemence the great tenor replied, "Caruso never does less than his best!"

✣ ✣ ✣

Cardinal Richelieu is said to have been an extraordinarily good judge of human character. "I've always marveled at how correctly you size people up," said a friend. "How do you do it?"

"With pictures," explained the French statesman. "I have two sets of paintings in my office. On one side of the room are hung beautiful landscapes and warm domestic scenes; on the other wall are violent scenes of battle. When I see a man carefully scrutinizing bloody scenes, I know he is a peaceful man at heart and is merely imagining himself a hero. However, those men who study the sentimental pictures are warriors basically, and I recommend them for dangerous or military posts."

—E. E. EDGAR.

✣ ✣ ✣

Two brothers were convicted of stealing sheep, branded on the forehead with the letters S. T., for "sheep thief."

One brother, unable to bear the stigma, tried to bury himself in a foreign land. But men asked him about the strange letters. He wandered restlessly, and at length, full of bitterness, died and was buried in a forgotten grave.

The other brother said, "I can't run away from the fact that I stole sheep. I will stay here and win back the respect of my neighbors and myself." As years passed he built a reputation for integrity. One day a stranger saw the old man with the letters branded on his forehead. He asked a native what they signified. "It happened a great while ago," said the villager. "I've forgotten the particulars; but I think the letters are an abbreviation of Saint."

—*Macartney's Illustrations* (Abingdon).

✣ ✣ ✣

In a Kansas town an Irishman was on trial for a traffic violation. When the judge asked if anyone present could testify to his character, he said, "Sure, your Honor, there's the sheriff." The sheriff said in surprise, "Why, I don't know the man at all." Replied the accused, "Isn't that a character for you, your Honor? I've lived in this town for twelve years, and the sheriff doesn't even know me yet."

—EDMOND M. KERLIN, *Telescope-Messenger*.

✣ ✣ ✣

Jonathan Smithers was a great fellow to whittle. A promising young man on a neighboring farm fell in love with his comely daughter and asked for her hand in marriage. To relieve his nervousness, the anxious suitor whittled while Farmer Smithers watched. The stick was finally whittled entirely away.

"Young man," said Jonathan, "had you made something out of that stick—just anything—you could have had my daughter; but you whittled it entirely away. Your property will go like that stick, bit by bit, until it is all gone. You have revealed your character—you can't have my daughter."

—*Nashua Cavalier*.

✣ ✣ ✣

A young girl said to her mother, just after a white-haired visitor had left their home, "If I could be such an old lady as that —so beautiful, sweet, serene, and lovable,—I should not mind growing old."

The discerning and keen-witted mother replied: "Well, if you want to be that kind of an old lady, you'd better begin now. She does not impress me as a piece of work that was done in a hurry."

—*Western Recorder*.

✣ ✣ ✣

"I cannot see why you esteem the character of Wordsworth so highly," a friend remarked to the poet Coleridge. "He appears to me to be a very small man."

"I don't wonder that he does," rejoined Coleridge. "He runs so far ahead of us that he dwarfs himself in the distance."

—ANDREW MEREDITH, *Christian Herald*.

✣ ✣ ✣

For fifteen hundred years the great wall of China stood unconquered. One day, by the gate, a guard was drunk, and a simple, harmless-looking shepherd came along and engaged him in conversation, corrupted and bribed him. The guard left the gate a moment, it was thrown back and hordes of barbarians poured in. They could not overcome China by bringing force against the wall, but they gained entrance through one man who was weak.

—DR. NORMAN VINCENT PEALE, *Guideposts* (Prentice-Hall).

✣ ✣ ✣

A farmer I know, living in the next town to ours in Vermont, has considerable skill as a carpenter. He has been working at that trade, lately, for a city man, who took his silent employe for just an employe, not a fellow human being. When the "employe" came into our general store, a group of neighbors asked, "What kind of man is the fellow that's bought the old Perkins place?" To which the Vermonter, who had been good at mathematics in high school, answered gently, "Well, I should say he's kind of an imaginary line drawn through a suit of clothes."

—Dorothy Canfield Fisher, *Holiday*.

✣ ✣ ✣

A visitor once watched a group of slaves slouching and shuffling off to their work. One tall, broad-shouldered fellow strode on, his head held proudly erect.

"Who is that?" the visitor asked.

"Oh," was the reply, "he's the son of an African king. He never forgets that."

—*Christian Herald*.

✣ ✣ ✣

Some years ago there was a heated struggle in the House of Representatives over an important bill. In the cloakroom Congressman Madden approached a junior Representative whose support of the bill had obviously been gained by unworthy means.

"Boy," he asked, "why did you vote as you did?"

"I had to, Mr. Madden," the young man answered. "I was under very great pressure."

Congressman Madden put his hand on the young colleague's shoulder: "But, boy," he asked, *"where are your inner braces?"*

The pressure of modern life against the inner spirit of man is great. It is likely to have disastrous results unless we as individuals and as nations buttress ourselves from within. Religious faith can give us those inner braces.

—Dr. Norman Vincent Peale, *Lifetime Living*.

✣ ✣ ✣

A scorpion, being a very poor swimmer, asked a turtle to carry him on his back across a river. "Are you mad?" exclaimed the turtle. "You'll sting me while I'm swimming and I'll drown."

"My dear turtle," laughed the scorpion, "if I were to sting you, you would drown and I would go down with you. Now, where is the logic in that?"

"You're right," cried the turtle. "Hop on!"

The scorpion climbed aboard and halfway across the river

gave the turtle a mighty sting. As they both sank to the bottom, the turtle resignedly said, "Do you mind if I ask you something? You said there'd be no logic in your stinging me. Why did you do it?"

"It has nothing to do with logic," the drowning scorpion sadly replied. "It's just my character."

—*Horizons.*

✤ ✤ ✤

Preceding my marriage to Livy, there were three or four proposals and as many declinations. However my suit went forward and we finally became engaged conditionally—the condition being her parents' consent. Mr. Langdon asked me for references—I furnished them.

In due course answers came and we had another conference. I had referred him to six prominent men. The results were not promising. All those men were frank to a fault. They not only spoke in disapproval of me but were quite unnecessarily enthusiastic about it.

I couldn't think of anything to say. Mr. Langdon was apparently in the same condition. Finally he raised his handsome head, fixed his clear and candid eye on me and said: "What kind of people are these? Haven't you a friend in the world?" I said, "Apparently not."

Then he said: "I'll be your friend myself. Take the girl. I know you better than they do."

—MARK TWAIN'S AUTOBIOGRAPHY (Harpers).

✤ ✤ ✤

CHEERFULNESS

A barefoot chap of four was walking along the street eating an ice-cream cone. Suddenly a group of older boys ran around a corner, knocked the boy down in their rush, and his cone was dashed to the ground.

The boy sat up and stared at the incomprehensible tragedy before him. There were no words, no tears; just mute, wide-eyed agony.

An old lady came down the steps of a porch and walked to

the child. "Well, laddie," she said, "the very worst has happened to you. But stand up, and I'll show you something."

The little boy got to his feet. "Now put your foot right on top of the ice cream, step hard, and watch it jump up through your toes," she said.

The boy stepped hard on the ice cream and it shot up through his toes. The old lady laughed with delight. "I'll bet there isn't another boy in town who has ever tickled his toes with ice cream," she chuckled. "Now run home and tell your mother about your funny experience. And remember," she added, "whatever happens you still can have fun!"

I was that little boy. I never knew who the little old lady was, but I never forgot what she did for me. The very worst has happened to me often since then, and the old lady's words have always come back. It *is* rather silly to take one's troubles too seriously.

—H. Middle Swarth.

✣ ✣ ✣

CHILDREN

Two women sat talking in a public park. One had three healthy children tumbling about in play; the other woman had none.

The woman who had no children watched wistfully while they romped like puppies on the grass. "I'd give ten years of my life to have three such wonderful children as yours," she said enviously.

"Well," the mother answered, after a few moments, "three children cost just about that."

✣ ✣ ✣

CHRISTIANITY

A soap manufacturer, who was also something of a cynic, said to a minister, "The Christianity you preach does not seem to have done much good. The world is still full of wicked people after all these years!" Just then they passed a small boy playing in the gutter. Looking significantly at the youngster, the preacher observed, "Soap hasn't done much good in the world, has it? There's still a lot of dirt and dirty people."

"Oh," said the manufacturer, "soap is useful only when it is applied." Said the minister: "Exactly. So is Christianity!"

✣ ✣ ✣

A small-town tradesman, habitually a non-church-goer, came to church one Sunday. The minister was delighted.

"Who brought you, Mr. Jones?" he asked.

"Reckon I just brought myself, Preacher," was the reply.

"I hope you like us well enough to come regularly."

"Reckon I might."

"Was there some special reason why you came?"

"Well, I'll tell you, Preacher. I've been doing business in this town for ten years, and five or six families have always been so pleasant and cheerful and happy-seeming, no matter how things were going, that sometimes I'd sort of tip the scales in their favor; I'd say the extra was a free sample and was one of my ways of advertising. In time I found they were members of your church, all of them. I reckon they'd been handing out free samples, too, because I finally had the sense to figure if their religion could keep them so pleasant and happy, it ought to be worth my while to give it a try. So I reckon I will."

—ALFRED I. TOOKE, *Good Business*.

✣ ✣ ✣

The King was debating whether or not to accept the new religion, Christianity, and consulted with his counsellors.

One old Pagan warrior said: "Do you remember, sire, how last midwinter King Edwin held festival in the great hall, with brands burning and the two huge fires on the hearths, while outside there was storm and utter darkness? And the windows by the roof being open, a bird flew suddenly from the darkness outside into the warm and lighted place and out on the other side into the outer darkness. Like that bird is the life of man."

—Old Saxon story, retold by GILBERT MURRAY,
Tradition and Progress (Houghton, Mifflin).

CHRISTMAS

There was once a German prince who wished to possess a Cremona violin; he offered a prince's ransom to purchase one. For months he had no success. Then one day an old man appeared at the castle with a worn case under his arm. The servants at first refused to admit him, but at length agreed to carry his message to the prince: "Heaven's music is waiting at your door."

So the old man was received by the prince. He drew from his shabby case a perfect Cremona, and created entrancing music. He was asked to name his price for the instrument. "The violin may be yours," he said, "only on condition that I pass my life within your house, and use the instrument every day." The prince accepted the violin on those terms.

The story is a parable. We have been hearing again at Christmastime the music of Heaven, proclaiming the Savior's birth and love and abiding presence in hearts that welcome and trust Him. Shall we not receive the Master Musician into our hearts and homes?

—W. Francis Gibbons, *The Christian World.*

✣ ✣ ✣

Last night John Elzy, watchman at the Grand Eagle Department Store, while making his rounds of the bargain basement, found the body of a man lying under a counter. He was thin to the point of emaciation, apparently in his middle thirties, and was shabbily dressed. His pockets were empty and there was no mark of identification upon his person. Store officials believe that he was trampled in the Christmas rush and crawled under the counter for shelter. But they were unable to account for what appear to be nail wounds in his hands. The police are investigating.

—*The Saturday Review.*

✣ ✣ ✣

CHURCH

One Sunday, Father O'Brien noticed from the sanctuary that there were no vacant seats for three women standing in the rear of the church. He recognized them as non-Catholic neighbors. Quietly, he summoned an altar boy to his side and whispered the order, "Three chairs for the Protestant ladies."

The altar boy looked puzzled, swallowed hard, and took two or three halting steps. When he saw that the boy did not understand him clearly, the priest beckoned to the lad again and whispered, "Three chairs for the Protestant ladies."

His face white as chalk, the altar boy drew a deep breath, turned to face the congregation, and shouted, "Three cheers for the Protestant ladies!"

✣ ✣ ✣

CHURCH—Attendance

A visiting minister was disturbed when a bird dog walked down the church aisle, looked all about and then dropped down for a nap under the pew. Afterward he rebuked the rural minister for not putting the dog out.

"Sir," the pastor replied, "that dog's owner is the chairman of our board of deacons and is quite ill. The dog saw people coming to church and having mourned his master since they took him to the hospital, he seems to think he may find his master here at church. Put him out? No, we think it is very beautiful that the dog identifies his master with his church."

—Dr. Louie D. Newton, *Word & Way*.

✣ ✣ ✣

CHURCH—Collections

The collections in the little Negro church had decreased to the extent that the pastor was obliged to go hungry part of the time. One Sunday morning he decided to make a short address before the collection plate was passed.

"Bredderen," he said gently, "ah don't want any man to give mo' than his share, but we must all give accordin' to what we rightly has. Ah say 'rightly has,' bredderen, cause we don't want no tainted money in this here box.

"Squire Jones told me that he done miss some chickens this week. Now, if any of our bredderen have fallen by the wayside in connection with these here chickens, let him stay his hand from the collection box. Deacon, please pass the plate while ah watches to see if anybody in this congregation needs me to wrastle in prayer for him."

—Friendly Chats.

♣ ♣ ♣

CHURCH—Contribution

A man pinned a note on a $1 bill, asking that all who spent the money write down exactly what it was spent for. The dollar bill was kept in circulation for two weeks, then came back to him with this list accompanying it:

It was spent five times for salary.
It was spent five times for cigarettes.
It was spent three times for candy.
It was spent three times for meals.
It was spent twice for haberdashery.
It was spent twice for haircuts.
It was spent once for groceries.
It was spent twice for laundry.
It was spent once for automotive repairs.
It was spent once for a magazine.
But not once did it come near a church.

♣ ♣ ♣

CITIZENSHIP

An Englishman moved to the United States after the end of World War II, and immediately took out his American citizenship papers. Several months later he was visited in this country by an English relative who sternly reprimanded him for giving up his British citizenship to become an American citizen.

"What have you to gain by becoming an American?" he questioned.

"Well," replied the former Britisher, "for one thing I won the American Revolution!"

CLARITY

"My father was a man of great intellectual energy," said Woodrow Wilson. "My best training came from him. I carried every thing I wrote to him. He would make me read it aloud. Every now and then he would stop me: 'What do you mean by that?' he'd ask. I would tell him, and of course in doing so would express myself more simply than I had on paper. 'Why don't you say so?' he would go on. 'Don't shoot at your meaning with birdshot and hit the whole country-side; shoot with a rifle at the thing you have to say.'"

✣ ✣ ✣

COMMUNISM

Otto Kahn, financier, art patron, and philanthropist, once said at a dinner in New York City:

"Communism, fascism, and other kindred movements are bound to fail, because they're based on hate, not love.

"As I understand it," he continued, "a man once said to a Communist: 'The fundamental idea of communism is to divide up with your neighbor.'

"'Nothing of the kind,' snarled the Red, 'the fundamental idea of communism is to make your neighbor divide up with you!'"

✣ ✣ ✣

COMPLACENCY

There lived in Nantucket some years ago an old-time whaler, Captain Coffin, who had had many thrilling adventures. Once he was harpooning a big sperm whale when the monster turned, crushed the boat and scattered the crew in the sea. For a moment the Captain was in the whale's great jaws, but pulled himself out and was rescued by his mates.

"Captain Coffin," said a friend, "what did you think when you found yourself in the whale's jaws?"

"What did I think?" replied the Captain. "I thought he'd make 100 barrels—and by the prophets, he did!"

—*Wall Street Journal.*

A member of an old Boston family, now 80, still lives on Beacon Hill and carries on the family traditions. Last winter she entertained a guest from the Middle West to whom she presented her small but select circle of friends. Shortly before leaving the guest remarked, "Emily, your friends are wonderful women, but tell me, where *do* they get their hats?"

"Oh, my dear," the Bostonian said with pained surprise, "we don't *get* our hats. We *have* our hats."

✤ ✤ ✤

COMPLIMENTS

A little girl, not quite 4 years old, asked her visiting grandmother to accompany her to her nursery school. The grandmother, delighted by the unexpected invitation, gladly put aside her other plans. As they entered the school, the child lifted her grandmother's hand toward the teacher's, stepped aside quite ceremoniously and, forgetting to include names, announced with great pride: "This is *my* grandmother. Her cheeks are rosy and she smiles a lot!" The grandmother has never forgotten the enchanting compliment.

—Dawn Crowell Norman, *Ladies' Home Journal.*

✤ ✤ ✤

A smart young officer, who was nothing if not efficient, was inspecting Selective Service Headquarters in the Deep South. Noting that the number of desks, telephones, and typewriters seemed far in excess of personnel, he asked one of the girls, "What is the normal complement of this office?"

The girl seemed puzzled, but only for a moment. "Well, suh," she replied slowly, "Ah reckon the most usual compliment is, 'Howdy, honey, you're sure luscious looking this mawnin'!'"

✤ ✤ ✤

COMPROMISE

An American woman visiting in Paris went to a bureau which provided American men as escorts. When informed that she could engage either a northerner or a southerner, she asked the difference and was told that the southerners were gallant and debonair, while the northerners were smooth talkers and romantic. "Well, then," she said, "I'll take a southerner from as far north as possible!"

—RALPH M. CRONIN.

✤ ✤ ✤

A Moscow Censor berated an American correspondent for writing that, during a Soviet parade, the American ambassador "stood within a stone's throw of Stalin."

"What do you mean by this outrageous insult?" the censor stormed. The correspondent finally managed to interrupt the tirade to explain the American idiom.

"So?" said the censor. "In that case we change it this way: 'The American ambassador stood near Stalin. He threw ***no*** stones!'"

—*The Best I Know* (Waverly House).

✤ ✤ ✤

CONCEIT

Mark Twain was in a restaurant one day and found himself next to two young men who were putting on a great many airs and ordering the waitress about in a most impressive fashion. One of them gave an order and told the waitress to inform the cook whom it was for. "Yes," said the other, "better tell him my name, also, so as to make certain of its being all right."

Mark, who disliked swagger, called the waitress in a loud voice, "Bring me a dozen oysters and whisper my name to each of them."

✤ ✤ ✤

A rather pompous city man, turned farmer, was showing a small lad over his acreage. He bragged incessantly of his accomplishments, finally concluding with the proud boast: "And I grew it all by myself, sonny. Started out with nothing, and now look at it!"

"From nothing?" echoed the duly impressed lad. "Golly, sir, without even a seed?"

—JOSEPH ZDERAD.

CONFIDENCE

Climbing the Alps one day a man and his guide came to a point where the trail narrowed to only a fraction of itself as it passed over a rock which projected over the precipice. The guide, laying hold of the rock with one hand and putting his other hand upon what was left of the trail, the hand extending out over the abyss, commanded the traveler to step upon it and his forearm and thus pass around the rock to safety. Fearful, the man hesitated, but the guide assured him: "Do not fear to stand on my hand. That hand has never yet lost a man."

—Edwin Frye, *Telescope-Messenger.*

✣ ✣ ✣

It was evident that the pretty school teacher on the television quiz was a very nervous contestant. The master of ceremonies sought to relieve tension by remarking kindly, "This is just like school and in school you know all the answers, don't you?"

"Well," replied the unconfident young woman, "in school I'm the one who asks the questions!"

—*Wall Street Journal.*

✣ ✣ ✣

A somewhat complicated machine had broken down and the village jack-of-all-trades was called in to look at it. "Can you fix it?" asked the owner doubtfully.

"A man made it," answered the local expert.

—*The High Road.*

✣ ✣ ✣

A friend of mine stopped in a country store in Tennessee just as a farmer came in and asked the storekeeper for a line of credit.

"Wilbur," said the storekeeper, "are you doing any fencing this spring?"

"Yes, Uncle Jake, I am."

"Are you fencing in or fencing out?"

"Fencing out, Uncle Jake. I'm taking in that old woodlot, down by the creek."

"All right, go in and tell Henry to give you what you need."

My friend couldn't make much sense of this. "I've seen all

kinds of credit systems," he told Uncle Jake, "But never one like that. How does it work?"

"Well," said the storekeeper, "if he's fencing in, that means the quackgrass and the broomsage and the sassafras is getting the best of him. If he's fencing out, then it means he's whipping *them*. It means he's winning the fight. I always give credit to a man that's fencing out."

—Robert M. Yoder.

✣ ✣ ✣

A few years ago we asked a likely lad to express his intentions as to his career.

"I am going to study medicine," he said, "and become a great surgeon."

"But," we objected, "isn't the medical field pretty crowded?"

"Yes," he agreed reflectively, "I suppose that's true. But, nevertheless, I shall study medicine, and those who are already in the profession will just have to take their chances!"

✣ ✣ ✣

A Vermont farmer was plowing a field with one horse, but he was yelling "Giddap, Jack. Giddap, Jerry. Giddap, Casey. Giddap, Cromwell."

A stranger passing by asked, "How many names does your horse have?"

"Oh," said the farmer, "his name is Jack, but he doesn't know his own strength. So, I put blinders on him and yell all those other names. He thinks he has other horses helping him."

—Can You Top This (Wor).

✣ ✣ ✣

CONFORMITY

Charles V, the powerful Hapsburg monarch who ruled half of Europe in the 16th century, occupied himself, after retirement to the secluded monastery at Yuste, by trying to synchronize two clocks. He found it virtually impossible to regulate them exactly.

One day, he turned to his assistant and exclaimed, "To think that I attempted to force the reason and conscience of thousands of men into one mold—and I cannot even make two clocks agree!"

—HAVELOCK ELLIS, *The Task of Social Hygiene.*

✣ ✣ ✣

CONGRESS

A housewife in the middle of her spring housecleaning was interrupted by the doorbell. Answering it, she was confronted by a smiling man with a brief case.

"Good morning, madam," he began. "I represent the Ajax Lightning Rod Company, and—"

"Not interested," she snapped, slamming the door.

She had been back at work only about ten minutes when the bell ran again. It was another man.

"Good morning, madam," he said. "I represent the Billings Bird Bath Company, and—"

"Not interested," she snapped, slamming the door once again.

Five short minutes later the bell chimed again. Furious, the woman went to the door, threw it open and shouted at the new man who stood there, "I suppose you're going to tell me you represent some idiotic outfit, too."

"That's for you to say, I guess," replied the man. "I'm your Congressman."

—*Wall Street Journal.*

✣ ✣ ✣

The comic magician was in need of an assistant to aid him in performing his mirth-provoking tricks, and was interviewing a young man who had applied for the job.

"I need a man to help me," stated the magician, "a man who can keep a straight face all through my performance, who will under no circumstances allow a smile to show on his face, no matter what silly things I might say or do. Now, what are your qualifications for this job?"

"Well," replied the young man, "I used to be a page boy in the House of Representatives."

—*Sunshine Magazine.*

CONSCIENCE

"Oh, yes," said the Indian, "I know what my conscience is. It is a little three-cornered thing in here"—he laid his hand on his heart—"that stands still when I am good; but when I am bad it turns around, and the corners hurt very much. But if I keep on doing wrong, by-and-by the corners wear off and it doesn't hurt any more."

—*Weapons for Workers.*

✣ ✣ ✣

CONSERVATISM

On maneuvers in rural England a soldier was being tried for shooting a chicken on prohibited ground.

"Now, my good man," said the commanding officer to the farmer who had brought the accusation, "Are you quite certain this is the man who shot your bird? Will you swear to his identity?"

"No-o," said the farmer deliberately, "No, I won't swear to that, but I will say he's the man I suspect o' doin' it."

"That's not enough to convict a man," the officer insisted. "You must tell us on what evidence you base your charge."

"Well," said the farmer, "it was this way: I heard a gun go off; then I seen this man puttin' the chicken in his knapsack. So it just didn't seem reasonable to conclude that the bird committed suicide."

✣ ✣ ✣

Conservatism is an admirable quality, but there are times when one may be a little too cautious; too deliberate in reaching a decision.

A witness in a railway accident case was asked by the defense to explain the circumstances leading up to the death of a companion.

"Well," said the witness, "Ole and I was walkin' down the railroad track when the train went by. When I got back on the track I didn't see Ole. So I kept walkin' along, and pretty soon I seen Ole's hat. I walked on and seen one of Ole's legs; then I seen one of Ole's arms, and then another leg. Then over to one side I seen Ole's head. So, right then and there I says to myself, 'Gosh! I suspect somethin' must o' happened to Ole'!"

✤ ✤ ✤

Cordell Hull was an extremely cautious speaker, striving always for scientific accuracy. One day, on a train, a friend pointed to a fine flock of sheep grazing in a field. "Look. Those sheep have just been sheared," he said.

Hull studied the flock. "Sheared on this side, anyway," he admitted.

—*American Magazine.*

✤ ✤ ✤

CONSIDERATENESS

My mother and father were deeply united, and very different. My mother loved people warmly—my father was interested in the way they behaved. Once, when my mother and he were walking along a street in San Francisco, she grew excited and clutched his arm.

"Jack!" she said. "Do you see that man ahead of us? Why, his pocket's on fire."

"Yes," said my father. "It does seem to be on fire. I've noticed it for some time."

"Noticed it for some time?" said my mother. "Then why didn't you do something about it?"

"Why, I didn't want to disturb him," said my father. "He may be the kind of man who likes to have his pocket on fire."

—STEPHEN VINCENT BENET.

✤ ✤ ✤

A group of seven-year-old campers were playing a game and one was selected to "count out." She began pointing from girl to girl, saying, "Eeny, meeny, miny, mo, catch a nigger by the toe." Following her words there was a silence of a few seconds. Then a little white girl blurted out, "My father and mother told me not to say that. I say, 'Eeny, meeny, miny, mo, catch a Negro by the toe.'" But the upshot of it was that the children decided to catch a monkey by the toe and they found that even more amusing. In such simple ways they showed their consideration for others.

—THOMAS W. PATRICK, *Parents' Magazine.*

✣ ✣ ✣

CONTENTMENT

In 1923, when Herbert Hoover was president of Better Homes in America (before it had become a department of Purdue University), that organization offered a prize for the best definition of a "better home" to be written by a school child.

The award was won by a Tennessee mountain lad, who wrote: "A 'better home' is a place my dad is proud to support, my mother loves to take care of, and we like to be in. It is a place to grow old in."

—MARIE M. MELONEY.

✣ ✣ ✣

At a crossroads hamlet in Georgia, we were so struck by a sign that we stopped and asked an elderly gentleman how the town got its name.

"It was like this," he replied courteously. "Our town used to be called 'Happy.' But tourists would stop and ask us what we had to be so happy about. I suppose all they could see was the *outside* of our little houses. Anyhow, we decided to change the name of the town. And we did."

The name which had attracted our attention was: "Suits Us."

—BILL TYUS, in "Life in These United States."

✣ ✣ ✣

A few months ago I had an experience that comes to all too many men around my age. The doctor took my blood pressure, counted my pulse, listened to my heart, and then told me there was a little red light shining up the road. I would have to slow down.

"Do you mean slack off on my work?" I asked.

"Yes, unless you can stop stewing about it. It isn't work but worry that puts men in the prime of life to pushing up daisies. You've got to get rid of this nervous tension. Can you do it?"

I didn't know.

A few days later, a business trip having taken me to Florida, I decided to do a little duck hunting—for relaxation, I told myself. I loved duck hunting but actually I had always worked as hard at it as though it were something important.

On two successive days I got the legal limit of ten ducks. On the third day I had eight ducks by four in the afternoon. I became so anxious to get the other two, to impress the fellows who would be at the boat landing, that I began to miss my birds clean, and soon was so tense that I couldn't have hit an ostrich.

Suddenly a violent reaction set in. "Why you fool!" I said to myself. "Here you are, throwing a fit because you haven't got two measly ducks! You already have eight ducks. What are you, a game-hog?"

Then I saw two ring-necks swing over the decoys at about 60 miles an hour and made a clean right-and-left. I had relaxed.

That night in bed I relived the incident and made a staggering discovery. In life, too, I already had eight ducks! At 49 I was close to the lawful limit of heart's desire. This is how I counted them:

One. A sweet wife.

Two. Children to be proud of.

Three. Reasonably good health.

Four. Friends.

Five. A livelihood.

Six. A fair share of honors.

Seven. Wide interests.

Eight. A hopeful outlook—hope for peace, of a better world, a future life, divine and human goodness, and all things dear to the human heart.

In fact, the only two ducks that I did not have were as much money and as much fame as some men possess. Was I going to stew myself into an early grave for these?

I certainly was not.

It occurred to me that most people of my age have about eight ducks. Most of us have good wives or husbands; creditable children; a fair share of honors, whether in the lodge, the church, community activities or the day's work; and a fair livelihood.

My list is the rule rather than the exception in this democratic country, where the bulk of the prizes do not go to a few game-hogs.

Now, every time I start to stew, I remember my eight ducks. Last week, when the doctor checked me again, my blood pressure was back to normal and that little red light had receded beyond the horizon.

So proudly count your ducks and live!

—EDISON MARSHALL.

✤ ✤ ✤

An oilman of my acquaintance approached an old Texas rancher to lease land to drill oil wells. The rancher, celebrated for his red-coated Herefords, gazed dreamily across his grazing lands, and to every increased offer grunted, "Nope."

"Consider," said the oilman, "consider all you could do with this money for your family—electrify the house, lay cement walks, buy laborsaving appliances. Wouldn't that be grand?"

"Nope," grunted the rancher.

Undaunted, the oilman tried again: "Just picture a forest of oil wells on this land, oil wells pumping up rich black gold day and night. Imagine how the lighted derricks would twinkle at night, like a thousand Christmas trees. Can you imagine anything prettier?"

The rancher nodded. "Yep," he said, and pointed toward the expanse of pasture land. "Red cattle grazin' on green grass."

—MILDRED TABER CLARK, in "Life in These United States."

✤ ✤ ✤

According to a Chinese legend the Judge of Purgatory decided that one of the spirits under his guardianship should return to earth as a rich man.

"But I don't want to be a rich man," protested the spirit. "I only ask for a regular supply of food, with no worries, that I may burn pure incense and drink bitter tea."

"Money I can provide in any amount," answered the Judge, "but this peaceful happy life you require is more than I can give."

—*Property.*

One summer evening, when Thomas A. Edison returned home from his work, his wife said, "You have worked long enough without a rest. You must go on a vacation."

"But where will I go?" he asked.

"Decide where you would rather be than anywhere else on earth, and go there," was the answer.

"Very well," promised Mr. Edison, "I will go tomorrow."

The next morning he returned to his laboratory.

—*Christian Science Monitor.*

✣ ✣ ✣

A Quaker put up a sign on a vacant piece of ground next to his house: "I will give this lot to anybody who is really satisfied."

A wealthy farmer, as he rode by, read it. Stopping, he said, "Since my Quaker friend is going to give that piece away, I may as well have it as anybody else. I am rich. I have all I need, so I am able to qualify." He went to the door.

"And is thee really satisfied?" asked the Quaker.

"I have all I need and am well satisfied."

"Friend," said the other, "if thee is satisfied, what does thee want with my lot?"

—*Sunday School Times.*

✣ ✣ ✣

For years, Grandpa had been stubborn and crabbed. No one could please him. Then overnight, he changed. Gentleness and optimism twinkled about him. "Grandpa," he was asked, "what caused you to change so suddenly?"

"Well, sir," the old man replied, "I've been striving all my life for a contented mind. It's done no good, so I've decided to be contented without it."

—*Radio Review.*

✣ ✣ ✣

Thornton Burgess, in one of his nature stories for children, tells of the meadow creatures' search for the best thing in the world. Each interpreted that best thing in his own way—the chipmunk thought it must be nuts or acorns; the rabbit, a pile of carrots; the coon, a field of sweet milky corn; and the fox, a pen full of young, tender chickens.

All day long—so the story goes—the animals hunted. When the sun had gone down they had not found that for which they sought. They were amazed to hear Mother Nature say, "The woodchuck has it—the best thing. It is just being happy with the things you have and not wanting things someone else has; it is called Contentment."

—*Telescope-Messenger.*

✣ ✣ ✣

A farmer, having lived on the same farm all his life, wanted a change. Having subjected everything there to his merciless criticism, he listed the farm with a realtor who prepared a flattering sales advertisement for the newspaper, but who first read it to the farmer before giving it to the newspaper.

"Wait a minute," said the farmer, "read that again slowly. I changed my mind. I'm not gonna sell. All my life I've been looking for a place like that."

—*Watchman-Examiner.*

✣ ✣ ✣

At a particularly dull academic meeting, a fellow guest remarked sympathetically to Albert Einstein, "I'm afraid you are terribly bored, Professor Einstein."

"Ach, nein," replied Einstein pleasantly. "On occasions like this I retire to the back of my mind, and there I am happy."

—*Wall Street Journal.*

✣ ✣ ✣

CONTROVERSY

One day Lloyd George, driving through North Wales with a friend, said to him, "The church I belong to is torn with a fierce dispute. One section says that baptism is *in* the name of the Father, the other that it is *into* the name of the Father. I belong to one of these parties. I feel most strongly about it. I would die for it, in fact—but I forget which it is."

—HARRY EMERSON FOSDICK.

CONVERSATION

The customer settled himself and let the barber put the towel around him. Then he told the barber, "Before we start, I know the weather's awful. I don't care who wins the next big fight, and I don't bet on the horse races. I know I'm getting thin on top, but I don't mind. Now get on with it!"

"Well, sir, if you don't mind," said the barber, "I'll be able to concentrate better if you don't talk so much."

—*Link.*

✤ ✤ ✤

As a young man, actor William Gillette studied stenography. He was living then in a boardinghouse, so decided to practice his shorthand evenings by taking down every word spoken in the drawing room. "Years later," Gillette told a friend, "I went over my notebooks, and found that in four months of incessant conversation, no one had said anything that made any difference to anybody."

—*New England Almanac.*

✤ ✤ ✤

CO-OPERATION

Jim leaned over, put his arm around Mary's neck and tried, unsuccessfully, to kiss her. Finally, after Mary had pulled and pushed herself away from three such attempts, she looked up with an injured air and said, "Why, Jim Healey, I believe you're trying to kiss me!"

"Well, Mary," replied Jim, "since that's clear to you, let's quit assaulting each other and co-operate a little bit."

✤ ✤ ✤

I was watching a flock of migratory cranes on the New Mexico plains watch a coyote staging a most extraordinary performance—running up and down, leaping, trotting in circles, capering and anticking like an animal gone mad. The cranes watched his preposterous show in utter fascination.

Then I saw a second coyote creeping up behind the birds with infinite stealth. Nearer and nearer he drew, while his performing teammate worked himself into a frenzy of acrobatics to hold the attention of his feathered audience. Finally the stalking coyote deemed himself near enough, broke into a streaking run, leaped among the cranes, and seized one.

As the other cranes flew off, the two coyotes settled down to share the feast their teamwork had secured.

—BOB BEVERLY.

✣ ✣ ✣

This story illustrates the importance of teamwork—and the need, at times, to do a little more than our specifically appointed tasks:

A midwestern university baseball team had lost seven games in succession. After the last defeat, the coach gathered his men together: "Boys," he said, "you all played magnificently—every man in his position. The trouble was in the spaces between your positions. That is where your opponents came through!"

✣ ✣ ✣

My cousin and I continually argued with each other while doing household chores. I was older and tried to tell her just how to do everything, and of course she resented it.

One day my grandfather took us out to the log pile and gave us a crosscut saw. Picking out a sizable log, he said, "Start sawing." We were both a little bewildered, but obeyed. I began to saw as fast as I could, thinking I would show up my cousin. But when I pushed the saw back faster than my cousin could pull it, the saw would bind, throwing me off balance. Then I realized that the more evenly I pulled without pushing the easier the saw cut. My grandfather, with a twinkle in his eyes, explained the principle of the crosscut saw: work together in harmony. Whenever you have a job to do, he said, work together and you will find the job goes easily and quickly.

—MRS. WILLIAM M. HOTCHKISS, JR.

✣ ✣ ✣

As a boy I lived on a farm in southern Ohio, and for recreation we would run the hounds Sunday afternoons. One memorable day the pack very soon picked up a fox trail and was hot on the chase. We scrambled to a knoll overlooking the valley, and saw the fox out ahead.

Right below us was a hollow log. The fox headed straight for it, scampered through, and ran on. The dogs sniffed at the entrance, then like good hounds ran to the other end, picked up the scent, and dashed on in full pursuit.

The fox led the hounds in a tremendous circle back to the hollow log, through which he ran again. He repeated this maneuver time after time. Finally the dogs visibly tired. But the fox seemed as fresh as ever.

All of a sudden we caught on. We ran to the log, poked in a long stick—and out sprang a fox. There were two foxes! Each time Fox No. 1 dashed into the log, No. 2 would come plunging out the exit, to lead the hounds on an exhausting chase while No. 1 caught his breath and awaited his turn to run.

—W. A. GEARHART.

✤ ✤ ✤

Basil Matthews, in his book, *Clash of Color,* tells of standing with the sports coach of an international college. They were watching the practice of a team of boys from all parts of the world. Matthews asked, "What special difficulty do you find in training a team like this?"

"These fellows," said the coach, "come from countries where the whole idea of team-play is unknown. Each, at the beginning of his football training, wants to dribble the ball down the field at his own feet and score the goal himself, for his own glory. So I have won the battle not only for the boy as a member of the team, but for his whole life job when I have taught him to pass."

✤ ✤ ✤

One bright, sunny Alabama day, two children came trudging down the street—an eight-year-old girl solicitously leading her younger brother, who had his eyes tightly shut. A watching passer-by asked, "What's the matter? Has he hurt his eyes?"

"Oh, no," was the girl's casual reply. "We do this every Saturday when the sun's so bright. He keeps his eyes closed and I lead him to the movies. Inside he opens his eyes and finds us both a seat in the dark."

—MRS. DONALD H. GUNTHER.

The late Will Hays used to tell about an experience he once had with George Eastman, the famous inventor, industrialist and pioneer in production of photographic supplies.

One evening Hays and Eastman were discussing a trip the latter had recently made to Africa.

"Would you like to see some of the motion pictures I took?" Eastman inquired. Hays opined he would, and, after the projector had been loaded, the two men settled back in their chairs to watch a film that included much of the wild life of the "Dark Continent." In one of the shots a savage lion charged the camera. The lion seemed to be leaping out of the screen and into the room, its huge jaws agape, its enormous claws reaching out to rip its victim into shreds. At the last moment, while in mid air only a few feet from the camerman, the lion dropped dead and a man with a rifle stepped forward to look at his kill.

Hays gasped. "Stop the film!" he said. And then, turning to Eastman, asked, "Who took that picture, George?"

"I did," Eastman calmly replied.

Now Eastman was then a man along in years, enormously wealthy, world famous for the products he had invented and was producing.

Hays looked at his friend in astonishment. "You must have been out of your mind," he said. "You could have been killed. Weren't you scared?"

Eastman thought a moment. "No, I wasn't scared," he replied. "I had a man with a rifle right beside me."

"But suppose he had missed?" Hays asked.

Again a pause. Then Eastman spoke. "I never even thought of that. Long ago when I was a young man I learned that no matter what you do or who you are you have to depend upon your organization."

—Editorial, *Social Education.*

✤ ✤ ✤

At Garmisch-Partenkirchen in Germany, scene of an Olympics meet before the war, the dead man's curve, called the Great Bavaria, is tricky. Bad weather had allowed the U. S. team only three trial runs before the race. On those trials they had negotiated the big bend only by use of the brake. And in a race, when hundredths of a second count, you don't use the brake.

On the morning of the race the American sled waited at the start high up on the pine-clad slopes of the Wetterstein. Beneath, the run looped like a great white ribbon down the slope.

The Americans' number was called. Captain Hubert Stevens gripped the wheel, the other three ran beside the sled, pushing it, and as it gathered speed, vaulted into place. Down the slope it shot, doing 40–50 miles an hour. They took the early curves perfectly. Then the long straightaway before the Great Bavaria. Stevens called the order for bobbing and his team swung back and forward in rhythm. They were doing better than 60.

The big curve came in sight, a sheer precipice of ice. Stevens knew that he had to jerk the sled at just the right moment and force it up onto the wall. But he was half a second too late. The sled was forced by terrific pressure up and up while Stevens fought with the wheel to bring it down. Three fourths of the way around, one runner was at the top, still mounting.

Then, with one impulse, the team put their hands under the upper runner. Heaving together, they literally picked up the flying sled and threw it back into the run. A photograph showed that one runner had been in the air, the other at the extreme upper edge.

Their shoulders struck the ice together down in the trough. The sled skidded violently for 50 feet on its side. With another heave, all together, they righted it. But the few seconds they had lost cost them first place.

To the onlooker the driver of the sled seems to be the whole show. But each man has his function, essential to the teamwork which means speed.

—EDWIN MULLER, *Kiwanis Mag.*

✣ ✣ ✣

An Indiana farmer whose prize corn took the blue ribbon at state fairs year after year was asked why he shared his best seed with neighboring farmers each season.

"Why," he replied, "it's a matter of self-protection. If I would grow good corn, I must encourage my neighbors to grow good corn. The wind picks up the pollen from ripening grain and swirls it from field to field. If my neighbors grow inferior corn, cross-pollination will steadily degrade the quality of my corn. Therefore, I see that they plant only the best."

—*Managers' Handbook.*

✤ ✤ ✤

A man who went into a bird store to buy a canary spotted a bright-looking bird that was singing merrily. "I'll take that one!" he said.

"Fine," agreed the clerk, "but you'll have to take the one in the cage below, too."

The customer protested: "I don't want that old battered, broken-down bird. I just want the singing one—the one in the cage above."

"Look," he said, "you can't take the one above without the other one."

"And why not?" asked the exasperated customer.

"Because," explained the clerk, "the one below is the arranger."

—*Minneapolis Star-Journal.*

✤ ✤ ✤

"For Miss Beard, from Jimmy and Bobby."

The teacher read the words written on tablet paper wrapped around a large apple. Calling the boys up to thank them, she inquired how both of them happened to give her one apple.

"Well, it was like this," began Jimmy. "We was comin' along to school. Bobby had the apple and he started to bite it. I said, 'Don't eat that apple. Let's take it to the teacher.' You see, it was his apple, but my thought!" he ended triumphantly.

—LEMAH S. JAMES, *Tracks.*

✤ ✤ ✤

On my way to the railway station in Seattle, it suddenly occurred to me that I hadn't enough money for the ticket I'd have to buy. But I had to catch that train—to meet an engagement in Portland.

I managed to get through the gate without a ticket, just as the train was pulling out. Throwing my suitcase onto the platform of the observation car, I climbed up over the rail—a slightly unconventional entrance. Entering the car, I decided to learn my fate at once. "Who," I asked, "is going to pay my fare to Portland?" Two men whipped out their wallets. Each said, "I will."

—William Trufant Foster, *Rotarian.*

✣ ✣ ✣

Two little ragged Negro boys stopped in at a candy store in Philadelphia one day. The storekeeper was attracted by their gentle manners; so when they asked if they could borrow three pennies, he offered them more. But they refused.

The next day the children returned with the three pennies. The man protested, but the boys argued: "If we didn't pay you back, we couldn't ask you again if we needed to."

The rest of the story was not learned until months later. It seems that the mother of a frail little Italian boy had to be taken to the hospital. While she was there, his two closest friends had provided his lunch at school. They did it by shining shoes after school and by serving a newspaper route before school. Only once did they fall short of the lunch ticket. It was then that the candy-store man helped out.

—*Christian Advocate.*

✣ ✣ ✣

Oliver Wendell Holmes was fond of telling the story that the people of the world decided to shout "Boo!" all at once at a specified moment, so that the voice of the inhabitants of the earth might be heard in the moon. When the time came for this mighty ejaculation, the people were so eager to hear the great noise that they failed to contribute their "Boos," and the great occasion passed as the most silent moment since creation.

—Julius Gordon, *Your Sense of Humor* (Didier).

✣ ✣ ✣

The various fruits had gathered to hold a discussion among themselves.

They wanted to discover the reason why no other fruit but the grape contains the juice from which the finest wines are made.

"Her drink is famous throughout the world and exquisitely pleasing to man's taste," they declared. "Why is she more worthy than we to be blessed with this gift of God?"

A cluster of grapes hanging nearby heard the complaint and replied, "All of you grow individually and produce your fruits independently but we grapes grow together in bunches and are faithful to each other. For that reason our substance is rich and capable of imparting such distinctive taste and fragrance to our wines."

—*Bluebird Briefs.*

✣ ✣ ✣

The instructor drew a chalk-line on the blackboard and turned to his psychology class. "I'm going to ask each of you to estimate the length of that line." Rapidly he polled the class. Estimates ranged from fifty-three inches to eighty-four inches. The instructor put them all down. Then he totaled them and divided the result by the number of students in the class. The average estimate, he announced, was sixty-one and one-eighth inches, although no one had given that exact figure.

Then he measured the line. It was sixty-one and one-fourth inches long. It's a practical example of the old saying that "two heads are better than one."

—*Property.*

✣ ✣ ✣

One merchant whose business always remained small boasted that he concentrated on his own business, never joined any associations or attended conventions.

"Those other fellows don't get any of my good ideas," he said firmly.

Another merchant, whose father started life as a pack peddler, built his store into a multi-million institution. "My business never really started to grow," this man said, "until I began to go out and exchange ideas with other merchants."

—*Wright Line.*

✣ ✣ ✣

Once when Sir Michael Costa was having rehearsal with a vast array of performers and hundreds of voices, some man who played the piccolo far away up in some corner, said to himself, "In all this din it matters not what I do," and so he ceased to play. Suddenly the great conductor stopped, flung up his hands, and all was still—and then he cried, "Where is the piccolo?"

—*Sunshine Magazine.*

✤ ✤ ✤

CO-OPERATION—Lack

I passed a building undergoing repairs. On one side workmen were removing large quantities of bricks which had crumbled away. Why, I mused, had some bricks disintegrated and not others?

"Fifty years ago, when the building was erected," said the foreman, "there came a day when the laborers at the brickyard had trouble with one another. And now, long years after the failure of those men to work together for a single day, a moral is written in crumbling brick."

—*Sunshine Magazine.*

✤ ✤ ✤

A flock of quail lived in the forest. They might have been happy, but they lived in great fear of their enemy, the quail-catcher. He imitated their call, and when they gathered together, he would throw a great net over them, stuff them into his hunting basket and carry them off to market.

One wise quail counseled: "Brothers, I have a plan. When the fowler puts his net over us, each one will put his head in the net and lift it up together and fly away with it. When we have flown far enough, we'll let the net drop on a bush and fly from under it."

All agreed. Next day, the fowler threw his net and the birds, working together, lifted it and flew away, later dropping it on a bush and escaping, according to plan.

This happened many days and the fowler's wife asked angrily, "Why is it that you never catch any more quail?"

The fowler replied glumly, "The trouble is that all the birds work together and help one another."

A few days later, one quail accidentally trod on the head of one of his brothers as they alighted on the feeding ground.

"Don't be angry," said the quail to his injured brother. "I didn't mean to tread on you."

But the brother quail went on quarreling. "I lifted all the weight on the net. You didn't help at all," he cried.

That made the other quail angry, and before long all of them were drawn into the dispute.

Nearby, the fowler saw his chance. He imitated the cry of the quail and cast his net over them. Still quarreling, they did not help one another lift the net. So the fowler lifted the net himself and crammed them into his basket.

—Adapted from the *Jataka.*

✤ ✤ ✤

Back in the olden days when organs were pumped by hand, a famous organist, leaving the platform after a long and brilliant performance, confided to a group of his admirers: "I really did some beautiful work this evening. I don't know when I ever played better!"

The young boy who had pumped the wind for the organ scowled but said nothing.

The next evening the artist placed his hands on the keys but no sound came forth. He tried once more. No response at all. He glared at the pumper and signalled angrily that wind was needed.

The boy grinned and replied: "Say WE, mister."

✤ ✤ ✤

COURAGE

The most promising student in our college in Vienna was a good-looking boy of 16 who was exceptionally gifted, industrious, ambitious, and well-mannered. We nick-named him "Metternich" in honor of our great diplomat because we were convinced that, with his superior intelligence, he had a brilliant public career before him. The only thing we disliked was his elegance: he always came to school in a newly pressed suit; if the weather was bad, his father's chauffeur brought and fetched him in a luxurious car. However, he was a nice fellow without any arrogance; we all liked him.

One morning "Metternich's" place remained empty. At lunch we knew the reason. The night before, his father, the head of a great financial enterprise, had been arrested: his business had been a gigantic swindle and thousands of small people found themselves robbed overnight of their hard-earned savings. The newspapers printed the news of the scandal with large headlines and photographs of the culprit and even of his family.

Now we understood why our unfortunate friend had not come to school. He was ashamed. Then one morning three weeks later the door opened; "Metternich" slipped in, took his place, immediately opened a book, and not once during the next two hours did he raise his eyes from it.

When the bell rang for the ten-minute recess we went out as usual into the corridors. "Metternich" went directly to the end of the corridor and stood alone, with his back to us, staring out the window as if absorbed. We knew he was avoiding meeting our eyes and that he was terribly alone. Evidently he was waiting for a sign of friendship from us. But uncertain how to approach him without hurting his pride, we hesitated. None of us had the courage to make a beginning.

After endless minutes the bell called us back to the classroom. "Metternich" strode in without a glance at us, his compressed lips still paler than before as he sat down and nervously opened his book. At the end of the session he left hurriedly so that none of us had a chance to speak to him.

We all felt a sense of guilt and began to deliberate how we could make up for it. He gave us no more opportunity, for the next morning his place was again empty. We learned that he had suddenly announced to his mother that he would not continue his studies. He left Vienna to become a dispensary apprentice in a small town and we never saw him again.

Had he been able to continue his studies, he would probably have surpassed all of us in life. Undoubtedly our hesitation and our failure to help had a considerable share in the breakdown of his career. One single word, one friendly gesture from us that morning might have given him strength to overcome his distress.

It was not lack of understanding, indifference, or unfriendly intention that made us let him down in that critical moment: it was but a lack of courage which so often prevents all of us from saying the right word when it is most needed. I am aware that it is difficult to approach a person whose soul is burning with shame at defeat or humiliation, but I learned from this early experience that one should never hesitate to obey the first impulse to give support, because a word or deed of compassion has real value only in the moment of utmost need.

—STEFAN ZWEIG.

✤ ✤ ✤

Emile Chartier, the philosopher who wrote as "Alain," had intellectual courage. No power on earth, he would say, should be allowed to destroy the personal, inner freedom which is every individual's birthright. One day he gave us remarkable proof of his independence. French professors are servants of the state; from time to time inspectors drop in to determine whether teachers are worthy of advancements. Alain was telling us why he disapproved of honors and decorations. "These toys," he said, "give a government too powerful a hold over the individual. There is a taint of bribery about them. How can a person who passionately desires a ribbon or rosette which the Minister alone can bestow live freely, uninhibited in action or judgment?"

At this moment the door opened and an inspector entered. He was a pompous, much-decorated individual. We looked at each other. Would Alain pursue the dangerous subject or would he elect to "play safe," since his future might be at stake? He greeted the inspector courteously, and then said gently, "I was explaining why I disapprove of decorations." We breathed more easily. Alain was still Alain. And, to the inspector's credit, be it said that Alain's boldness did not prevent his reappointment the following year.

—ANDRE MAUROIS.

✤ ✤ ✤

Though the heels of a wild horse seem limited weapons compared to the powerful jaws and teeth of many other beasts,

Frederick I of Prussia once demonstrated their effectiveness in battle. Seating himself, the Duke of Marlborough and some other guests safely behind metal gratings, he had the doors of several pens surrounding a small arena opened simultaneously. Out raced a lion, a bear, a bull, a tiger, a wolf—and a horse.

The first five at once charged one another, ripping at one another's throats, snorting and clawing, while the horse stood quietly watching. Eventually the bear, battle-scarred and furious, emerged victorious from the gory heap. Still the horse stood quietly, and the frenzied bear charged. The heels of the horse caught him a fearful blow, knocking him back. Again the bear attacked, and took a thunderous blow in the face. His mouth hung limply open: his jaw was broken, and the battle was over.

—ARTHUR VERNON, *The History and Romance of the Horse* (Waverly House).

✥ ✥ ✥

A dear old lady was about to have an operation for the removal of one of her eyes. Just as the surgeon was ready to administer the anesthetic, she stopped him and said: "I have a favor to ask of you, doctor." She looked up and smiled, "When you select a glass eye for me, be sure that it has a twinkle in it."

—CHARLES HANSON TOWNE, *Christian Herald.*

✥ ✥ ✥

During the Marshall Islands operations in the spring of 1942, five Jap dive-bombers swooped out of the clouds on Admiral Halsey's flagship. "I hit the deck," he recalls, "fustest and hardest. My staff trampled up and down my prostrate form."

Next day Halsey's eye fell on a first-class petty officer stationed at a near-by direction finder. "Rate that man a chief," he barked. "He had the guts to stand there and laugh at me when I was so scared yesterday!"

—GEORGE FIELDING ELIOT, *Pageant.*

✥ ✥ ✥

A marine who had lost his right arm on Iwo Jima lay on a bed in a California military hospital, silent, withdrawn.

Outside his window was a tall post to which was nailed, for some reason, a bit of three-ply cotton rope. A pair of linnets tugged and strained at this to get bits of it for their nest-building. Sometimes they succeeded in getting a scrap, sometimes they failed.

From his bed the marine watched quietly. Then suddenly one day he turned to his nurse. "You know, those birds make me ashamed of myself. Watch them tugging at that rope, will you! The only tool they have to work with is a bill less than an inch from their eyes! How much could I do if my hand was stuck on my nose instead of my wrist? And they sing on the job, too!" He grinned, for the first time in weeks, and asked: "What do we eat for chow tonight?"

—*Nature Magazine.*

✣ ✣ ✣

During World War II, a gnarled old French flower scientist developed a new rose and promptly, since he had nothing to lose but life, called it the Freedom Rose. This first angered, then amused, the Nazi masters. One day a colonel in the Paris division noticed that the Freedom Rose on its bush in Luxembourg Gardens was withering.

"See," he said to a French lad, standing near, "your Freedom Rose is dying."

"Yes, it is," said the boy, "but notice that buds have just sprouted below it. Sometimes one has to prune at the top—to keep healthy underground."

—IRVING HOFFMAN, *Hollywood Reporter.*

✣ ✣ ✣

"Can you fight?" Dr. Charles W. Eliot, president of Harvard University, once asked a young professor who had gone to him with a disconcerting problem.

"Why, yes," the man replied. "That is, I think I can."

"Can you fight when you are in the minority?"

"I have done so occasionally."

"Can you fight when everybody is against you—when not one man is ready to lend you support?"

"I am ready to try it if necessary."

"Then you need have no fear. But if you have convictions, it will sometimes be necessary to do no less."

—ROLLO WALTER BROWN, *Lonely Americans* (Coward-McCann).

✣ ✣ ✣

"I'm not afraid of anything," bragged Maurice. "Once I even cut off a lion's tail with my pen knife."

"Why didn't you cut off his head?" someone asked.

Maurice became rather sheepish. "Well, to tell the truth, someone had already cut it off."

—*L'Action Sociale,* Haiti (Droke House Translation).

✣ ✣ ✣

A few years ago I met a family in a city under military siege. Their house had been hit several times and the family was huddled in the bathroom, the least exposed place. A board had been laid across the bathtub to make a dining table. On the board was a spotless white cloth and a bowl of fresh flowers.

"In the very next hour," the woman told me, "we may be blown to bits. But in this hour we are living, and we will live as we always did."

—ZELDA POPKIN, *Coronet.*

✣ ✣ ✣

Napoleon often referred to Marshal Ney as the bravest man he had ever known. Yet Ney's knees trembled so badly one morning before battle that he had trouble mounting his horse. Looking down at them when he finally was in the saddle, he shouted contemptuously, "Shake away, knees! You would shake worse than that if you knew where I am going to take you."

—JOHN A. O'BRIEN, *Art of Courageous Living* (Declan X. McMullen Co.)

✣ ✣ ✣

My father had a natural affection for the kind of warrior who has no conception of defeat. On the battlefield of Gettysburg he bade me note and never forget the monument to the young Pennsylvania color-bearer who had led a charge and had become isolated when his regiment fell back. The major sent him a message: "Bring the colors back to the regiment."

The young man replied: "You bring the regiment back to the colors!"

—ROGER WILLIAM RIIS.

✤ ✤ ✤

At a dinner concluding a long and boring convention in Chicago a parade of reluctant speakers had been pried from their chairs to "say a few words." As the 16th orator took his seat, a sigh of expectation filled the room. Deliverance was in sight. But no! The chairman was on his feet again. "I'm sure this meeting does not want to break up without hearing from our good friend, Ken Roe."

Mr. Roe stood up. "Gentlemen," he said, "I am reminded of the story of the two skeletons. For days they had been imprisoned in the mustiest closet imaginable. Finally, one skeleton said to the other, 'What are we doing here, anyhow?' Whereupon, the other skeleton replied, 'I'll be darned if I know. But if we had any guts, we'd get the hell out of here.'"

—MATT ROBERTS, in *The Saturday Evening Post.*

✤ ✤ ✤

I was brought up on the family story about Cousin Abigail and the typhoid epidemic. Cousin Abigail had always had an easy life. She had a devoted husband, an excellent cook and a trustworthy nurse for her healthy children. Everybody thought this was providential, for Abigail was very delicate. It was in the days when fainting was approved of, and Abigail fainted easily.

Then typhoid fever struck the town. The children came down with it, the cook was summoned to her own sick family, the nurse fell ill, and finally so did Abigail's husband. There was nobody to care for five dangerously sick people except Abigail, who had always had her breakfast served in bed.

For weeks she sponged fevered bodies, gave medicine, scrubbed floors, cooked and served. One son died in the night. She kept the news from the others; stood alone beside the grave; and wiping the tears from her eyes went back to the stricken family.

The others gradually recovered. And what happened to Cousin Abigail after that? Instead of going back to her indolent ways she made it her business to find children whose parents had died in the epidemic and see that they had a fair chance at a happy life. And that led her to start the first farm-school home for orphans ever seen in that region.

Cousin Abigail could have gone on fainting and weeping—and her family would have died. She rose to the opportunity which turned her from a weak, selfish girl into a strong, beneficent woman. May we also rise!

DOROTHY CANFIELD FISHER.

✤ ✤ ✤

Spring before last I was passing through a small town in the fruit-growing section of the Rockies. The country folks were evidently having a picnic. There were games, singing and dancing to the old-fashioned music of a harmonica. I stopped beside a white-haired, sun-browned country woman in a faded dress.

"What are you celebrating?" I asked.

She looked me over. "You must be a stranger. Don't you know it's Apple Blossom Day?"

Looking around at all the bare trees, I said, "Where are the blossoms?"

She let out a tiny sigh. "They all froze last week, for miles around."

"Then what've you got to be so happy about?"

She squared her stooped shoulders, threw back a proud head. "It'd take more than a little frost to get us folks down. We had a mighty good harvest last year, and—God willing—there will be apple blossoms again next spring."

—SOPHIE PENNA, *Reader's Digest*.

✤ ✤ ✤

COURTESY

It was a lovely, mild spring day in Paris when Alexander Dumas, Sr., was told that the director of the city's largest theater wanted to see him.

The latter asked if it was true that Dumas' latest play was to be presented elsewhere, then stormed, ranted, offered higher and higher prices, and finally demanded, "Why the devil, if they didn't offer you more money, were you so stupid as to let them have it?"

Dumas replied, "Well, Monsieur Dartois used a simple, but very human, very meaningful gesture . . ."

"What was that?"

"He took off his hat whenever he talked to me."

—*Frankfurter Illustrierte,* Germany
(DROKE HOUSE translation).

✤ ✤ ✤

It was during a bargain sale and tempers were rising. "If I were trying to match politeness," said the customer to the salesgirl, "I'd have a hard time finding it here."

The clerk responded: "Will you kindly let me see your sample, please?"

—*Successful Farming.*

✤ ✤ ✤

In a Guatemalan office I asked for a pair of scissors. The young woman looked around her desk and then with a smile and an apology called to another woman. They talked and called a third. More discussion followed. Finally the answer came. They had no scissors, as I had begun to suspect. Ten minutes had been wasted. Annoyed and puzzled by the "act," I mentioned the incident to an American resident. "The girls were paying you a compliment," he explained. "They knew they had no scissors. They wanted to let you know that as a friend of their boss and guest in their country, your slightest wish would receive the greatest consideration from them." That was a lesson in courtesy.

—FRANCIS X. MARTINEX, *Holiday.*

✤ ✤ ✤

A New York bus driver, attending a company Courtesy and Safety School, cited an incident that "changed my attitude toward passengers." A woman got on the bus and asked a "bunch of questions."

"Can't you read, lady?" he growled.

Softly, she replied, "I can't read or write, sir. I never went to school."

"I felt about this high," the driver said, pointing to a small stool.

—*New York Times.*

✤ ✤ ✤

Fred stopped at Tony's house to play, and by supper time it was raining. Tony's mother got out her son's raincoat and rubbers for his little friend to wear home.

Fred seemed reluctant, and Tony's mother said, "I'm sure your mother would do as much for Tony."

"My mother," said Fred, "would ask Tony to stay to supper."

—*Christian Science Monitor.*

✤ ✤ ✤

An old crossroads merchant wrathfully wrote a debtor who had promised time and again to settle a long delinquent account.

"You are just a mule-eared liar. If you don't settle up, I aim to clobber you until there won't be nothing left but a pair of suspenders and a wart. I want my money and I want it now."

He signed his name with a flourish, reread the letter with grim satisfaction, then added the postscript, "Please excuse the pencil."

—*L. & N. Magazine.*

✤ ✤ ✤

"You short-changed that man," the storekeeper said to his teen-age son. Without waiting for the boy's confused look to deepen, the father explained: "This is your first day in the business. The first thing I want you to learn is this: a customer is short-changed unless you give him a smile—a really friendly, God-bless-you kind of smile. And that holds true even if he doesn't buy a thing; he still has a smile coming to him."

—ELLSWORTH KALAS, *Good Business.*

✤ ✤ ✤

A minister, a scientist, and a lawyer were adrift on a life raft in the tropics. At last they sighted land. But the wind died down while they were still a short way off the beach. The lawyer, the only one who could swim, volunteered to go ashore with a line and pull the raft to land. The minister knelt and prayed for his safety.

Then the lawyer dived in. His companions saw the black fin of a shark making straight for him. The shark disappeared, then came up on the other side, having passed under the swimmer. Shortly they saw an even bigger shark darting toward him, but this one also swerved just in time.

After the lawyer had reached shallow water, the minister said to the scientist: "There, you Doubting Thomas, there is proof of the power of prayer."

"Power of prayer, hell!" retorted the scientist. "That was just professional courtesy."

—ALEX F. OSBORN

✤ ✤ ✤

CRIME

The eight-year-old son of a professor of psychology was taken to see Fifth Avenue during a visit in New York. He stopped in amazement before the show window of a famous jeweler, where the use of invisible glass makes it appear that nothing but air separates the passer-by from the glittering display. The boy gazed for a while and then turned away, saying wistfully, "If I were not so well adjusted, I would reach in there and grab some of those jewels!"

—*Rockefeller Center Magazine.*

✤ ✤ ✤

A man who turned up at San Quentin with a "truth drug" which was supposed to revolutionize crime detection got a sympathetic hearing. A Sacramento lifer, convicted of murder, volunteered for the experiment. Doctor Stanley, the prison surgeon, recognized the serum, which was supposed to weaken the will while leaving the memory active.

As soon as the prisoner was under the effects of the drug, the "savant" began his questioning. "Did you kill that man?" he demanded.

"No," came the loud, clear answer.

The witnesses stared at each other. A gross miscarriage of

justice was about to be proved. The "savant" looked around triumphantly and then put his next question, "Who killed the man?"

"There was a pause, then the man's answer rang out firmly, "Dr. Stanley!"

The doctor says he hasn't tried any truth drugs since.

—IRENE SOEHREN, *Today's Health.*

✣ ✣ ✣

CRITICISM

The owner of a fish market ordered a new sign painted, of which he was very proud. It read: "Fresh Fish For Sale Here."

A passerby asked, "Why do you put in that word 'fresh.' Certainly you wouldn't offer for sale fish that were not fresh."

So the marketman painted out the word, leaving the sign: "Fish For Sale Here."

"Why do you say 'here'?" asked a second observer. "You're not selling them anywhere else, are you?"

So the marketman erased everything except the words, "Fish For Sale."

A third man asked, "Why use the words, 'For Sale'? You wouldn't have fish here unless they were for sale."

Then there remained only the word "Fish." Said the marketman, "Now, surely no one can find fault with that."

But another dissenter appeared. "I see no sense in putting up that sign, 'Fish' " he said. "You can smell them a block away!" So that's why the fish market has no sign!

✣ ✣ ✣

Among my pupils in a high school chemistry class was a lad who had a tendency to monopolize discussions. I decided that such a troublesome habit should be called to the attention of his parents. On his report card I wrote: "Allan is a good student but he talks too much."

Several days later the report was returned. Underneath my comment the boy's father had added: "You should meet his mother."

—HAROLD R. MAURER.

To a new Supreme Court judge who had just relinquished a very lucrative practice in New York to go on the bench, a rich clubman said: "I can't understand how you can give up your practice for the salary of a Supreme Court judge. Why, it costs me twice that to live."

"I wouldn't pay it, Harry. It isn't worth it," replied the judge.

—WATSON B. BERRY.

✤ ✤ ✤

When Sir George Adam Smith was visiting in this country, a reporter asked him: "When and how should matters of Biblical criticism be studied?"

"In the class room and the library," was the reply. "Not in the pulpit. I always warn my students of that. They must not come into the pulpit reeking with criticism; a child that smells soapy is not clean."

—*Church Management.*

✤ ✤ ✤

Alfred Hertz, the conductor, was once confronted by a lady after a concert who gushed, "Wasn't that modern quartet perfectly awful?" Dr. Hertz answered, "Not being an amateur, I can't tell quite so quickly!"

—ERICH WEILER, *Opera and Concert.*

✤ ✤ ✤

I deeply admired the late Hugh Jennings of baseball fame.

"You ought to have heard Ty Cobb knocking you the other day," one player told him.

Hugh's answer was immediate. "He's out there winning ball games, and the game is the thing. Whether he likes me personally is of no consequence. If you and some of the rest of the boys fought as hard to win as Ty does, I'd just as soon have less of your affection. The more games Ty wins, the more of a success I am as a manager. I don't think Ty does hate me. The only way he can prove that is by not winning games."

—MALCOLM BINGAY, *Detroit Free Press.*

✤ ✤ ✤

The great composer, Liszt, is said to have called upon Rossini with a letter of introduction. Rossini asked him to play, listened politely, and when he was done, asked him what the piece was. Liszt said, "It is a march which I have written on the death of Meyerbeer. How do you like it?"

Rossini replied, "I like it very much, but don't you think it would have been better if you had died and Meyerbeer had written the music?"

—Professor Bergen Evans, Northwestern University.

✤ ✤ ✤

Fierce as he was with his pen, Dean Swift was always kind to his servants. Even when he had to rebuke them he did so in a comical, kindly way. At dinner one evening, a joint had been overdone. Swift told the butler to call the cook, who presently appeared in the dining room trembling. Swift said to her: "Sarah, take the mutton to the kitchen, and do it less."

In utter amazement, she replied, "Sir, that is impossible."

Thereupon the Dean said: "Then for the future, if you must commit faults, commit faults that can be mended."

—*Times of Brazil.*

✤ ✤ ✤

A preacher kept on his desk a special notebook, labeled, "Complaints of members against other members." When someone called to tell him the faults of another he would say, "Here's my complaint book. I'll write down what you say, and you can sign it. Then when I have to take the matter up officially I shall know what I may expect you to testify to." The sight of the open book and ready pen had its effect. "Oh, no, I couldn't sign anything like that." And no entry was made. The preacher says he kept the book for forty years, opened it probably a thousand times, and never wrote a line in it.

—Rev. W. Wallace Downs, *Community Tidings.*

✤ ✤ ✤

I knew a young artist who had a genius for picking out another's weakness or affectation.

One night this young man had a dream. He saw himself on a barren road, struggling beneath a heavy burden. He cried out as he strove to support it: "What is this weight that I must carry? Why must I carry it?"

From somewhere he seemed to hear: "It is the weight of the faults you have found in others. Why do you complain? *You* discovered them—should they not belong to you now?"

—MAURICE MAETERLINCK, in *Cosmopolitan.*

✣ ✣ ✣

At an art show Max Weber met Abe Walkowitz, the artist with whom he had shared a Paris studio fifty years ago. "Abe," Weber greeted the seventy-three year old painter, "I hear you just had an eye operation. Will you be able to see well enough to paint?"

"I think so," Walkowitz replied. "And if I can't see, I'll become a critic."

—LEONARD LYONS, *New York Post.*

✣ ✣ ✣

When Polish Communist journalists visited West Germany, they were frequently told, "one of the differences between the free West and the communist East is that we in the West can criticize our governments, while you in the East dare not." The answer appeared soon afterward in the columns of the Warsaw papers. "It is true, the West can freely criticize the government and administrations. But such criticism is necessary because the capitalist governments do not represent the interests of the peoples concerned. We in Poland do not criticize our government, because there is absolutely no need for so doing."

—Sudeten Bulletin.

✣ ✣ ✣

Plutarch tells of a Roman, divorced from his wife, who was blamed by friends for the separation.

"Was she not beautiful?" they chorused. "Was she not chaste?"

The Roman, holding out his shoe for them to see, asked if it were not good-looking and well made. "Yet," he added, "none of you can tell where it pinches me."

✣ ✣ ✣

Once when Henry Ward Beecher was in the midst of an impassioned flight of oratory, a drunken man in the balcony waved his arms and crowed like a rooster. Instantly Beecher stopped, took out his watch, and remarked: "What, morning already? I wouldn't have believed it, but the instincts of the lower animal are infallible."

—EDGAR DEWITT JONES, *Lords of Speech* (Willett, Clark).

✣ ✣ ✣

One morning Professor John Berdan of Yale read to an English composition class a particularly inept theme and, as usual, called for comments. The students panned it unmercifully.

"Interesting," commented Berdan, "because I wrote the theme myself." As the critics began to blush, he continued: "You are quite right. This theme is incredibly bad. I spent two hours of painstaking effort last night to make sure I had not omitted a single feature of poor writing, and I believe I succeeded."

The professor paused for dramatic effect.

"What astounds me," he resumed, "is how you men can dash these things off day after day *in ten minutes*."

—BEIRNE LAY, JR.

✣ ✣ ✣

At the last big election, in a town in New Mexico, an old Mexican was standing near the curb on the public square, watching a political rally. The principal candidate was a notorious rabble-rouser. He hopped about excitedly, giving orders to his henchmen, complaining of this and that, waving his arms to real or imaginary friends in the crowd, and in every way trying to call attention to himself.

"Who is that?" I asked the old Mexican.

"*Es un hombre de muchas pulgas,*—He's a man with many fleas," he replied, in as pat a political comment as I've heard in many a day.

—STANLEY WALKER.

✣ ✣ ✣

Attending a church bazaar, Abraham Lincoln tendered a $20 bill to pay for a bunch of violets. The lady at the booth, making no attempt to return any change, gushed, "Oh, thank you, Mr. President."

Lincoln reached down from his great height, and gently touched the lady on the wrist, saying, "And what do you call this?"

"Why, Mr. President, that is my wrist. What did you think it was?"

"Well," drawled Lincoln, "I thought it might be your ankle. Everything is so high around here."

—ETHWELL EDDY HANSON.

✣ ✣ ✣

A judge who was on circuit at a certain town was always sure of being annoyed by some sneering remarks from a conceited lawyer. After one such occasion, someone asked the judge at dinner, why he didn't come down strong on the fellow. The judge dropped his knife and fork, placed his chin on his hands, and his elbows on the table as he gave emphasis to his story: "Up in our town," he said, "there lives a widow who has a dog which, whenever the moon shines, goes and barks and barks at it all night." Stopping short he quietly began eating again. One of the company asked, "Well, Judge, what about the dog and the moon?" "Oh, the moon kept on shining," he said.

—*Sunday School Chronicle.*

✣ ✣ ✣

CURIOSITY

Before the start of a particularly lurid French trial, the judge turned to the women spectators who packed the court room: "Perhaps you are not acquainted with the type of case to be tried today. Some things will be said which are the kind a respectable woman should not hear. In view of this, will all the respectable women please leave the court room?" Not a woman moved.

After a moment, the judge turned to an usher: "Now that all the respectable women have left, will you show the remaining women out?"

—DON DOWD.

✣ ✣ ✣

One summer day on a crowded Clyde coast steamer, young Tommy could not find a seat. Going to the rail, he shouted, "Dad! Look at the whale!" Everybody laughed but curiosity overcame them, and soon the rail was crowded. Then Tommy quietly strolled to a seat. But the throng at the rail continued to grow, and now Tommy himself feared he was missing something. He pushed his way to the rail, but only water and seagulls met his gaze. When he turned, every seat was occupied.

—D. STEWART, *Rotarian.*

✤ ✤ ✤

DEATH

Soon after my return from America to my native village in Yugoslavia my mother told me that Uncle Yanez, her favorite brother, was dying.

My mother went on, "The week before you arrived I went to Yanez' village to visit him, and he said to me, 'Well, Ana, I'll be gone before haying time; surely by the time buckwheat is ripe. But, taking one thing with another, I am not complaining. This is the first time I've really been sick in my life. I've plowed my share of furrows. I've worn thin many a scythe.

" 'But I should like to see my strange nephew before I go, the boy who writes books in English and has an American wife. He may be coming home just in time for my funeral.' Then he smiled, and said he would not die till you visited him; he would wait."

After we had visited him, outside Cousin Angela was placing an enlongated tub of water near the door. "That's for Death to wash his scythe when he leaves," she explained to Stella. "The idea is to be as accommodating to Death as possible."

During all this Stella and I could not help contrasting the attitude toward death in America with that of these people.

"Here," she said, "Death is a rather mild though inexorable fellow who comes and stands by the door with his scythe, waiting till his victim is through saying good-bye to everybody; then does his work because, somehow, it needs to be done . . . In America, Death is a gangster who puts one on the spot—then bang! He doesn't carry a scythe, but a sawed-off shotgun."

—LOUIS ADAMIC, *The Native's Return.*

When Michelangelo, already well along in years, was discussing life with an old friend, the latter commented, "Yes, after such a good life it's hard to look death in the eye."

"Not at all!" contradicted Michelangelo. "Since life was such a pleasure, death, coming from the same great Source, cannot displease us."

—*Temmler Werke* publication, Hamburg (Droke House Translation).

♣ ♣ ♣

Benjamin Franklin once wrote to a person with whom he shared the loss of a mutual friend:

"We are spirits. That bodies should be lent to us, while they can afford us pleasure, assist us in acquiring knowledge, or in doing good to our fellow creatures, is a kind and benevolent act of God. When they become unfit for these purposes . . . and answer none of the intentions for which they were given, it is equally kind and benevolent that a way is provided by which we may get rid of them. Death is that way. Our friend and we were invited abroad on a party of pleasure, which is to last forever. His conveyance was ready first, and he has gone before us. We could not all conveniently start together; and why should you and I be grieved at this, since we are soon to follow, and know where to find him."

♣ ♣ ♣

DECEPTION

My mother and aunts used to love to go blueberrying. I was a lazy child and always carried the smallest pail. While the others picked I lolled about. One day I filled my pail with moss and topped it off with a thin layer of berries. The pail looked full of berries, and I was highly commended for this unusual industry.

The next morning Mother made pies, and there was a "saucer pie" for me, with berries peeping through a slit in the crust. Imagine my chagrin to find beneath the tempting crust—moss!

Before I could fly into a tantrum, my mother said, "When you cheat others you are cheating yourself most of all. You are training your bad impulses; soon your good ones will cease to exist."

I have never felt any gain would be mine by cheating since that deceptive pie.

—M.H.L.

✣ ✣ ✣

Some students of biology laid devious plans to play a trick on their learned professor. They took the head of one beetle, the body of another of a totally different species, the wings of a third, the legs of a fourth. All of these members they joined together with glue. The result was a very credible monstrosity.

Then, pretending great excitement, they brought it to him as a new discovery. They eagerly asked him to identify it for them.

Adjusting his spectacles, the professor looked the creature over thoroughly. Then, clearing his throat, he turned and addressed his class. "I think I can identify this odd insect for you. It goes under the common name of 'humbug.' "

✣ ✣ ✣

DEMOCRACY

The students of social studies at the George School, Bucks County, Pennsylvania, were not convinced that democracy was the superior way of life, early in World War II. Democracy was ponderous, inefficient. Dictatorships got things done.

"Well," said the teacher, Richard McFeeley, "the only way to find out which is better is to experiment. As a starter, for the next two weeks this class will operate as a dictatorship."

Thenceforth, discussion was forbidden; questions were frowned upon; failure was severely punished. In addition, Mr. McFeeley organized a small Gestapo: four boys were appointed to circulate secretly among their fellows and take notes of what was said out of class. Then without warning, the teacher read aloud from their reports, quoting remarks boys had made in private about him and other members of the faculty, gossip about fellow students, violations of rules: an entire catalogue of intimate revelations never meant to be made public.

The students sat there stunned by the impact of dictatorship in all its ugly reality. Democracy was restored, by acclamation, at the end of the fifth day.

—GEORGE KENT.

✣ ✣ ✣

DESCRIPTION

The identity of the young lady is withheld, but the memory of her answer lingers on with the instructor conducting a science course at the high school. One of the requirements in the written quiz was, "Define a bolt and nut, and explain the difference." The girl wrote:

"A bolt is a thing like a stick of hard metal, such as iron, with a square bunch on one end and a lot of scratching wound around the other end. A nut is similar to the bolt only just the opposite, being a hole in a little chunk of iron sawed off short, with wrinkles around the inside of the hole."

The startled professor marked that one with an "A."

—*Sunshine Magazine.*

✣ ✣ ✣

DETERMINATION

George Leigh Mallory, master at Charterhouse School, near London, was perhaps the most famous mountaineer of his day and the only man to participate in all three expeditions to scale Mt. Everest in the early 1920's.

Slight, slim, with a boyish face, Mallory was far from the popular conception of a rugged outdoor man. Climbing was to him not exercise or amusement but a passionate devotion, less a physical than a spiritual adventure. His explanation of why men climb is the simplest and yet perhaps the most profound that has ever been given.

"Why," a friend asked him, "do you try to climb this mountain?"

Mallory answered simply, *"Because it is there!"*

—JAMES RAMSEY ULLMAN, in *High Conquest*
(J. B. Lippincott Co.).

Pasteur drove himself with relentless ferocity in exploration of the microbe world and suddenly fell victim of a hemorrhage of the brain. He nearly died—and he was only 45. But when he heard that work on the new laboratory being built for him in Paris had been frugally stopped in expectation of his death, he was furious and made up his mind to live. He staggered to his feet, and limped back to his new laboratory. Thenceforth, he was paralyzed on one side, but he set out to prove that "it is in the power of men to make parasitic maladies disappear from the face of the earth."

It was after this that he discovered the process of immunization and continued his microbe hunting which led to perfecting the process of immunization against rabies.

Let our young scientists and doctors remember the testament Pasteur left us in 1892 on his 70th birthday when a medal was given him at the Sorbonne. Lord Lister was there, and famous men from many nations, and galleries were packed. There was a hush as the old searcher limped up the aisle, leaning on the arm of the President of the Republic. The voice of the fierce microbe hunter was gone; his son read the words that were his heritage to the future.

"Do not let yourselves be tainted by a barren skepticism, do not be discouraged by the sadness of certain hours which pass over nations. Live in the serene peace of laboratories and libraries. Say to yourselves first: What have I done for my instruction? and as you advance: What have I done for my country? until the time comes when you may have the immense happiness of thinking that you have contributed in some way to the progress and good of humanity."

It was to the young people of today that Pasteur was calling.

—PAUL DE KRUIF in *Microbe Hunters* (Harcourt, Brace).

✣ ✣ ✣

One of the reasons why you can buy an electric light bulb today for 19 cents that in 1931 would have cost 40 cents, and would have delivered only half the present quantity of light, is the joke old-timers in General Electric's lamp division used to play on new engineers. They were assigned the "impossible" task of frosting bulbs on the inside. Such a bulb would diffuse more light with less absorption, but everyone knew it couldn't be done, and each perspiring neophyte forgave the snickers greeting his failure.

One day, however, Marvin Pipkin was initiated. And he not only found a way to frost bulbs on the inside, but developed an etching acid which gave minute rounded pits instead of sharp depressions, thus materially strengthening each bulb. No one told him it couldn't be done, and he took it so seriously that he did it.

—*Christian Science Monitor.*

✣ ✣ ✣

DEVOTION

Throughout his life, John Wesley went about preaching and doing good. During the most productive period of his career, he traveled 5,000 miles a year, preached fifteen sermons a week, and looked every hostile man full in the face. In his wide journeying he carried a Bible, a change of linen, and the implements of his simple diet. So deep was his devotion, so complete his consecration, that it has been movingly said of him: "When at length he came to die, he left only a knife, a fork, two spoons—and the Methodist Church."

✣ ✣ ✣

DILEMMA

Early in World War II a British gardener's boy reported the following incident: "We been laughing ever since they bombed the hall, for Sir John, he has the most terrible strict system about having the whole household roused as soon as there's a raid warning. Something slipped up and they didn't get no warning at all and the first thing they knew was a German plane dropping a bomb in the gardens and when they got out there they found the air-raid shelter blown to bits. So Sir John don't know rightly what to do, for the chap that didn't give the warning saved all their lives. And seeing what a proper martinet he is, we can't stop laughing."

—Rebecca West.

DILIGENCE

My greatest failing as a care-free youngster was in becoming too easily discouraged over a task that seemed difficult; I was not a plugger.

One evening my father handed me a thin board and a penknife, asking me to scratch a line across the width of the board. I followed instructions, and board and knife were then locked in Dad's desk. The performance was repeated every evening and at the end of a week I was overcome with curiosity. Still it went on. Each evening I would draw the knife once along the deepening groove.

Then came the night when there was no groove. My last light effort had cut the board in two. Dad looked long at me and finally said, "You never would have believed this possible with such little effort, would you? But the success or failure of your life depends not so much on how hard you try, but on whether you keep at it." It was an object lesson impossible to forget and one which even a ten-year-old could profit by.

—NOAH SEMONOFF.

✣ ✣ ✣

DIPLOMACY

With tears in her eyes his wife exclaimed: "I know you don't love me—you've forgotten my birthday!"

"Darling," replied the quick thinker, "I am more sorry than I can say, but it is really your fault."

"My fault?" she exclaimed. "How can that be?"

He took her hand in his. "How can I remember your birthday," he asked, "when there is never anything about you to remind me that you are a day older than you were a year ago?"

—*Kablegram.*

✣ ✣ ✣

The late David Lloyd-George, British statesman, had been a master at evading embarrassing questions. Once, while campaigning for a seat in Parliament, he was addressing an audience only half of whom were friendly to his views. He decided that it would be prudent to make a middle of the road speech. The crowd, however, would have none of his vacillating.

"Will you or will you not support the bill?" demanded one listener, when the future Prime Minister started to discuss a bill then being debated in the house.

"I will," said Lloyd-George. Half the audience cheered. "Not," he continued. The other half cheered. "Tell now," he concluded. At this the entire audience cheered loudly.

—E. E. EDGAR.

✣ ✣ ✣

When Voltaire visited England in the year 1727, feeling ran high against the French, and the great author felt this dislike keenly. Once he was accosted by an angry crowd of people as he went for a walk. "Kill him! Hang the Frenchman!" cried threatening voices around him. Voltaire stood on the curbstone and cried out: "Englishmen! You want to kill me because I am a Frenchman! Am I not already punished enough in not being an Englishman?"

The crowd applauded this speech and escorted him home in safety.

—*Toastmaster.*

✣ ✣ ✣

Franz Liszt, no less a diplomat than a musician, had a stock reply for young ladies, especially pretty ones, who demanded unmerited praise of their talents.

"Maestro," the young things would inquire, "do you not think I have a good voice?"

"Ah, my dear young lady," Liszt would reply, his voice ringing with enthusiasm, "good is *not* the word!"

—*Your Life.*

✣ ✣ ✣

"I don't know whether I like these photos or not," said the young woman. "They seem rather indistinct."

"Ah, but you must remember, ma'am," said the wily photographer, "that your face is far from plain."

DISCERNMENT

Li Yung Ku, my wise Tibetan teacher, told me this tale about his grandfather, who must have been a most reamrkable and delightful old man. Once his grandfather said to him: "You have two school books, both on the same subject. One is fat and full of footnotes but the other is quite brief. Which do you like best?"

"The little one," Li Yung Ku replied.

"Can you tell me why?"

"Because it is easier to read and it makes you think more. The other one says everything for you and you do not have to think."

"Very good." Then his grandfather recited two poems, and asked him which he liked best. Little Li liked the one he did not understand better than the one he did understand.

"Good," said his grandfather. "Now tell me which picture you like best, the one on this wall with the ducks among the reeds or the one with the mountains and the rain."

"The rain picture," said the boy.

"Why?"

"I don't know."

"Ah," said the wise old man. "Perhaps you really do know, only you do not have the words to say it. For how then could you have chosen the better one in each case? Remember that a thing should always be itself; but it cannot be a big thing unless it suggests more than it really is. The secret of greatness lies in the power a thing has to suggest more than it says. That is why we find pictures in good poetry and poetry in good pictures."

—Manuel Komroff.

✣ ✣ ✣

One incident in connection with the development of electrical lighting is especially interesting. Edison sold electric bulbs for forty cents each, while they cost $1.10. Then he got the cost down to eighty cents, but still sold them for forty cents. The third year the cost was reduced to fifty cents, with the losses skyrocketing because of rapidly increased sales. By the fourth year, costs were down to thirty-seven cents, and the losses were quickly recovered. Electric lighting would have been greatly retarded had Edison insisted on making a profit on the earlier lamp sales that were made.

✣ ✣ ✣

DISCIPLINE

In a Mother's Day contest conducted by a newspaper, the winning slogan was that of a boy who wrote: "My mother keeps on speaking terms with God and on spanking terms with me."

—Thomas F. Quinlivan, *Mary Immaculate.*

✣ ✣ ✣

If a Swiss boy sees a sign that to walk on the grass is forbidden, and the fine is a certain amount, he carefully keeps off, but an American boy feels in his pocket to see if he has that much.

—*Youth Leaders Digest.*

✣ ✣ ✣

A psychiatrist in a mental institution tells how physical discipline proved to be the healing factor in a sick mind. A patient was suffering from a severe psychotic condition. Neither psychotherapy nor shock treatment nor drugs were successful.

One night the patient was especially exasperating. In desperation the head orderly kicked him in the seat of the pants. The next day, for the first time, he began to respond to treatment and progress was steady until he was well enough to go home. Before leaving, the patient said to the orderly, in the presence of the psychiatrists and doctors: "They tried everything to cure me. But none of it did a bit of good until you gave me that kick in the pants."

—Kermit J. Nord, *Pulpit Digest.*

✣ ✣ ✣

In Chinatown where 8000 persons live in a few city blocks, juvenile delinquency is rarely a problem. A police captain gave me a reason: "Chinese children are trained to respect their parents and uphold the family ideals."

I wondered if this was the answer. I went to my friend Eddie Wu, for he had told me that when he was ten he had been arrested for truancy. Eddie suggested that I talk with his father.

"My son is known in Chinatown as 'Number One Bad Boy'" Mr. Fu told me.

Eddie sadly murmured, "Must I be reminded forever of my wild oat?"

"Yes—for I have eaten it," replied Mr. Wu. He explained that the first of all virtues is filial piety. It begins with serving one's parents, leads to serving one's kind, and ends in establishing one's character.

"When a child in Chinatown is bad-mannered and misbehaves," Mr. Wu went on, "it is the father who is criticized. It is his first duty to his country, his neighbors and himself to train his children properly."

"But suppose he is too busy, or doesn't care?" I asked.

"Then he loses face. His neighbors, his cousins, his friends and business associates would no longer invite him into their homes, nor would he be asked to feasts. And if he loses face with his family and friends he might as well go out and make a gun go pop into his heart.

"So we Chinese are very strict. What happened to you, my son, when you were arrested?" asked Mr. Wu, chuckling.

Eddie looked sheepish. "My father did not speak to me for two months. He took away all my playthings. I was not allowed to leave the house after school hours. My friends all laughed at me. I was very unhappy."

—Carl Glick, *Shake Hands with the Dragon* (Whittlesey House, McGraw-Hill).

✤ ✤ ✤

When I was in the penny-candy stage I spent many long minutes picking out my sweets, and sometimes even longer deciding whether to eat or save them. One day my grandfather, who often accompanied me on these pilgrimages, took out his watch and told me that hereafter my decisions must be made before the second hand had started on its next lap.

Grandfather explained that life is one choice after another, and that decisions should be made promptly and always with an earnest resolution that there would be no regrets if they turned out poorly. At first 59 seconds would tick away before I could take a breath and shout out my decision. But we played that game for years, and eventually my mental process was stepped up to a point where important decisions could be made instantly. Equally valuable to me has been the strength I have acquired in deciding "the die is cast; there shall be no regrets."

—George Gordon Paton.

✤ ✤ ✤

Little Claude's mother had reluctantly allowed her precious child to attend public school. She gave the teacher a long list of instructions.

"My Claude is so sensitive," she explained. "Don't ever punish him. Just slap the boy next to him. That will frighten Claude."

—*Philadelphia Bulletin.*

✤ ✤ ✤

DISCIPLINE—Self

A mother, who had just punished her child for not doing something he knew he ought to do, was somewhat taken aback when he turned a tear-stained face to her and asked, "How do you *make* yourself do the things you ought to do?"

—*Whatsoever Things.*

✤ ✤ ✤

DISCOURAGEMENT

The spirit of despair laid its withering hand on Martin Luther, and he almost lost his grit to grapple with life. While he was in this frame of mind, Mrs. Luther appeared before him dressed in deep mourning. When Luther looked up and saw her strange attire, he inquired the reason for her behavior; she replied, "God is dead and I am mourning His decease." "Nonsense," shouted Luther. "From the way you were acting," said she, "I thought God must be dead and that you were running the universe for Him."

—Strother A. Campbell, *The Grit to Gamble with Life.*

DISCOVERY

The great Eddie Stinson, back in 1916, discovered how to get out of a tailspin. Once in a spin no flier had ever recovered. However hard one pulled back on the stick, nothing would make a ship's nose come up out of that twisting, uncontrollable descent. Stinson, caught in a spin, thought he might as well die quickly. He pushed the stick forward for a steep dive. The spinning stopped and the ship recovered. Thus the suicidal reaction was the saving one.

—Wolfgang Langewiesche, in *Harper's Magazine.*

✣ ✣ ✣

DRINK—Drinking

Once upon a time a Mohammedan came to one of his religious leaders, called a Kadi, and asked, "If I eat dates, is that against the commands of religion?"

"No," said the Kadi.

"And may I add some water?"

"Certainly."

"And is it wrong to take a little yeast?"

"Oh, no."

"Well," went on the questioner, "date wine consists only of these three things. Why is it forbidden by the laws of our religion?"

The Kadi thought a moment and then said, "If I throw a handful of dust on your head, will that cause pain?"

"No."

"And if I add some water—will it hurt you then?"

"I think not."

"Now, if I mix dust and water together, burn it into a brick, and hit you on the head with it, what then?"

—*Dry Legion.*

✣ ✣ ✣

At a State dinner, a toast was proposed to an admiral who had just achieved a signal victory. As others present raised their glasses of champagne and drank, William Jennings Bryan lifted a glass of water. In explanation, he said: "The Admiral won his victory on water. So I toast him with water. When he wins a similar victory on champagne, I will toast him with champagne."

✤ ✤ ✤

You can get along with a wooden leg, but you can't get along with a wooden head. The physical value of man is not so much. Man, as analyzed in our laboratories, is worth about ninety-eight cents. Seven bars of soap, lime enough to whitewash a chicken-coop, phosphorus enough to cover the heads of a thousand matches, is not so much to see. It is the brain that counts! But in order that your brain may be kept clear, you must keep your body fit and well. That cannot be done if one drinks liquor. A man who has to drag around a habit that is a danger and a menace to society ought to go off in the woods and live alone.

—Dr. Charles Mayo, Mayo Clinic.

✤ ✤ ✤

If you cannot absolutely refrain from drinking, start a saloon in your home. Be the only customer and you will not have to buy a license. Give your wife $12.00 to buy a gallon of whiskey. There are 128 drinks in a gallon. Buy all your drinks from your wife at 40 cents each and in four days when the gallon is gone, your wife will have $39.20 to put in the bank and will have $12.00 to start up in business again.

If you live ten years and continue to buy all your booze from your wife, then die, your wife will have $35,750.40 on deposit, enough to bury you decently, bring up your children and marry a man who doesn't drink.

—*Christian Herald.*

✤ ✤ ✤

Old Ma Settles lived in a little cabin in the Ozarks, and was often asked by passing motorists how far it was to the nearest town.

"Well," she would reply, after some thought, "Pa figgers it's about twelve miles thar an' fou'teen miles back." Then she would explain, as the motorist would invariably question the variation in mileage: "That's on account of him walkin' straighter a-goin' than a-comin'."

DUTY

The time was the 19th of May, 1870. The place was Hartford, Connecticut. The day has gone down in New England history as a terrible foretaste of Judgment Day. For at noon the skies turned from blue to gray and by midafternoon had blackened so densely that, in that religious age, men fell on their knees and begged a final blessing before the end came.

The Connecticut House of Representatives was in session. As men clamored for immediate adjournment, the Speaker of the House, one Colonel Davenport, arose: "The Day of Judgment is either approaching, or it is not. If it is not, then there is no cause for adjournment. If it is, I choose to be found doing my duty. I wish, therefore, that candles may be brought."

—ALISTAIR COOKE, *One Man's America* (Knopf).

✤ ✤ ✤

Some years ago in our rural section of southern California, a Mexican mother died leaving a family of eight children. The oldest girl, not yet 17, was a tiny thing. Upon her frail shoulders fell the burden of caring for the family. Taking up the task with courage, she kept the children clean, well fed and in school.

One day when I complimented her on her achievement, she replied, "I can't take any credit for something I have to do."

"But my dear, you don't have to. You could get out of it."

She paused for a moment, then replied, "Yes, that's true. But what about the *have to* that's inside of me?"

—VERNA RALLINGS.

✤ ✤ ✤

During my interneship, the young daughter and only child of Dr. Walker, a lecturer on surgery at the medical school, was stricken with appendicitis. Dr. Walker decided to operate himself, with his classes present. I assisted as anesthetist, and toward the end of the operation whispered that the patient's heart was in a bad state. Dr. Walker told me to do what was proper under the circumstances, which I did, but the patient died on the table. When I told him, he nodded and finished the operation to the last detail—the incision was sutured, a dressing applied, and the bandage put in place. Then he turned to the students in the amphitheater above him and said:

"Gentlemen, the patient, my daughter, has been dead for perhaps ten minutes. I had only slight hope of saving her, but determined nevertheless to operate. My sole purpose in completing my work was to impress upon you the absolute necessity of doing this very thing, so that your future cannot be ruined by threats of malpractice for failure to continue an operation. Remember—always complete the operation, even if the patient dies on the table."

—DR. WILLIAM E. AUGHINBAUGH, *I Swear by Apollo* (Farrar & Rinehart).

✣ ✣ ✣

Someone tells the story about the time when a rider who headed a hunting party in England commanded a boy at a gate to open it.

"I'm sorry, sir," answered the boy, "but my father sent me to say that you must not hunt on his grounds."

"Do you know who I am?" demanded the man gruffly.

"No, sir," answered the boy.

"I am the Duke of Wellington."

The boy took off his cap, but he did not open the gate. "The Duke of Wellington will not ask me to disobey my father's orders," he said quietly.

Slowly the man took off his hat, and smiled. "I honor the boy who is faithful to his duty," said the great man, and with that he and his party rode away.

—*Nashua Cavalier.*

✣ ✣ ✣

DUTY—Devotion to

In Russia many years ago a certain Czar came upon a sentry standing at attention in a secluded spot in the palace gardens.

"Sentry, what are you guarding?" inquired the Czar.

"I do not know, sire," the guard replied. "I was ordered to my post by the Captain of the Guard."

Calling the Captain of the Guard to him, the Czar questioned him concerning the sentry's post. The Captain likewise could only reply that "regulations called for a sentry at that particular spot." Further inquiry revealed that no man at the court could tell why the sentry was there, or what he guarded.

Determined to find the reason for such an unusual post, the Czar ordered the archives to be opened and searched. Finally it was learned that Catherine the Great many years before had planted a rosebush there, and ordered a sentry to guard it so no one would trample on it. The rosebush was dead more than a hundred years, but the sentries still kept watch—not knowing why.

—*Sunshine Magazine.*

✤ ✤ ✤

ECONOMY

A banker lost all his money. He took the only job he could find, that of attendant in a gasoline filling station.

A customer stopped in front of a pump and said, "Gimme ten gallons."

"How far are you going?" the ex-banker inquired, eyeing the customer keenly.

The customer looked surprised at the question but good-naturedly supplied the information.

The former banker shook his head and suggested gravely, "I think you could get along with five instead of ten gallons."

✤ ✤ ✤

Each year for 10 years Mrs. Brown had made her visit to the local church for the christening of the latest addition to the family, and each year she gave the new baby five names.

On the eleventh occasion the vicar, laboriously entering all the names in the register, felt he must protest.

"Now, Mrs. Brown," he told the proud mother, "we can't go on like this, you know. It's the eleventh year in succession that you've come to me in this way. Next year you really must bring your own ink."

—*Tit-Bits,* London.

EDUCATION

A denizen of the hills of eastern Tennessee, was appearing as a witness in a lawsuit, and was being questioned as to his educational qualifications by the plaintiff's lawyer.

"Can you write?" asked the lawyer.

"Nope."

"Can you read?"

"Wa'al, I kind o' read figgers pretty well, but I don't do so good with writin'."

"How is that?"

"Wa'al, take these here signs along the road when I want to go somewheres: I kin read how fur, but not where to."

✣ ✣ ✣

A convict, faced with a 15-year-to-life sentence, settled down to books and study. As the years passed he learned to read and write not only English, his own language, but French and Spanish as well. Then came the discovery that he had been wrongly sentenced. After 16 years behind bars he walked to freedom, a high school diploma under his arm. Released from prison and from illiteracy he wrote this discerning tribute to education: "Through my learning came respect for the rights of my fellow man. When I was illiterate I would get violent with people, strike them when I had an argument with them. This was because I had no words to argue with. I could only assert myself through violence. I feel that I have been rehabilitated through education."

—*National Parent-Teacher.*

✣ ✣ ✣

The wife of a visiting professor of geography at Stanford attended a meeting of the Women's Faculty Club. One of the older members of the club asked her, "What does your husband do?"

"He teaches geography," answered the visiting professor's wife.

"Geography," declared the questioner. "I've always thought that the teaching of geography ended in the elementary school."

A month later, the guest wife went to the next meeting of the Faculty Club better prepared for the question, should someone ask it. Inevitably someone did, and she replied charmingly, "My husband teaches human ecology."

"Oh, my," beamed the questioner in envious approval, "that must be a very important subject."

—W. H. COWLEY, *Journal of Higher Education.*

✣ ✣ ✣

After one of his lectures, a woman came up to the distinguished educator, Francis Wayland Parker and asked, "How early can I begin the education of my child?" He asked her, "When will your child be born?" The puzzled woman replied, "Why, he's already five years old."

"My goodness, woman!" exclaimed the educator, "don't stand here talking to me. Hurry home! You have already lost the five best years!"

✣ ✣ ✣

Colonel Edward Davis was amused by a Chinese friend who was attending one of our colleges. After a short time, he wrote home to his friends and relatives, describing American institutions of various kinds as he saw them.

He defined an American university in these terms: "An American university is a vast athletic association where, however, some studies are maintained for the benefit of the feeble-bodied."

✣ ✣ ✣

EFFICIENCY

In the early days of the campaign, General MacArthur summoned an engineer and asked: "How long will it take to throw a bridge across this stream?"

"Three days," was the reply.

"Good," snapped MacArthur. "Have your draftsmen make drawings right away."

Three days later, the general sent for the engineer and asked how the bridge was coming.

"It's all ready," was the answer. "You can send your men across now, if you don't have to wait for them pictures. They ain't done yet!"

—WALTER WINCHELL.

EGOTISM

A certain Welshman, the proud possessor of a very fine bass voice, confided one day to a friend that he had had a remarkable dream. "I was in a mighty choir: 5000 sopranos, 5000 altos, 5000 tenors—all singing at once, double forte. Oh, magnificent! But suddenly," continued the singer, "the conductor stopped the lot, and turning to me said, 'Not quite so loud in the bass, Mr. Jones.' "

—*Wall Street Journal.*

✣ ✣ ✣

Few listeners—not even the woman who was supposed to introduce him—turned out for a lecture by Orson Welles in a small midwestern town. Welles undertook to introduce himself.

"Ladies and gentlemen," he said, "I will tell you the highlights of my life. I am a director of plays. I am a producer of plays. I am an actor on the legitimate stage. I am a writer of motion pictures. I am a producer of motion pictures. I am a motion-picture actor. I write, direct and act on the radio. I am a magician. I also paint and sketch, and I am a book publisher. I am a violinist and a pianist." Here Welles paused, leaned toward the small audience and said: "Isn't it a shame that there are so many of me and so few of you?"

—Sidney Skolsky, in *N. Y. Post.*

✣ ✣ ✣

ENCOURAGEMENT

Taking a walk in Galway, I stopped to ask an Irish peasant how far it was to Corrofin. "About a half mile down the road, Father. And God speed you!"

I walked a half mile, then another. Not until I had walked 12 half miles did I arrive at Corrofin. When I returned in the late afternoon I met the same Irishman. "What did you mean by telling me Corrofin was only a half mile away?" I asked indignantly. "It was six miles!"

"Well," he answered, "I gave you a half mile to Corrofin. That got you started. Somebody else gave you another half mile. That drove you on a bit further. In Ireland we do be always wanting to soften the journey of a stranger by giving him little dribbles of encouragement. Sure they'd be nobody going any place here on a hot day if people knew how far they had to go to get there."

—Leonard Feeney, *Fish on Friday* (Sheed & Ward).

✤ ✤ ✤

One day as a practical joke on certain guests, a hotel man who ran a small mountain inn for summer tourists put in several mileposts, less than three quarters of a mile apart, on nearby roads. Shortly afterward he noticed that guests who had been spending their vacations there for several seasons were remaining a week or so longer than usual. He did not know why until one day a guest remarked: "This place is doing me a lot of good this year. I can walk farther than I ever could in my life, and with less fatigue."

The proprietor quietly left the mileposts right where they were.

—Fred C. Kelly, *Human Nature in Business* (Putnam).

✤ ✤ ✤

To a young man learning to perform on the flying trapeze a veteran circus performer once said, "Throw your heart over the bars and your body will follow."

—*Happy Hours.*

✤ ✤ ✤

ENTERPRISE

A traveler in an isolated region found an unusual example of business acumen. In a rural section of the South the owner of a private ferry boat has posted a large sign at the dock. It reads: "Passengers must pay in advance as the boat leaks."

✤ ✤ ✤

Almost a century and a quarter ago, New York's new penny paper, *The Sun,* carried an ad reading: "A number of steady men can find employment by vending this paper. A liberal discount is allowed to those who buy to sell again."

This revolutionary new method of increasing circulation was the idea of Benjamin Day, publisher. Among the first applicants was a small boy named Barney Flaherty.

"But I advertised for grown men," Day told the youngster.

"I know," Barney said, "but I'm sure I can handle it."

The publisher was so impressed by the boy's sincerity that he gave him a job. Barney walked from the office with a bundle of newspapers under his arm and shortly New Yorkers heard the first cry of, "Paper! Get your *Sun* here! Paper!"

Next day he was at a downtown street-corner, again hawking papers. People stopped and stared, then bought. Little Barney Flaherty, America's first newsboy, had set a pattern for what would become an American institution.

—*Swing.*

✣ ✣ ✣

A prominent businessman was walking down the street toward his office after lunch one day when he was stopped by a stranger.

"You probably don't remember me," said the stranger, "but ten years ago I came to this city broke. I asked you for ten dollars and you gave it to me, saying that you never turned down a request to start a man on the road to success."

"I remember," said the businessman, interested. "Go on with your story."

"Well," said the stranger, "are you still game?"

—DAN BENNETT, *American Legion Magazine.*

✣ ✣ ✣

EQUALITY

Alexander the Great, seeing Diogenes looking attentively at a large collection of human bones piled one upon another, asked the philosopher what he was looking for.

"I am searching," said Diogenes, "for the bones of your father, but I cannot distinguish them from those of his slaves."

—*Smart Sayings of Great Personages.*

✣ ✣ ✣

ETHICS

When the senior Robert LaFollette was elected governor of Wisconsin, his old friend and teacher, John Bascom, wrote to him: "Robert, you will doubtless make mistakes of judgment as governor. But never mind the political mistakes so long as you make no ethical mistakes."

✤ ✤ ✤

A Los Angeles broadcasting station was rehearsing a commercial program in which the plug for the sponsor's product was to be delivered insidiously by one of the entertainers instead of by the announcer. According to the script, she was to say, "I had lunch the other day with Nelson Eddy, and he said to me . . ." This led gracefully to Eddy's endorsement of the product.

It happened that a delegate of the radio actors' union was present and inclined to make difficulties. "*Did* you have lunch with Nelson Eddy the other day, and *did* he say so-and-so?" he asked the actress. She said no, she was just reading the script. "Well, if it isn't true, you can't say it," the delegate said.

The masterminds producing the program wasted no time in argument, and it was too late to rewrite the plug: instead they got in touch with Nelson Eddy's studio. A property man hastily assembled a table, chairs, linen and silver. Mr. Eddy and the radio actress sat down and nibbled sandwiches, and he gravely said exactly what the script quoted him as saying. The commercial plug went on the air that night absolutely without deception.

—*The New Yorker.*

✤ ✤ ✤

A certain society in South Africa once wrote to David Livingstone: "Have you found a good road to where you are? If so, we want to know how to send other men to join you." Livingstone replied, "If you have men who will come only if they know there is a good road, I don't want them. I want men who will come if there is no road at all."

—*Church Herald.*

✤ ✤ ✤

A gentleman in the optical business was instructing his son in the technique of getting a fair and honest price out of a customer. He said, "Son, after you've fitted the glasses to the customer, and he asks, 'What is the charge?' you should say: 'The charge is ten dollars.' Then pause, and watch for the flinch. If the customer does not flinch, you say, 'That's for the frames; the lenses will be another ten dollars.' Then you pause again, but this time only slightly, and again you watch for the flinch. If the customer doesn't flinch, you say 'Each.' "

—*Virginia Spectator.*

✣ ✣ ✣

EXCUSES

Many stories have been told about the human tendency to invent excuses for minor wrongdoings. The best we've heard lately is about the native of a remote section of the U. S. who was riding his mule down a narrow lane. As he passed an apple orchard he spotted some branches laden with ripe fruit. From the mule's back he reached up to pick some apples, and at the same moment the animal lurched forward, leaving the man hanging perilously from the tree. Just then the owner of the orchard came along the road.

"Hey!" he yelled. "What are you doing up there in my apple tree?"

"Nothin', mister," replied the native. "I just fell off my mule!"

—*This Week.*

✣ ✣ ✣

EXPERIENCE

In a small New England secondary school, the dynamic young headmaster, faced with the task of selecting a department head, ignored seniority. After the announcement of the appointment, a disgruntled member of the department came to him, demanding to know why his 20 years' experience had been overlooked.

"My friend," said the headmaster, "in reality you haven't had 20 years' experience." Before the teacher could expostulate, he added, "You have had one year's experience 20 times."

—DAVID N. BEACH, III.

✣ ✣ ✣

One day a young Talmudic scholar who had just completed a learned work came to the Rabbi and begged him for a testimonial. The Rabbi regarded his visitor with gentle compassion.

"My son," he said, "you must face the stern realities. If you wish to be a writer of learned books you must be resigned to peddle your work from house to house like a vendor of pots and pans and suffer hunger until you are forty."

"And what will happen after I'm forty?" asked the young writer hopefully.

The Rabbi smiled encouragingly. "By the time you are forty, you will be used to it."

—NATHAN AUSUBEL, *A Treasury of Jewish Folklore* (Crown).

✤ ✤ ✤

There is a story of a ship captain and his chief engineer. The engineer said anybody could stand on the bridge and run a ship, and the captain said that any man could sit in warm quarters in the engine room and keep the power plant running. As a test they finally agreed to exchange places. The chief engineer went on the bridge and attempted to keep the vessel on its course, while the captain went below and took charge of the engine room. It wasn't very long before the captain had the engines fouled up, and, realizing the danger, he called the engineer to come down and take over. The engineer replied, "Come on up to the bridge, captain. We just ran aground anyway."

—WILLARD F. ROCKWELL, *Flowline.*

✤ ✤ ✤

"I suppose," probed the payroll supervisor, "that you and your wife have a joint checking account?"

"No," answered the new employee, "this is my second wife."

—*Kroehler News.*

✤ ✤ ✤

FAILURE

Centuries ago a great artist was engaged to paint a mural for the cathedral in a Sicilian town. The subject was the life of Christ. For many years the artist labored diligently and finally the painting was finished except for the two most important figures: the Christ Child and Judas Iscariot. He searched far and wide for models for those two figures.

One day while walking in an old part of the city he came upon some children playing in the street. Among them was a 12-year-old boy with the face of an angel—a very dirty one, but the face the artist needed.

He took the child home with him and day after day the boy sat patiently until the face of the Christ Child was finished.

But the painter still found no one to serve as model for the portrait of Judas. For years, haunted by the fear that his masterpiece would remain unfinished, he continued his search.

Then one afternoon as he sat in the tavern over his daily glass of wine, a gaunt and tattered figure staggered across the threshold and fell upon the floor. "Wine, wine," he begged. The painter lifted him up and looked into a face that startled him. It seemed to bear the marks of every sin of mankind.

Greatly excited, the old painter helped the profligate to his feet. Here at last was the model for Judas. For many days and parts of many nights the painter worked feverishly to complete his masterpiece.

As the work went on a change came over the model. A strange tension replaced the stuporous languor, and his bloodshot eyes were fixed with horror on the painted likeness of himself. One day, perceiving his subject's agitation, the painter paused in his work. "My son, I'd like to help you," he said. "What troubles you so?"

The model sobbed and buried his face in his hands. After a long moment he lifted pleading eyes to the old painter's face.

"Do you not then remember me? Years ago I was your model for the Christ Child."

—Retold by Bonnie Chamberlin in *The Saturday Review*.

✣ ✣ ✣

FAIRNESS

My brother and I always came home from school hungry. One day, when we asked for food, Mother set a small cake before us on the kitchen table. Placing a knife beside the cake, she said: "One of you divide it. The other has first choice."

My brother was quicker than I, and he started to cut the cake in unequal pieces. Suddenly he stopped, looking first at Mother and then at me. Then he cut the cake in exact halves and stood back for me to help myself.

From then on whatever there was to be shared—pie, cake, bread and butter—was divided in the same way. It taught us lasting respect for the other fellow's rights.

—JESSAMINE PARET KNIGHT.

✤ ✤ ✤

FAITH

Lou Gehrig, the famous home-run king of the N. Y. Yankees, visited a hospital for crippled children just before a World Series game. He told them, "You can do *anything* if you want to do it badly enough!"

One small, bed-ridden Yankee fan asked the great ballplayer to do him a favor. "Please knock two home-runs today," he pleaded.

"Two home-runs in a World Series game is a lot to ask," parried Gehrig. But he had committed himself on an item of faith. "All right," he agreed, "I'll knock two home-runs if you will tell me that you will walk." They shook hands on it.

Gehrig knocked his two home-runs that afternoon, but somehow never got around to going back to the hospital. One day, years later, he was entering the Yankee Stadium when a tall, good-looking young man stepped up and asked, "Do you remember me?" Lou couldn't place him. Then the young man said, "Well, then, look. *I can walk!*"

—*Tarbell's Teachers' Guide* (Revell).

✤ ✤ ✤

Anton Reicha, the great conductor, was rehearsing his choir for a production of *The Messiah*. The chorus was sung through to the point where the soprano takes up the refrain. The technique of the soloist was perfect—faultless breathing, accurate note placing, splendid enunciation. When the final note died away, Reicha walked up to the singer with sorrowful eyes and said quietly, "My daughter, you do not know that your Redeemer lives, do you?" The girl flushed and replied, "Why, yes, I think I do." Said Reicha: "Then sing it. Sing it so that all who hear you may know that you know." He motioned for the orchestra to play again. When the singer finished this time, the old man smiled. "Ah, yes, you *do* know. You have told me!"

—J. C. MITCHELL.

✤ ✤ ✤

On the wall of a cellar in Cologne, where a number of escaped prisoners of war hid for the duration, there was found this inscription: "I believe in the sun, even when it is not shining. I believe in love, even when feeling it not. I believe in God even when He is silent."

—LOIS BINSTOCK, *The Power of Faith* (Prentice-Hall).

✤ ✤ ✤

Alexander the Conqueror was once told through an anonymous note that his physician was plotting to poison him and that the lethal dose would be administered in his next draught of medicine. When the physician came and prepared the drug, Alexander took the glass, at the same time handing the physician the warning note. That expression of confidence naturally resulted in a firmer bond of friendship between the two, and it is said to have caused the physician to devote himself ardently and completely to the service of the king; for the medicine had not been poisoned.

—SHELDON SHEPARD, *Mind Digest.*

✤ ✤ ✤

In the orient they tell the story of a hell that is ten thousand miles deep. Every ten thousand years a god lets down a thread as thin as a spider's web, and every condemned soul who has faith can climb up ten thousand miles until he gets out. One time the god let down the thread and one poor soul saw it and had faith. He started to climb up and up until he saw daylight. Then, just as he was putting his foot over the edge, he . . . looked down and saw all hell climbing up after him on the same thread. He lost faith. "Let go! Let go! This is mine!" he yelled down, and the god snapped the thread and cast him and all the other condemned souls back into Hades.

Today the entire world is attempting to climb from the bottomless pit of international rancor and strife, and our only hope of rescue is the very thin thread of international cooperation. We shall win this struggle together or together we shall be plunged into the darkness of despair. We can reach our goal only if we have faith—faith in each other. It is the only means of escape offered so far.

—Richard C. Hedke, *Rotarian.*

✣ ✣ ✣

An old Scotchman operated a small rowboat for transporting passengers. One day a patron noticed that he had carved on one oar the word "Faith" and the other oar the word "Works." Curiosity led him to ask the meaning of this.

The old man said, "I will show you." He dropped one oar and plied the other called "Works," and they just went around in circles. Then he dropped that oar and began to ply the one called "Faith," and the boat again went around in circles.

After this demonstration, the old man picked up both "Faith" and "Works" and plying them together, sped swiftly over the water, explaining to his inquiring passenger, "You see, that is the way it is in the Christian life."

—*Canadian Churchman.*

✣ ✣ ✣

An Eastern story tells of a poor woman who asked the Sultan that she be recompensed for some property. "And how did you come to lose it?" he inquired. "I fell asleep, and while I was sleeping a robber entered my building," she replied. "And why did you fall asleep?" The reply of the woman so greatly pleased the Sultan he ordered her loss be made up. She answered: "I fell asleep because I believed you were awake."

—Edwin G. Frye, *Telescope-Messenger.*

✣ ✣ ✣

Frederick Douglass, famous ex-slave, never forgot the night he gave his most pessimistic speech in Boston. A packed house heard him lash the evils of slavery, then conclude hopelessly that the white people of America would never end the Negro's bondage. The only answer, he asserted gloomily, was armed revolt by the slaves, which could only result in wholesale manslaughter.

A giant, shabbily-dressed black woman arose. In her enormously deep voice, she roared, "Frederick, is God dead?"

The startled Douglass, usually quick to retort to hecklers, was momentarily silenced; the equally surprised audience was first to recover, and an avalanche of applause swept away the despair which had enveloped the hall. Sojourner Truth had saved the day.

—WALTER WHITE, *New Republic.*

✤ ✤ ✤

A girl reporter had heard of an unusual woman and called on her for an interview. The woman, a widow for years, had raised six of her own children and adopted twelve others. "How have you been able to raise all these children and do it so well?" asked the reporter. "It's been very simple," the widow replied. "You see, I'm in a partnership."

"A what?" asked the reporter.

To which the woman benignly replied: "A partnership. One day a long time ago I said to the Lord: 'Lord, I'll do the work and You do the worrying' and I haven't had a worry since."

—DR. A. AUGUSTUS WELSH, Christ Evangelical & Reformed Church, Bethlehem, Pa.

✤ ✤ ✤

In a school playground not long ago, some boys were taunting a lad who regularly attended church, taunting him because his shoes were broken through. They said, "If God really loves you, why doesn't He take better care of you? Why doesn't He tell someone to send you a pair of shoes?" The boy answered, "I think He does tell somebody, but they aren't listening."

—FREDERICK M. MEEK, *Zion's Herald.*

✤ ✤ ✤

When Mother Cabrini, at the end of the last century, arrived in New York to labor among the scorned Italian immigrants, she was penniless. A countess came to her aid, offering a house in the residential section to be used as a convent and orphanage. Archbishop Corrigan was rather apathetic. He didn't approve the location, and he was skeptical of the venture's support, even though the countess had also donated five thousand dollars.

"What of it?" he asked. "How long do you think that will last? It will all be spent within a year. What then?"

"Your Excellency," the countess exclaimed, "when we pray, we ask for our daily bread, not bread for a year!"

—*St. Anthony Messenger.*

✤ ✤ ✤

A happy Christian met an Irish peddler and exclaimed, "It's a grand thing to be saved!"

"Aye," said the peddler, "it is, but I know something better than that."

"Better than being saved?" asked the other. "What can you in your position possibly know that is better than that?"

Came the unexpected reply, "The companionship of the Man who saved me."

—Lora Lee Parrott, *Meals from the Manse Cook Book* (Zondervan).

✤ ✤ ✤

While walking along a mountain path with his little daughter, a man came to a small stream bridged by a fallen log. The father told the child to take firm hold of his hand for safety.

The little girl hesitated. Then she said, "If I take hold of yours I might let go; but if you take hold of my hand, no matter what happens, you will never let go of me."

—Minnie H. Griswold, *White Gold.*

✤ ✤ ✤

"If you don't believe in God, you ain't a whole man," said Elder Johnson. "A lot of smart people claim they don't believe nothin' unless they c'n see it. Look, friend, you cain't see electricity in that high-tension wire up yonder, but I dare you to tech it! No, you can't see electricity, but you c'n see the light!"

—*The Plugger.*

✤ ✤ ✤

Christopher, our old gardener, had many a story of miracles performed by a venerable preacher in a nearby village.

"It is the Lord Himself who tells the saint man things," he

whispered. "Every day, in the late afternoon, the door opens, the Lord comes in and they talk together."

"And have you seen this with your own eyes?"

Christopher frowned. "No; but the saint man told it to me himself."

"And you really believe him?"

"Do I believe him?" Christopher raised his voice. "How can you talk of such a thing? Do you suppose The Lord would come in every day and sit down and talk with a liar?"

—ANITA DANIEL, *American Mercury.*

✣ ✣ ✣

A certain doctor in the Middle West has received many compliments about his work from patients he has helped. Yet he likes most to remember one bit of tribute that was paid to his deceased father, who had been a doctor also.

Shortly after his father's funeral, the young doctor had stopped to visit a patient, a little boy about three. As the physician was about to leave, the little fellow called him back.

"Doctor, is God very sick?" the child asked anxiously.

The doctor's brow wrinkled in bewilderment. "Why, God never gets sick," he said, a trifle brusquely. "How did you happen to ask me that?"

" 'Cause your father died, and I guess God must have sent for him," the little boy replied.

—*American Medical Journal.*

✣ ✣ ✣

I was hunting with some friends in the hinterlands of Tunisia when an Arab galloped up and asked if there was a doctor in the party. I stepped forward and put myself at his service.

"Excellency, my wife dies," said the Arab. "Please come quickly."

I did. I examined the woman. I told her husband she had pneumonia and ought to be taken to a hospital in Tunis.

Before I left, the Arab implored me to write a prescription. "All right," I said, handing him one. "Give her some of this every hour. But get her to the hospital promptly."

Some time later I returned to the same region. My Arab friend greeted me with smiles and salaams. He said his wife was completely cured.

"You took her to the hospital?" I asked.

"Oh, no, Excellency," he said. "It was the magic of your writing. We knew it would bring her health."

"You mean my prescription?"

"Yes, wonder-worker," he replied. "I tore it in pieces and gave her some every hour, as you advised."

—LUDWIG C. KALNIN, *Medical Economics.*

✣ ✣ ✣

A little girl had reached the high point in school when she was being initiated into the wonders of arithmetic. Minus signs, plus signs, and division signs had made a deep impression on her. One day in church she looked intently at a gold cross on the altar. She whispered to her father, "What is the plus sign doing on the altar?" In one way she had her sign confused. But in a far deeper sense she was absolutely right! *The cross is a plus sign.* The redemption pictured by the cross has put a big plus sign into life.

—HALFORD E. LUCCOCK, *Christian Herald.*

✣ ✣ ✣

The late Dr. Jowett said that he was once in a state of perplexity and consulted Dr. Berry, of Wolverhampton. "What would you do if you were in my place?" he entreated. "I don't know, Jowett, I am not there and you are not there yet. When do you have to act?"

"On Friday," Dr. Jowett replied.

"Then you will find your way perfectly clear on Friday. The Lord will not fail you," answered Berry. And, sure enough, on Friday all was plain.

—F. W. BOREHAM, *Challenge.*

✣ ✣ ✣

In a summer's day tramp through a forest, a man came upon two small lads in Boy Scout uniform sitting forlornly by a small fire.

"Are you lost?" he asked.

"Well," said one of the boys hesitantly, "we do not know

where we are. But we are with the Scoutmaster and he knows the way home."

Is there not a lesson there for the lives of all? Sometimes we may grow bewildered by the events of the world about us or by the untoward circumstances that come into our own lives. But there is no need to become anxious or fearful. Our Master knows the way through.

—*Christian Observer.*

✤ ✤ ✤

A little boy rang the doorbell of a house one day. When the lady came to the door, he asked her to buy some greeting cards. When asked what he was going to do with the money he said he was building a church. "Alone?" she asked. "No," he said. "God is working with me, and besides Jimmy is working the other side of the street."

—MRS. J. RUSSELL HENDERSON, *Arkansas Methodist.*

✤ ✤ ✤

In our parish someone had been pilfering the poor box.

"This has got to stop," the pastor said grimly. He and his young assistant rigged an alarm that would ring in the rectory. The two priests were at lunch when the alarm went off. They looked at each other. "There's our thief!" muttered the pastor. "Let's go."

The culprit, a dark-eyed urchin of 8, had a good start on the priests—but they caught him just the same. Even though on the lam, he had stopped to genuflect before the altar.

—*Catholic Digest.*

✤ ✤ ✤

FAME

When Mrs. Calvin Coolidge went abroad after her husband's death, she feared there would be unnecessary fuss made over the wife of an ex-President. But the friend with whom she was traveling said, "Don't worry. In the little places where we'll be stopping they don't know one President of the United States from another. People won't bother you." And no one did—until in a small Italian town they received word that reservations for them were made in the next town. This sounded ominous. When they reached the hotel in question they were received pompously by the manager. Bowing profoundly, he said, "We are proud to welcome the wife of the great President of the United States. Will you register, Mrs. Lincoln?"

—MARGARET CULKIN BANNING.

✤ ✤ ✤

A distinguished actor had a large photo of Wordsworth prominently displayed in his dressing room. A friend regarded the picture with some surprise and remarked: "I see you are an admirer of Wordsworth."

"Who's Wordsworth?" demanded the actor.

"Why that's his picture," the friend pointed out. "That's Wordsworth, the poet."

The actor regarded the photograph with a new interest. "Is that old fellow a poet? I got him for a study in wrinkles."

—*Capper's Weekly.*

✤ ✤ ✤

When Dorothy and Lillian Gish were teen-age stars, their first realization that they were famous came when they found themselves followed by a crowd walking down Fifth Avenue.

The girls rushed home to their mother and reported this exciting experience. The wise Mrs. Gish, eager for her youngsters to remain unspoiled, told them: "So what if crowds do follow you on the streets? Remember this: The same thing would happen to any two people who walk down Fifth Avenue with rings in their noses."

—LEONARD LYONS, *This Week.*

✤ ✤ ✤

Somerset Maugham knows only too well how fleeting is fame. When his first novel appeared, shortly before the turn of the century, it was greeted with enthusiasm by one influential critic, who predicted that the young author would soon be at the top of the literary heap.

Twenty-five years later, when he was world-famous, Maugham met the critic in a theater lobby.

"Maugham, Maugham," murmured the critic. "Ah, yes, you're

the fellow who wrote that brilliant novel a quarter of a century ago. How is it that you haven't written anything since then?"

—IRVING HOFFMAN, *Hollywood Reporter.*

✣ ✣ ✣

A little boy, on being held up for a look at President Washington, exclaimed, with all the mingled relief and disappointment of a yongster who has been primed to expect deity and saw only human clay: "Why, he's only a man!"

Hearing this, the Father of His Country smiled. "Yes, son, that is all."

—CLARENCE W. HALL, *Link.*

✣ ✣ ✣

When the freshman returned a volume of Shakespeare to the library he was asked what he thought of his writing.

"I don't see why people make such a fuss over his work. All he has done is bring together a bunch of old, well-known quotations."

—*Parts Jobber.*

✣ ✣ ✣

An eight-and-a-half foot giant, who works for Roma Wine Company of California, was on his first visit to New York. At breakfast he was accosted by a man who questioned him for some time, then finally rose to leave after expressing his appreciation for the giant's patience in answering him.

"Oh, that's okay," returned the "big guy" carelessly. "When you're in the public eye you get used to it. If you'd ever gotten to be fairly well known, you'd get used to this sort of thing just as I have."

As the questioning stranger left, he put a card into the giant's hand. It read: "Admiral Richard E. Byrd."

—*Advertising Age.*

✣ ✣ ✣

Some years ago, when Donald Ogden Stewart was new in Hollywood, he prepared a script based on the life of Jane Addams, of Chicago's famed Hull House.

His superior looked up inquiringly. "Who's Jane Addams?" he asked. "Never heard of her." Then, turning to an assistant, he asked the question, "Ever hear of Hull House?" "No," said the aid, "what is it?"

The high mogul then turned to Donald with a smile, and said smugly, "See? Nobody ever heard of her. Get another subject."

—HEDDA HOPPER.

✤ ✤ ✤

The instructor of a course in cryptography was striving to explain an obscure point to his students. Finally he referred them to a particular textbook, saying, "I hope some of you will read it. I consider it one of the finest books on cryptography. I only wish I could remember the name of the author."

A meek little private in the last row raised his hand. "I wrote it, sir," he told the teacher.

—*Cleveland Plain Dealer.*

✤ ✤ ✤

This tale floats up (verified) from Tia Juana of the Chinese who was opening a new cafe. He asked a friend for a suitable name. After some thought the latter suggested, "Confucius Cafe."

Deliberating at length, the Chinese asked: "Who is Confucius?"

—MRS. TICK OTIS, *San Francisco Chronicle.*

✤ ✤ ✤

"What's your name?" the manager asked the young lad applying for a job.

"Ford," said the boy.

"What's your first name?"

"Henry."

"Henry Ford, eh?" the manager smiled. "That's a pretty well-known name."

"Uh-huh," replied the boy. "It should be. I've been delivering groceries in this town for nearly five years."

—*The Woman.*

✤ ✤ ✤

FAMILY LIFE

Wheaton Dudley has paraphrased Saint Paul's great Chapter 13 of *I Corinthians* for use in the family:

Though I speak about children in the lingo of Gesell, Ilg, and Spock, but do not truly love them, I am as futile as a radio commercial and as boring as a soap opera. Although I give every material advantage to the poor darlings, and give my patience until I am "burned up" but don't really love them, I get no thanks for my efforts. Truly loving parents don't berate their children, but put up with mistakes, believe the best of them, have great dreams for their future, and are the last to give up hope of their becoming mature, creative personalities. Now I know only a fraction of my child's personality, but some day, I shall know him fully, somewhat as I must be known and understood by God. Now abides three great capacities of the human spirit: faith in the future, hope in the significance of the past, and love, a creative companionship in the present—the greatest of these is love.

—Robert W. Burns, *The Foundation of a Christian Home.*

✣ ✣ ✣

FEAR

To celebrate Uncle Dudley's 75th birthday, an aviation enthusiast offered to take him for a plane ride over the little West Virginia town where he's spent all his life.

Uncle Dudley accepted the offer.

Back on the ground, after circling over the town 20 minutes, his friend asked "Were you scared, Uncle Dudley?"

"No-o-o-o," was the hesitant answer. "But I never did put my full weight down."

—Ralph P. Norton.

✣ ✣ ✣

As valedictorian of her high school class Margaret Lee Runbeck, the author, trembled with self-consciousness when she took her seat on the platform next to the guest speaker.

"I'm supposed to talk wittily to you," she whispered to the guest, "but I haven't a thing to say. I'm scared to death."

"I'm scared, too," the speaker confided. "I've got a speech written down, but I don't think it's much good . . ."

"But *you* don't have to be afraid," the girl interrupted.

"Neither do you," the speaker replied. "I'll tell you a secret; then you'll never need to be troubled again. Everyone on earth is shy and self-conscious. Everybody's timid about meeting strangers. So if you'll just spend the first minute you're with a stranger trying to make *him* feel comfortable, you'll never suffer from self-consciousness again. Try it."

Margaret Runbeck accepted the advice and now, years later, says that it works unfailingly.

—G. Ernest Thomas, *Faith Can Master Fear* (Revell).

✣ ✣ ✣

In his book, *Crusade in Europe,* Dwight D. Eisenhower tells us that he fell in beside a soldier marching toward the Rhine, for that last bloody assault on the German line. The boy was plainly afraid. He told his general that he had been wounded in a previous battle, and that he had only just been returned to the front lines. He admitted that he was nervous.

"Well, son," said General Eisenhower, "you and I should be good for each other. I am nervous, too. Suppose we just march along together." Then he told the private that the Allies had more power available for this battle than the Germans had, and that the attack was being supported by a tremendous air force and fire superiority. After awhile, just as they reached the banks of the Rhine, the boy said, "General, I mean that I *was* nervous. I am not now."

✣ ✣ ✣

During a bob-sledding meet at St. Anton, a girl volunteered to brake when the regular team member didn't turn up. She was a champion skier but had never been on a bob-sled. When the speed got above 60 the driver shouted for brakes. Frozen with terror, the girl just hung on. All the way down, despite agonized appeals from in front she never touched the brakes. They broke the course record for that season.

—Edwin Muller, *Kiwanis Magazine.*

✣ ✣ ✣

The director of a firm in Equatorial Africa took his native houseboy back to Europe with him. The first cold morning he was roused by the boy's cries. Rushing upstairs he found him in bed, wailing that he was on fire inside! But he was quite cool to the touch. "You haven't got fever," said his master. "Get up!"

"I can't, sir. Oh, the fire! Don't you see the smoke coming out of my mouth?"

In tropical Africa the boy had never seen his breath, and not until he was dragged out to the yard and saw the horses happily puffing smoke from their nostrils was he able to overcome his fear.

—Albert Schweitzer, *African Notebook* (Henry Holt).

✣ ✣ ✣

To me the most important feature of my life is its literary feature. There have been many turning points in my life, but my real crossing of the Rubicon occurred when I was twelve-and-a-half years old.

My father died that spring. Summer came, and brought with it an epidemic of measles. For a time, a child died almost every day. The village was paralyzed with fright, distress, despair. Children not smitten with the disease were imprisoned in their homes where there were no cheerful faces, no singing except solemn hymns, no voice but of prayer; no romping was allowed; the family moved spectrally in a ghostly hush. My soul was steeped in this awful dreariness—and in fear. At some time every day and night a sudden shiver shook me, and I said to myself, "There, I've got it! And I shall die."

Life on these miserable terms was not worth living, and at last I made up my mind to get the disease and have it over one way or the other. I escaped from the house and went to the house of a playmate who was very ill with the malady. When chance offered, I crept to his room and got into bed with him. I was discovered and sent back to captivity. But I had the disease and came near to dying. Everybody believed I would die, but on the 14th day a change came for the worse and they were disappointed.

This was the turning point in my life. For when I got well, my mother tired of trying to keep me out of mischief, decided to put me into more masterful hands than hers. She closed my school career and apprenticed me to a printer. It was a long road, but I can say with truth that the reason I am in the literary profession is because I had the measles when I was 12 years old.

—MARK TWAIN, in *The Family Mark Twain* (Harper).

✣ ✣ ✣

A member of a London bomb-disposal squad, lowered carefully into the crater of an unexploded German bomb, sat down calmly on the bomb and began removing its fuse. Suddenly he yelled:

"Get me out of here! Pull me up!"

His colleagues hauled him up in record time and ran for shelter. The man, however, remained at the edge of the crater, pointed downward and exclaimed: "Look at that big rat down there!"

—*The Newspaper P M.*

✣ ✣ ✣

A friend of mine had a little boy who was afraid of the dark. One night she had an inspiration. She took her son by the hand and instead of going upstairs to bed, walked outside in the yard with him. Together, they looked at the moon, the stars, and the fireflies. They looked for the flowers which bloom in the night and for those which seem to sleep. They felt the freshness of the dark and smelled the air. When she was putting him to bed, he said: "When I was little, I was afraid of the dark."

Joyously, this friend called to tell me that her little boy had lost his fear of the night.

—DEDE DE ARMAS, *American Home.*

✣ ✣ ✣

I know a woman who has a horror of height. Her son was amused at her inability to look into the Grand Canyon, her stubborn refusal to travel by air.

This lad was taken into the Army. From a remote training camp he sent his mother an honest confession that he was "afraid of being afraid."

On receipt of the letter, his mother climbed into a plane and flew to her son. "I thought you were afraid to fly," the boy said.

"I am," the mother replied, "but I flew to show you that fear can be conquered if the reason is good enough. A brave man is not a man who isn't afraid, but one whose will is stronger than his fear."

—CHANNING POLLOCK, *Guide Posts in Chaos* (Crowell).

✣ ✣ ✣

My mother never read a psychology book in her life, but she could have written one. Here's how she dealt with our fear of thunder. During a storm, she would seat us five children in a circle on the kitchen floor. Then she would distribute her pots and lids to us, one set apiece.

"See if you make more noise than the thunder," she'd say. "Go ahead; bang just as hard as you can and scare the thunder away."

How she endured the racket I'll never know, but diverted by our own din, we forgot to be afraid.

—MRS. LILY SANDROT, *Rotarian.*

✣ ✣ ✣

A sheep owner on a moorland farm in Scotland was searching for some lost sheep. His way took him near a cottage in which lived a shepherd, his wife and three-year-old son. The cottage was five miles from the nearest road; letters and supplies were left at the road, and never a visitor came. Now as the stranger approached the cottage the little boy spied him. He stared hard and then ran in terrible fright into the house: "Mither! There's a beastie laik ma feyther comin' up the gairden!"

—*Contryman* (England).

✣ ✣ ✣

On the eve of the opening of a new play, Sarah Bernhardt and her company sat silently in the greenroom. Marshal Francois Canrobert, a French hero of the Crimean War, entered and commented on their depression.

"We are on the eve of a great battle," Bernhardt explained. "We are afraid."

"Afraid?" echoed the Marshal.

"Oh, I beg your pardon, Monsieur," said Bernhardt. "I quite forgot." And summoning an usher she said, "Picard, please bring a dictionary for Monsieur."

—*The Christian Science Monitor.*

To the Chinese, the Dragon is a symbol of all that is good in nature and life. He is a symbol of the creative spirit of man escaping from a too realistic world to rediscover again his own soul; his ultimate acceptance of his identity with all nature.

For the Dragon is like nature. The rolling hills resemble his back; the waves of the ocean rush upon the shores like a hungry, devouring Dragon. The rivers twist as he does. Even the earth roars when there's an earthquake and volcanoes spit forth fire and smoke from their Dragon nostrils. But he is man's servant, not his master. And if you treat him kindly, he will be your friend. So the Chinese dance with the Dragon, twist his tail in good natured fun, and make of him a playful, kindly beast.

"If," as Mr. Wu said, "the Dragon is nature in all her terror and majesty, let us not be afraid. Let us go out and meet that fear. It is only the unknown that frightens us: we are afraid of what lies beyond the hill. Once we explore it, our fear vanishes. Shake hands with the Dragon—that's the way of peace."

—Carl Glick, *Shake Hands with the Dragon* (Whittlesey House, McGraw-Hill).

✣ ✣ ✣

Ivan was a timid little man—so timid that the villagers called him "Pigeon" or mocked him with the title "Ivan the Terrible." Every night Ivan stopped in at the saloon which was on the edge of the village cemetery. Ivan never crossed the cemetery to get to his lonely shack on the other side. The path would save many minutes, but he had never taken it—not even in the full light of noon.

Late one winter's night when bitter wind and snow beat against the saloon, the customers took up the familiar mockery. Ivan's sickly protest only fed their taunts, and they jeered cruelly when the young Cossack lieutenant flung his horrid challenge at their quarry. "Cross the cemetery tonight, Ivan, and I'll give you five rubles—five gold rubles!"

Perhaps it was the vodka. Perhaps it was the temptation of the five gold rubles. No one ever knew why Ivan, moistening his lips, said suddenly: "Yes, Lieutenant. I'll cross the cemetery!"

The lieutenant winked to the men and unbuckled his saber.

"Here, Ivan. When you get to the center of the cemetery, in front of the biggest tomb, stick the saber into the ground. In the morning we shall go there. And if the saber is in the ground—five gold rubles to you!"

The wind howled around Ivan as he closed the door of the saloon behind him. The cold was knife-sharp. Ivan pushed the cemetery gate open. He walked fast.

He recognized the large tomb and he kneeled, cold and terrified, and drove the saber through the crust into the hard ground. With all his strength, he pushed it down to the hilt. Ivan started to rise from his knees. But he could not move. Something gripped him in an unyielding and implacable hold. He cried out in terror.

They found Ivan, next morning, on the ground in front of the tomb. He was frozen to death. The look on his face was not that of a frozen man, but of a man killed by some nameless horror. And the lieutenant's saber was in the ground where Ivan had pounded it—through the dragging folds of his long coat.

—LEONARD Q. ROSS, in *The Saturday Review.*

✣ ✣ ✣

FORGIVENESS

A man lay on his death bed, harassed by fear because he had harbored hatred against another. He sent for the individual with whom he had had a disagreement years before, and then made overtures of peace. The two of them shook hands in friendship. But as the visitor left the room, the sick man roused himself and said, "Remember, if I get over this, the old quarrel stands."

—G. RAY JORDAN, *Pulpit Preaching.*

✣ ✣ ✣

The little boy had a new hearing aid, and his school work was progressing splendidly, but one day he had trouble with another boy. The teacher thought he ought to apologize, but he was reluctant. The teacher insisted. Finally, the little boy said, "I will apologize, but I shall turn off my hearing aid while I do!"

—JOHN A. FERRALL, *Volta Review.*

In his routine blessings, the six-year-old stopped before his brother's name and said to his mother: "I don't think I'll ask God to bless Cliff. He gave me an awful sock today." She gently reminded him that we should forgive our enemies. "But," he countered, "he's not my enemy, and that's what I can't forgive!" It is harder to forgive one's friends than one's enemies.

—*Pastor.*

✣ ✣ ✣

Some years ago, after a vigorous brotherly and sisterly disagreement, our three children retired only to be aroused at two o'clock in the morning by a terrific thunderstorm. Hearing an unusual noise upstairs, I called in to find out what was going on. A little voice answered, "We are all in the closet forgiving each other."

—Robert C. Tuttle, *Christian Advocate.*

✣ ✣ ✣

In the days of the American Revolution, a Baptist minister, Peter Miller, enjoyed the friendship of General Washington. In the same town was one Michael Wittman, an evil man who did all in his power to abuse and oppose the minister—But Wittman was involved in treason and was arrested, and sentenced to death. The old preacher walked 70 miles to Philadelphia to plead for the man's life. But Washington said, "No, Peter, I cannot grant you the life of your friend."

"My friend!" exclaimed the preacher. "He is the bitterest enemy I have!"

"You have walked 70 mi's to save the life of an enemy?" exclaimed Washington. "That puts the matter in a different light. I will grant the pardon."

✣ ✣ ✣

FRANKNESS

Old Tom Parker, a colored servitor, had been in the service of a certain family for a long time, and so, when he made the surprising announcement that he was "gwine to quit," his employer was for a moment startled into silence. When he had finally regained his composure, he asked: "But why do you wish to leave, Tom?"

"I'd rather not say, suh," replied Tom politely.

"But come, come, I insist upon knowing."

"Well, suh, ef yo' must know, I'se been heah now fo' mo' dan twenty yeahs, an', suh, I's absolutely sick an' tired at de sight of yo' and yo' fambly!"

—Arkansas Baptist.

✣ ✣ ✣

FREEDOM

I have on my table a violin string. It is free to move in any direction I like. If I twist one end, it responds; it is free. But it is not free to sing. So I take it and fix it into my violin. I bind it, and when it is bound, it is free for the first time to sing.

—Rabindranath Tagore.

✣ ✣ ✣

FRIENDLINESS

One summer our family was making a trip west, and when we reached Seminole, Texas, my father decided to look up a brother living in that vicinity. We pulled into a filling station.

"Could you tell me where Edgar Rollins lives?" my father asked.

"Sure can," the man said, pointing down the road. "He lives in the white house with a red roof, on the left-hand side, down this road about a hundred miles."

Sure enough, when we knocked, it was my Uncle Edgar who came to the door!

—Marigold Rollins Burns.

✣ ✣ ✣

Once, while visiting a hospital ward, the late Queen Mary stopped to speak to a sweet little girl with a large pink ribbon in her hair.

"Where do you live?" she asked the child.

"I live in Battersea, just over the river," explained the child. She looked at her visitor a moment, then added, "And where d'you live?"

Queen Mary was taken aback, but just for a moment.

"Oh," she answered, "I live just behind Gorringe's shop in Buckingham Palace Road."

—*Tit-Bits,* London.

✤ ✤ ✤

A few years ago, in a town in the deep South, the local chapter of the Ladies' Aid Society decided to bring a little sunshine into the state prison by writing cheery letters to the inmates. One dear lady didn't quite know how to go about addressing a total stranger, a man she knew only by a string of numbers. But finally she achieved what she happily believed to be a measure of friendliness:

"Dear 688395," she wrote. "May I call you 688?"

—*Crustene Courier.*

✤ ✤ ✤

FRIENDSHIP

Abraham Lincoln once dropped a few kind words about the Confederates. A woman flashed forth a question of how he could speak kindly of his enemies when he should rather destroy them.

"What, Madam, do I not destroy them when I make them my friends?"

—CARL SANDBURG, *Abraham Lincoln: The War Years.*

✤ ✤ ✤

When Socrates was building himself a house at Athens, being asked by one that observed the littleness of the design why a man so eminent would not have an abode more suitable to his dignity, he replied that he should think himself sufficiently accommodated if he could see that narrow habitation filled with real friends.

—SAMUEL JOHNSON.

✤ ✤ ✤

"Who is a friend like me?" said the shadow to the body. "Do I not follow you wherever you go? Sunlight or moonlight, I never forsake you."

"It is true," said the body; "you are with me in sunlight and moonlight, but where are you when neither the sun nor moon shines upon me? The true friend abides with us in darkness as well."

FUTILITY

A Boston surgeon visited a little inn in the tranquil village of Wellfleet, on Cape Cod. Old Captain Curran was in charge. The Cape was feeling the pinch of depression; summer folks were scarce and trade was at low ebb.

"Hello, Captain," sang out the surgeon. "And how is the hotel business?"

"Wall," drawled Captain Curran, "I ain't never yit made enough to quit and I ain't never yit lost enough to quit. I hope to the Lord I do one or the other this season."

—Dr. Robert M. Bartlett.

✣ ✣ ✣

An Englishman once went out shooting with a pointer he had borrowed from a friend who was a crack shot. He himself was a very poor shot, and missed again and again, the pointer each time looking at him in bewilderment.

Finally the dog set a pheasant, right out in an open field, and glanced back at the approaching man as much as to say, "Now, here's a perfectly good shot. For pity's sake, see if you can do anything this time." The pheasant rose and flew off; the man missed twice. Whereupon the pointer sat down on his haunches, raised his nose to high heaven, and howled long and dolorously. Then, with never another look at the amateur huntsman, he turned and trotted home.

—Samuel A. Derieux, *Animal Personalities* (Doubleday).

✣ ✣ ✣

GALLANTRY

A gallant old Arab chieftain, the Sheikh of Mohammerah, once gave a large reception in honor of Lady Blank, whose husband was the Governor of Bombay. She was a very beautiful woman.

Just at the moment when Lady Blank was being received by the sheikh, and was talking with him, something distracted her attention, and she turned her back on her host for a moment. Instantly realizing her unintentional rudeness, she said to her interpreter, "Please tell the sheikh I'm so sorry I turned my back on him."

Whereupon the old sheikh smiled and bowed. "Tell the lady," he commanded, "that a rose has no back."

—Colonel Edward Davis, *Sunshine Magazine.*

✤ ✤ ✤

GAMBLING

A minister told the children of his Sunday school a story about a shepherd who found a sick lamb and wrapped it in one of his garments and took it home to nurse it back to health.

"Now," he concluded, "do any of you know a similar story in which such a kind action was expressed?"

There was a prolonged silence. Then a little girl said: "I didn't see this myself, but I heard my daddy say he had put his shirt on a horse and lost it."

—*Virginia Mental Health.*

✤ ✤ ✤

A senator was arguing in the Idaho legislature in favor of a bill legalizing the operation of slot machines. He was interrupted by a fellow senator, who asked:

"Would you advocate putting a slot machine in your church?"

The senator replied: "I would just as soon, because there are some people who couldn't be pried out of a dime with a crowbar, but they might take a chance on a slot machine."

—*Parade.*

✤ ✤ ✤

"If we could only use the $2,000 in my savings account to buy a new car, we wouldn't have to pay any financing charges," a lady said to a bank teller.

"Then why don't you?" asked the teller.

"Because my husband would ask how I saved so much money. If I told him, it would spoil his fun. When he began playing the horses, I offered to place the bets for him. Instead, I took them myself. When his horse won, I paid him off, and when he lost, I put the money in my savings account."

—*New York Times.*

All horse players worthy of the name follow hunches. One race track classic is the story of the perfect inspiration which came to a bettor the time he visited the track on his birthday, the fifth day of the fifth month. On the program he found a horse named Quintuplets, in the fifth race and in the fifth position. At the five-dollar window he bought five tickets on her and settled back affably to collect on his "sure thing." Quintuplets did not spoil his perfect hunch. She came in fifth!

—*Fifth Wheel.*

♣ ♣ ♣

"Eddie," said a gambler to his friend, "I must tell you about this guy I met yesterday. He's figured out a system whereby a whole family can live without money."

The other gambler looked up eagerly. "Does it work?"

"No," admitted his friend sadly, "but that's the *only* loophole in his system."

—E. E. Kenyon, *American Weekly.*

♣ ♣ ♣

During the lull in the shooting between two fightin' hillbilly families, one group got out a worn deck of cards and chips, huddled low beneath a window and started playing poker.

Suddenly, without warning, a bullet whizzed by and got one of the players directly behind the ear. As he toppled over backwards, the player next to him sneaked a look at the dead man's hand.

"Pore Jim," he muttered, shaking his head sympathetically, "I believe he woulda made it!"

—E. E. Kenyon, *American Weekly.*

♣ ♣ ♣

GENEROSITY

Jacques, a young Parisian outdoor stall-keeper for a small shop, spent ten hours a day on the sidewalk, exposed to all kinds of weather. In winter the only way to keep warm was to stuff one's hands in one's pockets and stamp one's feet.

One bitter winter day Jacques, then 15 years old, was shivering at his stall, clad only in a threadbare suit and a flimsy scarf. Suddenly a well-dressed man stopped, examined him closely, and then entered the store. When he reappeared, he held out to Jacques a warm overcoat and a fur cap, saying, "These are for you. As a gift. Put them on right away, and don't ask me to explain. I am doing this for my own pleasure. Good-bye, my friend." Then he hurried away.

The incident made a great impression on Jacques. "That man had revealed to me," he said, "how rare a quality is the completely self-effacing goodness that asks for nothing in return. Better yet: I felt as if he had handed on to me some sort of secret formula, and that it was up to me to apply it and use it in my own life."

—JULES ROMAINS.

✣ ✣ ✣

One afternoon while driving through the hills of West Virginia, I spotted some beautiful old-fashioned flowers growing by a weatherbeaten shack. They were just what I needed for an arrangement I wanted to make for a flower show. I knocked, and a tiny old woman came to the door. I told her I admired her flowers and wanted to buy a few. Without a word she reached for a knife and proceeded to cut almost every flower. I protested, but with a sweet smile on her wrinkled face she said, "Can't ever remember having anything before that anyone else ever wanted."

—NAOMI P. HOSTERMAN.

✣ ✣ ✣

When John Barrymore lived at the Algonquin, he frequently levied upon the private wardrobe of Frank Case, owner of that caravansary.

Once Barrymore was asked by Wilson Mizner to describe Case. "He's great," said Jack. "There are no adjectives to describe him. He's . . . he's . . ." At a loss for superlatives, the actor resorted to a Broadway phrase. "Why he's the sort who'd give you his . . ." He paused, seemed to realize something amazingly co-incidental, pointed to his own bosom, then exclaimed, "My God! This *is* his shirt!"

—GENE FOWLER, *Good Night, Sweet Prince* (Viking).

Stopping for coffee at a small restaurant run by a blind veteran, I was amazed at the deft way he went about his business. Paying him, I handed him a dollar bill. He asked the denomination, then quickly gave me correct change. "Do you ever have trouble with people giving you ones and saying they're fives?" I asked.

"No, sir," he replied, "the only trouble I have is with people who give me fives and tell me they're ones."

—*Lionews.*

♣ ♣ ♣

A little boy once cried for the moon. His father, a kind and generous man and very wise, gave it to him. "You may have the moon," said the father, "only you must not be selfish about it. The very best place to keep the moon is up there in the sky, where it will give you light by night; and of course you want it to give light to your mother and me and to other people also. You may have the moon just as long as you are unselfish, but when you grow greedy, then the moon will belong to someone else who will make better use of it."

Another day the lad wanted the ocean, so the father gave him that on similar condition. "You must not bottle it up and carry it away," he said. "It is yours, but you must not be selfish with it. Let other people swim in it and sail boats in it."

When the boy wanted a great forest, his father gave it to him. When he asked for the mountains, his father granted the wish—one thing after another until soon he owned the whole universe, but always on condition that he would not be selfish, but would let other people enjoy these wonderful things of his.

—H. DaCosta Finley.

♣ ♣ ♣

This is a true story. Abdul Aziz Ibn Saud, King of Saudi Arabia, was making his annual pilgrimage to Mecca when his Packard sedan blew out a tire. His Majesty sat down in the sand while the tire was being fixed. A shepherd on a camel rode up and asked whether the King had gone by. Ibn Saud, unrecognized, asked why the shepherd wished to know.

"I heard that he was on his way to Mecca," the shepherd explained, "and want to see if he will give me some money so I can make the pilgrimage too."

Opening the bag of gold pieces which he kept about him for emergencies, the King fished out a handful. The shepherd stared at them, then looked at the King.

"Thanks, Abdul Aziz," he said. "I did not recognize your face but I know you by your generosity."

—NOEL F. BUSCH in *Life.*

✥ ✥ ✥

One of the most graceful bits of repartee on record was done with commas. Some years ago the talented actress, Margaret Anglin, watched the famous Mrs. Fiske do a wonderfully dramatic performance which impressed her so greatly that she scribbled a note on her program and sent it to Mrs. Fiske backstage. The note read: "Margaret Anglin thinks Mrs. Fiske is the greatest actress in America."

During the next intermission the note was returned to Miss Anglin, with two commas added. It now read: "Margaret Anglin, thinks Mrs. Fiske, is the greatest actress in America."

—*Whatsoever Things.*

✥ ✥ ✥

GENEROSITY/SELFISHNESS

There are two seas in Palestine.

One is fresh, and fish are in it. Splashes of green adorn its banks. Trees spread their branches over it, and stretch out their thirsty roots to sip of its healing waters.

Along its shores the children play, as children played when He was there. He loved it. He could look across its silver surface when He spoke His parables. And on a rolling plain not far away He fed five thousand people.

The river Jordan makes this sea with sparkling water from the hills. Men build their houses near to it, and birds their nests; and every kind of life is happier because it is there.

The river Jordan flows on south into another sea.

Here is no splash of fish, no fluttering leaf, no song of birds, no children's laughter. Travelers choose another route, unless on urgent business. The air hangs heavy above its water, and neither man nor beast nor fowl will drink.

What makes this mighty difference in these neighbor seas?

Not the river Jordan. It empties the same good water into both. Not the soil in which they lie, not the country round about.

This is the difference. The Sea of Galilee receives but does not keep the Jordan. For every drop that flows into it another drop flows out.

The other sea is shrewder, hoarding its income jealously.

It will not be tempted into any generous impulse. Every drop it gets, it keeps.

The Sea of Galilee gives and lives. This other sea gives nothing. It is named The Dead.

There are two seas in Palestine.

There are two kinds of people in the world.

—BRUCE BARTON, *McCall's Mag.* (Copyright 1928, McCall Corp. 230 Park Ave., New York 17, N.Y.)

✤ ✤ ✤

GENIUS

A young composer once came to Mozart for advice on how to develop creatively. "Begin writing simple things first," Mozart told him; "songs, for example."

"But you composed symphonies when you were only a child," the man exclaimed.

"Ah," Mozart answered, "but I didn't go to anybody to find out how to become a composer!"

—DAVID EWEN, *Listen to the Mocking Words* (Arco).

✤ ✤ ✤

Guglielmo Marconi, the genius of radio, was entertaining a friend one night in his laboratory. The two discussed the most intricate phases of wireless communication.

Finally, at dawn, the friend suggested they retire. As they were leaving the lab, Marconi looked back over his shoulder and said: "All my life I have been studying this phenomenon, but there is one thing I simply cannot understand about radio."

"Something you don't understand about radio?" smiled the other. "What is that?"

Marconi mused, "Why does it work?"

—*Milwaukee Journal.*

♣ ♣ ♣

It was a gala night, but the audience was apathetic. And then a catastrophe befell the violinist. In the middle of a performance, the E string snapped. Clawing furiously at the instrument, the artist deliberately broke the A and D strings. While the audience held its breath, the black-browed violinist strode recklessly to the front of the stage. Thrusting his violin under his chin, he then signaled the orchestra to proceed. "One string," he exclaimed, "and Paganini!"

Before, he had only been well known. Within a matter of weeks, Paganini was world famous.

—*Capper's Weekly.*

♣ ♣ ♣

Once when Paderewski played before Queen Victoria, the sovereign exclaimed with enthusiasm, "Mr. Paderewski, you are a genius!"

"Ah, Your Majesty," he replied, "perhaps; but before I was a genius I was a drudge."

—Hamilton *Spectator.*

♣ ♣ ♣

GIFTS—Giving

A clergyman wrote to a wealthy and influential businessman, requesting a subscription to a worthy charity. The man answered: "As far as I can see, this Christian business is just one continuous give, give, give."

"I wish to thank you," said the clergyman, in his response, "for the best definition of the Christian life that I have yet heard!"

—*The New Century Leader.*

♣ ♣ ♣

A missionary persuaded a London merchant of the great needs of his field. The merchant gave the missionary a check. In the morning the merchant learned that his business had suffered a heavy financial loss. Regretfully the missionary returned the check when the merchant requested it. Soon thereafter the missionary received a larger check. The merchant, who had torn up the first check, wrote, "God is teaching me that I must give while I can."

—EGBERT W. SMITH, *The Desire of All Nations.*

✤ ✤ ✤

A mother chided her small daughter, who had just returned from a visit to a pleasant neighbor lady up the street, her arms loaded with childish plunder.

"Oh, it's all right," the child insisted. "She likes me. I'm somebody she can give things to."

—*Whatsoever Things.*

✤ ✤ ✤

GOD—and Man

Abraham Lincoln used to tell the story of a balloon ascension that occurred in New Orleans some time before the war.

After sailing in the air for several hours, the performer, arrayed in silks and spangles, descended in a cotton field.

A number of Negro slaves, at work on the plantation, took to the woods in great fright. But one venerable old man was rheumatic and could not run. He stood staring in awed silence as this spangled specter from the heavens approached. Finally, remembering his manners, he took off his battered hat and bowed: "Good Mornin', Massa Jesus," he said, "How's yo' pa?"

✤ ✤ ✤

A young Communist girl once came to Dr. George Hedley, a college professor working with labor groups. She gave him the usual Communist line, saying that she didn't believe in God.

"What kind of a God don't you believe in?" Hedley asked.

It turned out she didn't think there was a grandfatherly gentleman sitting on a throne in the skies.

"Do you think the universe makes sense?" he asked the girl. "Do you think that effect follows cause regularly enough so we can count on it?"

She had to admit she did—or abandon the whole Marxist philosophy.

"Does it seem to you," the questioner continued, "that this kind of sensible universe may have been planned and set going by a conscious intelligence?"

"It must have been," said the girl.

"Well, then," concluded Dr. Hedley, "if you're confident of that, you're much surer of your belief in God than a lot of clergymen and professors I know!"

✣ ✣ ✣

After a hailstorm which severely damaged the tobacco in our section, I met one of the worst-hit growers. "Any of your crop saved?" I asked.

"No'm."

"But you did have it insured?"

"No'm. Not a penny."

"I'm sorry," I commiserated.

"Yes'm, thank you. 'Twas bad. Had a-been anybody else but the Lord had a-done it, I shore would a-been peeved."

—Louise Allen Harris.

✣ ✣ ✣

Daniel Webster once found himself in a group discussing Christianity. Webster said something about the divinity of Christ, and one of the group responded, "But, Mr. Webster, can you comprehend how Christ could be both God and man?"

The old statesman replied, "No, sir, I cannot. If I could comprehend Him He would be no greater than myself. I feel that I need a superhuman Savior."

—*Tarbell's Teachers' Guide* (Revell).

✣ ✣ ✣

After the bombing of World War II, the people of Frankfurt, Germany, began the rebuilding of their cathedral. Deep in the ruins they found a statue of the Christ which had stood in their chancel; it was intact except for the hands, which had been broken off as it fell. For a time they thought of engaging a sculptor to carve new hands for the old statue. Then they thought of something better. They set up the statue again, in its old place, and across the base of it they wrote, "Christ has no hands but our hands!"

—*Tarbell's Teachers' Guide* (Revell).

✤ ✤ ✤

In the course of my early ministry, I once spent considerable time in the sick-room of a dear old soul. One day, half in jest and half in earnest, she said to me, "Padre, I'm fed up with God. What can I do about it?" I replied, "Tell Him so. He will understand. He has a sense of humor, too. If not, it wouldn't be among His gifts to mankind."

Yes, if you are under the weather; if you are feeling exasperated and baffled, tell God. That is prayer; it is a wonderful help.

—John Short, *Triumphant Believing* (Scribner).

✤ ✤ ✤

George Muller, founder of Bristol Orphan's Home, in England, was said to be "a little queer" because he depended entirely on prayer for the support—even the financial support—he needed for his Home. One day a friend said to him, "You seem to be living from hand to mouth."

"Yes," replied Muller, "I do just that. It's my mouth, but it's God's hand."

✤ ✤ ✤

Eric Gill, the British sculptor, wrote in his autobiography: "I had a dream in which I was walking in heaven with my wife, Mary, and our children. We met Our Lord and I said to Him, 'This is Betty, and this is Petra, and this Joanna, and this is Gordian.' And He shook hands with them all. And then I said, 'And this is Mary.' And He said, 'Oh, Mary and I are old friends.' "

✤ ✤ ✤

A Negro preacher called on a hard-working parishioner, a farmer, each year, soliciting increasingly larger contributions for the church. One year, when he got the proposed levy past a point which the farmer thought he could bear, the preacher sought to persuade him by arguing, "Your farm's been good to you, and the Lord's been good to you. Part of this land belongs to the Lord. You're in partnership with Him, so you ought to give Him His share." To which the farmer replied, "I acknowledge that the farm is paying off, that the Lord's been good to me, and that He is my partner. But did you ever see this place when the Lord was looking after it Hisself?"

—ALBEN W. BARKLEY, *That Reminds Me* (Doubleday).

✣ ✣ ✣

Years ago, a young man named William Colgate left his home in Baltimore, Md., to go to New York to make his way in the world. Just before he left, he was talking with a friend of his family.

"What do you know how to do?" asked the friend.

"All I know how to do," answered young Colgate, "is to make candles and soap."

"Then make the best candles and the best soap you know how to make," advised the friend, "and make God your partner."

William Colgate took this advice and in time became the owner of a large and well-known soap company.

—JAS. E. SWEANEY, *You.*

✣ ✣ ✣

When St. Finnbarr's cathedral was being built in Cork, there was a workman who was inclined to cut the tiles on the spire a bit on the rough side, and the foreman spotted it. "It won't do, Jerry," said he.

"Why not?" asked Jerry. "Sure it is going up 200 feet and only the crows will see it."

"God will see it," said the foreman, "an' he's particular."

✣ ✣ ✣

The haughty man had decided that he would at least take some of what he had with him. He left specific orders that all his jewels and gold should be put in his casket. The casket was to be of solid stone. It was to be sealed so that it could never be opened from the outside. As a last assurance, a full-fledged curse was to be said over the grave.

All was done exactly according to his wishes. Surely he and his treasure were forever secure from man and nature.

But there was the faintest little crack in the stone cover of the tomb. Water seeped in and froze. Something had to give, and in the spring the crack was easily noticeable. The summer rains seeped through the crack, and the acorn that by chance had been left in the casket sprouted.

Slowly it grew toward the light that now filtered thru the crack. Watered and fed by nature, it grew through the opening and broke out into the sunlight. As it grew ever stronger, something had to give, and now a sturdy tree grows out of the tomb that was sealed and cursed for all time and eternity. Again the God who created all of nature had asserted his authority over the works of man.

—JOE DANA, *Link*.

✣ ✣ ✣

Dr. A. A. Hodge tells this story of the great Dr. Witherspoon, Presbyterian clergyman of the 18th century.

One day a man rushed into his presence. "Dr. Witherspoon," he shouted, "help me to thank God for His wonderful providence! My horse ran away, my buggy was dashed to pieces on the rocks, and behold I am unharmed!"

The good doctor smiled benevolently at the inconsistent, imperfect character of the man's religion. "Why," he answered, "I know a providence a thousand times better than that. I have driven down that rocky road to Princeton hundreds of times, and my horse never ran away and my buggy was never dashed to pieces."

—CHAS. E. BAYLEY, *Free Methodist*.

✣ ✣ ✣

Life is really simple, and yet how confused we make it. In old Chinese art, there is just one outstanding object, perhaps a flower, on a scroll. Everything else in the picture is subordinate to that one beautiful thing.

An integrated life is like that. That one flower, as I see it now, is the will of God.

—MADAME CHIANG KAI-SHEK in *The United States News*.

✣ ✣ ✣

On a small tropic island in the South Pacific an American airstrip was built. The chaplain and his crew tried to tell the natives about religion, but somehow they responded slowly. Christmas of 1943 came with orders to move on. The Americans gave a big farewell Christmas party with makeshift presents, and several tried to explain the origin of the Christmas spirit.

A few years later the same chaplain stopped at the island on his way to India as a missionary. He was greeted with excitement and taken to see something beautiful, a church. Over the doorway was this crude inscription: "This is our church built on the faith and brotherly love which we know is."

The chaplain stayed for a service. There were no seats, everyone stood in the presence of God. The songs were all Christmas carols, for these were the only ones they knew. One explained: "After you leave we build the church to worship Jesus. We worship him with only service we know, Christmas, the day he was born. Every day is Christmas here. Every day Christ child born anew. Our gift to give is love. Our church we call her Christmas Church."

—*Power.*

✣ ✣ ✣

Visiting a newly rich friend in the country, Wolcott Gibbs refused to be impressed by tennis courts, swimming pools, stables, and other forms of luxury. Finally, returning to the house, the owner pointed to a magnificent elm growing just outside the library window and boasted: "That tree stood for 50 years on top of the hill. I had it moved down here so on pleasant mornings I can do my work in its shade."

Said Gibbs: "That just goes to show what God could do if he had money."

—FRANK CASE, *Do Not Disturb* (Lippincott).

✣ ✣ ✣

Not long ago I was invited by a well-known surgeon to watch a complex operation he was about to perform. As he went through the laborious preparation for the operation—scrubbing for the allotted time and being helped into cap, gown and rubber gloves—he seemed confident but a little tense.

"All set?" I asked.

"Almost," he replied, and stopped and bowed his head for a moment. Then, calm and relaxed, he led the way to the operating room. During the operation his hand never faltered.

Afterward I said to him, "I was surprised at your praying before you went in. I thought a surgeon relied solely on his own ability."

He answered, "A surgeon is only human. He can't work miracles by himself. I'm certain that science couldn't have advanced as far as it has, were it not for something stronger than mere man. You see," he concluded, "I feel so close to God when I am operating that I don't know where my skill leaves off and His begins."

—KENNETH ROBERTS.

✤ ✤ ✤

GOLDEN RULE

A mother happening one day to overhear a group of little girls excitedly concocting a scheme of revenge against another little girl, who had apparently done something very "mean," was grieved to find her own child among the chief conspirators.

"Why, my dear!" she said, taking her child aside, "it seems to me you're going to do to Lottie just what you don't want her to do to you. I don't think this is the Golden Rule—is it?"

"Well, mamma," said the child, "the Golden Rule is all right for Sunday, but for everyday I'd rather have an eye for an eye and a tooth for a tooth!"

—*Watchman-Examiner*.

✤ ✤ ✤

GOVERNMENT

A Swedish farmer came into town to apply for naturalization papers. The judge asked if he was satisfied with the general conditions of the country. The farmer replied that he was.

"Does the form of government suit you?" the judge persisted.

"Yah, it bane all right," answered the Swede, "only I'd like to see a little more rain."

GOSSIP

A guest said recently, upon leaving: "I like to come here. It's the one place I can say anything I want to, knowing it won't go further." The compliment really should have gone to my mother.

One day, when I was about eight, I was playing beside an open window while Mrs. Brown confided to my mother a serious problem concerning her son. When Mrs. Brown had gone, my mother, realizing I had heard everything said:

"If Mrs. Brown had left her purse here today, would we give it to anyone else?"

"Of course not," I replied.

Mother continued: "Mrs. Brown left something more precious than her pocketbook today. She left a story that could make many people unhappy. That story is not ours to give to anyone. It is still hers, even though she left it here. So we shall not give it to anyone. Do you understand?"

I did. And I have understood ever since that a confidence or a bit of careless gossip which a friend has left at my house is his—not mine to give to anyone.

—CONSTANCE CAMERON, *Reader's Digest*.

✤ ✤ ✤

GRATITUDE

At one time my father worked as a dishwasher in a Denver hotel. He worked 14 hours a day, not getting through till midnight. He was then 60 years old. One of the other kitchen workers was a young Italian named Philip. My father studied an Italian grammar, and surprised the boy by addressing him in his language. Soon after that Philip came to Father and said: "You're to quit work at ten," explaining that he would take over my father's last two hours of dishwashing. Father remonstrated, but young Philip insisted.

In after years my father could never speak about Philip's great gift of *time* without tears in his eyes.

That story came to mind when a friend said, "In every man

there is a king and a pauper. Your father always spoke to the king, and the king came out."

—SIGNE TOKSVIG (biographer and novelist).

✣ ✣ ✣

One night at the turn of the century a young honeymoon couple dined at a small, obscure Paris restaurant. When it came time to pay the check, the husband was distressed to discover that his wallet had been stolen, particularly so when the waiter failed to believe him and took the couple to the manager. Something in the youth's manner appealed to the proprietor, however, and when he learned that they had lost their return tickets to Vienna as well, he offered to loan them enough to get home.

"You will not regret your wonderful generosity," said the young husband. "I promise I shall make both you and your café famous. My ambition is to write an operetta, and I shall put your restaurant in it." The manager smiled. His only hope was to get his money back.

But the youth—Franz Lehar—kept his promise. A few years later he wrote *The Merry Widow* with its famous Café Maxim song. And because its genial proprietor, Eugene Cornuche, had befriended a penniless composer, Café Maxim became the most popular night club in the world.

—*Romance, Rhythm and Ripley*, CBS, quoted in *Listen*.

✣ ✣ ✣

An old farmer tramped into a doctor's office at Huntington, West Virginia, one night, his lean, red face pinched with worry. A bachelor, he lived alone on a hilltop near the village of Milton, 20 miles away, but he had several nieces and nephews in Huntington, one of whom was stricken with infantile paralysis.

"What news, Doc?" the farmer asked uneasily.

"Good news," the doctor answered. "We've caught it in time, I think. I believe she'll walk again."

"Walk? Say, Doc, if you can make that girl walk—I'll—I don't know what I'll do!"

A year later the girl was walking. The farmer came back.

"Doc," he said, "here's the deed to my farm, best 200 acres in the state. I'm givin' you all else I own too. Not very much, just some cattle and implements, worth maybe a couple o' thousand dollars. But it's all yours, to use helping other kids like you helped ours. Maybe you could turn my old farmhouse into a hospital. It's shy a bathroom but you could put one in. I'll move right out. There's a little tenant house on the place where I can stay."

The farmer lived only four years more, but that was long enough for him to see the first 100 crippled children carried into his old farmhouse, long enough to see most of them come out walking. Some of them limped, to be sure. Some wore casts or braces. But they could work and play, tramp in the woods, go to school, grow into useful citizens.

Today a big modern orthopedic hospital stands on the farmer's hilltop. The "W. T. Morris Memorial" it is called, to honor the old bachelor who gave all he had in order that paralyzed children might walk again.

—KARL DETZER, *Reader's Digest.*

✤ ✤ ✤

A lady once wrote me that she had just had a baby—stillborn, and her heart was broken; she had no desire to go on living. Then, one evening her husband had turned on the radio and she heard my concert. It made her want to live again because there was beautiful music in the world. She did not sign her name, because she did not want me to think she wanted a reply—she only wanted to tell me.

The letter haunted me; I felt I must express my thanks. So my secretary called up every hospital in New York. We had nothing to go on but the date of the letter, but after hours of phoning we found her. The same day I sent her a photograph which I inscribed to her: "From Arturo Toscanini, Detective!"

—BERNARDINE SZOLD FRITZ in *Rob Wagner's Script.*

✤ ✤ ✤

H. G. Wells has such a big head that he has trouble getting hats to fit. Once when he found one that balanced nicely on his head he just walked off with it, and blandly penned a note to its owner, E. S. Peck, mayor of Cambridge, Mass.

"I stole your hat," wrote the author. "I like your hat; I shall keep your hat. Whenever I look inside it, I shall think of you and your excellent sherry and of the town of Cambridge. I take off your hat to you."

—Helen Morgan in *The Family Circle.*

✤ ✤ ✤

A middle-aged man rescued a small boy from the torture of teasing older children, comforted him with cookies, and gave him two old tennis balls to take home. The next morning his doorbell rang and there stood the little boy beaming. He walked to the nearest table and began to take keys out of his pocket—dozens of keys to nowhere, big keys, little keys, keys on rings, keys on chains, broken keys and junk pile keys.

"I came to tell you," he said gravely, "that if you ever need any keys, I can let you have some."

—Claire MacMurray, *Cleveland Plain-Dealer.*

✤ ✤ ✤

A couple had just been married. After the ceremony the bridegroom asked, "What do I owe you?" Replied the minister, "I have no set fee. Just pay me what it is worth to you." Beaming down on his bride, the groom said, "If I've got to pay what it's worth to me, you've bankrupted me for life."

—Edmond M. Kerlin, *Telescope-Messenger.*

✤ ✤ ✤

A woman displaced person stood gazing at the city's skyline as the ship neared American shores. With considerable emotion she said, "I understand Americans smile easily. I think it will take a while for me to quiet my gratitude for being here before I can smile."

—Harry C. Kenney, *Christian Science Monitor.*

✤ ✤ ✤

A traveler for a big publishing house couldn't wait to get to St. Louis where his oldest friend owned a prosperous bookstore. "Sam," he said to the owner the moment they were alone, "I want you to lend me two thousand dollars." "The answer, Joe," said Sam, "is positively no." "But, Sam," protested the salesman, "in 1929, when Bond and Share broke from 189 to 50, who gave you ten thousand dollars to keep you from being wiped out?" "You did," admitted Sam. "And in 1931, when your daughter Shirley had that tropical disease, who took her down to Florida because you couldn't get away from business, who did, Sam?" "You, my friend, you did." "And in 1933, when we were fishing together, who dove into the rapids and saved you from drowning at the risk of his own life?" "You did, Joe. It was wonderful!" "Well then, Sam, in Heaven's name, why won't you lend me two thousand dollars now when I need it?" "All the things you say are true," said Sam, nodding his head slowly, "*But what have you done for me lately?*"

—BENNETT CERF, *Saturday Review.*

✤ ✤ ✤

A lady, waiting for a bus, noticed the gentleman shuffling by. Obviously, he had seen better days. Tempering her charity with tact, she stooped as though to pick something up, then said, "Pardon me, did you drop this?" She held out a quarter.

"What do ya know?" said the man, taking the proffered coin and tipping his hat. "A lot of people would have kept that for themselves."

—*Way.*

✤ ✤ ✤

We were a group of friends in the midst of an after-dinner conversation. Because Thanksgiving was just around the corner and times were not prosperous, we were talking about what we had to be thankful for. One member of the group, a minister, asked, "What can I say in a sermon that is affirmative?"

That started us. One of us said: "Well I, for one, am grateful to Mrs. Wendt, an old schoolteacher who 30 years ago went out of her way to introduce me to Tennyson." She had, it appeared, awakened his literary interests and developed his gifts for expression.

"Does this Mrs. Wendt know that she made such a contribution to your life?" someone asked.

"I'm afraid not. I've never taken the trouble to tell her." "It would certainly make her happy, if she is alive, and it might make you happier, too. Far too few of us have developed the habit of gratitude."

Mrs. Wendt was my teacher, and I was the fellow who hadn't written. My friend's challenge made me see that I had accepted something precious and hadn't bothered to say thanks.

That evening, on the chance that Mrs. Wendt might still be living, I wrote her what I called a Thanksgiving letter. My letter was forwarded from town to town. Finally it reached her, and this is the note I had in return, in the feeble scrawl of an old woman. It began:

"My dear Willie: I can't tell you how much your note meant to me. I am in my eighties, living alone in a small room, cooking my own meals, lonely and like the last leaf of fall lingering behind.

"You will be interested to know that I taught school for 50 years and yours is the first note of appreciation I ever received. It came on a blue, cold morning and it cheered me as nothing has in many years."

I have continued to write my Thanksgiving month letters each November to people who had contributed something deep and lasting to my life. In ten years I have had more than 500 of the most beautiful answers anyone ever received. Thanks to the rebuke of a friend, I have learned a little about gratitude.

—William L. Stidger, *Reader's Digest.*

✣ ✣ ✣

A wealthy family in England, many years ago, took their children for a holiday into the country. Their host turned over his estate for the week end to the visitors. The children went swimming in a pool. One of the boys began to drown, and the other boys screamed for help. The son of the gardener jumped into the pool and rescued the helpless one.

Later, the grateful parents asked the gardener what they could do for the youthful hero. The gardener said his son wanted to go to college some day. "He wants to be a doctor," said the gardener. The visitors shook hands on that. "We'll be glad to pay his way through," they said.

When Winston Churchill was stricken with pneumonia, after the Teheran Conference, the King of England instructed that the best doctor be found to save the Prime Minister. That doctor turned out to be Alexander Fleming, the developer of penicillin.

"Rarely," said Churchill later, "has one man owed his life twice to the same rescuer."

It was Sir Alexander who saved Churchill in that pool.

—*Sunny Way.*

✣ ✣ ✣

GRATITUDE—Lack

Old Mrs. McCoy was an incurable grumbler. Nothing pleased her. But one fall her pastor heard of her excellent apple crop and figured that at last he had found one thing about which she could not possibly complain.

"Well, Sister McCoy," he said, "I know you are happy. I've heard a lot about that fine apple crop!"

The old woman glared at him as she replied: "Oh, I guess they'll do—but where's the rotten 'uns for the pigs?"

—LIBBY GATES, *Country Gentleman.*

✣ ✣ ✣

GREED

While we were touring the County Fair grounds a few years back, a group of visitors were leaning over the fence looking at Uncle Pete's prize fat hogs. They were by far the largest and fattest in the whole show. None of the others could hold a candle to Uncle Pete's. One of the group asked him, "How come your hogs are the biggest, Uncle Pete? You always win blue ribbons on them."

"Well," drawled Uncle Pete, "I feed them pigs all they can stuff into 'em. Then a couple of weeks before the Fair, I put a half-starved shoat in with them and when they see that shoat eatin', it rouses the greedy instinct in 'em and they start eatin' all over again."

—H. H. PICKETT.

✣ ✣ ✣

One of the artists at l'Opera de Pekin tells this new Chinese story: A saint had the power to transform stones by touching them with his index finger. One day a beggar came to him with a pebble, which the saint immediately turned into gold. The next day the beggar approached with a paving stone, which was again transformed. Every day the man would return with an increasingly larger stone, until finally he approached the saint apparently empty handed, said, "This will save time," pulled out a knife and cut off the saint's index finger.

—*Paris Match,* France (QUOTE translation).

✣ ✣ ✣

GROWTH

A visitor called at a friend's house, and asked the little boy, "What became of the tiny kitten you had?"

"Why, haven't you heard?" replied the little boy solemnly.

"No. Was it drowned?" asked the visitor.

"No."

"Lost?"

"No."

"Poisoned?"

"No."

"Run over?"

A shake of the head.

"Then what in the world happened to it?" asked the bewildered visitor.

"It growed up into a cat."

—*Shaw's Price List,* London.

✣ ✣ ✣

HABIT

A wise old man was once taking a stroll through a forest with a shiftless youth by his side. The man suddenly stopped and pointed to four plants. The first was a tiny sprout. The second had rooted itself quite firmly. The third was a small shrub. The fourth had grown into a well-developed tree.

The old man said: "Pull up this first plant." The youth pulled it up easily with his fingers.

"Now pull up the second," said the man. The youth obeyed, and with slight effort the plant came up, roots and all.

"And now the third," continued the elderly gentleman. The

boy pulled with one hand, then the other, but it would not come. Then he took both hands, and the plant yielded to all his strength.

"And now," said the old man, "try the fourth." The youth grasped the trunk with all his might, but hardly a leaf shook. "I cannot move it," he exclaimed.

"Just so, my son," said the wise old man, "with our bad habits. When they are young and small, we can cast them out but when they are full grown, they cannot be uprooted."

—*Uplift.*

✤ ✤ ✤

A well-dressed man came briskly into the restaurant. At once the waitress put before him a cheese sandwich, a baked apple, and a pot of coffee. In five minutes he had disposed of the food and was gone. "He must be a regular," I commented to the girl.

"Regular is no word for it," the waitress said. "For fourteen years he comes in at nineteen minutes past twelve, always eats the same thing and never talks. I don't say a word except in May and September. In September I say, 'We've got oysters.' He says 'Good,' and I give him an oyster cocktail instead of the baked apple. In May I say, 'No more oysters.' He says, 'Good,' and we go back to the cheese sandwich, baked apple and coffee."

Ruts dig deep graves!

—Joe Blandford, *Democracy in Action.*

✤ ✤ ✤

One cold, snowy morning an old man was seen, dressed in his nightshirt, vigorously chopping kindling.

His neighbor, amazed at the brevity of the old man's clothing in such severe weather, asked, "How come?"

The old man never missed a lick in his chopping as he replied: "For the last seventy years I have always dressed by a fire, and I'll be dad gummed if I'm gonna stop now."

—*Capper's Weekly.*

✤ ✤ ✤

"When I was young," remarked an old gentleman, "somebody gave me a cucumber in a narrow-necked bottle. I wondered how it got there. But in the garden one day I saw a bottle slipped over a tiny cucumber still on the vine and then I understood.

"I often see young people with habits that I wonder any strong, sensible person could form. And then I think that likely they grew into them when they were smaller, like the cucumber in the bottle."

—*Friendly Chat.*

✤ ✤ ✤

A hog buyer saw a drove of hogs, large but lean, acting quite peculiarly. They would run in a bunch to one part of the field, stay there a few minutes, then hump to a different place. Calling on the farmer, he mentioned their peculiar nervousness. The farmer, in a hoarse whisper, explained that he had always called the hogs to feed them, but when he took cold and lost his voice, he pounded on the fence with a stick to bring them. "Now," he said, "the darned woodpeckers are running those hogs to death."

—*United Mine Workers Journal.*

✤ ✤ ✤

In a certain school in New York there was a teacher, an energetic advocate of "Safety First," who opened her class each morning by rising and asking, "Children, what would you do if fire were to break out in this building?" The children would reply in chorus, "We would rise in our places, step into the aisle, and march quietly out of the building."

One morning when the children arrived at school they found themselves honored by the presence of the well-known and beloved Dr. Henry van Dyke. The teacher stepped before the class and instead of the usual fire drill question, said, "Children, what would you say if I were to tell you that Dr. van Dyke is to speak to you this morning?"

Instantly from the class came the resounding chorus, "We would rise in our places, step into the aisle, and march quietly out of the building."

—*Kablegram.*

✤ ✤ ✤

HANDICAPS

Wm. Prescott, at Harvard when only 15, was struck by a hard crust of bread, during an after-dinner frolic with schoolmates.

The blow destroyed one eye, and critically injured the other.

After months in a dark room, Prescott went back to school and managed to graduate. He started out in law in his father's law office, but had to give it up.

He turned to research. For 6 hours each day he sat in darkness while an assistant read from reference books. Tragedy struck early, but he would not give in to it. Today he is considered one of the finest historians ever to write in America. Darkness never conquered the light within.

—REV. A. PURNELL BAILEY, *Grit.*

✤ ✤ ✤

I have worked with many servicemen who were having a tough time returning to the world of business. Here was one who had broken almost every bone in his body and had lived to resume his old job with hardly any mental upset. Here was another whose injuries were trivial. If he carried a cane he could get around easily. But he loathed the cane. He seemed to regard it as a public confession of weakness. He was forever trying to do without it. Worse yet, he strove to walk without a limp. The strain was terrible. He insisted that life was empty for a cripple. Within two years he killed himself.

I reached two conclusions. Many people are better off with grave handicaps than with trifling ones. The grave handicap releases copious energies. The trifling handicap seems to stir the person too feebly to open up the big valves of nervous and mental power.

—WALTER B. PITKIN.

✤ ✤ ✤

One July afternoon at our ranch in the Canadian Rockies I saddled my horse and rode toward Helen Keller's cabin for my regular call. Along the wagon trail that ran through a lovely wood we had stretched several hundred yards of smooth wire, to guide Helen when she walked there alone, and as I turned down the trail I saw her coming.

I sat motionless while this woman who was doomed to live forever in a black and silent prison made her way briskly down the rough, uneven path, walking with her body completely relaxed, her face radiant. She stepped out of the woods into a sunlit open space directly in front of me and stopped by a clump of wolf willows. Gathering a handful, she breathed their strange fragrance; her sightless eyes looked up squarely into the warm face of the sun, and her lips, so magically trained, pronounced the single word "Beautiful!" Then, still smiling, she walked past me.

I brushed the tears from my own inadequate eyes. For to me none of the wonders of this exquisite high land had seemed beautiful: I had felt only bitter discouragement over the rejection of a piece of writing I had set much store on. I had eyes to see all the wonders of woods, sky and mountains, ears to hear the rushing stream and the song of the wind in the treetops. It took the sightless eyes and sealed ears of this extraordinary woman to show me beauty, and bravery.

—Frazier Hunt in *Redbook Mag.*

✤ ✤ ✤

General Melvin Maas, who is blind, served as chairman of the President's Committee on Employment of the Physically Handicapped for one year. Speaking to one convention crowd, he said, "Of course, I'm handicapped myself, you know."

The crowd looked sad for him, but then he added, "I have false teeth."

—Earl Wilson, *Minneapolis Tribune.*

✤ ✤ ✤

Arturo Toscanini, one of the greatest musical directors the world has ever produced, was so nearsighted that he grew weary of having to bend very close to his score sheet to play his cello. He resolved to memorize his music sheet. Not content with this, he memorized the parts for every instrument in the orchestra and their proper cues.

One night when the orchestra waited in the pit of the opera house in Parma, Italy, for the conductor, word came that the conductor had been taken very ill.

No one knew that Toscanini knew the entire score. Fellow students suggested that he do the conducting.

Although he had never done it before, the cellist calmly

mounted the conductor's stand. The audience was amused at the poise of this nineteen-year-old boy, and interested to see what he could do.

He closed the score book and conducted the entire opera from memory.

At the conclusion, he received an ovation from the audience and an appointment as permanent conductor. His cello's bow was replaced permanently by the baton. This nearsighted young musician became the world's greatest orchestra conductor.

—*Friendly Chats.*

✤ ✤ ✤

During World War II Colonel Rutgers Beekman, U.S.A. (this was almost his right name) and his son were in England, the former serving on Eisenhower's staff while the younger man, a naval lieutenant, had been flown in, badly wounded, during the day.

When the Colonel had begged to be permitted to see his son he had been told it was out of the question. It would excite his son.

"But he needn't know."

"He'll feel your nearness," the nurse had answered. "We shall call you right after the operation."

So now Colonel Beekman waited in his little flat walking up and down, up and down. And then there was, once more, the telephone bell. The operation was done. Would the Colonel come?

He hurried down the stairs. On reaching the street he noticed that a thick, pea-soup fog had dropped over London. Even in the few blocks to the hospital he missed his direction and was completely lost. The fog, accentuated by the blackout, wiped out the streets and buildings; the people he could hear and dimly see, shuffling, groping.

He called out, "I am an American Army officer. My son is in St. Gregory's Hospital. Won't somebody—"

Then a hand reached out and took his arm and he heard a voice: "Come along, sir!" The stranger guided him along, left, right, left, around a corner. A huge building loomed through the blackness. "Here you are, sir," said the voice.

Colonel Beekman thanked the Good Samaritan. Then, as he turned and started up the steps to the door of the hospital, he called back: "But how did *you* find your way?"

"Easily," was the answer. "I'm blind. Got it in both eyes. Dunkirk, sir."

—ACHMED ABDULLAH, *This Week Magazine.*

✣ ✣ ✣

I have, like other people, made resolutions which I have broken or only half kept; but one which I send you . . . is the key-note of my life. It is this—always to regard as mere impertinence of fortune the handicaps which were placed upon my life almost at the beginning. I resolved that they should not dwarf my soul, but rather be made "to blossom like Aaron's rod, with flowers."

—HELEN KELLER.

✣ ✣ ✣

When a young man, Robert Ripley was entering upon a career in big-league baseball. He fractured his arm in the first game he pitched. Doctors warned him not to do any work that would strain his arm.

Bob taught himself to draw. A job as a newspaper sports cartoonist was the first training for his highly successful feature. His radio work-pictures and pencil drawings of oddities have brought him world-wide fame.

Robert Ripley was inclined to regard his fractured arm at the first game of ball he pitched as a "lucky break."

—*Friendly Chats.*

✣ ✣ ✣

HAPPINESS

A rich and discontented lady found herself most unhappy. Finally, in desperation, she went to a famous psychiatrist and asked for help.

"Madam," said the doctor, after some prolonged consultation, "I cannot help you. But you can help yourself. My advice to you is to visit Niagara Falls and take a good, long look at something bigger than yourself!"

Recently I visited my uncle on his farm near Kingston, R. I. From dawn to dark he was busy with spring planting, but in spite of his endless chores and many cares, my uncle was always cheerful. Never have I seen a man who savored life with such terrific gusto.

One evening while we were enjoying a pipe together, I contrasted his happy temperament with that of a near relative, Vince, who seldom found pleasure in anything. "Some people," I said, "seem to enjoy life just once in a while, like Vince. Others, like you, seem to enjoy each day."

He smiled understandingly. "It's the way you grow up, mostly. When Vince was small, he liked to lick his spoon once after *finishing* his dessert. I used to lick my spoon after *each* mouthful."

—N. A. PETROCELLI

✤ ✤ ✤

Happiness depends on one's inner state, not on one's outward situation. Pleasure-seeking indicates heart hunger, but does not satisfy it. When Maxim Gorky visited America, some friends took him to Coney Island, to see the huge playground, swarming with hundreds of thousands of people. At the end of what may have seemed to them a perfect day, they asked their guest how he had liked it. After reflecting a moment, he replied, "What a sad people you must be!"

✤ ✤ ✤

A self-righteous man went to see a philosopher. "I was told once," he said, "that they who learned to do the right things are happy. I have not found it so. I am tired of doing the right things when I do not get rewarded for my sacrifices."

"I begin to see your difficulty," said the philosopher. "There is something yet for you to learn. It is not enough just to *do* the right things. If you would be happy, you must learn to *enjoy* doing them."

—REV. J. W. HOLLAND, *Progressive Farmer.*

✤ ✤ ✤

A mighty king was stricken with a strange malady, for which the physicians could find no remedy. A sooth-sayer told him that if he wore the shirt of a happy man, he would recover. With fresh hope, the king ordered the country searched for his happiest subject—but alas, when they found him, he had no shirt!

—*Employment Counselor.*

✣ ✣ ✣

A puppy said to a big dog, "I have mastered philosophy. I have learned that the best thing for a dog is happiness, and that happiness is my tail. Therefore I am chasing it; and when I catch it, I shall have it!"

Said the old dog: "I, too, have judged that happiness is a fine thing for a dog, and that happiness is in my tail. But I've noticed that when I chase it, it keeps running away from me; but when I go about my business, it comes after me."

—*Sunday School Times.*

✣ ✣ ✣

As my train was pulling into Pittsburgh one morning I heard the Negro porter singing joyously as he made up the berths. He had a big smile and a hearty "good morning" for everyone. I thought I would make an effort to discover his secret, so I asked, "What makes you so happy this morning?"

He seemed surprised by the question, as though happiness is a natural state of mind that should be taken for granted. He thought a moment, then answered, "Treat yo'self right and yo'll treat the other fellow right. I jes' like to be happy an' make someone else happy."

Which is just about all there is to it.

—WILFRED A. PETERSON, *Hoover Sphere.*

✣ ✣ ✣

We once counseled a successful and very egotistic businessman who could find no time to concern himself with the affairs and woes of his fellow men during his business day to go to the Grand Central Station in New York and to look for someone to help. Largely in a spirit of supercilious condescension he obeyed our prescription.

A poor woman from a country town had come to New York to meet her daughter. She had lost the slip with her daughter's address, and sat silently weeping in a corner. Our patient managed to find her daughter's address in the telephone directory, took the old lady and her bags and put her in a taxicab, and accompanied her to an obscure street in The Bronx. On the way he bought the old lady a few roses. She wept for sheer joy on his shoulder. He deposited her, smiling, in her daughter's house, rushed to the telephone to call us.

"Doc, I feel like a human being at last!" he blurted as he told us the story. Since then he has become one of the directors of a boys' club on the lower East Side of New York, and a member of various child welfare and civic organizations.

If we want to know what happiness is we must seek it, not as if it were a pot of gold at the end of the rainbow, but among human beings who are living richly and fully the good life.

—W. Beran Wolfe, M.D.

✣ ✣ ✣

A little girl of five said to her mother at bedtime, "I've had such a happy day, Mother, so much happier than yesterday."

"Really?" the mother replied. "What made it so different from yesterday?"

"Well," the wise cherub answered, "yesterday my thoughts pushed me around—today I pushed them around!"

—Margery Wilson, *Make Up Your Mind* (Stokes).

✣ ✣ ✣

"There is no duty we underrate so much," wrote Robert Louis Stevenson, "as the duty of being happy." Stevenson, a life-long invalid, found his happiness the sure way—by helping others to be happy. The last few years of his life he spent in Samoa, where his kindnesses won the deep love of the natives. When one of the chiefs was imprisoned by a European government, Stevenson visited him regularly, bringing him tobacco and other gifts. After his release, he and the other chiefs built, with their own hands, the "Road of Gratitude," through the wilderness to Stevenson's house. When Stevenson died, the natives buried him on a mountain top and the chiefs tabooed the use of firearms on that mountain, so that forever after the birds might sing undisturbed above his grave.

It might be well to remember another truth he wrote: "Perpetual devotion to what a man calls his business, is only sustained by perpetual neglect of many other things."

—*Whatsoever Things.*

✣ ✣ ✣

HASTE

We are new farm owners, and at first we were inclined to apply all the high-pressure hurry of our city living to our 60 acres. But Ben, our tenant farmer, took us down a peg. Asked if he had finished plowing the cornfield, he squinted at the setting sun and said serenely, "No, but the land'll be there tomorrow."

His bit of homely philosophy set me to thinking about the permanent values of life—the things that will be there tomorrow. Most of us pursue the temporary interests of our existence so frantically that we have little time to enjoy the everlasting ones. We rush to get waited on in stores, to beat others to a seat on the bus, to keep up with the Joneses. And all the time, unnoticed and unappreciated, stretch the eternal verities under our indifferent noses.

—CONSTANCE J. JOSTER, *This Week Mag.*

✣ ✣ ✣

HATE

"How much I hate that man!" Charles Lamb once exclaimed.

"Hate him?" asked his friend. "You don't even know him."

"Of course I don't know him," said Lamb. "If I knew him, how could I hate him?"

✣ ✣ ✣

A rattlesnake, if cornered, will become so angry it will bite itself. That is what the harboring of hate and resentment against others is—a biting of oneself. We think we are harming others in holding these spites and hates, but the deeper harm is to ourselves.

—E. STANLEY JONES, missionary and author.

HEALTH

A housewife developed a bad case of nerves. She suffered from severe headaches, especially when washing dishes, a chore she hated. She went to her doctor, and was given an unusual prescription: He simply told her, "Have a nice large window cut over your sink." She did—and no longer suffered headaches!

—*Tarbell's Teachers' Guide* (Revell).

✤ ✤ ✤

Lord Northampton, who had been a rather reckless young man, tottered out of a court one day complaining: "Confound these legs of mine; if I had thought that they would one day carry a Lord Chancellor, I would have taken better care of them."

✤ ✤ ✤

I doubt whether it is good for the ordinary man to know much of the details of how his body works. The man who has learned to think of his heart as a pump, with valves that get out of order, is on the way toward having a weak one. Better let him think of it as the seat of love and generosity and it will beat away happily till it stops.

Let him think of his stomach as where he puts his dinner, not as a fierce chemical furnace where acids are tearing up tissues and sending up exhaust gases. Let him think of his blood as part of his lineage, not as the battleground of a myriad of good and evil corpuscles, some on his side, some dead against him, and his bowels as the bowels of compassions, as gentle as the New Testament. Any man who has realized that he has in him about 25 feet of colon and semi-colon—a sort of string of sausages—can never think the same of himself again.

—Stephen Leacock in *Too Much College* (Dodd, Mead).

✤ ✤ ✤

Georg Christoph Lichtenberg, who suffered badly from gout, told his friends he could be cured if he could have the following prescription filled: "Take the handkerchief of a girl who never had a desire to marry, wash it 3 times in the pond of an honest miller, dry it in the garden of a protestant minister who had no children, write on it with ink from a lawyer who had never defended a dishonest cause, give it to a doctor who had never caused the death of a patient, and tie it around the gouty leg."

—*Auslese,* Frankfurt (QUOTE translation).

✤ ✤ ✤

Young Betsy ended her night-time prayers in all earnestness. "Please, Lord, can't you put the vitamins in pie and cake instead of in cod liver oil and spinach? Amen."

—*Vermont Marble Chips.*

✤ ✤ ✤

Disraeli, when prime minister of England, was out walking one day with a friend. As they went along the streets of London, they met a rather distinguished-looking elderly man whom Disraeli greeted very cordially and then inquired: "How is your old complaint?"

The man responded that it was getting worse and worse and he was sure that it was going to be the death of him.

As Disraeli and his friend walked on, his friend asked who the elderly acquaintance was. Disraeli said that he did not have the faintest notion who the man was.

"But you asked about his old complaint," persisted the friend. "How did you know about that if you did not know the man?"

The prime minister replied wisely, "I have found that almost all elderly people have some complaint, and they like to talk about it."

✤ ✤ ✤

Billie Burke was enjoying a trans-Atlantic ocean trip when she noticed that a gentleman at the next table was suffering from a very bad cold.

"Are you very uncomfortable?" she asked sympathetically.

The man nodded miserably.

"I'll tell you just what to do for it," she offered. "Go back to your stateroom, and drink lots of orange juice. Take five aspirin tablets. Cover yourself with all the blankets you can find. Sweat the cold out. I know just what I'm talking about. I'm Billie Burke of Hollywood."

The man smiled warmly, and introduced himself in return, "Thanks. I'm Dr. Mayo, of the Mayo Clinic."

HELPFULNESS

An incident is related of a company of people who gathered to pray for a family in great financial straits. While one of the deacons was offering a fervent prayer for blessings upon the family, there was a loud knock at the door. The door opened and there stood a sturdy boy.

"What do you want, boy?" asked one of the elders. "Pa couldn't come, so I brought his prayers in the wagon," replied the boy. "Just come and help me, please, and we'll bring them in." Pa's "prayers" consisted of potatoes, flour, beef, turnips, apples, and jellies. The prayer meeting was adjourned quickly.

—*Baptist Observer.*

✤ ✤ ✤

A sportsman's wife strongly objected to her husband gambling on horses, but he continued to back them secretly.

One evening an old friend, unaware of the prohibition, dropped in and said to the punter: "Well, did you have any luck with Sue the Second yesterday?"

Instantly the wife shot her husband an ugly look and went out of the room.

"You've torn it," groaned the husband. "My wife thinks I don't bet now. You'll have to square this with her."

In a few moments, when the wife returned, the friend said, breezily, "I say, Mrs. Brown, I'm awfully sorry if I misled you just now. Sue the Second isn't a horse, you know, she's a barmaid."

—*Tit-Bits*, London.

✤ ✤ ✤

A bus driver was making his usual run out of the city, through the suburbs and into the country. Along the way he tossed packages of newspapers to be picked up later by the distributors.

Suddenly a car pulled alongside, honking furiously. The bus pulled to a stop at the side of the road and waited for the motorist to come alongside. "Don't know what's the matter," the motorist called, "but you seem to be losing papers. I've been picking them up for the last hour." And he handed over the bus driver's entire morning delivery.

—*Balance Sheet.*

HISTORY

A young soldier returned a hero from Korea. One day, while chatting with a former professor, he was asked whether he had learned anything important from his war experiences.

"Yes, sir," the ex-student replied. "I have learned that it is easier to study history than it is to make it."

—*Nuggets.*

❖ ❖ ❖

Asked if he could summarize the great lessons of history in a single volume, famed historian Charles A. Beard replied that he could do it in four short sentences:

1. Whom the gods would destroy they first make mad with power.
2. The mills of the gods grind slowly but exceedingly fine.
3. The bee fertilizes the flower it robs.
4. When it is dark enough you can see the stars.

❖ ❖ ❖

HONESTY

In the mining country of West Virginia I stopped at a modest restaurant, during World War II, and was astonished by the menu which read:

Small, dry, tough steak .... 60¢
Thin pork chops, mostly bone & fat .... 50¢
Tasteless meat loaf .... 45¢
Fat, greasy spareribs .... 40¢

"Why do you list the meat like this?" I asked.

"Because that's what it is," the waiter said.

"But even if it is, couldn't you make it sound a little more attractive?"

"Look . . . if y'all was reg'lar here, you'd know better," he replied. "Our menus always tell ya just what ta expect. That's been our policy a long time and we don't reckon on changin' it fer no temp'rary thing like a war."

—BERNARD M. BOUR.

❖ ❖ ❖

A young Virginia woman who wished a pass to visit her brother, a Confederate soldier and a prisoner in the Union lines, was brought to Lincoln by old man Blair. He had warned her beforehand: she must not betray her Confederate sympathies. The President bent toward her, searched her face and said, "You are loyal of course?"

Her eyes flashed, met his gaze frankly, then, "Yes, loyal to the heart's core—to Virginia!"

He kept his eyes on her face a moment, went to a desk, wrote a line, and handed her a folded paper. She bowed herself out with Mr. Blair, who was saying: "Didn't I warn you to be very careful? You have only yourself to blame."

She unfolded the paper and read words to this effect, signed by the President: "Pass Miss ———. She is an honest girl and can be trusted."

—Carl Sandburg, *Abraham Lincoln: The War Years.*

✤ ✤ ✤

An Army private liked his furlough and wanted more. Resourcefully, he wired his commanding officer:

"No death, no emergency. Request extension of furlough. Having wonderful time."

Having heard all the usual alibis, his commanding officer responded: "Reward for honesty extension of five days on present furlough granted."

—*The Wolfe Magazine of Letters.*

✤ ✤ ✤

Recently a client went to his attorney and said: "I am going into a business deal with a man I do not trust. I want you to frame an air-tight contract which he can't break and which will protect me from any sort of mischief which he may have on his mind."

"Listen, my friend," said the attorney, "there is no group of words in the English language which will take the place of plain honesty between men, or which will fully protect either of you if you plan to deceive each other."

—Ernest Haycock, *Rotarian.*

✤ ✤ ✤

One of two women riding on a bus suddenly realized she hadn't paid her fare. "I'll go right up and pay it," she declared.

"Why bother?" her friend replied. "You got away with it—so what?"

"I've found that honesty always pays," the other said, virtuously, and went up front to pay the driver.

"See, I told you honesty always pays!" she said when she returned. "I handed the driver a quarter and he gave me change for fifty cents."

—*Alexander Animator.*

✤ ✤ ✤

On one occasion, before turning in a test paper, one of my boys called my attention to a question at the top of the page and urged, "Count that wrong. Someone told me the answer to that."

Noticing how painstakingly he had filled in the complete answer, I asked, "If you were going to tell me to count it wrong, why did you write it out in the first place?"

He grinned sheepishly. "It looked sorta bare up there," he explained.

—Dorothy Slade, *North Carolina Education.*

✤ ✤ ✤

Probably no man had a longer or more distinguished career in sports than the veteran coach, A. A. Stagg, for forty-two years the idol of students and graduates of the University of Chicago. Yet he is more admired for his rugged character and uncompromising honesty.

Stagg's champion baseball team was defending its college title. The batter had singled, and one of Stagg's men was racing home with the winning run. Stagg shouted, "Get back to third base. You cut it by a yard." "But the umpire didn't see it," the runner protested. "That doesn't make any difference," roared Stagg. "Get back!" It cost a game, but a character battle was won.

—*United Presbyterian.*

✤ ✤ ✤

A group of young schoolteachers were taking a routine efficiency test. When they came to Part III they found a long list of book titles and authors. "Check the books you have read," said the directions.

Later, the examiners scoring the papers discovered that one third of the teachers had checked almost every book on the list; some had checked every one. Such results didn't mean that these teachers were extremely well educated; they meant that they were liars—because twenty-five of the fifty book titles did not exist. They had been invented by the examiners as a means of checking the truthfulness as well as the efficiency of their subjects.

—Paula Philips, *This Week.*

✣ ✣ ✣

A baker living in a village not far from Quebec bought the butter he used from a neighboring farmer. One day he became suspicious that the butter was not of the right weight, so for several days he weighed the butter and found that the rolls were gradually diminishing in weight, and he had the farmer arrested for fraudulent dealing.

At the trial the judge said to the farmer: "I presume you have scales?" "Yes, of course, your honor." "And weights, too, I presume?" "No, sir." "Then how do you manage to weigh your butter?

"That's easily explained, your honor," said the farmer. "When the baker commenced buying this butter of me I thought I would get my bread of him and it is the pound loaves of bread I've been using as a weight for the butter I sell. If the weight of the butter is wrong, he is to blame himself."

—*Present Truth Messenger.*

✣ ✣ ✣

A nun dropped her pocketbook. After she thanked the panhandler who picked it up, she added, "I don't know why some people say you are not honest."

"Well, Sister," said the panhandler, "I'm honest to goodness."

—Helen Mull, *Catholic Digest.*

✣ ✣ ✣

At the end of the examination, the students were required to sign a pledge stating that they had neither given nor received aid during the examination. A rather dull looking boy lingered after the other students had left the room. He confessed to the teacher that he did not know if he could truthfully sign the pledge, since he had prayed to the Lord to assist him in the examination, and he did not know whether his prayers were answered. The amused teacher looked the paper over and said, "I think you can sign."

—JAMES MCBRYDE, *Coronet*.

✤ ✤ ✤

The politicians were discussing their honesty during the last campaign. "Well, you certainly can't say you ever heard that I was dishonest!"

"No, but I never heard that you were honest!"

—*Revue,* Munich (*Droke House Translation*).

✤ ✤ ✤

Anxious about a vessel which was long overdue, Jacob Barker, Quaker shipowner of Nantucket, called at the office of a local insurance company, and frankly admitting his concern, applied for a policy on vessel and cargo. The agent asked for time in which to investigate but on the day agreed upon for a decision, no news —good or bad—had been received by the insurance company. That morning Honest Jacob stopped in on his way to the wharves.

"If thee has not made out that policy, thee needn't, for I have heard from my vessel."

"But, Friend Jacob!" exclaimed the chagrined agent, "the underwriters have accepted the risk and the policy is here." He handed it to the old man.

The Quaker sighed. "A Friend's word is his bond," he said, and counted out the gold for the premium. "Yes, I have heard from her, Friend," he continued. "She went to the bottom last month, and with all aboard."

—ELEANOR EARLY, *An Island Patchwork* (Houghton).

✤ ✤ ✤

Abraham Lincoln, as a young lawyer, was pleading two cases the same day before the same judge. Both cases involved the same principle of law, but in one he appeared for the defendant, in the other he spoke for the plaintiff. In the morning he made an eloquent plea and won his case. In the afternoon he took the opposite side and was arguing with the same earnestness. The judge, with a half-smile, inquired the cause of his change in attitude.

"Your honor," said Lincoln, "I may have been wrong this morning, but I *know* I am right this afternoon!"

—NELLIE REVELL, *Right Off the Chest* (Doubleday, Doran).

✣ ✣ ✣

A plain little man clerking behind a dry-goods counter in Montreal many years ago, whom I knew only as Mr. Mathew, had a profound influence on my life. I was then 19, just over from London, with flashy ideas of making a fortune. My material possessions were an elegant broadcloth Inverness cape and $5, and I was glad to get a job as a clerk in a store for $6 a week and a commission on my sales. I didn't know chintz from chenille, or anything about selling, but I pretended I did.

Salesmanship, to my callow mind, meant talking in superlatives, so I exaggerated the qualities of the merchandise even to the point of misrepresentation, guaranteed the wearing quality of materials I knew nothing about, and used all my glibness to persuade a customer to buy.

I sold a fair amount by these tactics. Yet I noticed that plain old Mathew had a far better sales record at the end of the month. I asked him about it. He said: "It's because people believe me."

Surprised, I asked: "Why don't they believe *me?*"

"Remember, lad," he said, "whatever you are, it shows in your eyes!"

That brought me up with a jolt, and it came over me then, for the first time, that honesty meant something more than the fact that you did not steal money, that it also wasn't just a vague ideal teachers and parents talk about, but a part of plain everyday living.

I began to emulate Mathew and I was astonished to find it actually worked. My sales increased. One day a simply dressed customer began ordering high-priced goods rather recklessly, I thought. My commission would be considerable; but, bent upon following Mathew's precept of complete honesty, I urged her to consider the cheaper fabrics and to think about the entire purchase overnight. She bought what she wanted, however, and to my surprise, she paid cash on the spot.

Next day her husband came in, asked for me, and offered me a salesman's job at four times the salary I was getting. He said he was a diamond merchant. When I told him I didn't know a thing about diamonds, he said he didn't care because I had already learned the most important principle of salesmanship.

There has never been a period in my life that I have not been grateful for the lesson Mathew taught me. Now I have more than 650 salesmen. Again and again in conference with them I find myself paraphrasing Mathew's creed: "If you're not selling successfully, fix yourself up inside. You can't be top-notch unless your eyes show you are honest."

—Alfred E. Lyon.

❖ ❖ ❖

HONOR

An old Springfield friend of Lincoln, after an evening at the White House, asked, "How does it feel to be President of the United States?"

"You have heard," said Lincoln, "about the man tarred and feathered and ridden out of town on a rail? A man in the crowd asked him how he liked it, and his reply was that, if it wasn't for the honor of the thing, he would rather walk."

—Carl Sandburg, *Abraham Lincoln: The War Years* (Harcourt, Brace).

❖ ❖ ❖

HOSPITALITY

My sister, while doing mission work in a Kentucky mountain district, had to spend the night in one of the homes in that section. As she was preparing for her night's rest in the parlor bedroom, the hostess stuck her gaunt face in at the door, and said, "If you should want for somethin' you don't have, jest ask fer it. We kin show you how to do without it."

—Mrs. V. A. Crawford.

In 1875, a fleet of Chinese war junks set out to attack California. News had reached the Emperor in Peking that thousands of Chinese who had gone to California to work on the new railroads were being cruelly mistreated, and the outraged Emperor resolved to teach the United States a lesson it wouldn't soon forget. Eastward bound for Monterey sailed seven war junks armed with brass cannon. The Emperor, however, not realizing the size of the Pacific, had not sufficiently provisioned the fleet and before the voyage was half over the sailors faced death from thirst. Just in time a rainstorm came; quickly the sails were lowered and used as troughs to catch the rain.

At last the doughty fleet reached Monterey; 50 gunners stood by the cannon ready to blast the city to pieces if it put up a fight. But far from resisting, the people of Monterey were so delighted with this unexpected visit of Chinese war junks that the whole town came down to the shore to welcome the invaders. The pigtailed warriors, overwhelmed with hospitality, liked California so much that they refused to go home. The older men got jobs on the railroads, and the younger ones stayed on in Monterey as fishermen. The seven junks were ultimately broken up and burned.

—RICHARD HALLIBURTON, *Richard Halliburton, The Story of His Life's Adventure* (Bobbs-Merrill).

✤ ✤ ✤

In subscription courses the "word of introduction" custom can be at times diverting. At a university in California a professor made me feel at home by telling the assembly he didn't quite know how to introduce me as up to then they'd had "things of a cultural nature." And a New England chairman stated with Yankee brevity that "owing to the high price of Admiral Byrd we have Miss Skinner with us this evening."

—CORNELIA OTIS SKINNER, *New York Times Mag.*

✤ ✤ ✤

HUMAN NATURE

Farmer Jed was sitting on his porch steps moodily regarding the ravages of a cloudburst. A neighbor pulled up in a wagon.

"Say Jed," he yelled, "your hogs was all washed down the creek and they're all dead."

"How about Flaherty's hogs?" asked the farmer.

"They're gone too."

"And Larson's?"

"All washed away."

"Huh!" exclaimed the farmer, cheering up. "Tain't as bad as I thought."

—*Highways to Happiness.*

✤ ✤ ✤

A newspaper reporter in London is responsible for this story: Winston Churchill hailed a cab in the West End and told the cabbie to hurry to the BBC studios. The premier was scheduled to make a speech to the world.

"Sorry, sir," said the driver, "but ye'll have to get yourself another cab. I can't go that far."

Mr. Churchill was surprised and asked the driver why his operations were so limited.

"They hain't hordinarily, sir," he apologized, "but ye see, sir, Mr. Churchill is to broadcast in an hour, and I want to get 'ome to 'ear 'im."

Churchill was so pleased that he handed the man a pound note. The man was so pleased that he exclaimed, " 'Op in, sir! To blazes with Churchill!"

—*Capper's Weekly.*

✤ ✤ ✤

A woman once wrote Jacob Riis, the social reformer, that she had always admired Theodore Roosevelt until she heard that when he led his Rough Riders up San Juan Hill he had said, "Hell!" She hoped that Riis could restore her faith in her hero, with the assurance that the rumor was false.

To this communication, Riis made reply: "Madam, I do not know whether or not Colonel Roosevelt said 'hell' when he went up San Juan Hill, but I know that I did when I read your letter."

✤ ✤ ✤

The gatekeeper at a famous race track took $1200—his life savings—out of the bank to help his nephew through an eastern college. When asked how he could afford that gesture, he smiled sheepishly. "Day in and day out," he exclaimed, "I watch thousands of men bet on horses and lose their shirts. The way I figure it, a fellow might stand a chance to make a killing if he bets on a human being."

—FREDERICK VAN RYN, *Reader's Digest.*

✣ ✣ ✣

A floor-walker, tired of his job, gave it up and joined the police force. Several months later a friend asked him how he liked being a policeman.

"Well," he replied, "the pay and the hours are good, but what I like best of all is that the customer is always wrong."

—*Sales Scrap Book.*

✣ ✣ ✣

When an elderly businessman retired to his estate in an eastern farming section, he was depressed by the depleted soil, inferior stock and antiquated methods of his neighbors. He eagerly suggested new practices that promised better results, but they would have none of it.

Finally his farm manager, a native who knew the people, suggested building a fence around the place and following a policy of extreme reticence. The plan worked. The farmers climbed the fence by night and borrowed the ideas, as well as a little breeding from the foreign stock. The whole neighborhood was greatly benefited and every farmer felt it was a result of his own rugged individualism.

—BURGES JOHNSON in *North American Review.*

✣ ✣ ✣

Jack Dempsey was for a time one of the most unpopular champions that ever climbed into a ring. I remember the time and place when the switch occurred and the cult of Dempsey-worshipers was born.

It was some time between one and two o'clock in the morning of September 4, 1926, when Dempsey returned to a Philadelphia hotel room minus the heavyweight championship of the world. Gene Tunney had battered him almost beyond recognition.

Seconds, hangers-on, reporters, crowded into the room behind him. A lovely woman came to him with tenderness and took him into her arms for a moment. Lightly she touched his face. One side was completely shapeless, red, blue, purple in color, welted and bruised, the eyes barely visible between ridges of swollen flesh. "What happened, Ginsberg," she said. Ginsberg was Estelle Taylor's pet name for her husband.

Dempsey grinned out of the good corner of his mouth, held her off for a second, and then said: "Honey, I forgot to duck." From that moment on, everybody loved him.

—Paul Gallico, *Farewell to Sport* (Knopf).

✤ ✤ ✤

A rabbi, who lived nearly twenty years before Christ was born, set his pupils thinking by asking them this: "What is the best thing for a man to possess?"

One of them replied, "A kind nature." Another said, "A good companion." A third pupil volunteered, "A good neighbor."

But one of them, named Eleazer, said, "A good heart."

"I like your answer best of all," said the master, "for it includes all the rest."

—Francis Augusta Cox, *Friendly Chats.*

✤ ✤ ✤

HUMAN RELATIONS

Dwight Morrow was asked the secret of his success in dealing with others. He replied, "I never judge anyone until I discover what he would like to be as well as what he is."

—*Ladies' Home Journal.*

✤ ✤ ✤

Two boys fought. Finally one overpowered the other—got him down in the gutter and sat on top of him. As long as the victor held the vanquished down, the victor felt secure, but he was afraid to let his victim up for fear he might not be able to win a second time, if the fight were renewed. After a while the top boy began to realize that he could keep the other down only so long as he stayed down in the gutter with him. But he wanted to get up and play with some other boys. Finally he wanted to go home for supper. So he made terms with his enemy and let him up. The world has a hard time learning that he who enslaves another is tied to his slave. One who hates another is not free; rather, he is enslaved by his enemy.

—Dr. Frank E. Duddy, *Reveille.*

✣ ✣ ✣

HUMILITY

George Washington Carver, according to his own testimony, once asked, "Lord, what is the universe?" The Lord answered: "George, the universe is just too big for you to understand. Suppose you let me take care of the universe." Humbled, the Negro scientist asked, "Lord, if the universe is too much for me to understand, then what is a peanut?"

The Lord replied, "Now, George, you have something your size. A peanut you can understand. Now, go to work on the peanut—and I will help you."

For the remainder of his life George Washington Carver wrought miracles—with peanuts!

✣ ✣ ✣

At Sagamore Hill, Theodore Roosevelt and I used to play a little game together. After an evening of talk, we would go out on the lawn and search the skies until we found the faint spot of light-mist beyond the lower left-hand corner of the Great Square of Pegasus. Then one or the other of us would recite:

That is the Spiral Galaxy in Andromeda.
It is as large as our Milky Way.
It is one of a hundred million galaxies.

It consists of one hundred billion suns, each larger than our sun.

Then Roosevelt would grin at me and say: "Now I think we are small enough! Let's go to bed."

—William Beebe, *The Book of Naturalists* (Knopf).

✣ ✣ ✣

A friend once asked the famous conductor of a great symphony orchestra which instrument in the orchestra he considered the most difficult to play. The conductor thought for a moment. Then he said, "The second fiddle. I can get plenty of first violinists. But to find one who can play second fiddle with enthusiasm—that's the problem! And if we have no second fiddle, we have no harmony."

✣ ✣ ✣

Paul Cezanne never knew that he was "the father of modern painting." Having struggled 35 years without recognition, the shy old man was living in oblivion at Aix—giving away masterpieces to indifferent neighbors.

Then a discerning Paris dealer gathered several of these canvases and presented the first Cezanne exhibit. The great of the art world were stunned: they saluted a Master.

Cezanne arrived at the gallery on his son's arm. He gazed wonderingly at his paintings. Tears came to his eyes.

"Look," he whispered to his son. "They've *framed* them!"

—ROBERT OFFERGELD.

✣ ✣ ✣

A clergyman, meeting the President, hoped "the Lord is on our side."

President Lincoln: "I don't agree with you."

There was amazement.

The President continued: "I am not at all concerned about that, for we know that the Lord is always on the side of the right. But it is my constant anxiety and prayer that I and this nation should be on the Lord's side."

—CARL SANDBURG, *Abraham Lincoln: The War Years.*

✣ ✣ ✣

When William Allen White, editor of the *Emporia Gazette,* was standing in line at Columbia University, to receive an honorary degree, the man in front of him asked where he was from. "I guess I don't belong here," replied White. "I'm just a country editor from Kansas."

"Well," responded his companion in line, "I'm just a country doctor from Minnesota."

The "country doctor" turned out to be William J. Mayo of Rochester.

—DAVID HINSHAW, *A Man From Kansas* (Putnam).

When James Martineau was minister of Little Portland Street Chapel and was preaching to small but select congregations which included two or three of London's prominent intellectuals, an elderly domestic servant was observed to be unfailingly present at the services. A kindly man approached her, and after complimenting her on the regularity of her attendance, asked, "And do you understand the sermons?" She was greatly shocked, and answered, "God forbid that I should *presume to understand* Dr. Martineau!"

—J. M. LLOYD THOMAS, *Hibbert Journal.*

❖ ❖ ❖

A flight of stone steps is the last stage of a climb up a mountain in Sechuan, China, to a shrine. For more than a thousand years a steady stream of pilgrims has come and gone until the steps are worn and dangerous. Numbers of pilgrims have fallen, injuring themselves. The people of the neighboring city petitioned the monks to rebuild the steps, fearing their city might lose its profitable business of housing the pilgrims. But the Abbot of the monastery refused.

"It is to be regretted," he said, "that worthy pilgrims have suffered injury or death, but it is possible that they were holding their heads too high. Against these few are the millions who have learned that in life, one must walk carefully, holding the head high, but not so high that the pitfalls cannot be seen, and not so low as to lose sight of the sky."

—TOM ROBERTSON, *Fraternal Monitor.*

❖ ❖ ❖

A friar bemoaned to a friend the fact that his monastic order was not as famous as the Jesuits for scholarship, or the Trappists for silence and good works. "But," he added, "when it comes to humility, we're the tops."

—*Catholic Digest.*

❖ ❖ ❖

Through all his illustrious career, Anton Dvorak remained a simple, honest man, with a heart close to the common people of his native Bohemia. One day the admiring people of Prague brought him a wreath marked: "To the Greatest Composer in the World."

The composer was too moved to protest the honor too much, but when visitors came to his house a few days later, they discovered that Dvorak had placed the wreath where he believed it belonged. In a corner of the composer's study stood a bust of Beethoven, and upon its noble brow Dvorak had placed the treasured offering.

—*Wall Street Journal.*

✤ ✤ ✤

Michelangelo was seventy-two years old when he was appointed chief architect of St. Peter's, and commissioned to embellish the greatest temple in the world with his paintings and statues. For eighteen years he continued his work which made his fame as imperishable as the church itself. Toward the end, when his eyesight failed and he had become feeble, he had his servants carry him into the great halls and galleries and chapels, where he had labored with such vim and enthusiasm. He would run his hands over the statues and carvings, feeling out with his dexterous fingers the details which his eyes could no longer see; and he often exclaimed, "I still learn."

—*Sunshine Magazine.*

✤ ✤ ✤

When Thomas Mann was visiting America for the first time, one of Hollywood's literati abased himself before the novelist, emphasizing that he was nothing, a mere hack, his work not to be mentioned in the same breath with that of the master. Mann listened with infinite patience and courtesy. But when the party was over, he turned to his host, an old friend, and said, "That man has no right to make himself so small. He is not that big."

—*Life.*

✤ ✤ ✤

HUMOR

Walter Winchell's favorite story, which may be apocryphal, is about an editorial feud between the old New York *Sun* and *Post,* when both were conservative papers. One day the very proper and staid *Post* lost its temper and editorially called the *Sun* a yellow dog. The *Sun* replied in its starchiest manner: "The *Post* calls the *Sun* a yellow dog. The attitude of the *Sun,* however, will continue to be that of *any* dog toward *any* post."

—*Variety.*

✤ ✤ ✤

The London *Times* carries a so-called Agony Column. It is on the first page, and is used as a post office by persons who cannot communicate in the ordinary way. Some personals show a subtle British humor: "Invalided major requests loan of a cornet; object retaliation." Some show typical British politeness: "To the motorist who might have run over me in the King's Road on Sunday evening, Thank you."

—George Kent, in *The Christian Science Monitor.*

✤ ✤ ✤

IDEAS

Once, upon being complimented as a great inventive genius, Thomas Edison replied: "I'm a good sponge. I absorb ideas and put them to use— Most of my ideas first belonged to other people who didn't bother to develop them."

✤ ✤ ✤

IGNORANCE

The over-night millionaire wanted the best of everything. He went into a music shop and asked to see their most expensive violin. The assistant brought out a beautiful instrument, made in 1730.

"Wait a minute," said the millionaire, "you say this fiddle was made in 1730?"

"That's right."

"Then tell me; is the company that made it still in business?"

"Of course not!" exclaimed the assistant.

"Then it's no good," decided the rich man. "What would I do for spare parts?"

—*Tit-Bits,* London.

✤ ✤ ✤

An elderly man of convivial habits, also bookish, was hailed before a justice in a country town.

"You're charged with bein' intoxicated and disorderly,"

snapped the magistrate. "Have you anything to say why sentence should not be pronounced?"

"Man's inhumanity to man makes countless thousands mourn," began the prisoner in a flight of oratory. "I am not so debased as Poe, so profligate as Byron, as ungrateful as Keats, so intemperate as Burns, so timid as Tennyson, so vulgar as Shakespeare, so uncouth—"

"That'll do, that'll do," interrupted the magistrate. "Seven days. And, officer, take down that list of names he mentioned and round 'em up. I think they're as bad as he is."

—*Atlantic Courier.*

❖ ❖ ❖

ILLUSION

The first time I saw Maude Adams, she was playing in *Peter Pan.* I was six, and what enchanted me was her way of flying through the air. I believed that this was accomplished by what Peter himself called "flying dust," and to have been told that wires were employed would have shocked me beyond words.

When I met Maude Adams again she was playing at 67 the role of professor of dramatics at Stephens College, Columbia, Missouri. And again I was forced to crane my neck to see her, for she was standing atop a ladder. Under discussion was a plan to build rehearsal rooms in the attic above the stage and some doubt had been expressed as to the space available. "I'm going to see for myself," said Miss Adams, and up the ladder she went. But the ladder did not quite reach. She seized a rope and pulled herself up, hand over hand, and clambered through the opening above.

The sight of that trim dark figure dangling in the air totally *re*-illusioned me. All was not lost if Maude Adams, at an age when most of her contemporaries were either dead or retired, was still doing Peter Pan tricks. This time without wires or flying dust but out of some inner compulsion.

—George Kent, condensed from *Independent Woman* (National Federation of Business & Professional Women's Clubs, Inc.).

IMAGINATION

Often there is a job just waiting for somebody with imagination to come along and create it. This is a lesson I learned as a boy. Anxious to earn extra money, I asked all three drugstores in my town for a job—any kind of job. There were no openings. But a week later I found that one of these stores had taken on a new boy. Screwing up my courage, I asked the owner why.

"Well, I'll tell you, son," he said. "I didn't *think* I had a job open when you asked for one. But then Freddie came in with an idea. He owns a bicycle, and he suggested that I start a delivery service, meaning himself. That's a new notion for this town. It's going to make a hit."

Well, I had a bicycle, too, but Freddie had something I didn't have—an idea.

—JAMES D. WOOLF, in *Forbes*.

✣ ✣ ✣

I often think this "insomnia" business is about 90% nonsense. When I was a young man living in a boardinghouse in Toronto, my brother George came to visit me, and since there was no spare room, he had to share my bed. In the morning, after daylight, I said to George, "Did you get much sleep?"

"Not a damn minute," said he.

"Neither did I," I rejoined. "I could hear every sound all night."

Then we put our heads up from the bedclothes and saw that the bed was covered with plaster. The ceiling had fallen on us in the night. But we hadn't noticed it. We had "insomnia."

—STEPHEN LEACOCK, *Too Much College* (Dodd, Mead).

✣ ✣ ✣

Originality has been defined as a pair of fresh eyes. Have you ever tried to see the world through the eyes of your employer, your customers or the person you are careful to avoid? To do this improves your imagination and increases the pleasure of using it.

Take the barber who saw himself vividly through the eyes of his youngest customers as a tall dark stranger towering above them with terrifying scissors. He sawed the rockers off a rocking horse and he invited young customers to imagine they were knights or cowboys while they got their hair cut. Today his horse chairs are stabled in barber shops all over the United States.

—Ray Giles.

♣ ♣ ♣

IMITATION

The Japanese are acknowledged among races to be the world's cleverest imitators, but during the Korean conflict one U. S. Air Force commander was considerably provoked by this characteristic. The incident which brought this about occurred when a nervous pilot cracked a landing gear forging on a small but badly needed reconnaissance plane.

The officer, knowing that it might take months to obtain the necessary part from the States, called in a Jap mechanic.

"I want a part exactly like this one—quick," the commander said. "Can you make one?"

The mechanic, after studying the part, nodded gravely. In less than a week he was back at the hangar with the duplicate part, an exact copy of the original, including the inspection stamp impression.

The officer was elated until he took a second look at the forging—and then he was fit to be tied. The zealous workman had carefully, and with extreme accuracy, reproduced the crack in the duplicate part that had made the original part useless.

—*American Mercury.*

♣ ♣ ♣

IMMORTALITY

One day as I was lying in a canoe, a big black beetle came out of the water and climbed up into the canoe. I watched it idly for some time.

Under the heat of the sun, the beetle proceeded to die. Then a strange thing happened. His glistening black shell cracked all the way down the back. Out of it came a shapeless mass, quickly transformed into beautiful, brilliantly-colored life. As I watched with fascination, there gradually unfolded iridescent wings from which the sunlight flashed a thousand colors. The wings spread wide, as if in worship of the sun. The blue-green body took shape.

Before my eyes had occurred a metamorphosis—the transformation of a hideous beetle into a gorgeous dragonfly, which started dipping and soaring over the water. But the body it had left behind still clung to my canoe . . . I had witnessed what seemed to me a miracle. Out of the mud had come a beautiful new life. And the thought came to me that if the Creator works such wonders with the lowliest of creatures, what may not be in store for the human spirit!

—CECIL B. DE MILLE.

✤ ✤ ✤

INCONSIDERATENESS

The fat man and his wife were returning to their seats in the theater after the intermission.

"Did I tread on your toes as I went out?" he asked a man at the end of the row.

"You did," replied the other grimly, expecting an apology.

The fat man turned to his wife. "All right, Mary," he said, "this is our row."

—*The Highway Traveler.*

✤ ✤ ✤

INDEPENDENCE

The newcomer to our quiet corner of Maine didn't quite fit in. His car was a little too big and shiny; his clothes were a little too Country Club; his advances were a shade too effusive—and just a touch condescending. However, when he asked where he might get wood for his fireplace, we told him to try at George Ticknor's, down the road.

So he stopped his car in front of the Ticknor's place and blew the horn. After a while, he blew it again, longer. Eventually George strolled around from the back of the house. When he got within earshot our new neighbor called, an edge of impatience in his voice: "Look, I'm in a hurry. I hear you take orders for firewood."

George Ticknor looked the man over—the man and his car. Finally he spoke: "Well, I do have some firewood. And sometimes I accommodate my friends. But," and his voice grew crisper, "I dunno's I ever took orders from anybody in my life."

Whereupon he turned his back and walked away.

—DR. HARRY EMERSON FOSDICK.

✤ ✤ ✤

INDIFFERENCE

A story is often told of the Devil. He was auctioning his weapons to those who were interested. Hate, greed, and lust were among those weapons on his counter. Someone noticed that he was keeping one of them back and not showing it for sale. An interested spectator asked about this particular weapon.

"Oh," replied the Devil, "that is my favorite and most effective one."

On closer inspection, it turned out that this weapon carried the label, "Indifference."

✤ ✤ ✤

INDIVIDUALITY

My husband and I lived for a while in a California tourist camp consisting of long rows of identical cabins with identical little garbage cans by the door. One day I was sitting on my doorstep when a little boy of about four came running from the playground across the street. He lifted the lid of a garbage can near me and looked in. "No," he said and slammed it down. He picked up the lid of the next can and said "No" again, and slammed that down, repeating the process until he came to my garbage can, which he skipped, glancing at me briefly. Curiosity overcame me.

"What are you looking for, son?" I asked.

He lifted another lid. "I'm looking for our garbage," he explained shortly, "so I can find out where I live."

—MRS. NEAL SIMONS in "Life in These United States."

INFORMATION

A teen-age boy approached his father one evening and asked if he might interrupt his evening reading to ask a question. The father did not particularly care to be disturbed.

"Why can't you ask your mother?" he said.

"Oh," replied the boy, "I don't want to know that much about it."

✣ ✣ ✣

INGENUITY

During a Shriners' convention in Los Angeles one of the downtown boulevards was roped off for a parade. Only official cars with large signs such as *Potentate* and *Past Potentate* were allowed there; all other traffic was halted or rerouted. But one ingenious Californian got by the police blockade and drove nonchalantly down the street. His placard read: *Past Participle!*

—Milford P. Johnson.

✣ ✣ ✣

Lord Rothmere once made determined efforts to eliminate errors from his newspaper, the British *Daily Mail*. He was not too successful. Little errors appeared every day, in spite of all he could do. Finally he posted a notice on the bulletin board:

"Gentlemen: Hereafter we will print the first copy of the *Daily Mail* on a special paper and send it to His Majesty. That will be the royal copy; the million-and-a-half other copies will be exactly like it, except for the paper. And, gentlemen, His Majesty's copy must be errorless." Errors dropped ninety per cent.

✣ ✣ ✣

I like the story about the ventriloquist who was in theatrical parlance "between engagements"—which means between meals, or broke.

But he was ingenious, and a fine ventriloquist. So he spent his last dollar to buy a little dog and with the dog under his arm he made for the nearest bar. Here he took the bartender aside and said, "I have nothing in the world but this talking dog of mine. Would you give me $20 for him?"

The bartender was immediately on the defensive. "Whaddya mean, a talking dog?" he asked.

The ventriloquist went into his act. Apparently from the mouth of the puppy came a shrill bark, and then, "Sure I talk! I could say plenty about the free lunch in this joint. It's terrible! I've been here before!"

The bartender scratched his head in amazement. The ventriloquist smiled tenderly at the dog, and entreated the bartender: "I hate to give him up, but I've got to have the dough. How about it?"

"Twenty dollars is too much even for a talking dog. Here's ten." And the bartender lifted his apron and dug into his pocket for the money.

Our ventriloquist was in no position to quibble. He grabbed the bill, mumbled, "Thanks, pal," and hastened out.

But as he reached the door, the animal shouted at him: "I'm only worth ten bucks, eh? Just for that I'll never say another word as long as I live!" And he didn't.

—EDDIE CANTOR.

✤ ✤ ✤

Two pretty, earnest young school teachers went to Mexico last summer; they avoided all the tourist places, desiring only the real flavor of Mexico. They got it, too. Arriving in a highly flavored little inland city, they set out to explore. Coming to a street mellifluously named the Avenue of the Beautiful Springs and the Waterfall and the Bridge That is Music in Stone, they turned into it, only to be pounced upon by a policeman and hauled off to the police station. There the captain explained that their offense was trespassing on the redlight district. There was a fine of 300 pesos for any girl caught without a license on the Avenue of the Beautiful Springs and the Waterfall and the Bridge That is Music in Stone.

The girls protested that they were simply sightseeing and had no idea of muscling in, but the captain said the fine remained. Then he had an inspiration. "The fine is 300 pesos, but the license costs only 25. Why don't you apply for licenses?" he asked. The girls thought this a fine idea. For the Mexican equivalent of $5 each, they received handsomely engraved documents giving them access to the Avenue of the Beautiful Springs, etc.

—*New Yorker.*

✤ ✤ ✤

When Franklin Roosevelt was a young lawyer just getting started in New York, he was retained to handle a difficult civil case. The opposing lawyer was a very effective jury pleader and completely outshone his youthful rival in the argument to the jury. However, he made one fatal mistake: he orated for several hours. As he thundered on, Roosevelt noticed that the jury wasn't paying much attention. So, playing a hunch when his turn came, he rose and said:

"Gentlemen, you have heard the evidence. You also have listened to my distinguished colleague, a brilliant orator. If you believe him and disbelieve the evidence, you will have to decide in his favor. That's all I have to say."

The jury was out only five minutes and brought in a verdict for Roosevelt's client.

—Drew Pearson and Robert S. Allen, in *Washington Merry-Go-Round.*

✤ ✤ ✤

A man who was extremely successful in dealing with mule teams was once asked by General Booth of the Salvation Army how he managed the stubborn creatures. "Well, General," explained the man, "when they stop and won't go on, I just pick up a handful of soil and put it in their mouths. Of course they spit it out, but as a rule they start on."

"Why do you think it has that effect?" asked the General.

"Well, I don't know, but I expect it changes the current of their thoughts," the mule driver replied.

—W. Orton Tewson, in *An Attic Salt Shaker.*

✤ ✤ ✤

A woman appeared in the hat department of a big New York store not long ago and wanted the blue lace hat she had seen in one of the windows. The salesgirl didn't know of any such hat and appealed to the department head. He knew nothing about it either, but said he would check up. He found . . . the "hat" was really a ruffled lace collar which some imaginative assistant had stapled hatlike onto a mannequin. A few ingenious and surreptitious stitches were all that was required to convert the dollar-ninety-eight neckpiece into a twenty-dollar hat. The customer was satisfied.

—TINA SAFRANSKI, *Harper's Magazine.*

♣ ♣ ♣

When the inspector looked over my passport and entry permit, I was ready.

"Do you have friends meeting you?" he asked me. "Do you have money to support yourself?"

I pulled out a round fat roll of green American money—tens, twenties—a nice thick pile with a rubber band around.

"O. K.," he said. "Go ahead." He stamped my papers.

I got my baggage and took the money roll back again to Isaac's friend, Arapouleopolus, the money lender, so he could rent it over again to another man. One dollar was all he charged to use it.

—GEORGE PAPASHVILY, *Anything Can Happen.*

♣ ♣ ♣

A lady of our acquaintance commissioned a painter to decorate the bathroom of her apartment during a period when she was to be out of town. She gave the workman an ash tray enameled in the exact color desired.

For two days the painter struggled in vain to mix the required shade. But happily when the lady returned and gazed upon his handiwork, she was enraptured by the perfect match obtained. "And to this day," chuckles the painter, "she don't know that I repainted that fool ash tray with the same paint I put on the bathroom!"

—*Nuggets.*

♣ ♣ ♣

A business executive visiting Washington tried vainly to see the head of a federal bureau. Tiring of the run-around, he called the man's secretary:

"Please tell Mr. X," he directed, "that I must talk with him—and that I am not calling to remind him of that poker debt."

Within five minutes the bureau head was on the phone. Of course there was no poker debt.

—*Pageant.*

✤ ✤ ✤

Talma, the favorite actor of Napoleon, was famous for his ad-libbing. Once, while appearing in a duel scene, he was supposed to fall mortally wounded. However, the stage pistol in the hand of the other actor failed to go off. Having pulled the trigger several times, the thoroughly bewildered duelist, unable to think of anything else to do, rushed up to Talma and gave him a violent kick. The great actor with admirable composure exclaimed, "Mon Dieu, his shoe was poisoned!" and fell dead on the stage.

—*South Pacific Mail.*

✤ ✤ ✤

When Navy Chief Photographer Robert Parrish was taking official pictures of the Rhine crossings, an Army Officer pointed out a castle on a high bluff. He said it permitted an ideal picture of that section of the river. Parrish privately disagreed, considering the type of equipment he had. But "orders is orders," so he toiled up to the castle. As he had expected, his equipment was not suitable for that distance. But he found a caretaker who . . . gave him an old picture postcard of the Rhine from that view. He went back to the river and showed the card to the officer.

"That the sort of thing you wanted, sir?"

"Absolutely," the officer beamed. "I don't know how you fellows develop and print your pictures so fast."

—*American Legion Magazine.*

✤ ✤ ✤

Railways in the interior of Africa were laid by natives under the supervision of white engineers. The builders found their biggest problem was to get the lackadaisical natives to do any real work. They lit into their jobs as long as the boss was there to keep a stern eye upon them, but the minute he would leave, the men would lie back, chew grass, and dream about the next dance . . . One construction boss hit upon a brilliant idea.

He got a big glass eye, and when he left the gang he would

place it with great ceremony on a stack of ties and tell his languid crew that the eye would watch them while he was gone. It worked fine for three weeks. Then one day he came back to find his workers—every single last one of them—lying down on the job. Someone had covered the eye with a hat!

—MAUDE DAVIDSON, *Tracks.*

✤ ✤ ✤

A young matron we know was worried about her nine-year-old son. No matter how much she scolded, he kept running about with his shirt-tails flapping. On the other hand, her neighbor had *four* boys, and every one of them always wore his shirt neatly tucked in.

Finally our friend begged the neighbor to tell her the secret. "Oh, it's very simple," she replied. "I just take all their shirts and sew an edging of lace around the bottom."

—*This Week.*

✤ ✤ ✤

Some years ago Jean M. Douglas accompanied her doctor uncle on his sick calls through a wooded district of Eastern Canada. It was winter and the roads were often impassable. Additional hazards were created by teamsters hauling wood to market towns and frequently hogging the whole road.

Time after time the doctor was forced off the road. Finally he decided to assert his rights. Standing up in the sleigh he waved his whip dramatically. "If you don't give me half the road," he exclaimed, "I'll give you what I gave the last man we met!"

The teamster turned sharply and gave the doctor more than the lion's share of the road. As the vehicles passed, the teamster's curiosity got the better of him and he called out, "What did you give the last man?"

The doctor smiled. "The whole road."

—*Holiday.*

✤ ✤ ✤

Ephraim's front gate had always been rather difficult to open. His neighbors accepted the inconvenience and attributed it to his shiftlessness. A brash young newcomer to the village frankly asked why it wasn't repaired.

"There's nothing the matter with it," blandly replied Ephraim.

"Of course there is. Why, I can hardly push it open," sputtered the brash one.

"Naturally, young feller," came the answer, "that's because everyone who comes through that gate pumps a gallon of water into the tank on the roof."

—*Christian Science Monitor.*

✣ ✣ ✣

The mother went shopping with her small son, Charles. In the store, the grocer invited Charles to a handful of cherries but the boy seemed very backward.

"Don't you like cherries?" asked the grocer.

"Yes," said the boy.

The grocer put his hand in and dumped a generous portion in the little fellow's cap which he had promptly held out. Later, his mother asked him why he had not taken the cherries when first invited.

She quickly received the answer, " 'Cause his hand was bigger'n mine."

—*Journal of Education.*

✣ ✣ ✣

A certain doctor had ridden over a mile in a taxi when he suddenly discovered he had no money with him. He tapped the window and told the driver, "Stop at this cigar store a minute. I want to get matches so I can look for a ten-dollar bill I lost in the cab somewhere." When he emerged from the cigar store there was no taxi in sight.

—*Canadian Doctor.*

✣ ✣ ✣

Now that foreign travel is so popular, the following story may be of some service to those who experience difficulty paying off small obligations with unfamiliar currency and coin.

A wise and greatly experienced traveler was asked how he managed to pay the proper amount to taxi-drivers when he was abroad.

"Oh," replied he, "I take out a handful of small change and begin counting them in the driver's hand, keeping my eyes fixed on the man's face during the transaction. As soon as I detect a smile on his face, I stop doling out the money."

"I suppose," ventured the other, "that determines what you will pay him?"

"Not exactly," rejoined the experienced traveler. "I take back one coin and return it to my pocket, for when he smiles I know I have paid him too much."

—ANDREW MEREDITH, *Your Life*.

✤ ✤ ✤

A traveler, wishing to test the ingenuity of the Chinese, who are reputed to be able to do anything they are paid to do, arrived at an inn and, throwing down a copper, said to the innkeeper, "For this copper I want food, drink and entertainment."

The innkeeper returned with a slice of watermelon. Placing it before the traveler, he said: "You asked for food, drink, and entertainment. Here it is. You eat the pulp, drink the juice, and play with the seeds."

—THOMAS STEEP, *Chinese Fantastics* (Century).

✤ ✤ ✤

The little man was pushing his cart through the crowded market.

"Coming through," he called merrily. No one moved.

"Gangway!" he shouted. A few men stepped aside.

Ruefully he surveyed the situation and then smiled as a bright idea struck him. "Watch your nylons!" he warned. The women scattered like chaff in the wind.

—*Montreal Star*.

✤ ✤ ✤

An early settler, Richard Johnson, was dining with an Indian chief, Red Jacket, and the Indian said slyly, "I dreamed you gave me that coat." Johnson accepted the hint. Some months later, he met the chief again and said: "Last night I dreamed you gave me thirty thousand acres of your land."

The Indian ruefully fulfilled his part of the gentleman's agreement. Then he pleaded: "But do not dream again."

—*Eagle*.

An itinerant hawker was going about the villages of Brittany selling alarm-clocks. But he found the peasants very reluctant to buy. One day he engaged Malina, the gipsy fortune-teller, to go round among them reading their fortunes in their palms; "A strange man will come to see you and bring you good luck. A man with an alarm-clock!" Then, two days later, came the hawker himself.

From that time on business was so brisk that he couldn't get enough stock to satisfy his customers.

—*Constellation* (Paris).

✣ ✣ ✣

He was a bricklayer and had just finished a giant chimney. All the other workers had been lowered to the ground, when the ropes broke and he was left up there alone, with night and a storm coming. There was no way of reaching him. His wife had all the crowd yell up to him, "Unravel your socks. Start at the toe!"

She had knitted those socks. He tied a bit of brick to the end of the yarn as he unraveled and finally it reached the ground. They then attached stout twine, which he pulled up. After that, the ropes, and he was able to slide to safety.

—MALCOM BINGAY, *Detroit Free Press.*

✣ ✣ ✣

An Arabian sheik's entourage was minus one horse from a journey, so the sheik ordered that a horse be requisitioned from one of the villagers. Two horses were brought before him for inspection, but the owners were reluctant to part with them. They put up terrific howls, protesting that their horses were spavined, aged, and generally unsuitable for the sheik's purpose.

"There is only one way to settle it," said the sheik. "You will race your horses, and whichever wins, will be the one I will take."

"But your highness," whispered his adviser, "how will that settle it? Neither will put his horse to the supreme test."

"They will," said the sheik, "if each man rides the horse belonging to the other."

—*Judy's.*

Grimly Jack MacJockie listened to the listening-aid salesman's story. Patiently he heard him out until the end.

"Whoosh, lad, I dinna need your dee-vice," he then responded. Wherewith he pulled from his desk a loose thin wire attached to an earring; and then affixed the latter to the lobe of his left auricle.

"But, sir!" protested the salesman, "you can't hear through that empty wire."

"Dinna ye ken? When I put this on, people talk louder."

—*Air Conditioning and Refrigeration News.*

✣ ✣ ✣

A door-to-door salesman who always has trouble with chatty women got hold of an old, broken hearing aid which he wears when calling on prospective customers. If the lady of the house is a gabby kind who wants to talk, something always happens to the thing and he can't hear a word. Out comes a pencil and pad and the lady is asked to write down what she is saying.

Surprising how little a woman has to say when she has to write it down.

—*Louisville Courier-Journal Magazine.*

✣ ✣ ✣

A young lady applying for a position in a large establishment was given a very lengthy application blank to fill out. On the last page of the blank was a boxed space reserved for the employing official to fill in the amount of salary to be paid. Above it were the words: "Do Not Write In This Space."

The applicant, endowed with a sense of humor, wrote in: "Do Right In This Space."

She got the job.

—*Sunshine Magazine.*

✣ ✣ ✣

Repairs were being carried out on the roof of an asylum by a local builder who had asked for an inmate to assist him. All went well until lunchtime, when the builder's assistant clutched him around the neck and said: "Come on, let's jump down."

The builder was frightened almost out of his wits, but suddenly had an inspiration that saved his life.

"Oh, nuts," he replied, "anybody could do that. Come on down and let's jump up."

—*Lion.*

✤ ✤ ✤

A bus driver trying to make a turn found a woman driver about to move into his path. Leaning from the window, the busman whistled sharply and the woman stopped and looked, allowing him to go through ahead of her.

A passenger asked him why he whistled instead of using his horn. "About half the women drivers don't pay any attention to somebody honking," he said. "But there ain't a dame in town that won't stop when she hears a man whistle."

—*Louisville Courier-Journal Magazine.*

✤ ✤ ✤

Alexander Dumas, the French novelist, was once stopped in Paris by a beggar who asked for a handout. "Why do you not take off your hat to me when you ask for money?" asked the famous author.

"If I took off my hat to you," said the bum, "that policeman on the corner would know I was begging and arrest me. As it is, he thinks we are old acquaintances having a chat."

Dumas was so impressed by the man's logic that he quickly handed him a hundred francs.

—*Wall Street Journal.*

✤ ✤ ✤

Andy called at the employment office to apply for a job that he had seen advertised. "But, my dear man," said the manager, "you are much too late. Why, I've had over a thousand applications already!" Andy looked thoughtful. "Well," he said, after a while, "how about employing me to classify the applications?"

—*R.C.A. Victor Family News.*

✤ ✤ ✤

A chap was getting along fairly well in his mid-term history exam when suddenly he came upon the question: "How many Hessians did the British hire to help them fight our Revolutionary War?" Probably no one knows the correct answer, but the general idea was to find how many would try for a better answer than, "I don't know," or omit answering altogether. Our hero came up with, "I never heard how many the British brought over but they took back a dern sight less."

—*Employment Counselor.*

✣ ✣ ✣

A missionary fell into the hands of cannibals.

"Going to eat me, I presume?" asked the missionary. The chief grunted. "Don't do it," he advised. "You won't like me." Thereupon the missionary took out a knife, sliced a piece from the calf of his leg and handed it to him. "Try this and see for yourself."

The chief took one bite and choked.

The missionary worked on the island for 5 years. He had a cork leg.

—*Missionary Tidings.*

✣ ✣ ✣

The man at the football park had arrived well before the kick-off to get a front-row stance at the wall.

Just as the teams came out he was joined by a stranger, who bore two cardboard cups of tea.

"Want a drink?" asked the new arrival. "I jist bought them to get through the crowd. Ye can aye get tae the front if ye've twa cups o' tea in yer hand."

—*People's Journal,* England.

✣ ✣ ✣

My neighbor bought a new car about the same time we did. Six months later the doors of our car showed a rash of those little pits and scratches that most cars accumulate. Jim's still looked like new. I asked him how he did it. "A cinch," he repl'd. "I just always manage to park next to cars that are also new."

—HELEN HOUSTON BOILEAU, *Rotarian.*

✣ ✣ ✣

A Maine farmer spent the winter making wooden back-scratchers. He took a wagonful to Boston in the spring. Dealers laughed at him, told him there was no market and to go back where he belonged.

The most scornful and insulting of the dealers was visited a few hours later by an Egyptian, swathed in native raiment. He said his government had authorized him to purchase a thousand back-scratchers. He assured the dealer there was a great demand for them in Cairo.

"I'll have them for you by tomorrow," promised the dealer.

He found the farmer, who was apparently just about to go back to Maine. He bought the back-scratchers at a high price.

That evening the farmer returned the Arab outfit he had rented from a theatrical costumer, and had a satisfied look on his face as he drove back to the country.

—STANTON GRIFFIS, quoted in *Nashua Cavalier.*

✤ ✤ ✤

An aged merchant with two sons wished to retire from business. To determine which should be left in charge of his properties, he made this test: To each he gave a coin, saying, "Buy with this money something which will fill this house."

The elder son hastened to the market-place; learned that the cheapest, bulkiest thing he could buy was straw. He spent his coin for that, but had not enough even to cover the floor.

The younger son, perceiving his father had entrusted him with a commission which could be executed only by unusual shrewdness, deliberated and finally spent his coin for candles. These he took home and lighted, one in each room, so that the light they gave filled the house.

"To you," said the happy father, "I give over my business. You have shown true wisdom."

—*Toastmaster's Magazine.*

✤ ✤ ✤

A little old man laden down with parcels and a large umbrella boarded a Madison Avenue bus during the rush hour. After traveling several blocks insecurely suspended from a strap, he addressed a young woman sitting near him.

"Young lady, I'll be willing to pay you a nickel for your seat," he said.

The girl looked uncertain and unhappy and finally got up and pushed toward the rear of the bus without having expressed any interest in the five cents.

The little old man sat down and winked at one of his neighbors. "They never take it," he whispered.

—*New Yorker.*

✤ ✤ ✤

Oliver Herford had a neat knack of disposing of pestiferous people. One afternoon Albert Bigelow Paine was at Herford's studio when some one knocked at the door in a peculiar manner. "Sh-h-h," admonished Herford, and he and Paine were silent until the caller had left.

"He's a frightful bore," explained Oliver. "He comes here and talks all afternoon."

"But how did you get him to knock in that special way?"

"Oh," explained Herford, "I told him a lot of people came and bothered me, and that I was giving that knock to a few particular friends."

—*Liberty.*

✤ ✤ ✤

Two countrymen at a fair approached a stall where little balls bobbed about on top of water spouts. One tried his skill with a rifle, but could not pot the bobbing balls.

"Let's have a shot," said the friend, and taking the rifle, fired. Every ball dropped.

Walking away from the stall, the unsuccessful one said, "That was good! How did you manage to stop all the balls with one shot?"

"Easy," replied the friend. "I took a shot at the man who was working the pump."

—*Ireland's Saturday Night.*

✤ ✤ ✤

Pat was in the British army in France during World War I, but his anti-British sentiments were well known, so the censor and headquarters kept a wary eye on him.

Pat received a letter from his wife, Bridget, stating that it was nearly time to plant potatoes, but there was not an able-bodied man available for hire and she did not feel able to spade the potato patch herself.

Shortly she received a letter from Pat that said: "Don't dig in the potato patch. That's where the guns are buried."

Soon he received this news from his wife: "A lot of soldiers came and dug up the potato patch from end to end. What am I to do?"

Pat answered: "Plant the potatoes."

—*Good Business.*

✤ ✤ ✤

Women are supposed to be very conservative when it comes to passing out tips. But a certain waiter in a cocktail lounge is reported to be doing all right. Before he sets down the drinks for a table of middle-aged biddies, he always asks with a straight face, "Are you really sure all you girls are over twenty-one?"

—*Seng Fellowship News.*

✤ ✤ ✤

A newsboy was standing outside a ballpark when a sudden drizzle had crowds milling around, hesitant to watch their favorite pastime. The enterprising newsboy brought them in by shouting, "Buy a paper to sit on—seats are all wet!" He sold out in a few minutes by turning a minor calamity into a profit-opportunity!

—DALE CARNEGIE.

✤ ✤ ✤

Five minutes before the departure of the train there was still a long line of people at the ticket window. Then a gentleman went up to the head of the line in a business-like manner and called out, "Will everybody step back two steps." Those in line obeyed, slightly astonished and with a little grumbling, which grew louder when the man stepped up to the ticket window and requested "A second class ticket to Cologne."

—*Frankfurter Illustrierte,* Germany
(Droke House translation).

✤ ✤ ✤

Tired of waiting an unreasonably long time for jury verdicts, an Oklahoma City judge had hard-seated chairs substituted for the comfortable ones in the jury room. Then he timed the jurymen and found they reached verdicts in an hour less time. Deciding to keep up the good work, he had all chairs removed and discovered that juries which had to stand while deliberating reached verdicts in even less time. His final move reduced deliberation to a minimum: he had all windows in the jury room nailed down so that the air became stale in a short time.

—*The Wall Street Journal.*

✣ ✣ ✣

A young mother had trouble with a small son who had locked himself in the bathroom and either could not or would not unlock the door.

Finally she called the Fire Department and explained the predicament. When the fireman was told it was a little boy, he called into the bathroom, "You come out of there, little girl."

Promptly the door flew open and an indignant boy marched out. The fireman grinned, "Works nearly every time."

✣ ✣ ✣

The six-year-old daughter of a clergyman was sick and was put to bed early. As her mother was about to leave, she called her back. "Mommy, I want to see my daddy."

"No, dear," her mother replied, "your daddy is busy and must not be disturbed."

"But, Mommy," the child persisted, "I want to see my daddy."

The mother again replied, "No, your daddy must not be disturbed."

But the little one came back with even more determination. "Mommy," she declared, "I am a sick woman, and I want to see my minister."

—*Arkansas Baptist.*

✣ ✣ ✣

Charles R. Walgreen hated the small drugstore he owned, and decided one day to see if he could make a game of the business. "When someone who lived nearby would call up," he relates, "I would hold up my hand to attract my clerk's attention and repeat each item loudly as she gave it to me. When she finished, I'd start talking with her about anything I could think of;

meanwhile my clerk scurried around putting up the order and the grinning porter scrambled into his coat. Pretty soon, as we chatted, my customer would say, 'Just wait a minute, Mr. Walgreen, there's the doorbell.' In a minute she would be back. 'Why, Mr. Walgreen, that was the order I just gave you! I don't know how you managed to do it, but I think that's just wonderful service. I'll have to tell my husband about it tonight.'

"Folks began trading with us from right under the noses of druggists several blocks away. And soon other druggists were coming in to find out how I was building up my business."

Today Walgreen's is one of the largest drugstore chains in the country.

—John J. B. Morgan and E. T. Webb, *Making the Most of Your Life* (Long & Smith).

✣ ✣ ✣

Trial lawyers have more than a streak of the Thespian in their makeup, and will play any role from tragedian to clown in order to gain a favorable jury verdict. In Iowa recently, a lawyer turned himself into a pincushion to win a case. A man claimed that as a result of a head injury in a train accident he was lapsing into a mental decline. To prove it, he pricked the top of his head with a pin and testified that he felt no pain. Horrified jurors were ready to award juicy damages when the railroad lawyer asked for a recess. Returning to the courtroom with a paper of pins he thrust them into his own perfectly bald scalp till he resembled an animated porcupine.

"I'm going into a mental decline, too," he announced, parading clownishly before the jury.

Amid roars of laughter he won the case. The jury never suspected that a shot of pain-deadening novocain had been injected into the lawyer's bald pate during the recess.

—Henry Morton Robinson, in *Your Life*.

✣ ✣ ✣

In Glendale, California, a nice young couple, having decided they were made for each other, took steps which culminated in their friends and relatives' assembling at one of the fashionable churches. At this point the clergyman discovered he couldn't marry them. "Under California law you have to wait three days after getting your license," he explained. "Your license was taken out only day before yesterday."

The couple pleaded in vain. The bride remarked rather bitterly, that a couple of hundred guests, not to mention the bridesmaids and ushers, had appeared, confidently expecting a wedding. The minister urbanely agreed that the show must go on. "I'll just read part of the service," he said. "Nobody will notice anything wrong."

That's the way it worked out. The minister broke off just short of the I-do's and launched firmly into prayer. There was the reception, the throwing of the bouquet, and the shower of rice. The bride spent the next two days incommunicado with her aunt in a neighboring town, after which the ceremony was properly finished up.

—*New Yorker.*

✣ ✣ ✣

Mozart was one who could turn a musical joke when the occasion motivated it. The story is told how Mozart hoodwinked his friend Haydn with a piece he had just written. It seems Mozart dared Haydn to play it, and as the latter tried it out on the harpsichord he was stopped cold at a certain passage. On the manuscript Mozart had inserted a note to be struck in the center of the keyboard at precisely the time the right hand was playing in high treble and the left hand in low bass. When Haydn indignantly declared nobody could execute that passage because it necessitated the use of a third hand Mozart squatted on the harpsichord bench with a twinkle in his eye. As he reached the crucial part of the composition, he bent over and struck the central note with his nose.

—NINO LO BELLO, *Think.*

✣ ✣ ✣

The candidate for senatorial honors was scheduled to speak in a small town. Anxious to discover the religious affiliation of the majority of his audience, he addressed them warily in this manner:

"My great-grandfather was an Episcopalian (silence), but my

great-grandmother belonged to the Presbyterian church (more silence). My grandfather was a Baptist (silence), but my grandmother was a Congregationalist (continued silence). But I had a great-aunt who was a Methodist (loud applause)—and I have always followed my great aunt!"

✣ ✣ ✣

The boy who afterward became General Wood was once told by his grammar teacher, "Leonard, I will give you a sentence, and I want you to change it into the imperative mood. Here is the sentence: 'The horse draws the cart.'"

Young Wood quickly replied, "Giddap!"

✣ ✣ ✣

Several years ago, Ecuador wanted to erect a statue in memory of its national poet, Olmeda. Made-to-order statues, however, were found to be so highly priced that it was decided to buy an old one which had been discarded. Such a statue was found in a London junkyard, and promptly purchased.

Today it stands in Guayaquil, Ecuador, with Olmeda's name engraved on its base—but no Ecuadorian knows that it is actually a statue of Lord Byron.

—*Tit-Bits,* London.

✣ ✣ ✣

INITIATIVE (COURAGE)

When I was a young writer with a very uncertain income, I went into a quiet park to contemplate a serious problem. For four years She and I had been engaged but didn't dare to marry. There was no way of foreseeing how little I might earn in the next year; moreover, we had long cherished a plan of living and writing in Paris, Rome, Vienna, London—everywhere. But how could we go 3000 miles away from everything that was familiar and secure, without the certainty of *some* money now and then?

At that moment I looked up and saw a squirrel jump from one high tree to another. He appeared to be aiming for a limb so far out of reach that the leap looked like suicide. He missed—but landed, safe and unconcerned, on a branch several feet lower. Then he climbed to his goal, and all was well.

An old man sitting on the bench said, "Funny, I've seen hundreds of 'em jump like that, especially when there are dogs around and they can't come to the ground. A lot of 'em miss, but I've never seen any hurt in trying." Then he chuckled. "I guess they've got to risk it if they don't want to spend their lives in one tree."

I thought, "A squirrel takes a chance—have I less nerve than a squirrel?"

We were married in two weeks, scraped up enough money for our passage and sailed across the Atlantic—jumping off into space, not sure what branch we'd land on. I began to write twice as fast and twice as hard as ever before. And to our amazement we promptly soared into the realm of Respectable Incomes.

Since then, whenever I have to choose between risking a new venture or hanging back, those five little words run through my thoughts: "*Once there was a squirrel*——" And sometimes I hear the old man on the park bench saying, "They got to risk it if they don't want to spend their lives in one tree."

—Oscar Schisgall.

✣ ✣ ✣

One summer evening when a friend and I were out for a walk, we passed the city orphanage. A little redheaded boy about four years old called out to us, "Hello, Daddy!"

Dumfounded, we looked at each other, then at the child, who added resignedly, "It doesn't hurt none to try, does it?" We both laughed and walked on, but somehow I couldn't forget that little redhead.

A few weeks later I visited my friend and his wife, and discovered I wasn't the only one affected by the youngster's diplomacy. Playing in the yard was a new member of the family—the small boy who'd found out how true it is that it doesnt hurt to try.

—Roy O. Worrell, in "Life in These United States."

✣ ✣ ✣

A seventeen-year-old applied for a job with a road construction gang. He was slightly built and the boss eyed him critically. "Afraid you won't do, son," he said. "This is heavy work and you can't keep up with the heavier, older men."

The youngster glanced at the crew leaning on their shovels. "Perhaps I can't do as much as these men *can* do," he replied, "But I certainly can do as much as they *will* do." He got the job.

—*Executives' Digest.*

✣ ✣ ✣

A deck officer in the Merchant Marine, A. F. Mozier, started a one-man campaign some time ago to feed the hungry in five countries—Korea, India, Greece, Israel and Morocco—places where his ship put into port. It all began one day during a brief stop-over in India. He ran into a hungry farmer pleading for food. Mr. Mozier helped him, then in a practical way said, "Why don't you plant something to eat if you are starving?" The farmer was very practical in his reply: "Because we have no seeds."

Mozier started buying 10-cent packages of seed in the States and handing them out to needy farmers in the countries he visited. In six months he had handed out fifteen thousand packets. He surprised himself when he saw, from his own experience, what one person can do.

—*Christophers.*

✣ ✣ ✣

Once upon a time a man built a better mousetrap. Then he sat down and waited for the world to make a path to his door. Nothing happened. So he began to ask people why they had failed to turn to him.

One said "nuts"; another that his product was agin' nature, which had provided cats to take care of mice; another complained of the expense. A few were indifferent, and the druggist who sold rat poison was downright disagreeable.

So the man built a path himself, decorated it with descriptive signboards—and people started coming his way.

—*Salesman's Opportunity.*

✣ ✣ ✣

Long ago, so goes an historical legend said to have a basis in fact, a shipload of people were wrecked on an island in the Caribbean Sea. They found neither food nor fresh water, and their bones were soon bleaching on the scorching sands.

Years later a second ship was wrecked on the same coral reef.

This shipload found springs of fresh water. But they could find no food on the island; so they, too, after a while, perished from hunger.

Many years later still a third ship was wrecked on the same spot. But these people had initiative. They found the springs of fresh water. They found, too, that by diving deep among the coral reefs there were quantities of fresh oysters. And they discovered that an amazing number of oysters contained pearls. When they were finally rescued, they were not only well fed but enormously wealthy.

—*Friendly Notes.*

✣ ✣ ✣

A man lost his watch while cutting and storing ice in an old ice house many years ago. He knew he had dropped it somewhere in the sawdust, but he was unable to find it. He offered a reward, and others of the crew looked with lanterns and rakes, but no one could find it. Then, when the men went to lunch, a boy who had been watching them, went into the ice house. They were surprised, on their return, to learn the boy had found the watch. When questioned, he explained, "I just laid down in the sawdust and listened, and I heard the watch ticking."

—*Good Business.*

✣ ✣ ✣

INSPIRATION

The famous French tapestry weavers who wove those magnificent tapestries that we often see in the houses of the great were accustomed to doing all their work from the rear and all that they could see was a mass of loose thread and stitching. But sometimes a man would rise up from his work and pass round to the front to see the glorious design that was being wrought by their patient labor. And the heart of the toiler was satisfied.

—JOHN PATERSON, *The Book That Is Alive* (Scribners).

✣ ✣ ✣

INTEREST

The nurse in charge of a mental ward claimed a miracle was wrought by a bunch of pansies given to the hospital for Mary, a 14-year-old girl who had lost the urge to live. All attempts to interest her in anything had been met with "Nobody cares for me—let me alone."

The pansies brought a glimmer of pleasure to her eyes. As the worker turned to go, Mary called, "Those little faces are talking to me. *They* care!" That afternoon she asked for something to sew; gradually her interests broadened until finally she was restored to normal.

—LEIGH MITCHELL HODGES, in *Woman's Day.*

✤ ✤ ✤

INSTRUCTION

I was coaching my son in tennis. He tossed the ball, swung his racket, and pitched his first serve neatly into the net.

"You're hitting it into the net," I called.

He shifted his stance, took another grip, and tried again. Same thing.

"It's going into the net," I told him again.

He glared, and made another try.

"Still going into the net," I said pleasantly. He flung his racket on the ground.

"Look," he told me. "I can see that it's going into the net as well as you can. You don't need to sound like a broken record about it! Tell me what I can do to *keep it from going into the net!*"

—HENRY L. JORDAN, *Toastmaster.*

✤ ✤ ✤

INTEGRITY

At the close of the Civil War, a representative of a large insurance company offered Robert E. Lee the presidency of the firm at a salary of $50,000 a year.

Lee replied that while he certainly wished to earn his living, he seriously doubted whether his services would be worth quite so large a sum.

"We aren't interested in your services," the man told him. "We merely want your name."

"That," said Lee quietly but firmly, "is not for sale."

He accepted, instead, the presidency of a college at $1500 a year.

✣ ✣ ✣

In the city of Bagdad lived Hakeem, the Wise One. A great many people went to him for counsel which he freely gave to all, asking nothing in return. There came to him a young man who had spent much but received little, and he said: "Tell me, Wise One, what shall I do to receive the most for that which I spend?"

Hakeem answered by saying: "A thing that is bought or sold has no value unless it contains that which cannot be bought or sold. Look for the Priceless Ingredient."

"But what is that Priceless Ingredient?" asked the young man.

Spoke the Wise One: "My Son, the Priceless Ingredient of every product in the Marketplace is the Honor and Integrity of him who makes it. Consider his name before you buy."

—*Toastmaster.*

✣ ✣ ✣

IRONY

A lecturer of some renown was asked to speak at a nudist camp. He was greeted by ladies and gentlemen with no more on than nature saw fit to bestow upon them. They suggested that he would probably like to get ready for dinner. He went upstairs realizing that he must disrobe like the rest of them. He paced the floor in an agonized panic of indecision. The dinner bell rang. With the courage of utter desperation he stripped, and in Adamite splendor descended the staircase—only to find that all the guests had put on evening clothes to do him honor.

—DONALD CULROSS PEATTIE.

✣ ✣ ✣

When O. O. McIntyre got his first newspaper job with the Dayton *Herald,* he was terrified that he would lose it. He was sure that as soon as the Proprietor could catch him he would fire him, so whenever he had to pass the Proprietor's desk, he bolted by as though he had an epoch-making news story. One day the Big Boss asked the managing editor: "Who is that quick-stepping youngster who goes through here like a rocket?"

"That's Odd McIntyre, the new reporter."

"Say, you've been talking about sending to Cincinnati for a city editor. Why don't you try this boy? I'll bet he'll burn them up."

Odd was made city editor, boss of four reporters, three weeks after he took the new job in Dayton.

—Charles B. Driscoll, *The Life of O. O. McIntyre* (Greystone Press).

✣ ✣ ✣

JEALOUSY

Several Italian conductors, among them Toscanini and Mascagni, were once asked to participate in a gala festival in Milan honoring the composer Verdi. Mascagni, composer of *Cavalleria Rusticana,* was jealous of Toscanini's fame and agreed to direct on one condition—that he be paid more than Toscanini. He didn't care, he said, if it was only one lira more, but it had to be more. The management agreed. At the close of the festival, when Mascagni received his fee, he found it was exactly one lira. Toscanini had conducted for nothing.

—Edwin H. Schloss and Arthur Bronson.

✣ ✣ ✣

Oscar Wilde related the following story: The devil was once crossing the Libyan Desert when he met a number of people tormenting a holy hermit. The sainted man easily shook off their suggestions. Finally, after watching their failure, the devil said, "What you did is too crude. Permit me one moment." He whispered to the holy man, "Your brother has just been made Bishop of Alexandria."

A scowl of malignant jealousy at once clouded the serene face of the hermit.

"That," said the devil to his imps, "is the sort of thing which I should recommend."

—*Pastor's Wife.*

An old Negro was catching crabs. His fish box was over half full when a little boy told him the big ones were crawling out. "Thank you, son," the old man smiled, "but I ain't gwine to lose nary one. I knows crabs. When de big uns fights up to de top, de little uns catches 'em by de laig and pulls 'em down."

—MARION WILLIAMSON.

✤ ✤ ✤

JUSTICE

Many years ago, an alleged horse thief was brought up for trial in a rough and tumble Western frontier town. Before the proceedings began, the judge gave the usual instructions to the jury:

"Ladies and gentlemen, this here is a democratic country, and this feller is supposed to git a fair trial. You'll have to listen to the testimony and decide the verdict, guilty or not guilty. But remember one thing. There's somebody bigger'n you or me. There's a Divine Justice, above and beyond this courtroom, an Eternal Providence lookin' down here, and *He* ain't gonna be took in by no lyin' hoss thief."

—MRS. JOHN NALL, *Tracks.*

✤ ✤ ✤

The trials of various religious figures in Communist courts on charges of being "American spies" are similar to the story of an Italian brought into the court of an Irish justice who boasted of his hatred for Italians.

"Mike Costello," the justice said to him, "you are in my court charged with fighting. If you plead guilty, which you are, and which you know you are, you can expect the leniency of the court; but if you plead not guilty, which you are not, and which you know you are not, and which the court will find you are not, then you will catch the devil. Which way do you plead?"

—F. FISHER.

✤ ✤ ✤

Charles Haddon Spurgeon once refused a legacy of $150,000. A wealthy resident of Leeds was so deeply impressed by Spurgeon's sermons, he willed the bulk of his estate to him, leaving various needy relatives poorly provided for. Spurgeon immediately sent for a lawyer and distributed the entire bequest among the needy relatives. The newspapers of the day, reporting this, said: "Mr. Spurgeon has preached many great sermons, but none more striking than this. He would rather be just than rich."

—EDMOND M. KERLIN, *Telescope-Messenger.*

✤ ✤ ✤

At a Bar dinner, Judge Leibowitz and a group of his colleagues were analyzing a recent Supreme Court ruling. One member held the view that the phraseology was shot through with flaws. The judge agreed, but at the same time observed that in some localities the wording doesn't matter as long as justice is administered. He cited a frontier case:

A man was found dead in Leadville. The coroner's jury brought in the verdict: "We find that Jack Smith came to his death from heart disease. We found two bullet holes and a dirk knife in that organ, and we recommend that Bill Younger be lynched to prevent the spreading of the disease.

—BUSTER ROTHMAN, *Magazine Digest.*

✤ ✤ ✤

Out in Nevada a mining claim was pending before a certain old-time western judge with a reputation for a rather rough-and-ready brand of justice. One morning his honor made the following remarkable statement:

"Gentlemen, this court has in hand a check from the plaintiff for ten thousand dollars and a check from the defendant for fifteen thousand dollars. The court will return five thousand dollars to the defendant, and then we will try this case strictly on its merits."

—*Wall Street Journal.*

✤ ✤ ✤

A locomotive engineer in East Texas was climbing up to his cab one day when an enemy slipped up behind him and fired six shots into his back, killing him instantly. The man was convicted, without much trouble, of murder in the first degree. Some months later, in Austin, I had lunch with a judge of the appellate court which was hearing this man's appeal.

"The law is a funny thing," said the judge smiling. "Don't tell anybody, but I'm afraid we're going to have to reverse the conviction."

But how could that be? I wanted to know. The grudge was trivial, the man had a bad record, there were no extenuating circumstances.

"You forget something," said the judge. "If you remember the case, you'll recall that the engineer, at the time he was killed, had both hands on the supports leading up to his cab. He was clearly fixing to throw that big locomotive at that poor little man back of him. Obviously a case of self defense."

—STANLEY WALKER.

✣ ✣ ✣

After having a bowl of chowder and coffee at a restaurant of a well-known chain, a New York public relations man was charged ten cents for bread and butter which he hadn't eaten. He protested that he hadn't ordered the bread and butter, but the waiter said he was sorry, it was orders from the chain officials. Our hero—and to us he is a hero—asked for the manager, who said the waiter was right. Orders, sir, you know.

The man paid the dime, very ungracefully. Back at his office, he wrote a letter in public relations patter to the chain owners, telling them they were losing good will by charging for bread and butter, willy-nilly. A few days later, he sent the company a bill for professional services—$5000. By return mail came a letter from the restaurant's Wall Street lawyers pointing out that the whole thing was absurd, since they hadn't ordered any public relations service.

Our hero shot off a one-sentence reply: "Well, I didn't order bread and butter."

✣ ✣ ✣

JUVENILE DELINQUENCY

I've got a plan to lick juvenile delinquency. I propose that we bring into captivity every teen-ager, delinquent or undelinquent, and assign him to two adults, preferably a man and a woman. These adults would be given full authority over the teen-ager.

Adults and teen-agers would live together as a kind of cell (much like the old-time family) on a very friendly basis. The teen-agers would be made to feel at home (adults will have to be educated in how to communicate this feeling), but in all major things they would be subject to the orders of the adults. Major things would include attendance at school, attention to dress and manners, care in choosing friends, and being where the adults want them to be.

Somebody else thought of the plan before I did. It was summed up in a law handed to Moses, "Honor thy father and thy mother."

—JAMES D. ALBERSE, *Friar*.

✣ ✣ ✣

KINDNESS

We received a strange gift when we were children—something we still use. One winter afternoon Mother ran out of citron for fruitcake and sent us to the store. "I'll have to give you a $5 bill," she said. "So be careful of the change." We only half-listened to her instructions.

The clerk carved off a crescent slice of citron and we started home, scampering in the snow. Suddenly I remembered that he had given me only coins, no bills. We ran back. "Oh, no, little girl; you gave me a dollar bill," he said cheerfully but firmly, and went on weighing tea and spice. Utterly crushed, we huddled on the curbstone, crying. A big man with a white mustache asked us what was wrong.

"Wait here," he said. After quite a long time he came back with four dollar bills. We were stunned with relief. Then our manners prodded us, and we thanked him and said that Mother would be cross if we didn't get his name. He scribbled on a piece of paper. We gave it to Mother.

"Why there's too much money!" she exclaimed. "Yes, I did say I would give you a five but then I found a one." She said we'd take the money back after supper. The address was plain—439 Fourth Street. But there was no 439; the numbers ended at 325. And nobody on the street had ever heard of such a man.

Father put the money on the mantel. Mother said, "We'll do something kind with it." The money stayed there year after year. We did many good deeds with it without ever spending it. We would propose using it for this or that, but once the deed was done we somehow never reimbursed ourselves from the mantel.

Whenever Mother looked at the money, she said, "There are such kind people in the world." And when Anna cleaned on Saturday she picked it up and dusted under it. "Ach, such kind people yet." When visitors noticed it we told them the story and they, too, added it to themselves.

—MARGARET LEE RUNBECK in *Good Housekeeping*.

✤ ✤ ✤

Never overlook the power of a kind word.

A convict from Darlington, England, just released from jail, happened to pass Mayor John Morel on the street. Three long years had been spent by the convict in prison for embezzlement and he was sensitive about the social ostracism he expected to get from the people in his home town.

"Hello," greeted the mayor in a cheery tone, "I'm glad to see you! How are you!" The man appeared ill at ease and the discussion stopped.

Years later, according to the story told by J. H. Jowett, Mr. Morel, the mayor, and the released man accidentally met in another town, and the latter said, "I want to thank you for what you did for me when I came out of prison."

"What did I do?" asked the mayor.

"You spoke a kind word to me and it changed my life," replied the grateful man.

—REV. PURNELL BAILEY, *Grit*.

✤ ✤ ✤

I often think of the little boy I saw sitting outside of the walls of Versailles. He was holding a little sparrow with a broken wing. A kindly lady came along and she asked, "Sonny, would you like me to take this sparrow home and nurse it back to health? I promise I will bring it back to these gardens when it is healed and let it fly free again."

The little boy thought for a moment. Then he said, "If you

don't mind, Madam, I will take care of the bird myself." He paused momentarily and added, "Because, you see, I understand this bird."

The woman could not quite get what that boy meant until he stood up. Then she saw his left leg was in a cast. Because he was crippled he understood the suffering bird's problem.

—Reuben K. Youngdahl, *The Secret of Greatness* (Revell).

✤ ✤ ✤

One day in mid-winter, a friend came to visit the great scientist, Steinmetz, in his laboratory. There was no fire in the stove and zero weather was making itself felt unpleasantly. Steinmetz was bundled up in many coats, working at his desk with stiff fingers.

"What's the matter?" asked the friend. "If you're taking a fresh air cure, you'd better leave the windows open."

Steinmetz looked up from his work a trifle sheepishly. He pointed over his shoulder to the stove which was filled with a litter of paper from the wastebasket.

"A mouse has just had some children in there," he said. "I can't take them out until they grow up a little."

—Johnathon Norton Leonard, *Loki, the Life of Charles Proteus Steinmetz.*

✤ ✤ ✤

It was a bitter, raw day along the Thames, and an aged blind man, his fingers blue with cold, labored to play a cheap violin. Two well-dressed gentlemen paused. One, in broken English, inquired: "No luck, eh? Nobody give money? . . . Make them. Play until they open."

Suddenly he reached out and took the violin. He flourished the bow like a conductor's baton, then started along the streets. The cheap, cherry-red fiddle leaped to life. It became a thing of incredible animation; notes danced, raced in a mad tremendous scramble . . . Men and women listened, spellbound. Then the music stopped, and a hatful of silver clattered into the blind man's pockets.

"Your name?" pleaded the old fellow as fiddle and bow were

returned. The other gentleman spoke: "He is called—Paganini."

—Rev. Philip Jerome Cleveland, *Coronet.*

✣ ✣ ✣

During one of my childhood visits to the country I found a land terrapin and started to examine him, but the terrapin closed his shell like a vise. Seeing me trying to pry him open with a stick, my uncle said, "No, no. That's not the way."

Then he took the creature inside and set him on the hearth. In a few minutes he began to get warm, stuck out his head and feet, and calmly crawled toward me.

"People are sorta like terrapins," my uncle said. "Never try to force a fellow into anything. Just warm him up with a little human kindness, and more'n likely he'll come your way."

—Rilla Leggett.

✣ ✣ ✣

A lovely story is told about Her Royal Highness (now the young Queen of England) during her tour of South Africa. She had been invited to meet a gathering of Girl Guides, and noticed one group of girls that had been kept apart from the others. On being told that they were victims of leprosy, she at once, to the dismay of the officials responsible, made her way toward them and addressed to them a few words of recognition and good cheer. That gesture . . . will linger on when more spectacular events have been forgotten. The Princess spoke a language that everyone understood, and to which most people at once respond.

—John Short, *Triumphant Believing* (Scribner).

✣ ✣ ✣

A bus driver had to put on the brakes to keep from running over a tiny pup. A policeman aboard got off and placed the animal tenderly on the curb. But as he got back on, the pup followed him, wagging its tail.

Finally, after several attempts to leave the pup, the policeman carried it into the bus and told the driver to go on.

Turning to the passengers, the policeman asked, "Anybody want a pup?" Then, without waiting for answer, he smiled and said, "Well, I guess the kids can take care of one more dog."

—*St. Louis Globe-Democrat.*

I was familiar with the parochial grade school in a small Montana city, and knew it was like all the others across the country. I was greatly surprised, therefore, to see a group of sixth graders using the sign language.

"I didn't know deaf mutes attended this school," I remarked to a nun.

"Just one does," she smiled, "but our pastor feared he would be lonesome and shy, so he had an instructor teach the entire class sign language."

—E. F. BEAUDETTE, *Catholic Digest.*

✤ ✤ ✤

KNOWLEDGE

A sixth-grade pupil was experiencing more and more difficulty with arithmetic. "I want to give it up, pop," he pleaded. "It ain't no use anyway."

The father was properly horrified. "No use!" he exclaimed. "Do you want to grow up an ignoramus and not be able to figure football score, batting averages and racetrack odds?"

—*Journeyman Barber.*

✤ ✤ ✤

The candidate for a pilot's license stood before a board of old sea-dogs for his oral test—one famous for its tricky angles.

The examining officer asked, "You know, of course, where all the sand bars are in St. Simon's Sound?"

"No, I don't," he answered.

"Then how the hell do you expect to do any piloting?" the officer snapped.

"I know," said the candidate, "where the sand bars ain't."

—ESTELLE DANIELS, *True.*

✤ ✤ ✤

A New York socialite came into the salon of Walter Florell, mad milliner to movie stars and socialites, and announced she needed a hat at once for a cocktail party. Walter took a couple of yards of ribbon, twisted it around, put it on her head and said, "There's your hat, madam." The lady looked in the mirror and exclaimed, "It's wonderful."

"Twenty-five dollars," said Walter.

"But that's too much for a couple of yards of ribbon!" she gasped.

Florell unwound the ribbon and handed it to her saying, "The ribbon, madam, is free."

—Erskine Johnson, NEA.

✣ ✣ ✣

We were giving a concert in a hotel. After the last strains of Handel's *Largo* floated out, a fat motherly woman near me leaned over and asked, "Won't you please play Handel's *Largo?*"

"But, we've just finished playing it," I said.

The fat lady sank back in her chair. "Oh, I wish I'd known it," she sighed. "It's my *favorite* piece."

—Mary Browne.

✣ ✣ ✣

Driving through the mountains of Tennessee, we stopped to ask an elderly man the way to Coffee Hill School.

"Well, miss," said the native, "you go down here until you come to Hangin' Rock and then—you know where that is, dontcha?"

"No," replied my friend, "I don't believe I do."

"Well, that's where you turn off and go on two miles until you git to Tumblin' Creek. You know where that is, dontcha?"

"No, I don't."

"Im's sorry, miss," said the native shaking his head regretfully. "I don't think you know enough for me to tell you anything."

—Bradley Smith.

✣ ✣ ✣

At a recent international conference on technical assistance, there were prolonged deliberations concerning the necessity for "know how." Finally, the Turkish representative got up and said solemnly, "Let me tell you a story about Nasrettin Hoca, our traditional Turkish wit."

He began: "Once the Hoca was walking home carrying a neatly wrapped package of liver. As his wife's recipe for liver was renowned throughout the countryside, his mouth watered in anticipation of dinner. Suddenly, out of a clear sky, an eagle swooped down upon him, and snatched the package from the Hoca's hand. The Hoca was unperturbed. He smiled, and called after the bird, 'You've got the liver, but what good is it without the recipe?' "

There were no further arguments about the necessity for technical "know how."

—Nuri Kurt, Turkish Information Office, New York City.

✣ ✣ ✣

Whistler was in court trying to collect his fee for a painting which the purchaser, after he had accepted it, thought overpriced. Whistler was asked how long it had taken him to complete the canvas.

"About two days," he said.

"And for this you ask two hundred guineas?" said the lawyer in an attempt to embarrass him.

"Not at all," replied the artist with asperity. "I ask it for the knowledge of a lifetime."

—*Property.*

✣ ✣ ✣

LABOR AND MANAGEMENT

A nationwide strike of employers started last Thursday. This closes down every shop, store, and factory in the United States. Employees are beseeching owners and managers to resume business, but they persistently refuse until their demands are met.

It seems that the employers are asking only one thing, which is that the employees shall stand one-half the worry of the business. They say they lie awake half of the night, and sometimes all night long, worrying about how they are going to raise sufficient money to meet payrolls and necessary business expenses, while the employee, when the whistle blows at 3 o'clock in the afternoon, goes to his home without a worry so far as the business is concerned. The employers say it is unfair labor practice, and demand that responsibilities be shared equally.

—*Origin unknown.*

LAW

Curtis Bok, in one of his books, has recounted the historical fact that in one section of ancient Greece, it long was the custom that when a man proposed a law in the popular assembly, he did so on a platform with a rope around his neck. If his law passed, they removed the rope; if it failed, they removed the platform.

✤ ✤ ✤

LAZINESS

There is a legend at Harvard that the late Le Baron Russell Briggs, beloved dean of the College, once asked a student why he had failed to complete an assignment given to him.

"I wasn't feeling very well, sir," said the student lamely.

"Mr. Smith," said the Dean, frowning at the student, "I think that in time you may perhaps find that most of the work of the world is done by people who aren't feeling very well."

The Dean knew that there is such a thing as a sensibly prudent attitude toward one's health. But he also knew that the symptoms of fatigue and laziness are practically identical; that it is hard to tell the difference between not feeling well and not feeling like doing a hard job.

—*This Week.*

✤ ✤ ✤

On the Carolina Blue Ridge word was passed up the mountainside that there was a letter in the valley post office for Zeke. Days later, Zeke decided to fetch it. He started slowly. It was a sunny morning and several of Zeke's friends were lolling in the shade beneath the balsams where a steep slope forced Zeke into a jog.

Called out one of the hillbillies: "Look at Zeke—too lazy to hold back."

—Thomas Russell McCrea.

✤ ✤ ✤

LEADERSHIP

When a girl applies for admission to Vassar, a questionnaire is sent to her parents. A father in a Boston suburb, filling out one of these blanks, came to the question, "Is she a leader?" He hesitated, then wrote, "I am not sure about this, but I know she is an excellent follower."

A few days later he received this letter from the president of the college: "As our freshman group next Fall is to contain several hundred leaders, we congratulate ourselves that your daughter will also be a member of the class. We shall thus be assured of one good follower."

—*The Journal of Education.*

✤ ✤ ✤

A leader is best
When people barely know that he exists,
Not so good when people obey and acclaim him,
Worst when they despise him.
"Fail to honor people,
They fail to honor you."
But of a good leader, who talks little,
When his work is done, his aim fulfilled,
They will all say, "We did this ourselves."

—LAOTZU, *The Way of Life.*

✤ ✤ ✤

A tale is told of a man in Paris during the upheaval in 1848, who saw a friend marching after a crowd toward the barricades. Warning him that these could not be held against the troops, that he had better keep away, and asking why he followed those people, he received the reply, "I must follow them. I am their leader."

—A. LAWRENCE LOWELL, former president of Harvard.

✤ ✤ ✤

The question, "Who ought to be boss?" is like asking, "Who ought to be the tenor in the quartet?" Obviously, the man who can do the job!

—HENRY FORD, industrialist.

✤ ✤ ✤

LIFE

Motoring through the Arizona desert, where rippling water sang in the irrigation ditch beside the road, I noticed that the trees lining the roadside—trees 30 or 40 feet high—were all in line and evenly spaced. I remarked on this to a native of the state. "Oh," he said, "those were fence posts."

I thought he was joking, but he was stating what to him was a commonplace. Nature had so bountifully bestowed minerals in the earth and sunshine above it that when water was turned on this enchanted land, the fence posts reached out for it underground, drank, put forth roots and leaves and just grew into cottonwood trees.

—Frank Case, *Do Not Disturb* (Stokes).

✤ ✤ ✤

When a hospital in an English town ran out of sand for its sandbags during World War II, sacks were filled from the public gardens. Soddenly they protected the hospital walls all winter. But with spring came a change. Green shoots appeared through cracks of the sacking, and soon the whole grim barricade bloomed with yellow daffodils.

—V. Sackville-West, *Country Notes in Wartime* (Hogarth Press).

✤ ✤ ✤

A man walked into a rather exclusive antique shop and asked permission to look around. The visitor looked out of place because he was a poorly dressed laborer. At last he found just the thing he wanted: a beautiful piece of glass. A deposit was made, and each week he came in to make a payment until finally the article was his. The owner of the shop became curious, and engaged him in conversation in order to learn his story.

This unusual customer said he had bought the piece of glass to take to his little room. Through the years it had become his habit to take only the best and most beautiful to his room. "You see," he said, "that's where I live."

—Mamie Adams, *Power*.

✤ ✤ ✤

To dodge responsibilities is easy; the hard part comes in dodging the consequences of dodging them. We cannot escape from our lives; life has us cornered and we might as well make the best of it. We are in the position of the unhappy Negro recruit who, after the armistice was signed, applied to his superior officer for a discharge. "You see, suh," he explained, "Ah jes' 'listed fo' do duration ob de wah."

His superior eyed him pityingly and replied: "Dat's jes' de p'int. De wah am ovah, but de duration am skassly begun."

—*Nuggets.*

✤ ✤ ✤

LIFE—Living

In Edna Ferber's novel, *So Big,* a young woman teacher is having trouble getting along with herself. She wishes to run away from the problems of living. An old, mature Dutch housewife says to her, "You can't run away from life, missy; you can't run far enough."

✤ ✤ ✤

A minister on meeting a little boy one day asked, "Sonny boy, who made you?"

"'Well, to tell you the truth," the little boy replied, "I ain't done yet."

That sharp answer contains a very wise bit of philosophy. The lad realized he was still growing up. The longer he lived, the more opportunity life would give him.

—Reuben K. Youngdahl, *Secret of Greatness* (Revell).

✤ ✤ ✤

In making Persian rugs the artist stands before the rug while a group of boys stand behind to pull the thread after the artist starts it. If one of the boys makes a mistake, the artist adjusts the pattern accordingly so that when the rug is finished no one can tell where the mistake was made.

The same kind of adjustment will take place in our lives if we will but let go of the mental thread of each mistake and let God weave it into a successful, orderly pattern of life.

—James E. Sweaney, *Good Business.*

✤ ✤ ✤

LOGIC

A certain preacher's congregation flinches against his time-worn theme: the sin of staying away from church on Sunday.

One Monday not long ago this preacher buttonholed one of his young parishioners with the greeting that he had missed him in church the preceding day. He then launched into the subject of Sunday's sermon:

"Son, you don't stay away from the movies because it's too much trouble to get dressed, or you were out late the night before. Now, that's true, isn't it?"

"Yes, preacher, it is," agreed the unabashed young man. "But you don't go if you've already seen the picture."

✣ ✣ ✣

A member of the Bergdorf-Goodman staff came running up to Miss Dolan. "I just happened to be passing a fitting room and looked in," he said, "and there was a customer trying on a blouse with a blindfold on!"

"But of course," Miss Dolan replied. "She's getting it for her husband to give to her for her birthday. It's going to be a surprise."

—BOOTEN HERNDON, *Bergdorf's on the Plaza* (Knopf).

✣ ✣ ✣

A man walked into a restaurant and sat down at a table. "What will you have, sir?" asked the waiter.

The customer shook his head. "Not a thing," he replied. "I'm not hungry."

The waiter stared. "Then what's the idea," he grumbled, "of coming in here?"

The customer shrugged his shoulders. "It's very simple," he explained. "This is my lunch hour."

—*Farmer's Weekly* (South Africa).

✣ ✣ ✣

"I'm not really late, boss," said the tardy secretary, hanging up her hat. "I just took my coffee break before coming in."

—*Wall Street Journal.*

✣ ✣ ✣

"It's difficult to explain what a course in Logic will do for a person's thinking, but let me illustrate," the professor told a student. "Suppose two men came out of a chimney—one is clean, one dirty. Which takes a bath?"

"The dirty one, naturally," answered the student.

"Remember," chided the professor, "that the clean man sees the dirty one and sees how dirty he is, and vice versa."

"Now I get it," answered the student. "The clean one, seeing his dirty companion, concludes he's dirty, too—so he takes the bath. Am I right?"

"Wrong," said the professor nonchalantly. "Logic teaches us this: how could two men come out of a chimney, one clean and one dirty?"

—*Times of Brazil* (Sao Paolo).

✤ ✤ ✤

A woman who had taken her small nephew downtown was having trouble keeping up with him as he ran ahead of her and crossed the streets through the traffic. "Please slow down," she begged. "What would I tell your mother if a car suddenly came around a corner and killed you?"

"Well," he suggested reasonably, "you could begin by telling her I was dead."

—*Dixie Roto Magazine.*

✤ ✤ ✤

Cultivating logical thought development has its difficult moments.

One bright boy attending his first wedding asked his mother why the bride was dressed in white. "Because," she answered, "white stands for purity and joy."

"Then why," was the prompt retort, "does the groom wear black?"

—*Texas Outlook.*

✤ ✤ ✤

The emperor one day met a one-armed veteran. "How did you lose your arm?" he asked. "Sire, at Austerlitz."

"And were you decorated?"

"No, sire."

"Then here is my own cross for you. I hereby make you a chevalier of the Legion of Honor."

"Your Majesty names me chevalier because I have lost one

arm!" exclaimed the veteran. "What would your Majesty have done had I lost both arms?"

"Then," said the emperor, "I should have made you officer of the legion."

Whereupon the old soldier immediately drew his sword and with one stroke cut off his other arm.

This is one of the venerable European folk tales. No one, apparently, ever paused to consider how a one-armed man could draw his sword and sever his remaining arm!

✣ ✣ ✣

LONELINESS

We moved to a new town, and it was a new experience for our son, Mark, aged two and a half, not to have everyone speak to him as he walked down the street.

One day he stood it as long as he could. He stopped in front of one of the store windows, looked at his reflection for several seconds and then shouted, "Hiya, Mark!"

—MRS. ANNE DICKINSON, *Magazine Digest.*

✣ ✣ ✣

LOVE

A little eight-year-old girl in a Pennsylvania orphan asylum was a painfully unattractive child with annoying mannerisms, shunned by the children and actively disliked by the teachers. The head of the institution longed only for a legitimate excuse to get her out of the place.

One afternoon it looked as if her opportunity had arrived. The girl's roommate reported that she was conducting a clandestine correspondence with somebody outside the grounds. "Just a little while ago," she reported, "she took a note out and hid it in a tree." The head of the asylum and her assistant could hardly conceal their elation. "We'll get to the bottom of this," they agreed. "Show us where she left the note."

Sure enough they found it in the branches of the tree. It read: "To whoever finds this: I love you."

"Miss Hungerford is a woman to warm your heart by," the people of Cornwall, an old Hudson River town, told me. "She's a dedicated sort of woman, this teacher."

Everyone has wondered just what there was about Miss Hungerford that fired her pupils so. Somehow she made them believe they lived in a fine world, where a miracle could happen any morning, and they were fortunate and wonderful, with a lot of talent. "We've never thought so well of ourselves since," the Cornwall people say. And she sent out from that school a batch of youngsters who became important men and women all over the country.

I visited her when she was 85. I wanted to learn what it was about Miss Hungerford that had made people remember her all their lives. But, though I tried all day I couldn't get Miss Hungerford to talk about herself.

Then as I was leaving, for the first time, she spoke about herself. "You know, I feel ashamed," she said, "when I see all these bright modern teachers. Compared to them, I was not very well trained." She paused, "You see, all I had was *love*."

—DOROTHY WALWORTH in *Baltimore Sun.*

✣ ✣ ✣

Tennessee Ernie Ford was reading an article by a psychiatrist in which he explained how two young married people could determine whether they loved each other.

"Things have changed," said Ernie. "A few years ago people were so busy raising a family they didn't even have time to take the test."

—*Minneapolis Sunday Tribune.*

✣ ✣ ✣

Wheaton Dudley has paraphrased St. Paul's great Chapter 13 of *I Corinthians* for use in the family:

Though I speak about children in the lingo of Gesell, Ilg, and Spock, but do not truly love them, I am as futile as a radio commercial and as boring as a soap opera. Although I give every material advantage to the poor darlings, and give my patience until I am "burned up" but don't really love them, I get no thanks for my efforts. Truly loving parents don't berate their children, but put up with mistakes, believe in the best of them, have great dreams for their future, and are the last to give up hope of their becoming mature, creative personalities. Now I know only a fraction of my child's personality, but some day, I shall know him fully, somewhat as I must be known and understood by God. Now abides three great capacities of the human spirit: faith in the future, hope in the significance of the past, and love, a creative companionship in the present—the greatest of these is love.

—ROBERT W. BURNS, *Foundation of a Christian Home.*

✣ ✣ ✣

Five-year-old Mary underwent an operation and lost so much blood that it was necessary to resort to a blood transfusion. Samples of the blood of all the adults of the family were taken, but none was found to match Mary's. Then a test was made of her older brother's blood. It was found to match. Jimmy, a husky boy of thirteen years, was fond of little Mary.

"Will you give your sister some of your blood, Jim?" asked the doctor.

Jimmy set his teeth. "Yes, sir, if she needs it!"

The need was very desperate so the boy was at once prepared for the transfusion. In the midst of the drawing of the blood, the doctor observed Jimmy growing paler and paler. There was no apparent reason for this.

"Are you ill, Jim?" asked the doctor.

"No, sir, but I'm wondering just when I'll die."

"Die?" gasped the doctor. "Do you think people give their lives when they give a little blood?"

"Yes, sir," replied Jimmy.

"And you were giving your life for Mary's?"

"Yes, sir," replied the boy, simply.

—*Christian Herald.*

✣ ✣ ✣

The old gardener, engaged in breaking apart and re-setting rhubarb crowns, looked up as the little girl approached.

"How's the baby brother?"

Tears sprang at his words, for Mary was painfully jealous of the new baby. Mr. Wicks talked on as though he hadn't noticed. "Suppose your Mom and Dad are mighty busy with him now. Might even seem as though they'd be too busy to love you as much as they did, but love is like rhubarb. If it's divided, it grows better. Yes, sir," he continued, "I loved my mother a lot; then I met and loved a girl and married her. We had a baby pretty soon, and another one came along. But each time loving the new one didn't take a mite away from the old. Yes, love is like rhubarb; when it's divided, it grows."

—*Wall Street Journal.*

✤ ✤ ✤

What you say is not so important as how you feel, for all communication is not at the verbal level. Just as the little three-year-old said: "Daddy, when you tell me you love me, don't just say it with your mouth. Say it with your eyes."

—BLAINE M. PORTER, *Your Child's World.*

✤ ✤ ✤

A father was trying to read a serious book. His little son kept interrupting him. He would jump on his lap and say, "Daddy, I love you." The father would give him a hug and say rather absently, "I love you, too." But that did not quite satisfy the child. Finally he ran to his father and said, "I love you, Daddy, and I've just got to do something about it!"

—NELL and CAWTHON BOWEN, *Christian Home.*

✤ ✤ ✤

A little boy, six years old, recently introduced to the magic of numbers by his first grade teacher, applied that knowledge in a spontaneous expression of affection toward his mother. With all the conviction a boy of his age could command, he said, "Mother, I love you as many times as God can count!"

—FLOYD E. BOSSHARDT, *Telescope-Messenger.*

✤ ✤ ✤

I was traveling in eastern Colorado one day when I saw a small girl pulling a child's wagon. In it was a boy about four, a pale little fellow with a pair of thin useless legs. The girl dragged the wagon through the sand to a corner of the fence that paralleled the highway and the railroad.

I watched as she backed the wagon close to the fence, climbed upon the wire and anxiously scanned the horizon. Questioning her I found out that the boy had had infantile paralysis recently and that his sister, aged six, brought him to this place every afternoon to watch the streamliner *City of Denver* go by.

Presently we heard the hoarse whistle of the train and the little girl flew into action. Jumping into the back of the wagon she raised the helpless boy to a standing position so that he could grasp the top rail of the fence. Then, kneeling behind him, she lowered her head and pressed it against his back while she held to the fence in front. The little boy watched the train until it disappeared, then he relaxed his hold and his sister eased him gently down into the wagon. At this point I exclaimed, "But, darling, you didn't get to see the train at all!"

She gave me that look that precocious children reserve for adults as she said softly, "I saw it before he got sick."

—Carey J. Downing.

✣ ✣ ✣

A doctor was busy in his study when his small son came in and stood silently by. The doctor, preoccupied with his work, put his hand into his pocket, took out a coin and offered it to the boy. "I don't want any money, daddy," the lad said.

After a few moments the doctor opened a drawer of his desk, took out a candy bar and offered this to his son. Again he was refused.

A little impatient, the busy doctor asked, "Well, what *do* you want?"

"I don't want anything," replied the boy. "I only wanted to be with you."

—H. V. Larcombe, *Treasury of the Christian World* (Harper).

✣ ✣ ✣

LOYALTY

A skinny, hatchet-faced spinster, attending a Hollywood garden party, gazed out upon the incredibly beautiful landscape and gushed, "Oh, I just love nature!"

Groucho Marx overheard. "That's loyalty," he quipped, "after what nature did to her!"

—*Pure Oil News.*

✤ ✤ ✤

Grandfather was never known to admit that the weather in his native Ohio was anything but near-perfect. His infrequent trips out of the state strengthened his belief that we lived in the most agreeable spot on the globe.

One morning a few years ago we arose to find a full-fledged blizzard blowing. Grandfather went about his chores as usual, apparently unmindful of the driving wind and waist-deep drifts. When he returned to the house, Grandmother asked, "Pretty cold out, ain't it?"

"Cooled off pretty fast," Grandfather admitted, then added, in all seriousness, "from the looks of this they must be gettin' a bad storm over in Indiana."

—J. L. McManamy.

✤ ✤ ✤

LUCK

David, a second-grader, was bumped while getting on the school bus and suffered a two-inch cut on his cheek. At recess, David and another boy collided while running, and two of David's teeth were knocked loose.

Noon came and David, sliding on the ice, fell and broke his left wrist.

His parents were summoned and his father rushed David to the hospital. As they were waiting for x-rays to be taken, the father noticed that David was clutching something tightly in his good hand. It was a quarter.

"I found it on the ground when I fell," David said. "This is the first quarter I ever found. Dad, this sure is my lucky day!"

—*Milwaukee Journal.*

✤ ✤ ✤

Chauncey Depew used to tell of two friends of his—one an extraordinarily successful man of affairs; the other a speculator who won or lost more by instinct than through planned effort.

On one occasion these men were discussing whether success in life was attained by judgment or luck. The financier, naturally, said judgment. The speculator held out for luck.

Said the speculator: "You are a '49er; that was an adventure." "Not on my part," said the financier, "it was judgment."

"Well," persisted the speculator, "you came to New York at a time when investment of your money yielded the highest returns. Surely that was luck." The financier insisted it had been pure judgment. So the argument persisted. Finally the speculator concluded: "Well, you'll have to admit that you are mighty lucky to have such good judgment!"

✣ ✣ ✣

MAN

About the time I came to New York there occurred the *Titanic* disaster. You will recall how that great ship on her maiden voyage struck an iceberg and was sunk. One of our American publications carried two illustrations of that tragedy. One was a drawing of the ship striking the iceberg and breaking open like a fragile egg shell. Underneath this picture was written: "The weakness of man, the supremacy of nature." The other drawing placed beside it was a picture of one of the passengers on the ship, Mr. W. T. Stead, stepping back to give his place in the last lifeboat to a woman with a child. Underneath this picture was the caption: "The weakness of nature, the supremacy of man."

—Dr. Ralph W. Sockman, addressing a public relations group.

✣ ✣ ✣

MANNERS

George Washington was well known for his rather icy formality and impeccable manners. Once, while out walking with the Marquis de Lafayette, Washington doffed his hat and bowed to an old slave who had greeted him with a cordial "Good mornin', General Washington."

Noticing Lafayette's quizzical smile, Washington asked, "Could I permit a slave to be more gentlemanly than I?"

A guest at a dinner given in honor of Marshal Foch behaved rather rudely. "There is nothing but wind in French politeness," he observed.

Quietly, Marshal Foch retorted, "Neither is there anything but wind in a pneumatic tire. And yet it eases wonderfully the jolts along life's highway."

✣ ✣ ✣

MARRIED LIFE

Resting with his wife on the front stoop after the day's chores, a taciturn old Vermonter surveyed his spouse and said, "When I think of what you've meant to me for all these years, sometimes it's more than I can stand not to tell you."

—Adapted from *Vermont Is Where You Find It,* arranged by KEITH WARREN JENNISON (Harcourt, Brace).

✣ ✣ ✣

MEMORY

An ancient gentlewoman in Albemarle County, Virginia, frequently complains about the suffering and damage caused by the War. (Of course she is referring to "The War between the States.")

"We're still paying for that dreadful war," she exclaimed recently.

"But what made you think of that today?" she was asked.

"I'll tell you what made me think of it," she replied with spirit. "When those damyankees came through here they broke the hinges off our cellar door, and today the hogs got into the cellar and ate up all my butter."

—AGNES ROTHERY.

✣ ✣ ✣

Examining lesson papers, the professor found one which, instead of being covered with historical names and dates, had a crude sketch of a cemetery, with a large tombstone on which was written:

"Sacred to the memory that always deserts me on an occasion like this."

—*Catholic Fireside.*

The immortal Mozart had an extraordinary memory. He arrived in Rome on April 11, 1770, in Holy Week and went to the Sistine Chapel where he heard a *Miserere* by Allegri. The authorities had strictly forbidden anyone to take a copy of this music. But Mozart was so impressed by it that he brought every note away in his brain and wrote it out directly he reached home. Two days later he went to the chapel with the score concealed in his hat to correct any mistakes he might have made. He had made none. He had memorized accurately every note of the nine-part piece of music.

—WM. STRONG, *Tit-Bits,* London.

✣ ✣ ✣

Thomas A. Edison was notoriously absent-minded. One afternoon he got off the train at Orange, N. J., well pleased because for once he hadn't forgotten a thing. He had counted and checked his baggage, looked over his belongings carefully, and everything was there. Picking up a couple of bags, he had started down the platform when the ticket agent, an old friend, asked: "Sure you haven't forgotten anything, Mr. Edison? You didn't leave anything on the train by any chance?"

"Not this time!" Edison assured him. Then, casually glancing toward the train, he gave a startled exclamation, dropped his bags, and started on a run back to the car he had just left. For at the window he had seen the face of his bride of two weeks.

—LUBY POLLOCK, *Your Normal Mind* (Funk).

✣ ✣ ✣

A woman with a "terrible memory" recently told Dr. Bruno Furst, noted authority on memory training, a harrowing tale of how she once had to speak at a business function. Not only did she arrive late because she forgot the name of the hotel, but she also forgot the names of the people present, and when she rose to speak, couldn't recall the text of her remarks.

Dr. Furst asked what she had worn.

Without hesitation, she replied, "My navy silk-shantung suit, white straw hat, navy leather bag and shoes to match."

—CARL A. WINSTON, *Today's Woman.*

A boxer went to a psychiatrist because his memory was failing. The psychiatrist told him he could guarantee no cure, but if the pug would undergo treatment daily for two years, some improvement could be expected. At the end of that time the doctor told his patient he was ready to face the world. His memory was restored.

The fighter left the doctor's office happily. On the corner a man approached him and held out his hand. "Hello, Jack," the man said.

"Don't tell me," the fighter answered quickly. "Your name is Kid Robinson. I fought you in Toledo on the twenty-second of June in 1931; you weigh a hundred and fifty-six and a half pounds; you had a cut over your left eye; you wore purple trunks with a white stripe, and you had a green bathrobe with the name Murphy's Gym embroidered on the back and a hole in the right pocket. Right?" he concluded triumphantly.

"Jack!" shouted the other character despairingly. "Don't you recognize me? I'm your father, Sam!"

—LLOYD GOUGH.

✤ ✤ ✤

One day a visitor arrived in the home of Leonard Liebling, editor of *Musical Courier,* just as the family was about to sit down to dinner. Mr. Liebling, annoyed at such thoughtless timing, had the maid ask the guest to wait. After an unhurried meal, Mr. Liebling greeted his friend. "Sorry to keep you waiting," he said, "but we always eat at seven."

"That's what I thought," the friend replied, "when you invited me to dinner tonight."

—VERNON POPE, *This Week.*

✤ ✤ ✤

MISSIONARIES

Once, during the war years, Stonewall Jackson sent a message to the pastor of his home-town church. The pastor stood on the church steps and read it aloud to the people of the town, who thought it might contain some news of the battle and the course of war. But the letter read:

"My dear pastor: I recalled today that my gift to foreign missions was due. Find it enclosed. May the day soon come when this war is over, and may the right side win, that we may all go back to our primary task—which is the saving of the souls of men."

—*Tarbell's Teachers' Guide* (Revell).

✣ ✣ ✣

A missionary on furlough in the United States was raising funds to carry on his work in a foreign land. He met one of those individuals who do not believe in foreign missions. Said this man: "I want what I give to benefit my neighbors."

"How much land do you own?" the missionary asked.

"About five hundred acres."

"And how far down do you own it?"

The man was stumped, but finally said that he supposed he owned to a depth "about half-way through the earth."

"Well," observed the missionary, "you had better give to me, then. I want this money for men whose land adjoins yours at the bottom—the Chinese."

—*Tarbell's Teachers' Guide* (Revell).

✣ ✣ ✣

MISSIONS

An artist was once asked to paint a picture of a decaying church. To the astonishment of many, instead of putting on the canvas an old, tottering ruin, the artist painted a stately edifice of modern grandeur. Through the open portals could be seen the richly-carved pulpit, the magnificent organ and the beautiful stained-glass windows. Within the grand entrance was an offering plate of elaborate design for the offering of fashionable worshipers. But—and here the artist's idea of a decaying church was made known—right above the offering plate was hung a square box bearing the legend, "For Foreign Missions," and right above the slot through which contributions ought to have gone he had painted a huge cobweb!

—G. B. F. Hallock.

MODERN AGE

A four-year-old was told a story about a little boy who had an exciting adventure. When the story was finished, he asked, "But where was the little boy's mother?"

The story-teller said the adventure story didn't mention his mother. Perhaps she was dead.

The four-year-old nodded wisely and concluded: "I bet she was killed in a nervous wreck."

✤ ✤ ✤

MODESTY

Suffering from a stiff knee brought about by a fall, a prominent London matron consulted William Pennell, the famous specialist, in 1806. She was greatly embarrassed and almost fainted when Pennell explained he could not treat her knee without examining it. After a long pause, the lady reluctantly reached into her satchel and brought forth a fully-clothed girl baby-doll. With averted eyes she lifted the hem of the skirt and pointed to a spot on the doll's bare knee. "There, doctor," she gasped, blushing a fiery red, "that's where it hurts."

—WEBB B. GARRISON, *Today's Woman.*

✤ ✤ ✤

Toscanini was rehearsing Beethoven's Ninth Symphony with the New York Philharmonic. He gave his musicians such a new insight into the music that, when the rehearsal ended, they rose and cheered him. Desperately, Toscanini tried to arrest their ovation, waving his arms wildly, crying to them to desist. When there was a lull in the ovation, Toscanini's broken voice could be heard exclaiming—and there were tears in his eyes as he spoke: "It isn't me, men . . . it's Beethoven! . . . Toscanini is nothing."

—DAVID EWEN, *Dictators of the Baton* (Ziff-Davis).

✤ ✤ ✤

Orville Wright, never an aggressive publicity seeker, became, after the death of his brother Wilbur, in 1912, increasingly reticent. Once when a friend remonstrated with the pioneer aviation authority, on his refusal to address an important scientific conference, Orville smiled wryly and observed: "The parrot is the best talker and the worst flier in the kingdom of birds!"

✣ ✣ ✣

MONEY

An American symphony orchestra touring the Far East was about to give a concert in a provincial town where the Communists had been conducting a strong anti-American propaganda campaign. Just before the program was to begin, the man assigned to help the American manager with the seating arrangements for the orchestra rushed up to him in great agitation and said, "Sir, there has been a great oversight, I'm afraid. Where are the cash registers to be set up?"

"We have no need for cash registers," smiled the manager. "This is a free concert."

"Yes, I know that," replied the man. "But we understood that the music Americans liked most was the ringing of cash registers. Why have you none in your orchestra?"

—*Executives' Digest.*

✣ ✣ ✣

MOTHERHOOD

A little boy, after reading Bunyan's *Pilgrim's Progress,* asked his mother which of the characters she liked best.

"Christian, of course," she replied. "He is the hero of the story."

The child responded, "Mother, I like Christiana best, because when Christian set out on his pilgrimage he went alone, but when Christiana started, she took the children with her."

—*Baptist Observer.*

✣ ✣ ✣

NATURE

William Jennings Bryan once observed: "I was eating a piece of watermelon some time ago and was struck by its beauty. I took some of the seeds and dried them and weighed them. I found that it would require five thousand of those seeds to weigh a pound; then I applied mathematics to that forty-pound melon. One of those seeds, put into the ground, takes off its coat and goes to work. It gathers from somewhere two hundred thousand times its weight, and forcing the raw material through a tiny stem, constructs a watermelon."

✣ ✣ ✣

NEIGHBORLINESS

One day the richest woman in town went to visit an old woman living in a tenement, who was in great need. There was no food in the dingy kitchen; no money for rent. "I'll see that a settlement worker visits you in the morning," said the grand dame, as she planned a hasty exit. The old woman proudly replied: "You needn't trouble yourself; I need no help."

At that moment another woman, from "upstairs" in the tenement, entered with food and clothing. She was warmly welcomed. When the rich visitor asked for an explanation, the tenement-dweller replied, "You see, she's a ***neighbor.***"

✣ ✣ ✣

OBEDIENCE

West Point's Drawing Department is intended to teach young officers-to-be engineering drawing, map reading, and photo reading, but every so often some cadet attempts to express a sprightly artistic originality. On one occasion a cadet, required to make a drawing of a bridge over a rural stream, playfully sketched in a couple of children sitting on the bridge rail. Naturally this did not meet with the approval of his instructor who sharply directed him to "take those children off the bridge."

The next time the instructor made his rounds, he found that his orders had been obeyed to the letter—the children had been transferred to the riverbank. "No, no!" he protested. "Get rid of them!"

On the third trip the instructor found that the children had indeed been done away with. In their place stood two pathetic little tombstones.

—KENDALL BANNING, *West Point Today* (Funk & Wagnalls).

Washington once complained that his plans were held up because his soldiers would not obey until time was taken to explain why the commands were necessary. He hoped, he said, that a time would arrive when they would trust his leadership enough to obey his commands without delay or argument. That time did arrive, and then the army became efficient.

—Bishop GERALD KENNEDY.

✣ ✣ ✣

A kindly gentleman of advanced years encountered a four-year-old standing on the street corner in deep perplexity.

"I want to run away," confided the tot.

"Oh," said the gentleman understandingly, "why don't you?"

"Well," said the perplexed youngster, "I'm not allowed to cross the street."

—EARL WILSON.

✣ ✣ ✣

OBSERVATION

The late Governor Folk of Missouri, accompanied by a friend, arrived at his office one morning to find a number of men waiting for him in the anteroom. He paused as he passed through and told a very ancient joke. In the Governor's office, the friend said, "That was an awfully old chestnut you pulled out there."

"I know it," the Governor replied, "but I wanted to find out how many of those fellows were here to ask favors."

"And did you?"

"Oh, yes," said Folk. "They were the ones who laughed."

—*Wall Street Journal.*

✣ ✣ ✣

"You do not use your faculties of observation," said the professor, pushing forward a dish containing an offensive smelling chemical. He put a finger into it, then into his mouth. "Taste it," he said.

Reluctantly, one by one, the class dipped fingers into the concoction, grimaced at the taste.

"I must repeat," chided the professor, "that you do not use your faculties of observation. Had you looked more closely, you would have seen that the finger which I put into my mouth was not the finger I dipped in the dish."

—*Chicago News.*

✤ ✤ ✤

While on government duty, I visited various forest regions. A summer was spent with Kentucky hillbillies with whom I made friends. One of them refused to believe that the world was round. "What happened to the sun the other day?" he asked, referring to a recent solar eclipse. I explained in terms of Copernicus. He shook his head and quoted the Bible.

"Apparently," said I, "you believe the earth is flat."

"Well," he drawled, "it's been flat in every place that *I* ever was."

—BENTON MACKAYE, *Survey.*

✤ ✤ ✤

When I'm sick of myself and other men, I tuck my wife under my arm and go places—maybe as far as Saturn, via the dime-a-squint telescope on the street corner, maybe to the excitement in an anthill, or to watch the shore birds beat each oncoming wave to dinner. Always I take a jaunt outside the sphere of human affairs. There I see how well the world wags beyond the scope of human worry. So I get into focus again and see mankind as only a part of nature, and nature as an eternally successful experiment.

—DONALD CULROSS PEATTIE.

✤ ✤ ✤

The woman had been bumped by the fender of a passing car. She was uninjured but indignant. A police officer came to investigate and asked, "Did you get the number of the car that touched you, madam?"

"No, I didn't," spluttered the woman, "but the hussy that was driving it wore a three-piece tweed suit lined with canton crepe, and she had on a periwinkle hat trimmed with artificial cherries!"

✤ ✤ ✤

OBSERVATION—Lack of

Fred Stone and his young daughter, lunching with a group at the Algonquin Hotel, fell to discussing the anonymity of waiters.

R. H. Burnside, the producer, contended that only one person in 50 notices the waiter who serves him.

A well-known painter present maintained that this goes for household servants too, recalling that early in his career when he and his wife were living in very modest circumstances in England, his wife was startled in the middle of her morning housework to see a local duchess coming up the garden path on her first social call. After a moment's panic at being caught in her dustcap, she opened the door, admitted the duchess with a murmured, "Madam will be down shortly," and whipped up the stairs. A few moments later she came down in a presentable costume, and the duchess gave no sign of ever having seen her before.

While the painter told the story, a waiter took the dessert order, cleared the table. When he arrived with the dessert, Stone's daughter suddenly exclaimed, "Daddy—isn't that Mr. Burnside?"

It was: the producer had waited on his friends for ten minutes without their recognizing him.

—PEGGY McEVOY.

✣ ✣ ✣

OBSTACLES

An elderly woman, watching a tennis game, saw how often the ball hit the net. Exasperated, she declared, "Why don't they take down the net?"

Some folks cannot comprehend the value of obstacles or opposition. They never realize the satisfaction and exhilaration experienced by those winning against odds.

—*Capitol Life Contact.*

✣ ✣ ✣

OBSTINACY

Some years ago an old Boston family was persuaded to take a trip to California. Never previously had they considered it worthwhile to travel farther than Lexington, Concord, Dedham and other Boston suburbs.

When they arrived in Los Angeles, their friends inquired: "By which route did you come to California?"

The man turned to his wife and asked, "Darling, didn't we come by way of Dedham?"

—John Homer Miller.

✣ ✣ ✣

OPINION

In a country church, the story goes, there was a quarrel over a new organ. Somebody asked an elderly man of strong convictions how he felt about the issue.

"I have not yet made up my mind," said the deacon. "But when I do, I shall be very bitter!"

—Clyde R. Miller, *The Process of Persuasion* (Crown).

✣ ✣ ✣

Listening to an important law case one day, I feared the opposing attorneys would come to blows any minute. I had no doubt they were bitter enemies. Later, I saw the two lawyers going down the corridor arm in arm to have lunch together. I pointed out to a friend how they were double-crossing their clients, and expressed the opinion that their verbal clawing was only so much hypocritical action, designed to conceal that the case was fixed, and division of the spoils agreed upon in advance.

"If these men became unfriendly to every man whom they oppose at the bar," explained my friend, "no lawyers would be on speaking terms. But these men have learned how to hold difference of opinion and still remain friends."

—J. S. Royer, *Chips of Inspiration.*

✣ ✣ ✣

It had been a rather stormy session of the board and some very harsh things had been said, but one man—always highly respected and unusually wise in his judgments—had said nothing.

Suddenly one of the leaders in the debate turned to him and said: "Brother J——, you have not said a word. I would like to have your opinion in this matter." Whereupon the wise man said,

"I have discovered that there are many times when silence is an opinion."

—ROY L. SMITH, *Christian Advocate.*

✣ ✣ ✣

When President Jefferson Davis asked General Robert E. Lee for his opinion of a fellow officer, Lee spoke of the man in the highest terms. This greatly astonished another officer, who said to Lee afterwards, "General, don't you know that that man is one of your bitterest enemies and that he misses no opportunity to malign you?"

"Yes," replied General Lee, "but the President asked for my opinion of him; he did not ask for his opinion of me."

—*Sunshine Magazine.*

✣ ✣ ✣

My wife, whose feminine logic always baffles me, returned from a shopping trip lyrical in her description of a "dream dress" she had seen in a shopwindow. After a week of badgering I gave in as usual, and she went gaily off to buy her heart's desire. But to my amazement she returned empty-handed. "It was still in the window," she explained. "So I decided that if no one else wanted it, neither did I."

—DONALD L. WHITEAKER, in "Life in These United States."

✣ ✣ ✣

There is a story of a salesman trying to sell radio sets in Russia. He explained to a peasant that with this set in his home, he could listen to what was being said in Moscow. "Yes," said the peasant, "but haven't you something so that the people in Moscow can listen to what we are saying?"

This story, probably apocryphal, illustrates the need in every human heart to register his opinion; the hunger to be heard.

✣ ✣ ✣

OPTIMISM

Two men were talking as they rode their morning train to work.

"That school principal is certainly a confirmed optimist," said one.

"I never noticed it," said his neighbor. "What makes you think so?"

"Well," was the reply, "he lives in the block next to me, and he's trying to raise roses, vegetables, chickens, two cocker spaniels and three boys, all on the same lot."

—*Texas Outlook.*

✤ ✤ ✤

OPTIMISM—Pessimism

The old mountaineer and his wife arrived at a railway station, and for the first time in their lives beheld a train of cars, which was standing there. The husband looked the engine over carefully, and opined, "She'll never start!"

The conductor waved, the bell rang, the locomotive puffed—and the train moved, quickly gaining momentum.

The couple watched, fascinated, as it disappeared in the distance. "Well, Pa," said the wife, "what do you think of it now?"

The old man shook his head. "She'll never stop," he declared, "she'll never stop!"

✤ ✤ ✤

A Massachusetts newspaper editor remarked one morning to his landlady, "I think we'll have a good potato crop this year." She took issue with him, replying firmly, "I think the crop will be poor."

When he got to the office the editor had a filler set reading, "An excellent potato crop is expected this fall."

To his delight, that night the landlady said apologetically, "I was wrong about the potato crop. I saw in the paper that the crop will be excellent."

—I. D. Smith.

✤ ✤ ✤

OPPORTUNITY

The governor of North Carolina was complimenting Thomas A. Edison one day on being a great inventor. The modest Edison looked discomfited.

"I am not a great inventor."

"But you have over a thousand patents to your credit."

"Well," explained Edison, "I guess I'm an awfully good sponge. I absorb ideas from every source I can, and put them to practical use. Then I improve them until they become of some value. The ideas I use are mostly the ideas of people who don't develop them."

—*Rainbow.*

✣ ✣ ✣

An Indian princess, on coming of age, was given a basket and told she might pick the finest ears of corn in a given row. The only condition: she was to choose as she went along. She could not retrace her steps. She admired the fine quality of the corn before her; and as she felt one ear after another she left them on the stalk, always thinking what better ears lay ahead. Suddenly, and to her dismay, she came to the end of the row—and she had gathered none.

—*Pipe Dreams.*

✣ ✣ ✣

One night three horsemen were riding across an Eastern desert. As they crossed the dry bed of a river, a voice called "Halt!" They did so and the voice continued, telling them to dismount, pick up some pebbles and put them in their pockets. Then the voice said, "You have done as I commanded. Tomorrow at sun-up you will be both glad and sorry."

Mystified, they rode on, as directed. At sunrise, they reached into their pockets, and found that the pebbles were diamonds, rubies and other precious stones. Then they thought of the warning, and they were both glad and sorry—glad they had taken some, sorry they had not taken more.

—*Link.*

✣ ✣ ✣

A faucet leaks. I cannot close it tight. Good. I call my seven-year-old son to take another lesson in one of the most important courses I have to teach him. He seizes the faucet, tries to turn it off, can't. He grins.

"What's the matter, Pete?" I ask.

He looks up happily, and gives the answer. "Grownups, Daddy."

Propaganda, of course. I have taught him that we, his elders, cannot make a fit faucet. But he may. There's a job for him and his generation in the plumbing business. And in every business.

I teach my child and I tell other children of all ages—pre-school, in school, in college, and out:

That nothing is done finally and right.

That nothing is known positively and completely.

That the world is theirs, all of it. They are glad, as I am, that there is something left for them to discover and say and think and do. Something? There is *everything* for youth to take over and it is an inspiration for them to learn this. It gives purpose to their studies, to their work, to their life.

—Condensed from *Lincoln Steffens Speaking.*

✣ ✣ ✣

My brother and I were still youngsters when our parents brought us to the United States. We were fascinated by the American scene. Never will I forget the summer's evening in 1916 when we made our first Saturday night pilgrimage downtown in that New England textile city. The good-natured crowd, the shiny automobiles, the clang of the streetcars, the alluring shop-windows, the blinking of the electric signs made me actually jump with joy. It was then that my brother turned to me and said, "If we get all this for nothing, *how much will we get for a dime?*"

—Matthew Turnbull.

✣ ✣ ✣

Waiting in a steamship office to be interviewed for a job as wireless operator, a group of applicants filled the room with such a buzz of conversation that they were oblivious to the dots and dashes which began coming over a loud-speaker. About that time another man entered and sat down quietly by himself. Suddenly he snapped to attention, walked into the private office, came out smiling.

"Say," one of the crowd called out, "how'd you get in ahead of us? We were here first."

"One of you would have got the job," he replied, "if you'd listened to the message from the loud-speaker."

"What message?" they asked, surprised.

"Why, the code, the stranger answered. "It said, 'The man I want must always be alert. The first man who gets this message and comes directly into my private office will be placed on one of my ships as operator.' "

—*National Canvas Goods Manufacturer's Review.*

✣ ✣ ✣

A friend of mine was rhapsodizing about man's wonderful ingenuity. "Just think!" he exclaimed. "We've conquered the air, enslaved lightning, destroyed space . . ."

"True," I put in; "but remember the barnacle."

The barnacle is a symbol of all those things we have *not* done. For centuries that tiny marine organism has taken expensive joy rides on the bottoms of our ships. He slows down our sea defenses and costs us millions yearly. A fortune awaits the man smart enough to outwit him.

The list is endless. Nothing is anywhere near perfect. Industry and research are crying for good men, and fame and fortune hide in every test tube, under every microscope.

—WILLIAM D. COOLIDGE, *The American Magazine.*

✣ ✣ ✣

A doctor in Sequatchie Valley in Tennessee was called to examine the young wife of an elderly, deaf mountaineer. "Your wife is pregnant," he told her husband.

The mountaineer, hand behind his ear, queried, "Eh?"

The doctor shouted, "I said your wife is pregnant."

"Eh?"

Finally the doctor screamed, "Your wife is going to have a baby."

The man walked to the edge of the porch, spat out a mouthful of tobacco juice, and drawled, "I ain't a bit surprised. She's had ev'ry opportunity."

—DOLCE OGDEN.

✣ ✣ ✣

A woman salesman went into a retail jewelry store and said: "I want a gem that is ugly on one side and beautiful on the other." That sounded like a funny request, but the jeweler strove to please, and sold her a geod—a stone with a homely rough outside and a beautiful crystal inside. Then he asked what she was going to use it for.

She told him when she had difficulty getting attention, she merely showed her prospect the stone, and said, "If you saw this stone in the street, you wouldn't pick it up, would you?" "No." Turning it over, she would ask: "But if you knew the other side was composed of these beautiful, valuable gems you would, wouldn't you?" "Oh, yes." "You don't know what I'm going to tell you, or its importance until you hear it. It may be one of these gems." She usually got in.

—Charles B. Roth, *Canadian Business.*

✤ ✤ ✤

ORIGINALITY

A company that manufactured soap and perfume offered a prize for the best slogan submitted for the advertising of its products. The judges easily agreed on the best slogan, but did not give it the prize. The slogan was, "If you don't use our soap, for heaven's sake use our perfume!"

—*Good Business.*

✤ ✤ ✤

"Why ruin your disposition twisting your hair into such a mess?" inquired my father, when he found me weeping with ill temper because I was too young and inept to cope with the coiffure of my high school days.

"It's the fashion!" I wailed. "Only mine never turns out right!"

Studying me gravely, Father directed: "Part your hair in the middle. Brush it back and tie it with a ribbon." I humored him, albeit ungraciously. "Now," he said, "wear it like that a week, and if half the girls in your class aren't copying you I'll give you ten dollars."

I thought him unbelievably naive. Yet ten dollars was a fortune I could not resist. Had I arrived in class wearing my nightgown, the agony would not have been any more acute. But when the week had ended, almost every girl in my class wore simply parted hair, tied back with a ribbon! Said my father: "Don't be commonplace. The world has enough mediocrity. Never be afraid to have an idea of your own, and if it's right, carry it through, no matter what the crowd does."

—MRS. BROOKS CAIRNS.

✤ ✤ ✤

PATIENCE

John A. Brashear, as a child, had been shown a view of the heavens through a telescope. Years later, after he became a steel worker in Pittsburgh, he acquired a five-inch piece of glass and a book of instructions, and started to make his own telescope. Every night for three years, after his exhausting days at the mill, Brashear ground and polished at his lens. At last it was ready. Mounting it in an improvised frame, he aimed the home-made instrument through an open window and saw again, with the intimacy of his first view, the stars and planets in their courses.

The director of the Allegheny Observatory examined Brashear's lens and gave him others to grind. Soon scientists everywhere were ordering lenses from this steel worker, for there were none more accurate. Even today lenses ground by Brashear are in use at observatories all over the world.

Brashear became acting head of the Allegheny Observatory; and he built there an observation room where other youngsters too poor to buy a telescope could view the heavens nightly without charge.

—RUTH AND EDWARD BRECHER, in *The American Scholar.*

✤ ✤ ✤

I shall never forget my first weeks as a student in Dr. William J. Beal's laboratory. He handed me a plant fresh from the river-bank—leaves, roots, flowers—and told me to study it, make sketches, and write down what I saw. I was impatient. In 15 minutes I showed what I had to the professor. "Go on," he said, "you've only just begun."

After using the hand microscope, I went up again with my notes. "Go on," he said, "you haven't begun to see all there is in that plant."

This continued for three or four days. It seemed a great waste of time to me, but presently I began to find, to my surprise, that the plant, a blue lupin, was far more interesting than I had dreamed. The veining of the leaves, their arrangement, the channels in the stem began to fascinate me. I was making all those discoveries; it was as though I were exploring a whole new world.

Impatience, restlessness, were among the chief faults of of my youth. In Doctor Beal's laboratory I learned that impatience is the enemy of thought, and that everything is in anything. Now I know how far a man can travel in ten miles, the number of things one can see, hear, smell and taste. When I came across a remark of Rodin, the sculptor, "Slowness is beauty," I knew what he meant. Dr. Beal taught me that.

—RAY STANNARD BAKER, *Native American, The Book of My Youth* (Scribners).

✣ ✣ ✣

"How's school going, Henry?" asked an old veteran of the Cross of a young seminary student.

"Oh, I don't know, Mr. Fayne. Seems it's a long, hard grind before one has anything to offer for the Lord."

"Don't be discouraged, son. You know your dad wasn't grinding out loaves of bread when he threshed that wheat last week."

—NAOMI A. DALLAS, *Moody Monthly.*

✣ ✣ ✣

"Give me some milk! Give me some milk!" the little girl yelled, banging her cup on the table.

"Why, Daughter, haven't you any patience?" one of her parents mildly chided her.

"Yes, I have," shouted the child, "but I haven't any milk!"

—*Fifth Wheel.*

✣ ✣ ✣

Most of us can afford to take a lesson from the oyster. The

most extraordinary thing about the oyster is this: Irritations get into his shell. He does not like them. But when he cannot get rid of them, he settles down to make of them one of the most beautiful things in the world. He uses the irritation to do the loveliest thing that an oyster ever has the chance to do: he makes his irritation into a pearl. There are irritations in our lives today—and there is only one prescription: make a pearl. It may have to be a pearl of patience, but anyhow, make a pearl. And it takes faith and love to do it.

—Harry Emerson Fosdick.

✣ ✣ ✣

A doctor was once asked by a patient who had met with a serious accident, "Doctor, how long shall I have to lie here?"

The physician answered cheerfully: "Only a day at a time."

—Andrew Murray, *Religious Telescope.*

✣ ✣ ✣

Robert G. Ingersoll, the brilliant atheist of the last century, once stopped in the middle of one of his eloquent lectures, took his watch out of his pocket and said to the audience: "I will give God five minutes to strike me dead for the things I have said." He was not struck dead; the five minutes ran out, and he resumed his discourse.

Someone told Theodore Parker about that; Parker smiled and said, "And did the gentleman think he could exhaust the patience of the Eternal God in five minutes?"

✣ ✣ ✣

PATRIOTISM

When Elihu Root was called into Teddy Roosevelt's cabinet to serve as Secretary of State, he was already a well-known and well-thought-of man in the United States. In fact, an intimate friend wrote Root, "Why not wait three years and get the substance instead of being the shadow now?"

In a return letter, Mr. Root replied, "I have always thought that the opportunity to do something worthwhile is the substance, and trying to get something is the shadow."

Elihu Root's willingness to serve his country in any capacity, however enticingly fame beckoned from the future, is a form of patriotism which political aspirants might do well to remember.

—*Property.*

✤ ✤ ✤

John Hancock, first signer of the Declaration of Independence, was an earnest worker for the cause of freedom.

During the siege of Boston, General Washington consulted Congress upon the propriety of bombarding the town. His letter was read to Congress, of which Mr. Hancock was president. At first, there was silence. Then a member made a motion that the house should resolve itself into a committee of the whole, in order that Mr. Hancock might give his opinion, since all of his property was located in Boston.

Leaving his chair, John Hancock addressed the chairman of the committee as follows: "It is true, sir, nearly all of the property I have in the world is in houses and other real estate in the town of Boston: but if the liberties of our country require their being burnt to ashes—*issue the order for that purpose immediately!*"

—Mabel-Ruth Jackson, *Treasures.*

✤ ✤ ✤

PEACEFULNESS

Philippe Vernier, the great French Pacifist, Protestant Clergyman, was before the judge, not for the first time, because he had refused service in the French army. He had told the judge of his belief in brotherhood and love, and the judge had listened patiently. Finally he said, "But we don't live in that kind of a world." Philippe Vernier replied, "I do."

—James Bristol, *New Outlook.*

✤ ✤ ✤

PERFECTION

"Here," announced the engineer, displaying the latest novelty dreamed up by his staff, "we have combined: an inkwell, a small clock, a pencil sharpener, a memo pad, an interest table and a calendar. On top is a miniature elephant with a cask on his back for holding postage stamps, matches and buttons, while on top of the cask is a pin cushion. Don't you think that's a dandy combination?"

The prospective manufacturer stared at the weird contraption, a frown on his brow. "There's something lacking," he finally announced. Then he smiled: "I know what it needs! From somewhere should come music!"

—*Christian Science Monitor.*

✤ ✤ ✤

There once was a restaurant famous for a steak which came as close to perfection as sirloin was intended to come. There was a widespread rumor that the chef used some complicated abracadabra to turn out the beef wonder. For years enterprising fellow chefs tried to worm the secret out of him.

In time the great chef retired, and in a moment of sentimental generosity, agreed to tell a few close associates the "how" and "why."

"I use the best meat I can get," he said, "take plenty of time and care in trimming it and preparing it for the fire. I watch and baste it carefully until it's done just right. That's all . . . there isn't any secret to it!"

—*Type Talks.*

✤ ✤ ✤

In a biographical sketch of Enrico Caruso by Claudia Cassidy, music critic of the *Chicago Tribune,* that came with an album of his immortal recordings, I came across this significant paragraph:

"It happened in the wings of the Metropolitan Opera House early in 1916, when Edith Mason was beginning her career, as his was approaching its tragic end. She was singing Oscar the Page to his Riccardo in "The Masked Ball" and as they waited for their entrance she was amazed to see that the most idolized of tenors was trembling.

" 'Why, Caruso,' she exclaimed incredulously, 'are you nervous?'

" 'Mason,' he replied in utter sincerity, 'other singers must sing 100%. Caruso 150.' "

To attain greatness a man must excel. And to hold his position he must keep right on excelling. When a man does a job superbly well, he sets a standard that people expect him to live up to. The price of being a top-notcher is terrific. Few of us are willing to pay it.

—WILFERD A. PETERSON, *Friendly Adventurer.*

✣ ✣ ✣

Thorwaldsen, the noted Danish sculptor, was once asked by an admirer, "Which do you consider is your greatest statue?"

Without hesitation, the famous Dane replied, "My next one."

✣ ✣ ✣

PERSEVERANCE

Some years ago a Midwestern university unveiled a tablet to one of its alumni who had been an undistinguished man. His scholastic average had been in the B's; he had never been president of anything, or outstanding in any collegiate activity. When the war came he served in a minor capacity in a medical unit, and one day met his death trying to help a wounded man under fire. The French Government posthumously conferred upon this man the *Croix de Guerre.* So his alma mater unveiled a tablet in his honor, and on it the inscription is written: "He played four years on the scrubs—he never quit."

—DR. HARRY EMERSON FOSDICK.

✣ ✣ ✣

A monkey named Charlie which lives in the Baltimore Zoo was always beating up the other monkeys. So zoo officials put him in a cage with a porcupine named Wilton. They figured a faceful of Wilton's needle-sharp quills would kill Charlie's love of battle.

But they misjudged Charlie's perseverance. He kept on the offensive. After each assault on Wilton, he would retire to a corner and patiently, one by one, remove the quills. Finally Wilton ran out of quills. They buried him next day.

—*Capper's Weekly.*

✣ ✣ ✣

When Justice William O. Douglas was a youngster he was a

puny lad, with spindly legs, due to an attack of infantile paralysis. To overcome his handicap he began to take long walks and to climb mountains. When he began, he used the foothills as one uses weights or bars in a gymnasium. He says: "First, I tried to go up the hills without stopping. When I conquered that, I tried to go up without change of pace. When that was achieved, I practiced going up not only without any change of pace, but whistling as I went."

—*Wright Line.*

✤ ✤ ✤

Charles F. Kettering, vice-president of General Motors, tells this story of the origin of Duco paint:

We used to finish cars with the same kind of varnish that you put on pianos. It took 17 days for cheaper cars and 35 days for more expensive ones. I called in all the paint experts and said, "We want to shorten the time required to paint a car."

They said, "You can't do much about that. We can shorten it a couple of days. How long do you think it ought to take to paint a car?" I asked, "Why can't you paint a car in an hour?"

"The paint won't dry," they said. "Nothing in the world you can do to speed it up."

"I don't believe it," I told them. So I was always looking for paints that would dry fast. Walking down Fifth Avenue one day I saw some little pin trays with a new type of lacquer on them. I asked the manager, "Where do you get this lacquer?" He didn't know so I went to the pin-tray manufacturer. He got it from a fellow over in New Jersey.

I found a little bit of a laboratory back of a business block and I said to the fellow who was running it, "I want a quart of that material." "My goodness," he said, "I never made a quart of it before. What do you want to do with it?"

"I want to finish an automobile door with it."

"You can never do it in the world," he said. "If you put it in one of your spray guns, it will dry before it reaches the door."

"Can't you do anything to slow it down?"

"Not a thing in the world."

So the thing you call Duco is simply halfway between the paint they couldn't speed up and the paint they couldn't slow down, and we have finished many automobiles in an hour's time.

✣ ✣ ✣

When I was halfway through writing my first book a sudden desolation struck me like an avalanche. I asked myself: "Why am I wearing myself out with this toil for which I am so preposterously ill-equipped? What is the use of it?"

I threw down my pen. I saw finally that I was a presumptuous lunatic, that all I had written, all that I could ever write was wasted effort, sheer futility. I decided to abandon the whole thing. Abruptly, furiously, I bundled up the manuscript, went out and threw it in the ash can.

I went for a walk in the drizzling rain. Halfway down the loch shore I came upon old Angus, the farmer, patiently and laboriously ditching a patch of the bogged and peaty heath which made up the bulk of his hard-won little croft.

When I told him what I had just done and why, his weathered face slowly changed, his keen blue eyes scanned me with disappointment and a queer contempt. His words when he spoke were cryptic.

"No doubt you're the one that's right, doctor, and I'm the one that's wrong . . ." He seemed to look right to the bottom of me. "My father ditched this bog all his days and never made a pasture. I've dug it all my days and I've never made a pasture. But pasture or no pasture," he placed his foot dourly on the spade, "I canna help but dig. For my father knew and I know that if you only dig enough a pasture can be made here."

Suddenly my trivial dilemma became magnified, transmuted, until it stood as a touchstone of all human conduct. It became the timeless problem of mortality—the comfortable retreat, or the arduous advance without prospect of reward.

—A. J. Cronin.

✣ ✣ ✣

Louis Pasteur was sensitive, raw-nerved against human pain. As a nine-year-old boy he had run away, crying, from the edge of a crowd that blocked the door of a blacksmith shop of Arbois. Above the awed excited whispers of the people he had heard the crackling "s-s-s-z" of a white-hot iron on the flesh of a farmer who had been bitten by a rabid wolf. The iron was cruel and useless against rabies and it didn't save that farmer from dying in the agony of hydrophobia. But it did sear a lifelong hatred of death into Pasteur.

That hatred hardened him against the sneers of the medical world when (only a chemist) he promoted his then silly theory that microbes are the worst menaces of humanity.

—Paul de Kruif in *Microbe Hunters* (Harcourt).

♣ ♣ ♣

In Stewart Edward White's novel, *Blazed Trail,* there is a description of the hero Thorpe's march through the forest with the Indian. The Indian walked in front, Thorpe following blindly. The white man became fascinated watching the easy, untiring lope of his companion. There was never the slightest variation in speed or stride; he seemed to be made of steel springs; he never appeared to hurry, but neither did he rest.

Thorpe tired in a few hours, and became so weary he felt he must drop. Suddenly he gained his second wind.

Says Mr. White, "Second wind is only to a very small degree a question of breathing power. It is, rather, the response of the vital forces to a will that refuses to heed their first grumbling protests."

♣ ♣ ♣

PERSISTENCE

Following a talk to some high-school students, Christy Mathewson took the boys out to show them something about the game of baseball. "Here," he said to one boy, "Can you catch?" The boy was given a glove and the fun began. Mathewson amazed the boys with his famous curves. No matter where the boy held his catcher's mitt, the ball always landed in it. Christy knew how to make it curve and land just where he wanted it.

"Show us how to do it!" the boys pleaded.

In answer to their request, Mathewson made this simple statement: "You can do it only when you pitch, and pitch, and pitch."

—Hazen Werner, *Live With Your Emotions* (Abingdon).

Jacob A. Riis, a man of known stability, was once asked the secret of his calmness in times of trouble. He replied: "When nothing seems to help, I go and look at a stone-cutter hammering away at his rock—perhaps a hundred times without so much as a crack showing. Yet, at the hundred and first blow it will split in two, and I know it was not the last blow that did it, but also all that had gone before."

✣ ✣ ✣

If Columbus had turned back after sixty-five days of sailing on the uncharted seas, no one could have blamed him. But then, no one would have remembered him, either! Even if you have a good excuse for giving up, remember that all the rewards go to those who stick until they get what they are after.

✣ ✣ ✣

PERSONALITY

You are very watery. Your brains are 79 percent water, your body as a whole is 70 percent water. It is the other 30 percent of ingredients that make all the difference between a puddle and a person.

—*You.*

✣ ✣ ✣

PESSIMISM

A peppery old "odd-job" man in our community has a reputation as a chronic pessimist. As I passed by a neighboring yard one day last summer, the old fellow was engaged in mowing the lawn, cussing a blue streak the while. I asked him what was wrong.

"Wire in the grass," he grumbled. "Slows me up; ruins the mower."

Surveying the lawn I saw no evidence of wire and remarked to that effect.

"No," agreed the pessimist reluctantly, "there ain't no wire here—but there's sure to be in the next lawn I mow!"

—David H. Smith.

PESSIMISM—Optimism

Johannes Brahms and Gustav Mahler once took a walk together. The old master contended that there were no great composers any more, and that the end of creative music had occurred. The two had just arrived at the bridge of the Ischl River. Mahler pointed down to the stream and said, "Look! Here comes the last wave!"

—THEODORE REIK, *A Psychologist Looks at Love* (Rinehart).

✤ ✤ ✤

PHILANTHROPY

When Jo Davidson, the famous sculptor, was a struggling young artist, a wealthy friend financed him for a year. Later, when Davidson had achieved fame and fortune, his benefactor brought up the matter of the loan and asked for repayment. The sculptor declined to pay it back, saying that if he did, the matter would end right there. Instead, he preferred to use the money to help other artists on their way up, lending them money when they most needed it and extracting from them a promise that, instead of repaying *him,* they would, in turn, help some other needy artists. Thus, with his financial assistance to Davidson, the original benefactor had started a chain of kindness, and had made a contribution to the arts far greater than he had ever imagined.

—*Whatsoever Things.*

✤ ✤ ✤

PHILOSOPHY

There are people who have traveled round the world and brought back no vivid memories except of quarrels over small sums with taxi drivers, clerks and waiters. Contrast these with an acquaintance of Ralph Waldo Emerson's who, when he set out on a journey, made a budget of his probable expenses and added a certain percentage "to be robbed of." Having established this reserve in advance, he proceeded in equanimity and peace.

—BRUCE BARTON, in *Your Life.*

POLITICS

A surgeon, an architect and a politician were arguing as to whose profession was the oldest.

Said the surgeon: "Eve was made from Adam's rib, and that surely was a surgical operation."

"Maybe," said the architect, "but prior to that, order was created out of chaos, and that was an architectural job."

"But," interrupted the politician smugly, "somebody created the chaos first!"

✤ ✤ ✤

POVERTY—Abundance

David Lloyd-George, the British statesman, commenting at one time on the bounties of America, told of an old Welsh peasant who had lived inland all his life and had a very hard time of it on his small farm. Finally, late in life, he was permitted for the first time to visit the seaside. When he beheld the vast expanse of shore and water he exclaimed: "Thank God for something of which there seems to be plenty!"

✤ ✤ ✤

POWER

Biographer of Robert Fulton tell us that when he was working on his first model of the steamboat, friends who deemed his theory impracticable suggested that he concentrate on some device to increase the speed and efficiency of sailing vessels.

"No," said Fulton, "I will not bother with anything that must depend for its progress on power from outside sources. The power must come from within."

—G. B. F. HALLOCK.

✤ ✤ ✤

Thurman "Dusty" Miller once told a story about his two sons: "How does it happen, Pa," the elder lad asked, "if an automobile can make juice enough to start itself, and light itself, why can't it make enough power to run along without any gasoline?"

"Can you lift Harry, there?" countered his father.

"Yes," said Gene.

Turning to Harry, he asked, "Can you lift Gene?"

"Sure I can lift Gene," replied the brother.

"Now, if you boys can lift one another, you ought to be able to lift yourselves. Try it."

—*Nuggets.*

✣ ✣ ✣

PRACTICALITY

At the end of a state banquet in Moscow during World War II, after Churchill, Roosevelt, Stalin, the Armies, the Navies, and the Air Forces—almost anyone and everything the celebrants could think of—had been toasted, Marshal Stalin rose.

He spoke quickly and eloquently, and apparently with humor, judging from the smiles on the faces of the Russians present. The British and Americans sat with their fingers around their glasses, ready to get to their feet, but waiting for an interpreter to translate.

Marshal Stalin sat down. The interpreter rose and said simply: "Gentlemen, Marshal Stalin says the men's room is on the right."

—DON IDDON in London *Daily Mail.*

✣ ✣ ✣

A father took his little son on his knee and told him the story of the lost sheep: how it found the hole in the fence and crawled through; how glad it was to get away; how it wandered so far that it could not find its way back home. And then he told him of the wolf that chased the sheep, and how, finally, the shepherd came and rescued it and carried it back to the safety of the fold.

The little boy was greatly interested. When the story was over, he asked, "And did they nail up the hole in the fence?"

✣ ✣ ✣

In a Washington school, a teacher was giving her class a review of the story of the British attack on our national capital in the War of 1812. "With the approach of the British forces," she related, "all the congressmen left the city. Of course, they all came back later."

"Teacher," interrupted one little chap, wise in Washington ways, "did they get mileage both ways?"

PRAISE

The parish priest called unexpectedly and the housewife had nothing in the way of food on hand but the remainder of a not-too-successful effort at homemade pie. Bravely, however, she brought it out and to her surprise the clergyman praised it highly. Some weeks later the same priest was coming out to family dinner. This time the housewife made certain that her pie would be superlatively good. The priest ate it without any comment. After dinner, when she got him aside, she couldn't help complaining about the pie. "And you praised the bad one," she complained, "but said not a word about the good one served to-night." The priest nodded. "That's right," he agreed. "The truth is, that other pie needed praising."

—John A. Ferrall, *Volta Review.*

✣ ✣ ✣

A judge in a court of domestic relations tells the story of a middle-aged couple who were seeking a divorce and whose differences he was trying to reconcile. "Are you sure you want this divorce?" he asked the woman. "Yes," she replied, "I sure do want it." "Why?" the judge persisted. "We've been married fifteen years," she replied. "All that time I've kept his house and got his meals and mended his clothes and . . ." As she paused tearfully at the recollection, the judge prompted, "And he has found fault with you?" "No," she said, "it's not that, but in all that time he's never once said, 'You've done a good job!' "

—Florence Hale, *Grade Teacher.*

✣ ✣ ✣

Some months before her death, Madame Ernestine Schumann-Heink invited me to have dinner with her in Chicago, and promised to cook the dinner herself. Then she added, "If you tell me I am a great singer, I will like that; but if you have dinner with me and then say, 'Schumann-Heink, that is the best soup I ever ate,' then you will be a friend forever."

—Dale Carnegie, *Five Minute Biographies* (Greenberg).

✣ ✣ ✣

Johnny Figarro, thirteen-year-old Italian boy, was a problem. He reveled in fighting; spoiling games of younger children. He was insolent to teachers. The more he was punished, the more defiant he became.

In the sixth grade he encountered a quiet, demure woman teacher. One day Johnny was sent inside at recess. He clumped noisily to his seat. Miss A regarded him quietly, then said pleasantly, "Johnny, how nice you look today in that clean shirt."

He squared his shoulders and sat erect. At noon a frayed black tie was clumsily fastened under his collar. Miss A was quick to notice and approve. Next day, his knotted shoe laces were replaced with new ones, and his scuffed shoes shone. "Praise Johnny Figarro," Miss A whispered to the other teacher.

Johnny Figarro became president of a state university in the middle west. An encouraging boost saved a boy.

—*Christian Union Herald.*

✤ ✤ ✤

PRAYER

I have a friend who took his little 7-year-old boy fishing with him one day. They put out the line and then went up to the cabin. After an hour, they went back down to the river to see if they had caught anything.

Sure enough, there were several fish on the line. "I knew there would be, Daddy," said the boy.

"How did you know?" asked the father.

"Because I prayed about it," said the child.

So they baited the hooks again and put out the line and went back to the cabin for supper.

Afterward, they went back to the river; again, there were fish on the line. "I knew it," said the boy.

"And how?" asked his father.

"I prayed again."

So they put the line back out into the river and went to the cabin. Before bedtime, they went down again. This time there were no fish.

"I knew there wouldn't be," said the child. "How did you know?" asked the father.

"Because," said the boy, "I didn't pray this time."

"And why didn't you?" asked his father.

"Because," said the boy, "I remembered that we forgot to bait the hooks."

—Robert E. Goodrich, Jr., *What's It All About* (Revell).

✣ ✣ ✣

In a little town in the French Pyrenees is a shrine celebrated for miracles of healing. One day shortly after World War II an amputee veteran appeared at the shrine. As he hobbled painfully along the way to the shrine, someone remarked: "That silly man! Does he think God will give him back his leg?"

The young veteran overheard the remarks and, turning, replied quietly: "Of course I do not expect God to give me back my leg. I am going to pray to God to help me live without it."

—*Forward.*

✣ ✣ ✣

Dr. John Sutherland Bonnell, as pastor of New York's Fifth Avenue Presbyterian Church, pioneered in pastoral psychiatry. Within every one of us, Dr. Bonnell believes, there is some spark of religious aspiration, even if we haven't been in church or prayed for many years. Many persons pray like children writing to Santa Claus, asking only for material blessings and failing to realize that their deepest needs are spiritual. There was the businessman who lost his customers and was praying desperately for new ones. Dr. Bonnell taught him, instead, to pray for courage to stand up to his problem and for the wisdom to overcome it. Step by step the new prayer was answered. The young woman who prayed merely for "lots of friends" was advised instead to pray and strive for the qualities which attract friends and the changed prayer was answered.

—Ray Giles, in *Christian Herald.*

✣ ✣ ✣

Lincoln's own favorite story among the many that circulated about him during his lifetime was about two Quakeresses discussing the Civil War leaders, Lincoln and Jefferson Davis.

"I think Jefferson will succeed," declared one.

"Why does thee think so?"

"Because Jefferson is a praying man."

"And so is Abraham a praying man."

"Yes, but," countered the first, "the Lord will think Abraham is joking."

—DIXON WECTER, *The Hero in America* (Scribners).

✣ ✣ ✣

My mother lived very close to God, and her example has influenced me greatly. When we asked her advice about anything, she would say, "I must ask God first." And we could not hurry her. Asking God was not a matter of spending five minutes to ask Him to bless her child and grant the request. It meant waiting upon God until she felt his leading. Whenever Mother prayed and trusted God for her decision, the undertaking invariably turned out well.

One day during World War II, I was talking with Mother about the imminent Japanese menace, and I suddenly cried out: "Mother, you're so powerful in prayer, why don't you pray that God will annihilate Japan—by an earthquake or something?"

Looking at me gravely, she said: "When you pray, or expect me to pray, don't insult God's intelligence by asking Him to do something which would be unworthy even of you, a mortal!"

—MADAME CHIANG KAI-SHEK in *The United States News.*

✣ ✣ ✣

A British soldier one night was caught creeping stealthily back to his quarters from the nearby woods. He was taken before his commanding officer and charged with holding communications with the enemy. The man pleaded that he had gone into the woods to pray by himself. That was his only defense.

"Have you been in the habit of spending hours in private prayer?" the officer asked.

"Yes, sir!"

"Then, down on your knees and pray now!" he roared. "You never needed it so much!"

Expecting immediate death, the soldier knelt and poured out his soul in prayer that for eloquence could have been inspired only by divine power.

"You may go," said the officer simply, when he had finished.

"I believe your story. If you hadn't drilled often, you could not do so well at review."

—*Gospel Herald.*

✤ ✤ ✤

He asked for strength that he might achieve; he was made weak that he might obey.

He asked for health that he might do greater things; he was given infirmity that he might do better things.

He asked for riches that he might be happy; he was given poverty that he might be wise.

He asked for power that he might have the praise of men; he was given weakness that he might feel the need of God.

He asked for all things that he might enjoy life; he was given life that he might enjoy all things.

✤ ✤ ✤

He-man Connie Mack told me that he couldn't go to sleep without saying his prayers. He-man Eddie Rickenbacker told me that he believed his life had been saved by prayer; he prays every day. He-man Edward R. Stettinius, former high official of General Motors and United States Steel, and former Secretary of State, told me that he prayed for wisdom and guidance every morning and every night.

These he-men discovered the truth of William James' statement: "We and God have business with each other; and in opening ourselves to His influence, our deepest destiny is fulfilled."

—Dale Carnegie, *Christian Herald.*

✤ ✤ ✤

George Adam Smith tells us that he was once climbing the Weisshorn above the Zermatt valley with two guides on a stormy day. They had made the ascent on the sheltered side. Reaching the top, and exhilarated by the thought of the view before him, Smith sprang to the top of a peak—and was almost blown away by the gale. The guide caught hold of him and pulled him down saying, "On your knees, sir! You are safe here only on your knees."

—J. W. Roberts, *The Christian World.*

Dr. Rufus Jones, the great Quaker leader, once spoke on the importance of a radiant countenance. After the services a plain little woman asked, "What would you do if you had a face like mine?"

Without a moment's hesitation Rufus Jones replied: "I'd pray. If you light it up from within, any old face is good enough!"

✤ ✤ ✤

A Scottish laborer went to work for a wealthy farmer. It was regarded as something of a favor to be employed by him, as he was a prompt and liberal paymaster, and was regarded by his neighbors as a very superior farmer. The Scotsman remained with him only a few days.

"I'm told you've left Farmer McAndrew," said a neighbor.

"Yes, I have," was the reply.

"Was the work too hard?"

"There was nothing to complain of on that score."

"What then? Were the wages too low?"

"No."

"Then why did you leave?"

"There was no roof on the house!"

And he went on his way, leaving his questioner to ponder on the strange answer he had given.

The Scotsman's meaning may be found in the saying of an old writer, who affirms that a dwelling in which prayer is not offered to God daily is like a house without a roof, in which there can be no peace, shelter, or comfort.

✤ ✤ ✤

PREACHERS—Preaching

The young preacher thrilled his congregation with his first sermon—a challenge to "gird their loins" for Christian service and living. Then, to their dismay, he preached the same sermon the following Sunday. When he confronted them with the same ringing message on the third Sunday, his flock felt something must be done.

"Don't you have more than just one sermon?" blurted a spokesman to the pastor.

"Oh, yes," he answered quietly. "I have quite a number of sermons. But you haven't *done anything* about the first one yet!"

—W. W. Reid, *Arkansas Methodist.*

✣ ✣ ✣

A sexton cleaning up the pulpit after Sunday service took a peek at the preacher's manuscript. Along the left margin were instructions such as "Pause here," "Wipe brow here," "Use angry fist gesture," "Look upward." Near the end was a long paragraph of texts, opposite which the preacher had marked in capital letters: "ARGUMENT WEAK HERE. YELL LIKE HELL!"

—Alex F. Osborn.

✣ ✣ ✣

A dear woman was weeping copiously as she parted with her pastor of several years.

"Now, now," said the pastor, consolingly, "don't cry. The bishop is sending you a good pastor, a much better one this time."

The woman continued to wail, "That's what they told me the last time."

—Robert Griffith, *Pastor.*

✣ ✣ ✣

The pastor had just been telling his visiting grandchildren a most fascinating bedtime story. The little ones listened to him breathlessly, but when the tale was finally ended, Johnny took a deep breath and asked, "Grandpa, was that really a true story, or were you just preaching?"

✣ ✣ ✣

A clergyman who was visiting a church apologized profusely after the service for the shortness of his sermon.

"You see," he explained to several church elders, "when I got into the pulpit I discovered that my dog had eaten several pages of my address."

"Well, sir," said one of the churchmen, "all I can say is that you would be doing us a tremendous favor if you'd send our parson a pup."

PRECISION

The late Vladimir de Pachmann, most capricious of pianists, always fussed over his piano stool in full view of the audience. On one occasion, he fiddled and fumed and called for something to sit on. When a thick book was handed him, he tried it, shook his head. Then he carefully tore off a single page, tried it again, and smiled happily as he began his first number.

—JOHN SHELBY, in *Cue*.

✣ ✣ ✣

PREJUDICE

When the Peruvian llama takes a dislike to the person riding it, it stops dead in its tracks, twists its head round, and ejects with considerable force and excellent aim a portion of its acrid saliva. A llama at the London Zoo developed a strong objection to top hats, and whenever one got within spitting distance the unfortunate owner received a charge of malodorous saliva, delivered with the force of a garden syringe, full on his offending headgear.

—FRANK W. LANE, *Nature Parade* (Jarrolds).

✣ ✣ ✣

During a discussion about contemporary English writers, Irvin Cobb asked Oliver Herford his opinion of Arnold Bennett.

"To tell you the truth, Irvin," said Herford, "something I wrote once, in a critical way, concerning Arnold Bennett so prejudiced me against the man that I never could bear to read a word he wrote."

—ELISABETH COBB, *My Wayward Parent* (Bobbs-Merrill).

✣ ✣ ✣

PREPAREDNESS

The circular parks interrupting all the main streets in Washington, D. C., which often annoy tourists, are actually part of the city's defense system. The French engineer who designed Washington, Pierre Charles L'Enfant, originated the idea after watching the mobs of the French Revolution tear unhindered through Paris. He planned Washington's circles so that cannon placed in them would block entry to the city from any direction.

—SIGRID ARNE, in A.P. feature.

✤ ✤ ✤

Mrs. Blossom of our Bridal Salon has a rather baffling case. Seems a pretty girl came in some time ago and had Mrs. B. help her choose one of Saks' best Lohengrin get-ups—shell pink satin embroidered with little pearl wedding rings. The girl paid for it, asked to have it held, and now she writes Mrs. B. cheery little notes every few months, saying: "Haven't found a man yet, but hope to make it by June."

—From an advertisement of Saks-Fifth Avenue.

✤ ✤ ✤

Some years ago a tourist was traveling along the shores of Lake Como in Northern Italy. When he reached the castle, Villa Asconati, a friendly old gardener opened the gate and showed him the grounds, which the old man kept in perfect order. The tourist asked when the owner of the castle had last been there.

"Twelve years ago."

"Does he ever write to you?"

"No."

"From whom do you get your instructions?"

"From his agent in Milan."

"Does he come?"

"Never."

"Who, then, comes here?"

"I am almost always alone; only once in a while a tourist comes."

"But you keep this garden in such fine condition just as though you expected your master to come tomorrow."

The old gardener promptly replied: "Today, sir, today!"

—F. T. RUHLAND, *Walther League Messenger*.

✤ ✤ ✤

A farmer, interviewing a hired man, asked his faults. "Well," the man answered, "the last fellow I worked for said I was awful hard to wake up during a bad wind storm at night."

The farmer hired him, but a few weeks later had reason to remember the man's statement. A heavy wind storm hit the area and the farmer woke instantly and went to waken the hired hand so they could check on stock and equipment. But the man would not wake up. Finally the farmer went out alone. To his amazement he found the barn doors securely fastened. The hay stack was tightly anchored with a heavy tarpaulin. The lumber pile had heavy stones on top.

A great light dawned on the farmer. He now knew why his hired man slept soundly while the wind blew hard at night.

—*K.V.P. Philosopher.*

✣ ✣ ✣

While walking in the country one summer morning when I was a young man, I learned what it means to use—*really to use*—the magic gift of sight. Attracted by a marvelous mist of fragrance borne by the breeze, I left the road and discovered nearby a wondrous garden.

In the path leading from a little house in the midst of the flowers stood an old and very tiny woman; I knew instinctively that she was the creator of this incredible garden. "This is a wonderful place you have," I called to her.

"Do you like flowers?" she answered. "Then do come in—"

She told me the history of each flower. Some had been brought by merchant-adventurers from the Indies, Mexico, Persia and Syria in the 16th century. In like manner the tulip came from Constantinople; later arrived the pansy, sweet pea, and Indian pink. I thought, as I listened, that I had never really seen a flower before. So luminously did she describe them that had it been blackest night I would have seen them clearly.

"Notice that hooked spur of the columbine," she said. "No bee can reach in to drain it except the bumblebee. Over there is the campanula, my favorite among the tall plants; its flowers are so fine in texture that if you hold one close to your eyes it seems transparent. And see the leaves of the flax—they're shaped like little lances."

Marveling, I asked her how she knew her myriad flowers in such precise detail. "I learned to use my eyes each day as if, the next morning, I would no longer be able to see," she said. "Then I found that nothing I had seen could ever be taken from me."

Many years have passed, but I have remembered her words. I could not easily forget them, if only because of that last moment when smiling, she lifted her head to say good-bye and I saw the cataracts in her sightless eyes.

She had used them well, before the dark morning came.

—MAURICE MAETERLINCK.

✤ ✤ ✤

Even as a young officer in Panama, President Eisenhower was preparing himself for future events. One hot afternoon he remarked to a friend: "It's very quiet here now, and I've been thinking I should go into the hospital to have my appendix out."

"Has it been bothering you?" the friend asked.

"Oh, no," Eisenhower replied. "But it might rear up and put me out of action sometime when things aren't so quiet."

—DEMAREE BESS in *The Saturday Evening Post.*

✤ ✤ ✤

In 1908 Lord Northcliffe took over the London *Times*. One evening, as he was leaving the building, he almost collided with a little man with a satchel. The little man moved quickly along the main floor corridor, stopped in front of an unlabeled door, took a latchkey out of his pocket and let himself in. Northcliffe followed him into the room which turned out to be a bedroom complete with old-fashioned washstand and shaving kit. The little man was putting food beside a gas plate in the corner.

"Who are you?" asked Northcliffe.

"I am Shorter from Coutts Bank."

"And what are you doing here?"

"Well, sir, I go into the bank at closing time Saturday, they give me the satchel and I walk over here. I stay until 9:30 Monday morning and then I go back to the bank. I've been coming for 23 years."

"And what's in the satchel?"

"Gold coin. You may look, sir." And Northcliffe looked at about 25 pounds weight of gold—roughly a thousand pounds sterling.

Lord Northcliffe called the bank and discovered that other

little men with satchels had been occupying that room over weekends for nearly 100 years. They told him the reason:

The battle of Waterloo was fought on June 18, 1815—a Sunday—and the enterprising editor of *The Times* thought he should get a man over to cover it. Plenty of sloops were available, but all the banks were closed and he couldn't raise enough money to finance the expedition. So the next day he made an arrangement with Coutts Bank whereby whenever the bank was closed, a man with a thousand pounds would be available at the Times Building. By the time private vaults became commonplace, the deal with the Coutts Bank was forgotten. But the little man with the satchel continued his vigil.

—Adapted from ROBERT J. CASEY, *Such Interesting People* (Bobbs-Merrill).

✣ ✣ ✣

In the old days when a certain Dr. Bancroft practiced medicine at Evergreen, Colo. in the Rockies, his patients often came a long distance under great difficulties. One of them, a cowhand, arrived one day, unconscious, slung across the saddle horn of his buddy.

"His horse throwed him on a rock," the rider said, "and then fell on him. His leg's all smashed to hell."

The doctor took a look and got ready to amputate, while the friend sat and sweated.

"Doc," the friend said at last in a voice hoarse with emotion, "if this man dies, you go with him." Bancroft turned to see him placing a .45 gently on a little table at his elbow.

The doctor regarded it for a moment over his glasses and then left the room. He returned with a tray of instruments. Among them was a six-gun of his own. "My friend," he said, patting it, "if this man is going to die, I'll know it five seconds before you do"; and proceeded to operate—successfully.

—WALTER B. PITKIN.

✣ ✣ ✣

The closest call Carl Akeley ever had came high in the bamboos on Mount Kenya, where he had gone to make photographic studies of the elephants' habitat. "Suddenly," he wrote, "I was conscious that an elephant was almost on top of me. My next mental record is of a tusk right at my chest. I grabbed it with my left hand, the other tusk with my right hand, and swinging in between them went to the ground on my back. The action was purely automatic—the result, many a time on the trails, of imagining myself caught by an elephant's rush and of planning what I would do.

"The elephant drove his tusks into the ground on either side of me, with his curled-up trunk against my chest. As I looked into one wicked little eye above me I knew I could expect no mercy. I heard a wheezy grunt as he plunged down and then—oblivion.

"Of course, I should have been crushed as thin as a wafer if his big tusks had not struck something in the ground that stopped them. Apparently he thought me dead, for he left me and charged after the boys, who had scattered like a covey of quail.

"I firmly believe that my imaginings saved my life. If a man imagines and plans what he would do in a crisis he will, I am convinced, when the occasion occurs, automatically do what he planned."

—Mary L. Jobe Akeley, *The Wilderness Lives Again* (Dodd, Mead).

✣ ✣ ✣

"Does it *always* look as neat as this?" asked the overawed city visitor of a Vermont housewife.

"Yes, indeed," firmly replied the Vermont matron, glancing around her spotless kitchen. "I never go to bed without leaving my house in dying condition."

—Gladys C. Britten, in "Life in These United States."

✣ ✣ ✣

When new port facilities were inaugurated at Aarhus, Denmark, King Christian X honored the occasion with his presence. All along the route of the royal car, school children waved banners and kerchiefs and shouted loudly. The sidewalks were swarming with them.

"My goodness," the King cried in wonder, "where do all these children come from?"

"Your Majesty," said the Mayor humbly, "we have been preparing for this great day for many years."

—*New York Times.*

✤ ✤ ✤

PRESTIGE

"No," said the wealthy Baron Rothschild to a man who wanted to borrow money from him. "But this I will do for you. I will walk arm in arm with you across the floor of the Exchange."

✤ ✤ ✤

PRETENSE

A delegation from Kansas, calling upon Theodore Roosevelt at Oyster Bay, was met by the President with coat and collar off. "Ah, gentlemen," he said, mopping his brow, "I'm delighted to see you, but I'm very busy putting in my hay just now. Come down to the barn and we'll talk things over while I work."

When then reached the barn, there was no hay waiting to be thrown into the mow. "James!" shouted the President to his hired man in the loft. "Where's that hay?"

"I'm sorry, sir," admitted James, "but I just ain't had time to throw it back since you forked it up for yesterday's delegation."

—*Christian Science Monitor.*

✤ ✤ ✤

PROCRASTINATION

A boy scout troop was being used as "guinea pigs" in a civil defense test in a Western city. The mock air raid was staged and the scouts impersonated wounded persons who were to be picked up and cared for by members of the defense organization.

One scout was supposed to be on the ground and await his rescuers, but the first aid people got behind schedule with their work and the scout lay "wounded" for several hours.

When the first aid men finally arrived on the spot where the casualty was supposed to be, they found nothing but a penciled note:

"Have bled to death and gone home."

An automobile mechanic with a sense of humor used to tell his prospects: "Well, sir, I can reline your brakes today for $22.85 (or whatever the price was), or I can do the job tomorrow for you for $122.85."

Very frequently the customer would "blow his top" and ask how come. To which the obvious answer was: "By tomorrow you may also need a front bumper and radiator grill."

—Ed Packer, *Automotive Service Digest.*

✣ ✣ ✣

Doing nothing about duty or opportunity is doing something: indecision is decision—the wrong way.

No man ever said, "I will be an ignoramus." He just looked at the books he ought to read and said, "I will read them—some other time."

No man ever said, "I will go to the devil." He just said, "Moral standards? Christian principles? I will attend to them all—some other time."

—*The Church Herald.*

✣ ✣ ✣

PROFANITY

It was with a troubled conscience that the young divinity student confessed to the bishop he had used profanity.

"You see, it was like this," he explained. "It was the big game, the ball had been passed to me . . . a long pass . . . and I caught it right under my arm. There were only two men between me and the goal line. I dodged one and interference handled the other. Within two yards of the goal post I looked down and the ball wasn't under my arm. It just simply wasn't there, Father. Before I realized, I heard myself saying: "Where the hell's that ball?"

Cried the Bishop impatiently: "Well, where the hell was it, boy?"

—*Super Service Station.*

✣ ✣ ✣

When I was about twelve years old, I reached the place where I felt that profanity would add a manly flavor to my conversation. My father, with an insight which would have done credit to Solomon, did not scold or threaten but said something which has kept me from using profanity ever since.

"When you feel that some particular bit of profanity would pep up your conversation," he said, "mentally substitute an ordinary word such as 'chair' or 'house' in the sentence and see how ridiculous it sounds. That is precisely how profanity sounds to someone else."

To this day, when I say to myself, "Chair, chair, it's hotter than house," the words I planned to use stay unsaid.

—Robert C. Hickle, *Better Homes and Gardens.*

✤ ✤ ✤

The first and second grade boys were using pretty naughty language on the playground. Finally the superintendent called them together and said he would not tolerate the use of swear words or dirty words. "Now," he concluded, "do you all know what I mean?" One little fellow replied: "Yes, you don't want us to talk like our daddies do at home."

—Gordon Gammack, *Des Moines Register.*

✤ ✤ ✤

A certain parson in the Australian bush country took exception to the contention that bullocks cannot be successfully driven without blasphemy.

Challenged to prove his case, the parson cracked his whip, cleared his throat, and in roaring tones addressed the animals: "You rapturous archangels! You sublimated cherubims! You sanctified innocents! Get ye up and hence!"

The bullocks slowly gathered themselves together and moved off!

—*Capper's Weekly.*

✤ ✤ ✤

Supreme Court Justice Stone went golfing with a distinguished Washington bishop, who missed four straight shots in a bunker without saying a single word. Justice Stone watched him with some amusement and remarked, "Bishop, that is the most profane silence I ever heard."

—Bennett Cerf, *Saturday Review.*

PROGRESS

Once upon a time there was a man who thought that it would be better for him to creep on all fours rather than to walk. After all, he argued, man has four limbs like the animals, so why not use all four. He decided to try and he not only succeeded in creeping fast but even, through intensive training, to creep twice as fast as he did at the beginning. This proved to him that his theory was right, and he could already, through a simple arithmetical calculation, foresee the moment when he would run on all fours, as fast as a hare. He was so occupied with his training and planning that at first he did not notice that the men who still walked on two legs were advancing much faster than he, and this in spite of the progress he had actually been making and was so proud of. He was compelled to realize that he was not, as he had thought, a forerunner, but that he was lagging considerably behind.

—Gunnar D. Kumlien, *Commonweal.*

✣ ✣ ✣

Legend has it that the change-over from silk to paper was not as "smooth as silk." The silk makers were understandably hostile. A big chunk of their business was going the way of the horse and buggy in our own time. Feeling ran so strong that save for some skullduggery on the part of T'sai Lun, the inventor, we might still be writing on silk or bark or bamboo.

The wily T'sai said it was evident this was either an invention inspired by the gods or by the devils. If by the devils, it ought to be forgotten. If by the gods, who would dare oppose?

He offered a test. He would take some poison, a fatal dose. Two days after burial, he would be dug up. If still dead, there would be no doubt about it, the invention was of the devils. If alive, paper was on the side of the gods.

The silk makers agreed. T'sai Lun took the poison. He was buried. Two days later they exhumed him. "Kinda dark down there," says T'sai when they got the lid off. "Cold, too. How about a spot of tea?"

It was later suspected, to be sure, that somebody had swapped arsenic for aspirin, and that somebody else had contrived to work a long hollow bamboo tube from the open air down into the casket, but these are doubtless rumors spread by the disgruntled silk makers. Anyway, T'sai Lun's invention prevailed.

—*K.V.P. Philosopher.*

✣ ✣ ✣

Old Spaeth kept up a lifetime's interest in Princeton crew affairs. When he retired, someone said to him: "Rowing must mean more to you than mere exercise. It must have some symbolic meaning. What is it?"

Answered he: "Yes, I had rather be a member of a society of eight men facing backward and going forward than a member of a crowd facing forward and going nowhere."

—GOODWIN B. BEACH, *Education.*

✣ ✣ ✣

A young soldier carried the flag far ahead of the rest of the regiment and placed it near the enemy lines. The captain cried: "Bring back that flag, you fool!" But the soldier said: "Never! You bring up the regiment!" When the regiment of soldiers finally arrived at the place where he was under heavy shell fire, they found him dead, but the flag was flying triumphantly in the breeze.

—*Pulpit Digest.*

✣ ✣ ✣

Recently a trade journal in the leather industry carried a feature story of a veteran who had spent half a century in the employ of one of the large processing houses.

"Well," commented a reporter, "in your time you must have seen some vast changes in this business."

"Yes," agreed the old man meditatively, "yes, I have. In the old days, I used to have to go down in the cellar and carry the leather up three flights of stairs. But now," he brightened, "they bring it up to me."

—CLINTON CAMPBELL.

PROGRESS—Prejudice

When Edison announced his first public exhibition of the electric light, the story got into the *New York Herald* before it was seen by the managing editor. When he did see the item, he rushed in wrath to the city room. Pushing the paper under the nose of the city editor, he shouted: "How did that get into the paper? Light strung on wires, indeed! You have made a laughing stock of the *Herald!* Oh, what will Mr. Bennett say?"

—*Wright Line.*

✣ ✣ ✣

PROTOCOL

When I, with four other Americans, was received in audience by the late Pope Pius XI, the Rome correspondent for the United Press instructed us in Vatican protocol—which, in the matter of apparel, is rigorous. The men wear full dress suits with black waistcoats; the ladies wear a covering for the head, a high-neck dress and long sleeves. The United Press man, himself a devout Catholic, remarked when he saw us properly attired: "I've always believed it would be much easier and less expensive just to blindfold the Pope."

—STANLEY HIGH, *Simpson Sphere.*

✣ ✣ ✣

PSYCHOLOGY

One day while mailing routine advertising brochures, an enterprising secretary decided to see what would happen if she sent out several hundred envelopes completely empty. Next day the phones began jangling as customers who ordinarily would have discarded the advertising matter without a glance called to find out what had been forgotten. The secretary was quick to seize this opportunity to give detailed information, create interest—and take orders.

—MRS. D. E. WINDEN, *Rotarian.*

A New York City bus driver learned how to disperse passengers who insisted on crowding to the front of his vehicle. He simply yelled, "All intelligent people please step to the rear!"

—*This Week.*

✣ ✣ ✣

PUBLIC RELATIONS

A man had been badly bitten by bugs while a passenger on a railway sleeping car. Indignantly, he wrote to the railway company to complain about the situation.

Back came a prompt reply from the public relations office. Soothingly, they explained: "It was the very first complaint that the company had ever received about such a matter. Inquiry had failed to reveal any explanation for the most unprecedented occurrence. Nevertheless, the stringent precautions taken in the past would be redoubled in the future."

He felt much better after he had read the letter—until he noticed a small slip of paper which had fallen out of the envelope. On it was this notation: "Send this guy the bug letter."

✣ ✣ ✣

PUNCTUALITY

On a day memorable to me, I boarded a tiny tugboat that I used often in crossing a southern river and saw that we had a new Negro engineer. He sat in the doorway of the engine room reading the Bible: he was fat, squat and black, but immaculate and in his eyes was the splendor of ancient wisdom and peace with the world.

As I paused to talk with him I noticed that the characteristic odors that had always emanated from the engine room were no longer there. And the engine! It gleamed and shone; from beneath its seat all the bilgewater was gone. Instead of grime and filth and stench I found beauty and order. When I asked the engineer how in the world he had managed to clean up the old room and the old engine he answered in words that would go far toward solving life's main problems for many people.

"Captain," he said, nodding fondly in the direction of the engine, "it's just this way: I got a glory."

Making that engine the best on the river was his glory in life, and having a glory he had everything. The only sure way out of suffering that I know is to find a glory, and to give to it the strength we might otherwise spend in despair.

—ARCHIBALD RUTLEDGE, *It Will be Daybreak Soon* (Revell).

✤ ✤ ✤

As a child I was slow to respond when my mother called me from play or reading. I would answer, "In a minute"—but the "minute" usually lengthened into many more.

One day my mother hung upon the wall a clock-face made of cardboard. It had but one hand, which she set at 12 o'clock. Then she explained that for every minute I was late in coming when called, the hand would be moved forward that much. In the evening, the total would be subtracted from my day, thus making it necessary for me to go to bed earlier.

After having to leave the family circle and retire soon after dinner a few evenings, the words "in a minute" were dropped from my vocabulary. I had learned the lesson of promptness.

—ELLEN PUTNAM.

✤ ✤ ✤

QUALITY

An American traveler in Italy stood watching a lumberman at work. As the logs floated down a swift mountain stream, the man jabbed his sharp hook into an occasional one and drew it carefully aside.

"Why do you pick out these few?" inquired the onlooker. "They all look alike."

"But they are not alike," answered the lumberman. "The logs I let pass have grown on the side of a mountain, where they have been protected all their lives. Their grain is coarse; they are good only for lumber. But these few logs, sir, grew on the very top of the mountain. From the time they were mere sprouts and saplings they were lashed and buffeted by the winds and so they grew strong with fine grain. They are not just ordinary lumber. Those few we save for choice work."

✣ ✣ ✣

Quality may accompany quantity, but it need not.

"I could eat you at a mouthful," roared a brawny opponent to the small and sickly Alexander H. Stephens. But Stephens did not react as the bully expected him to do.

"If you did," replied Stephens quietly but clearly, "you'd have more brains in your belly than you ever had in your head."

✣ ✣ ✣

RACE RELATIONS

In St. Joseph, Missouri, a minister and a student from India were waiting for a train which would take the young student to California where he would board a ship for his native land. Since the train wasn't due for fifty minutes, they decided to get their lunch in a nearby restaurant.

After sitting at a table for nearly ten minutes without being served, the minister became concerned that they might not have enough time to eat before train-time. He called over the manager and asked to have their order taken.

The manager said, looking at the young colored student, "Don't you know we can't serve you because of him?"

The minister stood up and in a clear voice addressed the people sitting in the restaurant:

"This young man came all the way from India to study American democracy. He spent one year here, and now on the eve of his return home, you have given him another lesson in democracy. Even though we are hungry, we will have to leave."

They walked out of the restaurant and headed for the train station. Behind them the dining room became empty as all the other patrons walked out, too.

—*Work.*

✣ ✣ ✣

Seven years ago, while I was on tour, I stopped in a prejudice-filled town and brought a wrist-watch into a jeweler's to be repaired. The jeweler eyed me with cold contempt. "I don't work for your kind," he snapped.

Last year my tour brought me to the same place. I feared some repetition of humiliation, but after my concert a group of autograph-hunters approached me. While signing the autographs, I noticed a man watching me. "You don't know me," he said at length, "but I'm the man who once refused to fix your watch. I'm here to apologize." We talked. He confided that he'd been tortured for years by the hate in him, until he learned that hate becomes self-hatred.

—BILLY ECKSTINE, in *Guideposts.*

✤ ✤ ✤

A friend of mine got tired of hearing a certain man say, "Isn't that just like a Jew?" Now he always asks, "Which Jew do you mean—Shylock or Jesus Christ?"

—JOHN G. SIMONS.

✤ ✤ ✤

REALISM

An elderly woman was shopping for a hat and the salesgirl kept showing her new types of headgear which didn't suit the old lady at all. Finally she said, "Listen, I wear a corset and I wear drawers, and I want a hat to match."

—CEDRIC ADAMS, in *Minneapolis Tribune.*

✤ ✤ ✤

When Calvin Coolidge was in the Massachusetts legislature another member in session asked him whether the people where he came from said, "A hen lays, or a hen lies."

"The people where I come from," Mr. Coolidge replied, "lift her up to see."

—WILLIAM LYON PHELPS in *The Rotarian.*

✤ ✤ ✤

George Bernard Shaw's extraordinary correspondence with Ellen Terry in the early nineties, were love letters to a woman he had seen but never met. He merely knew her by heart. In the explanatory preface written by Shaw himself when the correspondence was published years after Ellen Terry's final exit, there was one sentence which I copied out:

Let those who may complain that it was all on paper remember that only on paper has humanity yet achieved beauty, truth, knowledge, virtue, and abiding love.

I sent that sentence as my wedding present to furnish the house of two young people who would have no house at all—two loving young people, with the sundering sea already between them and never a hope of seeing each other until the war was over. It would, I thought, be as useful as a silver teapot, say, and last much longer.

—ALEXANDER WOOLLCOTT.

✣ ✣ ✣

The teacher whose pupils will remember him and his lessons the rest of their lives is always somewhat of a showman. During a journalism class at the University of Missouri, a student suddenly rose, pulled a revolver from his pocket, and shouted at the instructor, Professor Roscoe Ellard: "You can't do that to me!" Thereupon he fired, and Dr. Ellard slumped down behind the lecture stand. Then an assistant went to the blackboard and wrote: "Describe in complete detail the murder which has just occurred."

—GEORGE KENT.

✣ ✣ ✣

Nehru is not a messiah, like Gandhi. Any messianic feeling would have been quickly scotched by his wife and daughter, who took to calling him around the home by the names the people used: "O Jewel of India, what time is it?" or "O Embodiment of Sacrifice, please pass the bread."

—JOHN AND FRANCES GUNTHER, in *Life*.

✣ ✣ ✣

John Ford is as ingenious as anyone in Hollywood at tricking his actors into giving realistic performances. The high point of *The Informer* was the court-martial scene in which Victor McLaglen breaks down under the merciless questioning of his accusers. Ford approached this scene with misgivings. Was McLaglen artist enough to convey the swift dissolution of a human soul? The night before the scene was to be shot, Ford told McLaglen not to spend much time learning his lines, because only a few simple scenes would be run through, without dialogue. But Ford instructed all the other members of the cast to be letter perfect.

Next morning, Ford announced that the head office wanted the court-martial scene done at once. "But don't worry," he reassured McLaglen, "Go out there and ad lib when you get stuck."

The cameras clicked; the precise, deadly questions of his accusers began to weave about McLaglen the network of his guilt. When he tried to answer, the panic he was supposed to portray became inextricably mixed with the genuine confusion of an actor who did not know his lines. In the middle of the scene he blew up completely, and gave a performance unequaled for the reality of its helpless terror and tortuous embarrassment.

Indeed Ford will go to almost any length to get a realistic result. In *Hurricane,* Jon Hall, the hero, makes a thrilling attempt to escape from prison camp, diving into the ocean as guards open fire across him. Before the scene was shot, Ford told Hall: "You've got to make the audience believe you're swimming for your life."

"I'll do it," answered Hall.

"I *know* you will," said Ford.

When Hall plunged in and started swimming for liberty, a rifle bullet suddenly smacked the water in front of him. Another sang viciously past his ear. He dove, stayed under as long as he could, came up with his lungs bursting. "Plop" went another bullet in front of him. Then a volley whipped the water round him into a froth. The look of fear and despair which the cameras caught upon his face was the real thing. For the usual extras with blank cartridges, Ford had quietly substituted loaded rifles in the hands of sharpshooters.

—J. P. McEvoy, *The Baltimore Sunday Sun.*

✤ ✤ ✤

Donatello, Italian sculptor, was sought by his native city of Florence to create a masterpiece that would fitly represent the spirit of Italy. He accepted the challenge, and after many days completed the work. The people of Florence, wishing the creation to be above criticism, asked the greatest of all sculptors, Michelangelo, to inspect the work and offer criticism.

It was a gala day in Florence when Michelangelo came. Throngs of people lined the streets as the famous artist passed along on his way to the cathedral where the work of Donatello stood. As he mounted the inspection scaffold men and women held their breath in an agony of suspense. The future history of art in Florence was at stake.

Slowly the curtain shielding the work of art was drawn, and there stood a marvel in marble, the like of which even Michelangelo had not seen before. It was the portrayal of the Italian army, man after man, artillery without end, every soldier's face drawn taut, every nerve a-tingle. Even the veins of the drummer boy's face stood out bold in cold, pure marble. The Italian marble army, tense and alert, was ready to march.

And the people of Florence stood tense and hopeful. What would Michelangelo say? Then suddenly, in the deathly stillness of the great cathedral, the great sculptor clicked his heels, saluted the marble slab, and gave the command, "Forward March!"

—EVERETT W. HILL, *Friendly Chats.*

✤ ✤ ✤

When Michelangelo had completed his painting on the ceiling of the Sistine Chapel in Rome, he made a careful examination of the supporting walls, and was alarmed to see that they were in danger of crumbling, thus destroying his work. He appealed to the authorities, asking them to construct a series of buttresses which would shore up the walls and make them safe. But the authorities paid no attention to his requests.

Nearly a year passed, and the artist became convinced that perseverance alone was not enough. He would have to figure out some supplementary method of persuasion.

During the next few days he had his ladders brought back into the building, presumably to "retouch" parts of the painting. Working at night, he painted cracks into the picture so realistic that when the building committee came to view the painting again, they were horrified at the result of their neglect. They immediately ordered the necessary brick reinforcements.

Anyone who has visited the Sistine Chapel will remember seeing the brick buttresses, and also the painted cracks, which are still there as a testimony to the painter's imagination.

—*Friendly Chats.*

✣ ✣ ✣

REALITY

A beautiful young girl dreamed that a sinister but handsome dark-haired man appeared at her bedside. Before she could protest, he yanked her from the satin covers and carried her away to a luxurious limousine waiting at the door. Hurling her into the back seat, he drove swiftly into the country, drawing up at last in a secluded, moon-flooded lane. The man turned and stared menacingly at the beautiful girl.

"What are you going to do now?" she asked quivering.

"How should I know?" he retorted. "It's your dream."

This was the story told by Lt. Col. Harold Hinton, public relations man for the army's European theater during World War II, when asked about a second front.

—*Newsweek.*

✣ ✣ ✣

On one occasion, when Cecil B. DeMille issued orders for the purchase of a large amount of royal brocade at $200 a yard, someone asked him, "How will the customers know if it's real brocade or a $2 substitute?"

DeMille smiled. "They won't know. But my actresses will. Can you imagine a woman wearing $3000 worth of brocade and not giving her best performance?"

—Frederick Van Ryn, in *Liberty.*

✣ ✣ ✣

RECOMPENSE

On a mountain road near Wooton, Kentucky, I met a big woman leading a tiny donkey loaded with rugs. "Did you make all those rugs?" I asked.

"Yes, I did, an' a heap more. Last year I wove a cow."

I followed her to the Community Center to learn the meaning of her amazing statement. There I saw the director examine the rugs and say to her, "Well, Molly, you've made some mighty pretty rugs. I'll take 20 of 'em. Now tell me what you've been hankering for while you've done all this work."

"Well, Mr. Deaton, I was a-hopin' I had wove a porker."

And a porker she got. She put it in a gunny sack, swung it up on the donkey's back, hoisted herself on board and rode off up the mountain trail.

"And what about the cow she says she wove?" I asked the director.

"Well, ma'am, the women up Wooton Creek come here for old cloth. They dip it in dyes they have made from berries and root juices, and then weave these rugs from patterns handed down for generations from their Scottish and Irish ancestors. Last year this woman made 45 rugs. She had her heart set on a cow, and she got a choice one. She was telling the truth when she said she 'wove a cow.' "

—ZYLPHA S. MORTON.

✤ ✤ ✤

RECREATION

Eisenhower has not been the first president-General to take an interest in golf. Nearly a century ago, U. S. Grant was introduced to the game in Scotland. To demonstrate what a fine, manly sport it was, Grant's host took him out on a nearby links, placed a leather-and-feather ball on the tee and took a mighty swipe at it. Turf and dust flew through the air. The ball remained implacably inert. Again the host swung mightily and again the turf flew, but not the ball.

Grant was fascinated. Finally he remarked, "Mmmmmmmmh. There does seem to be a fair amount of exercise in the game. But I fail to see the use of the ball."

—*Property.*

REFORM

Thomas Carlyle, the "great impatient" of the Victorian age, repudiated much of the Christian orthodoxy of his day and had some hard things to say of the Church and its preachers, even though the essential stuff of Scotland's Calvinism never ceased to smoulder, and sometimes to blaze, in his deepest being. Seated once with his aging mother by her fireside at Ecclefechan, and inveighing against the preachers of his day, he exclaimed: "If I had to preach, I would go into the pulpit and say no more than this: 'All you people know what you ought to do; well, go and do it.' " His mother continued knitting in silence, and then replied: "Aye, Tammas; and will ye tell them how?"

—John S. Whale, in *The Protestant Tradition* (Cambridge).

✤ ✤ ✤

A friend found John Dewey, the philosopher, standing with his small son who was ankle deep in a puddle of water. Dewey was looking perplexed. "John," said the friend, "you'd better get that boy out of that puddle or he'll catch cold."

"I know, I know," said Dewey, "but it won't do any good to *get* him out of the puddle. I've got to get him to *want* to get out out of the puddle, and I'm trying to figure out how."

—Milton Mayer, *Negro Digest.*

✤ ✤ ✤

RELATIVITY

At a party, the learned creator of the theory of relativity was asked by his hostess to explain it "in a few well-chosen words." Einstein told a story instead.

"I was once walking with a blind man," said the scientist, "and remarked that I would like a glass of milk."

"What is milk?" asked my friend.

"A white liquid."

"Liquid I know. What is white?"

"The color of a swan's feathers."

"Feathers I know. What is a swan?"

"A bird with a crooked neck."

"Neck I know. But what is crooked."

Einstein then explained that he took his friend's arm, straightened and then bent it to demonstrate what was crooked.

"Oh," said the blind man. "Now I know what you mean by milk."

"So," said Einstein to his hostess, "do you still want to know what relativity is?"

♣ ♣ ♣

RELAXATION

A man devoted so much to making money that he had a nervous breakdown. Finally, he arranged to visit a world-renowned psychiatrist daily. At the end of the month he received a bill for fifteen hundred dollars. On his next visit he paid it and remarked, "It was really worth it, doctor. I feel great."

"Yes," said the doctor, "lying relaxed on a couch for thirty minutes every day for a month often works wonders in such cases as yours."

—John A. Ferrall, *Volta Review.*

♣ ♣ ♣

RELIGION

This allegorical story comes to us out of the Middle Ages.

When Jesus returned to heaven at the end of his earthly sojourn, he was met at the gates of heaven by Gabriel, who welcomed him home, and who then asked, "Have you finished the work you set out on earth to do?"

"No," Jesus replied, "I didn't finish my work, but my Father had need of me, so I had to come home; but I have told my plans to Peter and James and John, and the other disciples, and have told them to tell others, and eventually the whole world will know and believe."

After a period of consideration, Gabriel again asked, "But what if Peter and James and John fail to pass the Word on, what alternate plans have you made?"

Without a moment's hesitation Jesus replied, "I have made no other plans; I am counting on men."

REPENTANCE

The picture "The Light of the World," painted by Holman Hunt, shows Christ in a garden at midnight. In His left hand He is holding a lantern and His right hand is knocking on a heavily paneled door.

When the painting was unveiled, an art critic remarked, "Mr. Hunt, you haven't finished your work. There is no handle on that door."

"That," said the artist, "is the door to the human heart—it can be opened only from the inside."

—FAIRFAX DOWNEY, *Disaster Fighters* (Putnam).

✤ ✤ ✤

RESPONSIBILITY

A king hired a blind man and a lame man to guard his fruit garden. One day the lame man sighted some fruit and told the blind man exactly where it was. Both men enjoyed the rare delicacy. When the king learned of the stolen fruit he summoned both men. The lame one denied taking it on the grounds that he could not walk. The blind one denied the theft on the grounds that he could not see. The king spoke to his guards, "Place the lame one on the blind man's shoulders." This done, he sentenced both as one.

—ARNOLD FINE, *American Hebrew*.

✤ ✤ ✤

A father had purchased a globe of the world for his small son. One night, during World War II, while the war news was being broadcast, the father decided he would get the globe and follow the movements being described by the news commentator. He went into the son's room on tiptoe, picked up the globe and started out. Just then the boy sat up in bed and asked, "Daddy, where are you going with my world?"

—REV. JOHN G. SIMMONS.

✤ ✤ ✤

A mother with four children in the Sunday School approached the pastor with bitter complaints about the conduct of the school. "I think they ought to get better teachers," she concluded.

"I quite agree with you," said the pastor. "And for the last two years I have been trying to persuade you and your husband to take posts in the church school. But you have refused to accept any responsibility. Do you really feel you have the right to come to me criticising the people who are doing their best, even if they are inefficient?"

—Roy L. Smith, *Christian Advocate.*

✤ ✤ ✤

RESOURCEFULNESS

A young Japanese compositor, employed by a Japanese paper in New York, was riding downtown in a subway one morning. Engrossed in his morning paper, he paid no attention to the other passengers. But an impertinent young fellow, sitting next to him, suddenly asked:

"What sort of 'nese' are you, anyway; a Chinese or a Japanese?"

The smart young Japanese was not caught napping. He retorted:

"What sort of a 'key' are you, anyway; a monkey, a donkey, or a Yankee?"

The young man suddenly decided the next stop was the one he wanted, as the chuckle of the other passengers was heard.

✤ ✤ ✤

D. A. J. McDonnell, chief surgeon of Roowoomba General Hospital in Queensland, Australia, read a longish telegram one day in 1910 and shook his head sadly. Sister Elizabeth Kenny, graduate nurse, working alone in the bush country 100 miles away, needed advice in treating four children striken by a strange disease whose symptoms she described. Dr. McDonnell scribbled a reply: INFANTILE PARALYSIS . . . NO KNOWN CURE . . . DO BEST YOU CAN.

A year later, young Elizabeth Kenny returned on leave from the lonely outlands where she served as visiting nurse, midwife, and counselor to the sparsely settled families. Dr. McDonnell inquired anxiously about the polio cases.

"There were two more—worse than the first lot," said the young nurse. "But all six are well now."

"Splendid!" said the doctor. "How badly are the children crippled?"

"Why they're not crippled! They're entirely normal."

Dr. McDonnell looked hard at Sister Kenny. Then took her telegram from a file.

"These read like severe cases—some of them already in the paralytic stage," he said. "Good heavens, nurse, such cases just don't recover as completely as that!"

"But they're all right," the nurse insisted.

"What did you do?" the surgeon demanded with mounting excitement.

"I used what I had—water, heat, blankets and my own hands," the nurse said. "The children recovered."

—LOIS MATTOX MILLER.

✣ ✣ ✣

A young servant lass was being considered for a situation at the farm when she was brusquely informed by the farmer that she would need to produce a reference from her previous employer.

The reference was not forthcoming by post and nothing more was heard from her. Some time later the farmer met her in the village and asked if she now had her "character."

"Ay," she replied, "—but I've gotten yours as weel—and I'm no comin'."

—*Scotland Laughing.*

✣ ✣ ✣

A missionary was captured by aborigines and condemned to death. To decide the manner of execution, it was the tribal custom that a victim must make an affirmative statement. If the high priest considered the statement true, the victim was shot with a poisoned arrow. If the statement was considered false, the victim died by fire. But the missionary, thinking fast, made a short statement so perplexing that it was impossible to carry out the execution.

Said the missionary: "I will die by fire." If the high priest decided that this statement was true, execution would have to take place by shooting. But that would make the statement false, and so the victim would have to be burned. But if he were burned, the statement would become true, thus prohibiting an execution reserved for liars.

—Harold Hart, *Invitation to Fun* (Stokes).

✣ ✣ ✣

At the close of a talk on King Hezekiah, a New York clergyman asked if there were any questions.

A lady rose. "I've never been clear," she said, "how old Hezekiah was."

The clergyman hesitated, then said, "Well, when? Hezekiah was different ages at different times, you know."

"Oh," said the lady, "I never thought of that," and contentedly sat down.

—Ethel Tilley.

✣ ✣ ✣

A traveler was telling of his experiences in Africa. "One day I landed among the wildest natives. The chief had me tied up, while others sharpened their knives and still others built a fire under the kettle."

"And how," asked one of the listeners (female), "did you get away?"

"Simple. I showed the chief my appendectomy scar and said, 'I'm not edible. The chief of the next tribe over tried not long ago, see?' "

—*Revue,* Munich (Droke House Translation).

✣ ✣ ✣

The prize for quick thinking is awarded to Juano Hernandez, who played the Lord in *Green Pastures* for "Theater Guild on the Air." When a fellow actor couldn't find his lines and froze, Hernandez came to the rescue.

"Son," he said reassuringly, "you is nervous before me and I can understand that. But I is de Lord, and I knows what is in your mind." Whereupon he supplied the missing lines.

—*This Week.*

One of Queen Victoria's grandchildren, Prince Alexander of Battenberg, was attending a boys' school in England in the 1890's when he ran short of funds. He applied to Grandmother for help. She properly rebuked him. Little boys, she wrote, should keep within their allowances and he must wait until his next one came.

The prince was resourceful and the Queen received this reply: "My Gear Grandmamma—I am sure you will be glad to know that I need not trouble you for any money just now, for I sold your letter to another boy here for thirty shillings."

—H. J. Haskell, *Kansas City Star*.

✤ ✤ ✤

It was one of those quiet hotels that cater to sedate, elderly people, and the desk clerk was profoundly shocked when a page boy trotted through the lobby whistling.

"See here, my boy," he admonished in a tense undertone. "You know that whistling on duty can cost you your job."

"But I wasn't whistling, sir," the boy whispered back. "I was just paging old Mrs. Vandersnort's dog."

—*Conveyor* (Australia).

✤ ✤ ✤

When a species of small crab inhabiting the Great Barrier Reef is hungry, it seizes an anemone and holds it aloft. The anemone waves its tentacles distractedly, and presently catches a tidbit. The crab promptly takes this away, eats it, and again brandishes the anemone until his hunger is satisfied.

—Frank W. Lane, in *Nature Parade* (Jarrolds).

✤ ✤ ✤

Two Chinese, Chung and Yung, arrived in the United States at about the same time, and set up restaurants side by side. Both did quite well, but each was troubled about the amount of business he was losing to the other.

At length, when the two competitors could endure the situation no longer, they met and discussed how they might operate their respective establishments in peace and contentment.

"You manage my restaurant," Chung finally suggested, "while I manage yours." The idea proved mutually agreeable;

each man took over the management of the other's business. After that, each was perfectly happy to see patrons enter the restaurant next door.

—*Wall Street Journal.*

♣ ♣ ♣

A little boy sat turning the pages of a travel magazine. "I wish," he mused, "I had the wings of an angel. I'd fly to the top of this mountain pictured here. It is beautiful." Then, after brief meditation he observed, "I haven't any wings. But I have feet and legs. I can climb to the top of a mountain with them! "

♣ ♣ ♣

For homework, I was required to make a drawing of a flight of stairs. I finished it, and just as I was putting away the ink, a blot dropped right in the middle of my picture. It was too late to draw another. I felt so discouraged I burst into tears.

My father, learning the trouble, said gently, "Don't worry—the ink blot looks just like a black patch on the side of a terrier—all you have to do is draw a dog around it. Don't get so easily discouraged, honey. Often it only needs a little grit and imagination to turn the bad into the good. Remember, few things are as hopeless as they may seem at first."

I sketched a dog around the ink blot. The next day my picture was voted the best in the class. "You see what a little imagination will do," the teacher said. "That little fox terrier just completes a good drawing."

When things look black or go wrong, I still remember my black-patched terrier, and can hear my father's encouraging words: "It only needs a little grit and imagination to turn the bad into the good."

—SUSAN COOPER.

♣ ♣ ♣

While visiting an Indian Reservation in New Mexico several years ago, I noticed an old Indian striding back and forth across a plowed field, his hand dipping into the grain sack at his side, and his arm swinging rhythmically as he apparently broadcast the seed in the time-honored fashion. But to my surprise, the sack was empty; no grain fell from his hand.

Mystified, I asked an Indian standing nearby what he was doing.

"Him fool crow," was the reply.

Then I noticed the large flock of crows following the sower, seeking the grain that wasn't there.

The old Indian continued this performance for three days at the beginning of the planting season every spring. Then, when the black robbers gave up and departed for more profitable fields, he sowed his grain without loss.

—J. M. Terrass.

✤ ✤ ✤

RETICENCE

Oliver Herford, humorist, disdained being used as an exhibition piece. A society woman, widely known as a collector of celebrities, once gave a large dinner party at which the guests of honor were Herford and a famous military man. Bulbous and beaming, the lady rose at the end of the meal and unexpectedly announced: "Mr. Oliver Herford will now improvise a poem in honor of the hostess."

Oliver seemed visibly to shrivel. "Oh, no," he murmured. "Have the general fire a cannon."

—Julian Street, *The Saturday Review.*

✤ ✤ ✤

REVENGE

Not so many years ago, George Bernard Shaw, poking fun at all things American, came out with some unusually caustic comments. A number of newspapers howled in protest, but one editor held his fire until Mr. Shaw paid his much publicized visit to Miami. This editor's paper published a lengthy report of the arrival of Mrs. George Bernard Shaw. Mrs. Shaw went to this dinner. Mrs. Shaw attended that function. Mrs. Shaw said this, and Mrs. Shaw did that. Then at the bottom of the long article was this casual afterthought:

"With Mrs. Shaw was her husband, George Bernard Shaw, a writer."

—*Christian Science Monitor.*

Joe Jackson is an enterprising young cashier in the bank of my home town. Joe supplements his income with part-time bookkeeping jobs in the evening, and one of his important clients happens to be the town's most disreputable tavern, Red-Neck Kelly's.

The local society queen, being unmarried and living alone, had little else to do than gossip, and she soon made it known she didn't quite approve of Joe's client. In fact she announced at one of her cocktail parties she'd seen Joe's car parked in front of Kelly's Bar every night recently. She sighed she wouldn't be surprised if Joe had also turned into a drunkard.

When Joe heard this remark he knew exactly what to do. The following night, and every night thereafter, he parked his car in front of the society girl's home, and walked home to bed.

—Bob Bowman, *True.*

✣ ✣ ✣

It happened one night in a port somewhere west of Suez.

British sailor tipsy. Goes in saloon. Meets three U. S. sailors. Limey slams U. S. Navy. Yankees buy him a drink. Limey slams U. S. Navy again. Yankees buy him another drink. Limey slams U. S. Navy third time. Yankees buy him third drink . . . buy him tenth drink.

Limey passes out. Yankees sympathetic. Take him back to ship. Stop en route at tattoo shop. Limey still out.

Limey comes to. U. S. battleship on chest. Also red, white and blue inscription, "God Bless America."

—*Yank.*

✣ ✣ ✣

Composer Edward MacDowell at one time owned a clever dog that was capable of learning many tricks. One day a composer friend, irritated by the dog's antics, kicked the animal viciously. MacDowell was enraged by this brutality, but said nothing to the offender.

A year later, he again invited that composer to a musicale, at which that composer's music was to be played exclusively. The man was flattered greatly at the prospect of having his music performed before such a distinguished gathering.

The moment the quartet started to play one of his compositions, his host's dog let out a dismal howl. From the beginning to the end of the concert, the animal's yowls echoed through the house. When the composer-guest finally departed, a humiliated man, MacDowell chuckled softly to himself. For one solid year he had played the composer's music to the dog and had taught her to howl when she heard it.

—W. E. Golden, *Your Life.*

✤ ✤ ✤

A peasant helped an old man carry a heavy burden. When their ways parted, the stranger said, "I am the Lord, and for your reward you shall receive whatever you ask for, but on condition that your worst enemy have double."

The peasant thought for a few seconds. "Lord," he said, "gouge out one of my eyes."

—Douglas Woodruff, *Tablet* (London).

✤ ✤ ✤

An employe of a Middle West blueprinting concern quarreled with its owner, M. W. Mills. After denouncing his employer, he quit the job and invested his savings in starting a competing firm, circulated false and bitter stories about his former boss. In competitive bids for public work the disgruntled man, by sacrificing his own profits, managed to cut heavily into Mills' business volume.

Fire struck the plant of Mills' competitor. Mills volunteered his own facilities, completed his "enemy's" contracts, generously offered to lend his rival money to rebuild the damaged plant.

An odd way to get even? Yes . . . But there is a sequel: The man who was out to wreck Mills is back on the Mills pay roll, its hardest worker, its biggest booster.

—Roger Baster, *Good Business.*

✤ ✤ ✤

In the fall of 1897 a traveler named Jones dined at La Junta and, spurning the steaks, demanded beans. Under the Harvey rule, he got beans, but was charged the price of the regular meal.

He protested that beans were worth only a dime, but the manager held out for six bits, the standard price of a meal. The customer went away sore and in a few hours the House got a collect wire and paid eighty-five cents to learn that Mr. Jones was still sore. Hours later it got another wire from San Francisco and paid two dollars and a quarter to learn Mr. Jones' sentiment. Several days later, it paid five dollars and sixty-seven cents to be apprised from Mexico City that: "I still think you charged me too much for those beans."

—JAMES MARSHALL, *Santa Fe, The Railroad That Built an Empire* (Random).

✣ ✣ ✣

One of those incredible, dreams-come-true things happened recently to a man we know. He was bowling along a highway when a prowl car with two cops in it hurtled through an intersection, passing a red light and almost smashing him. When the squeal of brakelinings had died down, one of the cops leaned out and said gruffly, "Go along."

"The hell I will," the citizen said, and continued firmly, "pull over to the curb, you!" He had to repeat the command before the cops finally obeyed. The man then got out of his car, put his foot on the running board of the prowl car, and gave the cops a little lecture. "Now I know you men weren't on an emergency call, because your siren wasn't on," he said. "I don't ask to see your license and identification, because you look dumb enough to be real cops."

At this point, one of the cops feebly asked: "Who are you?"

"Never mind who I am. Right now I'm just a citizen," the man replied. Then he turned to the man who wasn't driving and said, "Write your friend a ticket." He stayed until the cop hauled out a pencil and pad, then got in his car and drove off, pausing only to yell, "And see that it doesn't happen again!"

There's still some happiness to be found in this world.

—*The New Yorker.*

✣ ✣ ✣

The owner of some beautiful white birch trees was walking down the road, when he came upon a man who had stopped his car, and was cutting off large pieces of birch bark.

Without a word the tree owner took out his knife, and cut a

gash in the rear tire of the car and took off a strip of the protruding inner tube.

The car owner let out a wild yell of protest.

"Why all the anger?" asked the tree owner, calmly. "You slashed my trees without asking my permission, so I naturally assumed that you would not object if I took a souvenir from one of your tires. Now, my advice to you is to get that spare tire on as fast as you can and get out of this neighborhood before I decide to cut another souvenir for myself."

✤ ✤ ✤

RULES

A spry little old gentleman was smoking in the bus, much to the annoyance of several passengers. The conductor finally approached and said, "Don't you see the sign that says, 'No Smoking Allowed'?"

"Yes, I do," replied the old man tartly, "but how can a man keep all your rules? There's another sign right by it that says, 'Wear Stay-red Lipstick.' "

✤ ✤ ✤

An old-fashioned clergyman was driving a horse and buggy along a country road in Canada, accompanied by a young man who felt very modern and exact.

"So you object to the Ten Commandments, eh?" asked the clergyman.

"No, not exactly, but a fellow hates to have a 'thou shalt' and 'thou shalt not' flung in his face on every hand. They sound too arbitrary."

The old minister clucked to his horse, and smiled to himself. Suddenly the youth said excitedly, "You've taken the wrong road; that signpost said 'This way to Toronto.' "

"Oh," chuckled the minister, "I hate to be told to go this way or that way by an arbitrary signpost."

An embarrassed laugh from his red-faced young companion told its own story as they turned back and obeyed the arbitrary signpost.

—*War Cry.*

SACRIFICE

In the West Riding of Yorkshire in England on the rolling grounds of Fountain Abbey, is a home, Fountains Hall. It once rang to the shouts of two children. They were called upon at the ages of eighteen and nineteen to take part in World War II. The girl, Elizabeth, at eighteen, and the boy, Charles, at nineteen, died in active military duty.

There is a new stained glass window in the entrance hall to their memory. Carved in stone below are words of service, of sacrifice, and of love. These words are, "When you go home tell them of us and say, 'For your tomorrow, we gave our today.' "

—*Rotarian.*

✤ ✤ ✤

When I was a boy in Carolina I was cured forever of caging wild things. Not content with hearing mockingbirds sing from the cedars, I determined to cage a young one and thus have a young musician all my own.

On his second day in the cage, I saw his mother fly to him with food in her bill. This attention pleased me, for surely the mother knew how to feed her child better than I did. The following morning my pathetic little captive was dead. When I recounted this experience to Arthur Wayne, the renowned ornithologist, he said:

"A mother mockingbird, finding her young in a cage, will sometimes take it poisoned berries. She thinks it better for one she loves to die rather than to live in captivity."

—Archibald Rutledge.

✤ ✤ ✤

SAFETY

A sexy color picture of a woman's lovely leg was passed around by the plant safety director to his workers for their whistled appreciation. Then he made a simple statement: "Looks good, doesn't it? But it makes no impression on a blind man."

That one comment was worth a thousand lectures on eye safety.

Another safety director was equally simple, equally dramatic.

He took a handful of glass eyes out of his pocket, passed them around, and said, "We furnish these eyes in all different colors. But we prefer that you use goggles while you work."

—RALPH G. MARTIN, *Pageant.*

✤ ✤ ✤

SALESMANSHIP

An American and a British shoe salesman traveled on the same boat to West Africa, each representing different shoe companies. After landing, they looked around, and what struck them first was that all the natives were barefoot. The Britisher cabled his head office: "Nobody here wearing shoes. Coming home by next ship."

The American salesman cabled his chief: "Nobody here wearing shoes. Send one million consignment. Market wide open."

—BRIANT SANDO, *Fruit and Vegetable Review.*

✤ ✤ ✤

I like the story about the salesman who was told he was working in a territory where all the farmers were poor and that his chance of selling his merchandise—milking machines—was one in a thousand. He was told, in particular, that the farmer on whom he was going to call that day owned only one cow.

"I'll sell him," he said confidently. He did. And came away with the cow as down payment!

—JERRY FLEISHMAN, *Buck Bits.*

✤ ✤ ✤

A serious-looking man haunted New York's second-rate office buildings. In each he got into an elevator, went to the top and took another down. On the way down he would insist the elevator was not working properly and would demand to see the renting agent. "I was considering renting an office here," he would say, "but that's out now. If the elevators are in such bad shape the whole place is probably run down."

The visitor was finding out for an elevator service company what elevators needed attention and was making the agent vulnerable to later salesmanship.

—JOHN ALLEN MURPHY, in *Advertising & Selling.*

One day an Indian came into the store of a Gallup trader, blinking from the brilliant noonday sun. The trader sold him a pair of black sunglasses.

After the usual dallying, for an hour or so, and the usual bottle of pop, the Indian started home. Almost at once, he was back. He hadn't realized it was getting dark outside; he was a long way from home, in a strange country. Whereupon the trader said a few well-chosen words of comfort—and sold him a lantern and a quart of kerosene.

—Alberta Hannum, *Spin a Silver Dollar*.

♣ ♣ ♣

The clerk in a hardware store had a quick, sharp tongue, and he was proud of it. One day an unobtrusive-looking man came into the store. "Do you keep flashlight batteries?" he asked.

"No, we sell them," snapped the clerk.

"Well," said the prospective customer, turning on his heel, "you'll keep the ones you might have sold me!"

—H. I. Wheelock.

♣ ♣ ♣

A man once owned a very fine horse which was the envy of all his acquaintances, one of whom, a shrewd trader, often asked to buy the animal. The owner always refused, but when the horse died, he had it sent to the trader. Some time later the two men met and the practical joker asked the other how he had liked the gift. The trader replied, "I made $3600 off him."

"How did you manage to make that off a dead horse?"

"Oh," said the trader, "I sold raffle tickets."

"My dear fellow, didn't anyone object?"

"Oh yes," the trader answered calmly, "but the only one who objected was the man who won the horse, and I gave him back his money."

—M. M. Brown.

♣ ♣ ♣

A New York man who was looking for a country place found an ad in the paper for an old salt-box house on a couple of acres at Sherman, Conn., near the lake and also near the general store.

The ad was a blind—signed with a box number in care of the

newspaper—but the man immediately set out for Sherman. He went to the general store and described the house to the old gentleman behind the counter. "Must be Fred's place," the grocer said, pointing outside helpfully. "You can see it right out the window there."

"That can't be it," the New Yorker protested. "The lake must be four miles from here. And that house isn't like the ad."

He handed over the clipping to prove his point. The grocer studied it for a moment, then handed it back. "Nope," he said, "the house ain't like the ad, but, by Godfrey, the ad is like Fred!"

—HERBERT A. THOMPSON.

♣ ♣ ♣

A tailor was eager to sell off a batch of remainders at the end of the year. But the suits had been picked over all year and were badly cut and made. One, in particular, was atrocious. But the proprietor did not give up easily.

"Why don't you sell that suit, Sam?" he demanded of his helper. "Now I'm going to lunch. Let's see you concentrate. Sell that suit while I'm out."

When he returned from lunch the suit was gone. In spite of himself, he showed amazement.

"So you sold it!" he exclaimed. "That shows what application will do, Sam! But your face is cut—your clothes are torn. Did the customer put up a fight? Did you have a struggle?"

"No," replied the faithful Sam. "The customer didn't mind taking that suit at all. But I had a terrible time with his Seeing Eye dog."

—*New Republic.*

♣ ♣ ♣

Bargain-hunting for things to add to my collection of rare bric-a-brac, I stopped one day at the little curio shop of Sam Cohen, where from time to time I had picked up valuable pieces. Browsing around, I saw nothing of interest and was about to leave. Then just inside the door, I noticed a cat lapping milk out of a saucer. One glance told me that the saucer was a priceless antique. With a wild hope that Sam was unaware of its value I said, "That's a nice cat you have there, Sam. Would you sell him to me?"

"I'd sell him for five dollars."

I paid the five, put the cat under my arm and then added, "I'll just take the saucer along. The cat is probably used to eating from it."

"Oh, no," said Sam, "I couldn't give you the saucer."

"Well, then, I'll buy it from you."

"Oh, no," said Sam. "I couldn't sell it to you."

"That's ridiculous, Sam. Why can't you sell me this old saucer?"

"Because," replied Sam, "from that old saucer, I already sold 139 cats."

—JULES M. SMITH.

✣ ✣ ✣

A sidewalk flower vendor was not doing any business. Suddenly a happy thought struck him and he lettered this sign: "This gardenia will make you feel important all day long for 10¢."

All at once his sales began to increase.

—JAMES KELLER, *Just For Today* (Doubleday).

✣ ✣ ✣

A very pretty redhead window-shopping on Fifth Avenue was being followed by a smooth Latin type.

At Sloane's she turned on him, indignant. "You've been following me for three blocks—I saw you. You can stop right now. I'm not the type of girl you can pick up."

The Latin bowed, and smiled. "Madame," he said, "I am not picking you up. I am picking you *out.*"

It worked!

—PM.

✣ ✣ ✣

A farmer walked into the hardware store of a midwest town and asked to see an axe. After carefully examining a half-dozen, he chose one and asked its price.

"It is $1.50," said the storekeeper.

Producing a page torn from a mail-order catalogue, the farmer said, "Here is the same axe for only $1.33."

The hardware man looked at the picture, pondered, then said, "If they can sell it for that, so can I."

"O.K. I'll take it," said the farmer.

The storekeeper picked up the axe, weighed it on a scale and began to make out a sale bill, $1.33, plus 15 cents, total $1.48. "Hey!" shouted the farmer. "What's that 15 cents for?"

"For postage. If you sent off for it you'd have to pay postage, wouldn't you?"

The farmer had to admit he would. He counted out the $1.48. The storekeeper wrapped up the axe—and calmly laid it on a shelf.

"Say, what is the big idea?" asked the farmer.

With a twinkle in his eye, the storekeeper replied, "Come back in three days and you can have it."

—Ben Shatzman.

✤ ✤ ✤

Door-to-door salesman: "Do you have children, madam?"

Housewife: "Two small boys."

Salesman: "Then you will be interested in our new Space Soap, especially concocted to remove rocket grease, interplanetary smudge, comet grime and stellar dust."

—*Woodmen of the World Magazine.*

✤ ✤ ✤

He works alone among outsiders, yet he belongs to a team.
He produces nothing, yet he greatly increases production.
He employs no one, yet he prevents unemployment.
He is not supervised, yet he is responsible for results.
He influences people over whom he has no authority.
He does much to raise the standard of living.
He is a maker of better balance sheets.
He is the man who sends in orders. He is *the salesman.*

—*Best's Insurance News.*

✤ ✤ ✤

She wanted to buy a stove.

She listened meekly to the sales patter. She heard about noncorroding bolts and patented insulation material and the gauge of steel used, and tricky controls, and over-size combustion chambers, and all the other things that are so startlingly new in an old lady's world that you'd think they would impress her mightily. Finally, the salesman paused, and she still waited with patient expectancy.

"Well, madam, I've told you everything about the stove," the salesman declared. "Is there anything else you'd like to know?"

"Yes," she answered. "Will it keep an old lady warm?"

—*The Casualty and Surety Journal.*

✣ ✣ ✣

The insurance salesman was on the point of writing a large policy. The prospect said he recognized the need, meant to buy the insurance, but was inclined to wait a while. "Later, later," he said. "Come back in November."

The insurance man's hand was on the doorknob. As he was leaving he spun around and said: "Whom shall I ask for if you are not here in November?"

—*Postage Stamp.*

✣ ✣ ✣

Perhaps our gravest sin in selling is the overlooked opportunity. Let me illustrate with a personal experience.

On a rainy morning, a month or so ago, I was forcibly reminded that I needed a raincoat. I clipped an ad from the paper illustrating a likely-looking coat. That noon, as it was still raining, I visited a haberdasher in our office building. I handed the ad to a clerk with the comment that I wanted a coat something like the one pictured. He glanced at the ad and said, "Oh, sir, you are in the wrong place! The store you are looking for is four blocks down the street." If I hadn't taken the initiative and *insisted upon buying,* he would have sent me out in the rain to walk four blocks for a coat I really wanted to purchase then and there!

—E. F. O'Brien.

✣ ✣ ✣

Stopping for gas in an Iowa town, I found a line of cars at a filling station which displayed a sign: "Your tank full free if you guess how much it takes." After I had guessed—and lost—I asked the busy proprietor how his plan had worked out. "Fellow guessed right about two years ago," he said, "but it only cost me $1.30. And we don't get any 'Gimme a dollar's worth' customers any more. Everybody makes a guess and fills up."

—M. F. McGrath, *Rotarian.*

✤ ✤ ✤

When James H. Rand, Jr., chairman of today's gigantic Remington Rand, Inc., was a salesman of bank equipment, he called on Frank A. Munsey, then preparing to open Munsey banks in Baltimore and Washington. Young Rand was thoroughly quizzed on the merits and demerits of different types of equipment. Then Munsey said, "I'll give you a letter to my manager in Washington and you can go after him for the order."

Elated, Rand jumped on a train to Washington, told his story, and got a $25,000 order—forgetting to present the letter. Coming across it later in his pocket, he opened it and read, in effect: "Learn all you can from this man, but don't buy anything from him if you can help it."

—B. C. Forbes, *Forbes.*

✤ ✤ ✤

A good many persons engaged in selling might find a moral, I think, in an experience I had on a fishing expedition in Colorado. An associate, who accompanied me, had just about bought out a sporting-goods shop. He had rods, reels, and a weird assortment of lures.

I had made no elaborate preparations, but instead consulted a rustic I encountered on the front porch of our lodge. "Well, mister," he said, "if you want to catch mountain trout *sure-fire,* you've got t' give 'em the bait they're hankerin' fer—and that's grasshoppers. Reckon I kin fix y' up fer a dollar."

He did. I came back with a nice string of rainbows. My friend, sad to relate, returned with an empty creel.

—James D. Woolf, *Advertising Age.*

✤ ✤ ✤

During World War II, L. L. Bean (an authority on outdoor apparel) was in Washington as a consultant to the armed forces.

For cold weather wear the Army wanted leather-topped rubbers with sixteen-inch tops. Bean thought twelve-inch tops and a lighter rubber would be better.

Getting nowhere with verbal argument, he whipped out a pencil and began furious calculation. "Gentlemen," he said presently, "do you realize that if you insist on the higher-topped boot, in a day's march of 36,980 steps, each soldier in the Army will be lifting 4,600 unnecessary pounds?"

Awe-stricken by this Down-East way of figuring, the Army capitulated.

—EARLE DOUCETTE, *Coronet.*

✤ ✤ ✤

An attractive young woman had an amazing record in the house-to-house sale of vacuum cleaners. Questioned as to her success, she confessed to an effective stratagem:

"I always make it a point to address my sales talk to the husband—in tones so low that the wife won't want to miss a single word!"

—*Wall Street Journal.*

✤ ✤ ✤

A few years ago, the late Arthur Kudner, founder of the Kudner Advertising Agency, made a pitch for a big, midwest account. To make a first-rate showing, he took his whole agency "circus" along with him: verbal acrobats, client-tamers, copy-riders and the like. The midwest executive—for whom it had all been given—looked dazed when the show was over, but he was determined not to be "pushed" into anything.

"I'm sorry," he said, "but I believe we should have an agency whose president can give his personal attention to our account. We need a small agency."

Arthur Kudner's answer was quiet, but to the point: "I have never known one that was small by choice."

—*Television Age.*

✤ ✤ ✤

Salesmanship is not always a matter of "putting on the pressure." It may be manifested in resisting pressure from the buyer who seeks unwarranted concessions. I recall a personal experience. An overcoat was priced at a little more than I cared to pay. I asked the proprietor of our local men's shop to reduce the price, pointing out that we had been friends for a long time.

"Verne," he said to me, without hesitation, "don't you realize that I must pay all of my expenses and make my living from the patronage of my friends? My enemies, the lousy so-and-sos, never come into my store!" I bought the coat and paid the full price.

—VERNE R. MARTIN, sales consultant.

✣ ✣ ✣

The world's best salesman recently made his outstanding sale to a seventeen-year-old soldier at Ft. Lewis, Washington. The soldier's father back in Idaho complained to the Prosecutor's office that the salesman sold his son a five-hundred year subscription to a magazine for fifty dollars.

The Deputy Prosecutor couldn't decide immediately what kind of charge to file, but said: "I'd sure like to meet a guy who can sell a five-hundred year subscription to anything."

—JACK HEISE, *True*.

✣ ✣ ✣

SELF-CONFIDENCE

Admiral Dupont was explaining to Farragut his reasons for not taking his ironclads into Charleston Harbor. "You haven't given me the main reason yet," said Farragut coldly.

"What is that, sir?" asked Dupont.

And Farragut replied: "You didn't think you could do it."

✣ ✣ ✣

SELF-DISCIPLINE

A mother, who had just punished her small child for not doing something he knew he ought to do, was somewhat taken aback when he turned a tear-stained face to her and asked, "But Mummy, how do you make yourself do the things you ought to do?"

—*Whatsoever Things*.

SELF-CONTROL

"How did you keep from crying?" someone asked a little girl who had fallen and hurt her knee.

"Oh," she answered, "I just said to myself, 'Stop that,' and made myself mind me."

—*Sunshine Magazine.*

✤ ✤ ✤

SELF-ESTEEM

Walter Damrosch, renowned orchestra leader, once told this tale: "Early in my career I made what I fancied was remarkable progress as a conductor, and came to consider myself the irreplaceable leader of my fine little orchestra. But one night I was disillusioned. I was preparing to conduct a particularly ambitious programme, when I discovered that I had forgotten my baton. I told my assistant to get it for me, when three violinists held up restraining hands. 'Don't mind,' each said, 'here's a baton,' and each produced one from an inner pocket. Never since that moment have I considered myself indispensable."

✤ ✤ ✤

SELF-Reliance

I once saw a mockingbird mother go into a rage at her offspring's insistence on a prolonged adolescence. Food was at the young bird's feet, but it cried lamentably and ruffled his feathers and opened his mouth for the manna to be dropped into it. The mother patiently picked up the feed and dropped it and picked it up again, to show her child the manner in which it was done. He opened his bill the wider. Suddenly she flew at him in a fury, pecked him several times, and flew away. He must shift for himself. He looked over his shoulder disconsolately, then he went to work and fed himself with perfect efficiency.

—MARJORIE RAWLINGS, in *Cross Creek.*

✤ ✤ ✤

What would you think of a baseball player who insisted on four strikes as his just due, while all other players were limited to the conventional three strikes? Well, our country today is full of people who want four strikes. The labor lobby in Washington wants four strikes for labor against three for industry. The manufacturers would get four strikes to labor's three if they could. Farmers want four strikes against three for consumers. Renters want four strikes against three for the landlord.

The tragedy of our revolt against personal responsibility is that we are becoming less and less competent to bear the burden of our freedom.

—Dr. Harold B. Walker.

✤ ✤ ✤

SELFISHNESS

A farmer imported some especially fine seed-corn and produced a crop that was the envy of his neighbors. When they sought some of the seed, he refused, fearing to lose the competitive advantage he had gained.

The second year, his crop was not so good; the third year, results were even worse. Suddenly, it dawned upon him that the poor grade corn of his neighbors was pollinating his prize corn. His selfishness had caught up with him.

—*Business Efficiency.*

✤ ✤ ✤

A famous Indian chief, Blackfeather, once spoke these worthy words to his tribe: "I have lived long. I have seen many things. What I know I speak. Selfishness is the great enemy of peace. Selfishness walks by itself and no one walks with it. Selfishness never goes unseen. It raises flags and banners as it goes. People are quick to see these signs. They are like the hiss of the rattlesnake that the wise avoid. What I have said is true. Selfishness is the enemy of peace."

✤ ✤ ✤

Two very young boys climbed on a small hobbyhorse. After a few minutes, one said to the other, "If one of us got off, I could ride much better."

SELFLESSNESS

One of the best sermons I have ever heard was delivered by a country preacher in a little country church. He said: "People talk to me about the problem of evil, but I will tell you an even greater problem: the problem of goodness. How do you account for the fact that in such a world as this there should be so much self-sacrifice, so much unselfishness, so much love? By what miracle has man, who only a few thousand years ago was living on the level of the beasts, risen to a point where he will literally 'lay down his life' for his family, for a cause, for a friend?"

As the years accumulate do you find yourself more sympathetic and tolerant, with a higher reverence for the nobility of your fellow men? That is the essential test of growth.

—Bruce Barton in *The American Magazine.*

✣ ✣ ✣

In the cemetery office a uniformed chauffeur approached the clerk at the desk.

"The lady is too ill to walk," he explained. "Would you mind coming out with me?"

Waiting in the car was a frail, elderly woman whose sunken eyes could not hide some deep, long-lasting hurt. "I am Mrs. Adams," she said. "Every week for the last two years I have been sending you a five-dollar bill—"

"For the flowers!" the clerk remembered.

"Yes—to be laid on the grave of my son. I came here today," Mrs. Adams confided softly, "because the doctors have let me know I have only a few weeks left. I shall not be sorry to go. There is nothing to live for. But I wanted to drive here for one last look, and to thank you."

The clerk blinked at her irresolutely. Then, with a wry smile, he spoke: "You know, ma'am, I was sorry you kept sending the money for the flowers."

"Sorry?"

"Yes—because the flowers last such a little while! And nobody ever sees them."

"Do you realize what you are saying?"

"Oh, indeed I do. I belong to a visiting society. State hospitals. Insane asylums. People in places like that dearly love flowers—and they can see them and smell them. Lady, there are living people in places like that."

The woman sat in silence for a moment. Then, still without a word, she signaled the chauffeur to drive away.

Some months later the clerk was astonished to receive another visit; doubly astonished because this time the woman was driving the car. "I take the flowers to the people myself," she announced, with a friendly smile. "You were right; it does make them happy. And it makes me happy. The doctors don't know what is making me well—but I do! I have something to live for."

She had discovered what most of us know and forget; in helping others she had helped herself.

—Fulton Oursler, in *Christian Herald.*

✣ ✣ ✣

SERVICE

A charming girl said to me, "You know, Doctor, I give out too much of myself; everybody tells me so."

That was just the trouble. Everybody had told her so and the suggestion had worked. It did not take her long to learn that it was not her "giving out" but the "see how much I am giving and how tired I shall be" attitude which was exhausting her. A real self-expression and the fulfillment of a real desire to give are never anything else than exhilarating.

—Dr. Josephine A. Jackson and Helen M. Salisbury,
Outwitting Our Nerves (Appleton-Century).

✣ ✣ ✣

There was a very wealthy woman who lived in a palatial home, surrounded by fine tapestries, linens, imported china, expensive bric-a-brac, and who indulged in every luxury. She died and went to the gates of Heaven, but to her astonishment there was no fanfare of trumpets when she arrived. An angel was chosen to accompany her to the home that was to be her permanent abode. They passed down a beautiful street of indescribable grandeur and magnificence. Finally they came to a street of much less glamor, and way down at the end of it was a very humble little cottage. They turned to enter, and the woman stopped and looked about with tragic disappointment on her countenance. The angel said to her, "This is to be your eternal home." "Oh but," she said, "I have been accustomed to a mansion on earth. I had the most beautiful home on our street. I had everything; all that wealth could give me. I am accustomed only to the finest and most expensive. There are many, many beautiful homes which we passed similar to mine on earth. There must be some mistake." "Ah," said the angel, "but we built your eternal home here out of the material which you have sent us from earth, and this is the best we could do with what you have sent."

—DR. PRESTON BRADLEY, *General Federation Clubwoman.*

✤ ✤ ✤

A housewife sent her best colored luncheon cloth and two of the matching napkins to the laundry. They came back miserably faded. She stormed into the laundry and got into line at the complaint desk. When her turn arrived, the clerk informed her seriously, "If you'll bring in the remaining napkins, madam, we'll be glad to fade them to match the rest of your set."

—MARCIA WINN in *Chicago Tribune.*

✤ ✤ ✤

One night a man took a little taper out of a drawer and lighted it, and began to ascend a long, winding stair.

"Where are you going?" said the taper.

"Away high up," said the man, "higher than the top of the house where we sleep."

"And what are you going to do there?" said the taper.

"I am going to show the ships out at sea where the harbor is," said the man. "For we stand here at the entrance to the harbor, and some ships far out on the stormy sea may be looking for our light even now."

"Alas, no ship could see my light!" said the little taper. "It is so very small."

"If your light is small," said the man, "keep it burning bright, and leave the rest to me."

Then he climbed the stairs to the top of the lighthouse—for

this was a lighthouse they were in—and he took the little taper and lighted the great lamps that stood ready there with their polished reflectors behind them.

You who think your little light of so small account, can you not see what great things it might do?

—*Highways of Happiness.*

✠ ✠ ✠

At the time of the Crimean War many eagerly joined Florence Nightingale under the inspiration of a great patriotic cause.

As the ship sailed into Scutari harbor, a young nurse, enthusiastically effervescent, rushed up to the leader: "Oh, dear Miss Nightingale, let there be no delay! Let us go straight to nursing the poor fellows!"

The great nurse looked at her young charge and made disillusioning reply: "The strongest will be wanted at the washtubs."

—FRANK H. FAGERBURG, *Is This Religion?* (Judson).

✠ ✠ ✠

A doctor hesitated when a call for help came on a particularly inclement night, but his love for humanity was strong, and he went through a drenching rain to the distant home of a farmer. His services saved the life of a small child. Years later the doctor said: "I never dreamed that in saving the life of that farm child I was saving the life of the leader of England." That child was David Lloyd-George, onetime British prime minister.

—CHARLES L. WALLIS, *Treasury of Sermon Illustrations* (Abingdon-Cokesbury).

✠ ✠ ✠

The old doctor had never refused a call, from rich or poor, but now he was tired.

"Have you any money?" he asked the midnight caller.

"Certainly," he replied.

"Then go to the new doctor. I'm too old to get out of bed for anybody who can pay for it."

—*United Mine Workers Journal.*

✠ ✠ ✠

The largest hotel, in one of the southern Mexico cities, is five stories high. As there is no elevator, rates are progressively cheaper as one ascends; the higher the room, the lower the price. An American tourist in a second floor room, not minding an extra climb and wishing to save a few pesos, asked to be transferred to a room on the fourth floor. The manager replied that he was sorry, but all of the fourth floor rooms were occupied.

"But, senor," he said, after a moment's consideration, "we can from now on pretend that you are on the fourth floor, and will reduce your rate accordingly."

—RALPH E. OGDEN, *Pan American.*

✤ ✤ ✤

Sarah, my once-a-week cleaning woman, had several times referred to a quiet little widow in our neighborhood as "a mighty 'stravagant woman."

Finally I pressed for an explanation. "Mrs. Kenney can't be *very* extravagant," I insisted. "She gets only a small pension; hasn't any money to speak of."

"Yes'm," agreed Sarah readily. "Ah knows that. But it ain't money Ah means. Dat woman all de time doin' fo' othah peoples. Yes'm, she's wondahful 'stravagant—not with money, but with herse'f!"

—MRS. A. GORDON.

✤ ✤ ✤

In China an American woman journalist watched a frail Sister cleansing the gangrenous sores of wounded soldiers. "I wouldn't do that for a million dollars!" the visitor remarked. Without pause in her work, the Sister replied, "Neither would I."

—*Catholic Digest.*

✤ ✤ ✤

A young girl of sixteen lay dying. She had been an elder child in a large motherless family. She spent her childhood bearing the burdens of the home. She literally was tired to death, dying of tuberculosis. A visitor asked her if she had been confirmed? Had she gone to church? To which she answered, "No."

Taking a serious view of the whole situation, the visitor asked, "What will you do when you die and have to tell God that?"

The child, taking out her thin, transparent hands, stained and twisted with work, laid them on the coverlet, and said: "I shall show Him my hands."

—Rev. John Craig Roak, *Everybody's Weekly.*

✤ ✤ ✤

An English writer tells of a blind man who always carried a lantern. People used to ask of what use the lantern could be to his sightless eyes. "I do not carry it to prevent my stumbling over others," he replied, "but to keep them from stumbling over me." . . . Let your light shine so that somebody else will not stumble because of you.

—Rev. Peter Pleune, *Christian Observer.*

✤ ✤ ✤

One day an old umbrella-mender knocked at the back door; and we gave him a job. As he mended the broken and torn umbrella, he seemed to take unusual pains, testing the cloth, carefully measuring and strongly sewing the covers, so we remarked:

"You seem unusually careful."

"Yes," he said without looking up. "I try to do good work."

"But," we suggested, "your customers would not know the difference until you were gone . . . Perhaps you expect to come back this way again some day?"

"No, I shall probably not come back."

"Then why are you so particular?"

"So it will be easier for the man who follows me," he answered simply. "If I put on shoddy cloth or do bad work, my customers will find it out in a few weeks, and the next old umbrella-mender who comes along will get the cold shoulder."

—*Religious Telescope.*

✤ ✤ ✤

The day on which this story begins was cheerless; the air was thick with swirling snow, and my heart was heavy. We had within three years lost two baby daughters; David, our young son, had been so ill that for months his life hung in the balance; and I, suffering from arthritis, was faced with life as a house-bound invalid, a burden to those I loved.

As I sat staring out into the dusk, a tiny gray bird lit on the icy porch railing. He was battered by the storm, and probably had known scant rations for days. Yet he clung there singing at the top of his lungs: "Chickadee-dee-dee!"

His courage and need pulled at my heart. Every motion had been agony; but somehow I dragged myself to the door with a handful of crumbs. He ate just enough to refresh himself, then flew off. In a few moments he was back with every relative and friend he could gather. With quickened interest, I tossed out crumbs by the handful.

Next morning I forgot the pain of arising in my anxiety to get to the window. Would they be there? They were, bless them. My heart was flooded with gratitude that I, so nearly helpless, had been able to give help. I was good for something. That moment marked the rebirth of hope.

—Ada Clapham Govan, *Wings at my Window.*

✣ ✣ ✣

"Is your father home?" a lad sitting on the country doctor's doorstep was asked. "No," said the boy, "He's away." When the visitor asked where the father could be found the lad replied, "Well, you've got to look for him someplace where people are sick or hurt, or something like that. I don't know where he is, but he's helping somewhere."

—W. L. Phillips.

✣ ✣ ✣

A man was to meet a missionary at a railway station. Since the visitor was unknown to him, he asked a friend for a description. "Oh, you will know him all right," said the friend. "He'll be helping someone off the train."

✣ ✣ ✣

My mother was a Christian minister—the first woman ordained by the Congregational Church in New York State. Her sermons were so simply and directly spoken, from her heart to yours, that she seemed to have no art at all. In one of them she began by telling the congregation of the hard time she had finding a theme for that Sunday. There seemed to be nothing in the house, or in the garden, or in fact anywhere in town to suggest it.

She finally went out into the country and walked down an old road through the woods.

"I was walking very fast when all of a sudden I heard a slow drawling voice that said: 'Why—don't—you—saunter?' "

It was the old road itself speaking. "I am a worker; I have no time for dallying," was her reply.

The road laughed rudely, and said: "I suppose you think there's nothing worth while in a road but its end! Believe me, no road has any end, only another beginning.

"A lot of people in the church," the road said at last, "are so intent on getting to heaven that they haven't time to be good on the way. I'm afraid they will be turned back when they get there because they have no wedding garment. You have to get your wedding garment, your immortality, as you go along. If you do not find love and joy and peace on the road, they will not be waiting for you at the end."

That is the way she would preach, for she realized that the Christian ideal, if you really mean it, demands more of you than "life" does. She tried to live a life the core of which was doing, and not just being, good.

—MAX EASTMAN.

✣ ✣ ✣

A visitor passing through an English war factory during World War II was startled to see at a lathe a man who bore a striking resemblance to the king. Greater was his astonishment to learn that it *was* the king. Each day, after his official duties were over, the King of England took his place in the factory and worked with his people.

—HENRY F. POLLOCK.

✣ ✣ ✣

William D. Boyce, a Chicago publisher, became lost one night in a London fog. A boy touched him and asked, "Can I help you, sir?" He escorted the publisher to his hotel, and upon arrival refused pay for his services. "I am a Boy Scout," he explained. "We do not accept pay for rendering a service to anyone in need."

Boyce was impressed. He called on Sir Robert Baden Powell,

founder of British scouting, to learn more about the movement. Returning to America, he became one of the leaders in establishing Boy Scouting in this country.

✤ ✤ ✤

My mother had a stroke and found herself suddenly paralyzed. The neighbors all came to call. Anna Kerns was one of them. When she left she didn't say to my Aunt Mary, "Now, if there's anything at all I can do . . ." She said, "Mary, I'll be here at seven-thirty in the morning to do the washing for you." She was there, too, and stayed all day. She got down on her knees and waxed the linoleum, and then sat all afternoon with Mother.

—Ernie Pyle, *Home Country* (Wm. Sloane).

✤ ✤ ✤

Grandmother, on a winter's day, milked the cows and fed them hay, slopped the hogs, saddled the mule, then got the children off to school; did a washing, mopped the floors, washed the windows, and did some chores; cooked a dish of home-dried fruit, pressed her husband's Sunday suit.

Swept the parlor, made the bed, baked a dozen loaves of bread, split some firewood, and lugged in enough to fill the kitchen bin; cleaned the lamps and put in oil, stewed some apples she thought would spoil; churned the butter, baked a cake, then exclaimed, "For Heaven's sake, the calves have got out of the pen"—went out and chased them in again.

Gathered the eggs and locked the stable, back to the house and set the table, cooked a supper that was delicious, and afterward washed up all the dishes; fed the cat and sprinkled the clothes, mended a basketful of hose; then opened the organ and began to play, "When You Come to the End of a Perfect Day."

—*War Cry.*

✤ ✤ ✤

SINCERITY

In ancient Rome there were many fine sculptors and stone-carvers—and there were some who were not so fine. Some would let their chisels slip and cut unintentioned lines in the stone. They developed a trick to cover up these mistakes: they just filled the chipped places with wax, and sold the finished product as faultless.

But the better artists, willing to sell only perfect wares, stamped their work with the words *sine cera* (without wax). From their custom—and honor—comes our word "sincere."

✤ ✤ ✤

John Barrymore once asked the great Russian director, Constantin Stanislavski, how he selected his artists. "I choose them by means of this," said Stanislavski, picking up a pin. "Now, you go into the next room."

Barrymore went out, and in a moment Stanislavski said, "You may come in now. Please look for the pin."

The Russian watched as Barrymore picked up the glasses from the table, looked under them, and lifted each plate. He felt along the surface of the tablecloth, lifted the corner, and there was the pin.

Stanislavski clapped his hands: "Very good—you are engaged! I can tell a real actor," he explained, "by the way he looks for a pin. If he prances around the room, striking attitudes, pretending to think very hard, looking in ridiculous places—exaggerating—then he is no good."

—ALMA POWER-WATERS, *John Barrymore* (Messner).

✤ ✤ ✤

SPEECH—Introduction

The speaker was introduced in a lengthy and flowery fashion, his various degrees and accomplishments appended like the tail of a kite. Being a humble man, when he arose to start his speech, he began with this story:

A farmer of Italian descent was leading a calf to market. When he came to a bridge, the calf balked, and nothing could induce it to go beyond the middle of the bridge. The calf was too large to carry, and the stream was too swift and deep to ford. At this juncture a huge car came by, and the driver, finding the way blocked, asked if he could be of any assistance. After some discussion, it was agreed that the driver should blow the horn, which he did lustily.

The poor calf, frightened at this unexpected blast, jerked loose from the farmer, jumped over the railing of the bridge and was drowned in the stream below.

The two men compared notes sorrowfully. The ultimate conclusion, as voiced by the Italian farmer, was this: "Too bigga da honk for so smalla da calf."

✤ ✤ ✤

SPEECH—Speakers

"Once in Virginia," said a speaker who had received an introduction that promised more than he felt he could deliver, "I passed a small church displaying a large sign. It read: 'Annual Strawberry Festival,' and below in small letters, 'On account of the depression, prunes will be served.' "

—Boston *Transcript*.

✤ ✤ ✤

In all the debates that I have attended I have never been fortunate enough to hear any very witty interruption, and wish I had been in the House of Lords when Lord Haversham told me their Lordships had been bored to extinction at some copious Peer who usually opened his speeches with:

"And now, my Lords, I ask myself this question—"

At which a young Peer said in a loud voice:

"And a damned dull answer you'll get!"

—MARGOT ASQUITH, *More or Less About Myself* (Dutton).

✤ ✤ ✤

A fledgling public speaker illustrated his sense of inadequacy with this story.

A small boy was strolling down the street with his still smaller niece when a neighbor stopped to comment on the little girl's growth.

"Can she talk yet?" asked the neighbor.

"No," replied the little boy seriously. "She has her teeth, but her words haven't come in yet."

When Edmund Burke was delivering his famous speech against Warren Hastings, he suddenly stopped in the very middle of an idea. Slowly and impressively he raised his hand and pointed his index finger at Mr. Hastings. He stood for almost a minute with that dramatic pointing finger while the audience almost held its breath. Then he went on.

Afterward, one of the opposing advocates said, "Mr. Burke, that was one of the most effective pauses I have ever seen. We in the audience simply held our breaths, wondering what you were going to say next."

"That," responded Mr. Burke, "is exactly the way I was feeling."

—*Better English.*

✣ ✣ ✣

SPEECH—Speaking

Speakers, lecturers and toastmasters alike suffer dire distress when addressing an unresponsive audience. I once asked Christopher Morley if he was immune from the failing. "No," he said. "Not long ago, in the middle of a lecture I was giving at a club in Cleveland, I was horrified to see the occupants of the back rows marching out of the hall with almost military precision. You can imagine my intense relief on learning that the matter was not really serious. They were leaving, not because they found me lacking in charm, but merely bacause the house was on fire."

—Frank Crowninshield, in *Vogue.*

✣ ✣ ✣

Years ago, when I first came to New York, Mark Twain gave a dinner in my honor. There were some 30 distinguished guests present, and as the dinner progressed, I became panicky.

"Don't you feel well?" asked Mr. Clemens.

"I'm scared to death," I said. "I know that I shall be called upon to speak, and I'm sure I shan't be able to rise from my chair. When I stand up, my mind sits down!"

"Eddie," said my host, "it may help you if you keep one thing in mind—just remember they don't expect much!"

I have never since been self-conscious when I get on my feet.

—MAJOR EDWARD BOWES, quoted by W. ORTON TEWSON in *An Attic Salt-Shaker.*

✣ ✣ ✣

SPEED

The Navy Department shares private business's idea that pressing documents can be hurried through the barricade of office red tape if specially marked for immediate attention. The trouble with this system, as the Navy Department discovered, is that people get used to any sort of immediate-attention mark, and you have to resort to a more stimulating one. Long ago, a Navy Department official got some little pink slips marked "EXPEDITE." Its novelty wore off, and the slips next said "URGENT." This was followed by "RUSH." Came the inevitable time when documents marked "RUSH" were discovered days later, buried in somebody's desk, and the high command realized that a new word was in order. Pressing papers were then marked "FRANTIC."

—*The New Yorker.*

✣ ✣ ✣

SPIRIT

The late Charles J. Connick, the master stained-glass craftsman, was once approached by a young artist who had been studying with him in the craft. The young man asked the master if he might have the privilege of using some of the master's tools with which he worked.

"Why do you want to use my tools, son?" asked Mr. Connick.

"Oh, I just want to use them to see if it will make any difference in the work I do," replied the young man.

A week later the master walked into the young man's presence and said, "Well, son, how are you doing with my tools?"

"Not so good, Master. In fact, my work is not one whit better than it was, even working with your tools." And the young man looked dejected.

A gray-haired artist, overhearing the conversation between the craftsman and the apprentice, said to the young man, "Son, perhaps it isn't the tools of the master that you need; it's the master's spirit."

—WILLIAM L. STIDGER.

✣ ✣ ✣

I once asked an orchardman who specialized in raising apples whether he grew a certain variety. He replied that he did not because trees of that variety got into the habit of bearing only every other year. When I asked what caused that, he explained that when a tree was heavily loaded with fruit, it did not have sufficient energy to grow that crop and at the same time develop under the bark the buds that were necessary for the next crop. Thus it developed the habit of bearing apples only every other year. It was so busy with the outward fruit that it had no time for the inward. That is true of many a Christian life. We are so busy with outward activities that we have no time for development of the inward fruits of the spirit.

—REV. WALTER L. LINGLE, *Christian Observer*.

✣ ✣ ✣

SPORTS

He was obviously a novice at boxing, and when he entered the ring and saw his opponent he felt far from happy. As he went to his corner he saw a man with a towel thrown over one shoulder.

"Who are you?" he asked.

"I'm the second," was the reply.

Over the novice's face there flashed a look of relief. "No," he said firmly, "you go first. I'll go second!"

—*Tit-Bits,* London.

✣ ✣ ✣

STRATEGY

A Brigade Major with General Allenby's forces in Palestine during World War I was reading his Bible one night by the light of a candle, looking for the name "Michmash." His brigade had been ordered to capture a village of that name which stood on a rocky hill just across a deep valley. The name had seemed vaguely familiar.

Finally, in Samuel I, Chapter 13, he read: "And Saul, and Jonathan his son, and the people with them, abode in Gibeah of Benjamin: but the Philistines encamped in Michmash." The major went on to read how Jonathan and his armor-bearer went over to the Philistines' garrison alone one night, through a pass that had "a sharp rock on the one side, and a sharp rock on the other side: and the name of the one was Bozez, and the name of the other Seneh." They climbed the rocky hill till they came to "a half acre of land, which a yoke of oxen might plow." Then the Philistines awoke, thought they were surrounded by the armies of Saul, and "the multitude melted away."

Saul then attacked with his whole army, and "so the Lord saved Israel that day."

The major thought to himself, "This pass, those two rocky headlands and the flat piece of ground are probably still there." He woke the brigadier, and they read over the story. Scouts were sent out and found the pass, thinly held by the Turks; rocky crags were on either side—obviously Bozez and Seneh—and high up in Michmash moonlight showed a small flat piece of ground.

Then and there the general changed his plan of attack: instead of sending the whole brigade, one company alone was sent along the pass at dead of night. The few Turks met were silently dealt with; the hill was climbed; and just before dawn the company found itself on the flat bit of ground. The Turks awoke, thought they were surrounded by the armies of Allenby, and fled in disorder. Every Turk in Michmash was killed or captured that night.

And so, after thousands of years, the tactics of Saul and Jonathan were repeated with success by a British force.

—MAJOR VIVIAN GILBERT, *Romance of The Last Crusade* (Appleton-Century).

✤ ✤ ✤

Members of the theatrical profession are the worst hypochondriacs in the world—and the most gullible. Of all people they are the last to admit that most of their ailments are purely imaginary. The acknowledged dean of theatrical hypochondriacs was Albert Lewis, producer of many successful plays.

In the summer of 1928 I was rehearsing for *Whoopee*. After a particularly long run-through one night, the late William Anthony McGuire, who wrote the show, went with me to a restaurant for a refresher. This was during my baby-food period, when I theorized that one could remain healthy as a child by eating as children do; so I ordered cereal and cream. Bill McGuire gave me a frightened look and promptly ordered Scotch and ginger ale.

Then he gazed about the room and spied our mutual friend Al Lewis at a corner table. Weary as we were, we fell to exchanging stories about Lewis's famed "ailments." Seeing him coming over, we decided to do something for good old Al's benefit—in a hurry. Casually I poured half my bottle of cream into the glass brought for Bill's drink, and filled the glass with ginger ale.

Immediately Al asked, "What's that you're drinking."

"What I drink every night," I answered. "Half cream and half ginger ale."

"What good is that?" he asked.

"It's just the best tonic in the world, that's all."

"Where's that waiter?" chimed in McGuire who meanwhile had hidden his jigger of Scotch. "Why didn't he bring my cream and ginger ale?"

"You, too, Bill?" Lewis gasped.

"Of course!" he replied. "I've been sleeping like a baby since Eddie introduced this drink to me."

"But Eddie said it was a tonic."

"That's the beauty of it, Al," I said. "When you want pep, you drink it; and when you want to relax, you drink it. I guess I really owe my health to that Swiss doctor who first made me try it."

When Lewis bade us good night, he had the appearance of a man who has just struck oil.

It was two years before I saw Albert Lewis again. I hardly recognized him. He walked with a youthful buoyant step. The familiar lines of worry had vanished from his face. His handclasp made me wince. I was delighted to see him looking so well and told him so.

"Thanks to you," he returned. "You made me what I am today."

I was puzzled, and he laughed at my foggy expression.

"The cream and ginger ale!" he explained. "You know how ill I was. Well, I've been drinking that combination every single night for two years, and I've never felt better in my life. I sleep like a log, I'm full of energy and I accomplish more in one day than I used to in a month. Really, Eddie, it saved my life!"

—EDDIE CANTOR.

✤ ✤ ✤

During the war, foreign diplomats in Berlin took it for granted that their embassies were wired with dictaphones and their telephones tapped. They took advantage of this to get messages to the German government which they did not want to deliver direct. When Field Marshal Goring, convinced that he would make a big hit in New York, was angling for an official invitation—the last thing Washington wanted—it was arranged that an American visiting in Berlin should telephone the American Embassy and inquire whether Goring was going to the United States. The voice at the Embassy replied, "Yes, the Marshal seems bent on going over. He doesn't seem to realize what he'll be up against. Of course, the government can mobilize enough police to protect him. But the Marshal is apparently wholly unaware that in the U. S. he is one of the most hated men in the world."

Two days later the official German press service carried a statement that Goring had abandoned his plans to visit the United States.

—DREW PEARSON & ROBT. S. ALLEN.

✤ ✤ ✤

SUCCESS

When P. T. Barnum, as a young man, left Danbury, Connecticut, to make his way in the world, he left numerous unpaid bills behind him. To one creditor the imaginative showman said with great intensity: "I'll pay you what I owe you as soon as I get rich."

The other laughed and eyed the young chap disdainfully. "That will be when a sieve holds water," he jeered.

But in a few years the master showman was well on the road to success, and with great satisfaction wrote the man the following note: "Dear Sir: I have fixed that sieve."

—*Richland Press.*

✤ ✤ ✤

Malcolm Bingay once explained success to a young man with this story: Years ago the Bingays hired a maid, big as a bulldozer and about the same shape. She spoke only Finnish and received her instructions in signs. Shortly after, Detroit had a three-foot snowfall and Bing—a little man weighing only 210—decided to let the maid shovel snow.

"I showed her how. She got the idea, so I went inside to eat breakfast. When I came out the big troll from Finland was out of sight three blocks away and still shoveling."

"Thank you, sir," said the young man. "I shall remember that lesson. 'Work hard and do more than is expected of you.' "

"Jumping Jehosaphat, NO!" yelled Bingay. "The lesson is to get some muscle-headed mutt to do your work for you!"

—FRED BECK, *Pageant.*

✤ ✤ ✤

"To what," asked the interviewing reporter, "do you attribute your remarkable success in this business?"

"To my laziness," answered the proprietor. "I've always hated hustling and scheming and dickering. So I decided to be content to make just a simple, honest living. I figured I wouldn't have much competition, and, by cracky, I didn't!"

—*Nuggets.*

✤ ✤ ✤

The name Joseph Jefferson is synonymous with the play *Rip Van Winkle.* It was this play that added his name to the theatrical greats in America, yet if Jefferson had been easily discouraged, he would never have played the part.

One day after rehearsal, he was stopped by Dion Boucicault, the author of many hit plays, who warned that this play was lacking in audience appeal and would never succeed.

"The trouble, Joseph," said Boucicault, "is that you are shooting over the audience's heads."

"You couldn't be more mistaken, Dion," answered Jefferson. "I am not even thinking of their heads. I am aiming at their hearts. That way I cannot fail."

The play that everyone thought could not succeed ran for forty years.

—STELLA KAMP.

✤ ✤ ✤

"Prince" Michael Romanoff resents people who ask: "How does it feel to be a success?"

"I was a success when I was sleeping on a park bench," he tells them coldly. "You are confusing success with comfort."

—*American Weekly.*

✤ ✤ ✤

Two college classmates met for the first time in twenty years, and after the usual pleasantries, one asked, "What's the dope on those four fine sons of yours?"

"Well, the oldest," reported the father proudly, "has a brilliant legal mind. He's working in the district attorney's office now. The salary is very low, but the training will enable him to get to the top.

"My second son is an engineer. You should see the structures and bridges that boy has designed! He's worked only for a government agency so far, but his break is bound to come soon.

"My third son is going to be a renowned surgeon. He's an interne now, and we have to support him, but that will all be changed one day."

The father showed no inclination to continue, and his friend had to remind him, "But what about your youngest? You haven't told me about him."

"Oh, him," said the father with a noticeable lack of enthusiasm. "He finished high school and took a job with a railroad company. He's an assistant superintendent and makes several hundred dollars a month salary, but what kind of a profession is that for a son of mine?" Then he conceded, "Of course, if it wasn't for him, the rest of us would be starving to death."

—*T. & P. Topics.*

✤ ✤ ✤

SUPERSTITION

Many years ago, the reluctance of seaman to sail on a Friday reached such proportions that the British government decided to prove the fallacy of the superstition. They laid the keel of a new vessel on Friday, launched her on Friday, named her H.M.S. *Friday,* and sent her to sea on Friday.

The scheme had only one drawback—neither ship nor crew was ever heard of again.

—*Our Navy.*

✤ ✤ ✤

SUSPICION

A new settler missed his ax, the most important piece of equipment he owned. His suspicion at once was directed to one neighbor, whom he didn't care for. And from that time on he kept spying on his neighbor through the slits in his fence. There was no doubt, it seemed to him, that the way the neighbor moved, the way he placed his feet, the way he coughed, the way he used his hands, was typical of a thief, especially a thief who would steal an ax. He became more and more convinced, and more and more angry, until one day he decided to have a talk with the neighbor and force him to admit the theft. However, that very day he found the ax in the weeds between his flower beds. And from that time on there was no doubt; it seemed to him, that the neighbor no longer moved, placed his feet, coughed, or used his hands like a typical thief. Meanwhile, the neighbor had not changed at all. He himself had changed only his attitude.

—Chinese story told by WERNER HELWIG, *Rheinische Merkur,* Cologne (Droke House translation).

SYMPATHY

One American boy, Sam Stewart, of Schenectady, N. Y., speaks for American youth in a simple letter. Wrote twelve-year-old Sam to seventy-two-year-old Lt. Governor Joe R. Hanley, of N. Y. State, after the latter had his right eye removed: "I want to let you know there is nothing to worry about, as I went through the same thing three years ago. I play all the games the other boys do. I read a lot and can see better with my one eye than a lot of people can with two. Dad has taken me to New York two times, and a lot of people don't realize I have a glass eye."

Then Sam added: "If you have any questions, I'd be glad to come and see you."

—HENRY LEE, *Coronet.*

✣ ✣ ✣

The other day a friendly lady whom I have known for more than a quarter of a century, called on me at my office.

She said: "Isn't it too bad about the elevator man's baby?"

"What about the baby?" I asked.

"Why, did you know he is in the hospital for a dangerous operation?"

I have ridden with the elevator man every day for years. I didn't know he had a baby. She rode up just once. Subconsciously, he realized that she had compassion. Her sympathy, moreover, was given concrete but unobtrusive expression by doing something about that sick baby.

—BRUCE BARTON in *Your Life.*

✣ ✣ ✣

E. V. Lucas tells of a school in England where sympathy is taught. In the course of a term every child has one blind day, one lame day, one deaf day, one day when he cannot speak. The night before the blind day his eyes are bandaged. He awakes blind. He needs help and other children lead him about.

Through this method he gets a grasp on what it is really like to be blind. And those who help, having been "blind" themselves, are able to guide and direct the blind with understanding. This method accomplishes what all of us need—daily training in how we can establish a sense of real fellowship with others.

—GELETT BURGESS, *Reader's Digest.*

✤ ✤ ✤

As a schoolboy, Sir Walter Scott was far from being a brilliant scholar; in fact, he lingered dangerously near the foot of his class.

One day long after he had become famous, he made a surprise visit to his old school. The teacher tried to make a good impression, putting her brightest pupils through the paces; but the effect was somewhat marred by a small boy who sat disconsolately in the corner. He wore a dunce cap!

Sir Walter tried to give his complete attention to the star performance being given but his attention kept wandering again and again to the unhappy lad in the corner. When, at length, the exhibition was finished, the author hastened to the boy, took his hand and said with great kindness, "My good fellow, I know just how you feel. Here's a crown for keeping my place warm."

—*Christian Science Monitor.*

✤ ✤ ✤

Madame Chiang Kai-shek was educated in the United States, not only at Wellesley but also at Wesleyan College in Georgia, where she absorbed an understanding of American regional life. "Tell me something about Sherman's march through Georgia," a European once asked, trying to trip her on American history.

"You will excuse me," she replied, "but I am a Southerner and that subject is naturally very painful to me."

—ELSA MAXWELL.

✤ ✤ ✤

TACT

Cattleman Cy Ferrin had been ill for one of the few times in his stalwart life, so my wife and I rode down country one afternoon to inquire about him. As we approached his gate, about a quarter of a mile from the ranch house, we saw what looked like a new white headstone.

"Why . . . good Lord!" I said. "That can't be true. We'd have heard . . ."

I got off my horse, opened the gate and examined the headstone. On it was neatly lettered: "Here lies the last man who left my gate open. REST IN PEACE."

—STRUTHERS BURT.

✤ ✤ ✤

To make friends with an audience, slowly and step by step is something of a trick. But to do so instantly—perhaps in one's very opening sentence—is a much more difficult feat. In 1937, a little after the second Roosevelt tidal wave, Mrs. Theodore Roosevelt, Junior (who chances also to bear the name Eleanor), made an address at the Dutch Treat Club.

Though I had purposely introduced her without referring to the recent unpleasantness at the polls, she began her talk with this polished gem: "I feel it only right to tell you that I belong to the Oyster Bay, or out-of-season, Roosevelts!"

The applause that followed was, of course, due to a really happy feat of phrasing.

—FRANK CROWNINSHIELD, in *Vogue.*

✤ ✤ ✤

After a speech a famous lecturer and wit was approached by a little white-haired woman who told him how much she had enjoyed his talk. "I take the liberty to speak to you," she admitted, "because you said you loved old ladies."

"I do, I do," was the gallant reply, "and I also like them your age."

—*United Mine Workers Journal.*

✤ ✤ ✤

A New Hampshire sheriff presented President Eisenhower with a revolver on behalf of the National Sheriffs' Association, declaring, "It's the first time I've ever presented a gun to a Democratic President." Recognizing his mistake, he quickly added, "Go ahead, Mr. President, you may use the gun now—on me!"

—*R. & R. Magazine.*

A lady of uncertain age had been offered a seat by a gentleman of about the same age. "But why," she asked, "should you be so kind to me?"

The gallant reply: "Because, madam, I myself have a mother, a wife and a daughter."

—*Crucible.*

✣ ✣ ✣

Tact is a prime requisite in dealing with church dignitaries, but a child's unpredictable answers may thwart the most carefully laid plans.

The children had been primed for the monsignor's visit, and Sister Rita smiled confidently when he asked, "Does anybody know what a monsignor is?"

"A monsignor," Judy began in precise phrases, "is someone who has done great things for God . . ."

She caught the pleased smile her questioner turned on the parish priest and felt encouraged to continue.

"And," she added, cheeks burning with excitement, "he's just a *little bit* ranker than a priest."

—SISTER MARY GILBERT.

✣ ✣ ✣

A society woman brought her daughter to a renowned piano teacher for an audition. The master listened attentively to the girl's playing, and then said gravely: "The young lady is not without a lack of talent."

—NICOLAS SLONIMSKY, *Etude.*

✣ ✣ ✣

A Friend in a meeting heard proposed (for an office) the name of a member whose fitness he strongly questioned. He merely cleared his throat and murmured: "That is a name which would not have occurred to me."

—I. C. POLEY, *Word Study.*

✣ ✣ ✣

A young man of the diplomatic corps, discouraged at the impasse in world affairs, went into life insurance selling. One of his first prospects, a woman, became coy when asked her age for the application. "Guess," she urged, "you must have some idea."

"I have several ideas," he said with a smile, his training coming to the fore. "The only trouble is that I hesitate whether to make you ten years younger on account of your looks, or ten years older on account of your brains."

—*R. & R. Magazine.*

✣ ✣ ✣

A New York couple decided to spend their vacation in Baltimore, where they were born and raised. En route they visited the battlefield at Gettysburg, Pa. The guide who showed them around waxed eloquent about Northern strategy and Northern heroism. They thanked him, paid the usual fee, and happened to drop the remark that they must be getting home to Baltimore before dark.

The guide's face dropped. "Gosh, from your license plates I took you for New York folks. I should have given you the Southern lecture—matter of fact, I like it better myself."

—*This Week.*

✣ ✣ ✣

James Whitcomb Riley came down the steps of his Lockerbie Street home in Indianapolis one day to be confronted by a hunchbacked little boy with a tear-stained face. "Mr. Riley," his voice shook, "you've seen some crooked soldiers, haven't you?"

The poet looked around, saw an "army" of youngsters, with wooden guns and swords waiting intently for his verdict.

"Of course I have. Not very many, though," he added, "because crooked soldiers are the bravest, the best and the very hardest to get."

—JOSEF CHEVALIER, *Coronet.*

✣ ✣ ✣

TACTLESSNESS

At a prayer meeting shortly after the minister and his wife had returned from a long trip, an elder offered up thanks for their safe return—but put his foot in it.

"Oh, Lord," he said, "we thank Thee for bringing our pastor safely home, and his dear wife, too, dear Lord, for Thou preserveth man and beast."

—*Watchman-Examiner.*

✤ ✤ ✤

TASTE

"You know," said an author, fishing for compliments, "my books are selling better and better, but I think my work is falling off. My new work is not so good as my old."

"Oh, nonsense!" said his friend. "You write just as well as you ever did. Your taste is improving, that's all."

—*Senior Scholastic.*

✤ ✤ ✤

TAXES

Six schools tried and failed to cram formal education into Will Rogers. After he became famous, a woman listener reproached him for bad syntax.

"Syntax?" Rogers repeated, obviously wrestling with a strange new word. "It must be bad, havin' both sin and tax in it."

—Homer Croy, *Our Will Rogers* (Little, Brown).

✤ ✤ ✤

A congressman explained the difference between tax evasion and legitimate tax avoidance this way:

A man approaches a river which can be crossed by two bridges: one, a toll bridge, the other, a free bridge. If, however, he exercises his right of choice and passes over the free bridge, this is tax avoidance.

—*Property.*

✤ ✤ ✤

TEACHERS—Teaching

The little lady remained calm despite the young man's impatience. "But what is your occupation," he demanded, shuffling the forms he held.

"Oh, I do many things."

"Housewife?"

"No."

"Employed?"

"Oh, yes."

"What do you do?"

"A little of everything in a small way. Today—"

"And what did you do today?" the superior young man urged.

"Banking, editing, typing, filing—"

"You are an office clerk?"

"No. I did a bit of housekeeping, nursing, mending, laundering—"

"Ah, then you must be a home economist."

"Oh, no. Part of my day was spent as playwright, stagehand, actress, musician—"

"You work in the theater?"

"Not exactly. At times I paint, print, bind books—"

The young man snapped his fingers. "I've got it. Of course. You are a librarian."

"And somewhat of an electrician, machinist, engineer, architect, cement mixer, plasterer, paperhanger—"

"Madam, surely you are not a builder? Yes? Then I suppose you are also a chemist, explorer, nationalist, and maybe even an internationalist, or—or—a politician?"

"Oh, yes. Yes, indeed," she smiled. "And also a pretty good psychologist, detective, lawyer, judge, umpire, jailer and policeman, as well."

"That is all?"

"Well—"

"Please, madam." The young man held up his hand. His face flushed. His jaw worked. His voice came through clenched teeth. "Please, madam. You say you did all those jobs today. But yesterday—what did you do yesterday?"

"Oh, the same. You see I teach children."

—BEULAH HELEN BEERS, *Journal of Education.*

✣ ✣ ✣

At the end of my university studies when I was leaving for

my first professorial job, I went to say good-bye to my old teacher, William Peterfield Trent.

"I can give you no theoretical advice in pedagogy," he said, "but I'll tell you one thing from experience. It will frequently happen when you are holding forth that some boy in the class will disagree. He will probably shake his head violently. You will be tempted to go after him and convert him then and there. Don't do it. He is probably the only one who is listening."

—John Erskine.

✤ ✤ ✤

TEMPTATION

A little boy had been severely punished by his mother for a misdeed. "You should turn a deaf ear to temptation when it calls," she scolded.

In tears, the little fellow protested, "But Mummy, I don't have a deaf ear!"

✤ ✤ ✤

THEORY-Practice

The difference between theory and practice is well illustrated by the story about the young man who thought that he knew a great deal about child education. As a student of child behavior, he frequently delivered a lecture called the "Ten Commandments for Parents." He married and became a father. The title of the lecture was altered to "Ten Hints for Parents." Another child arrived. The lecture became "Some Suggestions for Parents." A third child was born. At this point, the lecturer gave up lecturing.

✤ ✤ ✤

"Figures can't lie," said the instructor. "For instance, if one man can build a house in twelve days, twelve men can build it in one."

A puzzled student interrupted: "Then 288 will build it in one hour, 17,280 in one minute, and 1,036,800 in one second. I don't believe they could lay one brick in that time."

While the instructor was still gasping, the "ready reckoner" went on: "And again, if one ship can cross the Atlantic in six days, six ships can cross in one day. I can't believe that either."

—*Sunshine Magazine.*

✣ ✣ ✣

According to the theory of aerodynamics and as may be readily demonstrated through wind tunnel experiments, the bumblebee is unable to fly. This is because the size, weight and shape of his body in relation to the total wingspread make flying impossible.

But the Bumblebee, being ignorant of these scientific truths, goes ahead and flies anyway—and makes a little honey every day.

—Sign in a General Motors plant.

✣ ✣ ✣

One night a stargazer wandered on the outskirts of a town. Gazing up at the stars, he fell into a well. For long hours he shouted for help. Finally a villager came to see what was the matter. He peered into the well and saw the helpless astronomer, struggling to get out. "How did you ever manage to get in there?" he asked. The man explained. The villager smiled and said: "My good man, while you are trying to pry into the mysteries of the skies, you overlook the common objects that are under your feet!"

—PHIL MANN, *York Trade Compositor.*

✣ ✣ ✣

A well-known British minister once told of a certain Londoner who was forever sitting around, telling anyone who would listen, how the British Commonwealth should be run.

One day as this man sat spouting his theories, his hard-worked wife found her nerves a bit on edge. She tossed the crying baby into his lap and said, "Here, take your bit of the British Empire and see what you can do with it. I've got to get dinner."

—RALPH W. SOCKMAN.

✣ ✣ ✣

A railway bridge had been destroyed by fire and it was necessary to replace it. The bridge engineer and his staff were ordered in haste to the place. Two days later came the superintendent of the division. Alighting from a private car he encountered the old master bridge-builder.

"Bill," said the superintendent, "I want this job rushed. Every hour of delay is costing the company money. Have you got the engineer's plans for the new bridge?"

"I don't know," said the bridge-builder, "whether the engineer has the picture yet or not, but the bridge is up and trains are passing over it."

✤ ✤ ✤

A modern business firm had just hired a psychologist as personnel manager. The first job was to hire a new secretary for the head of the firm, and the boss was looking on while the expert gave a psychological quiz to three feminine applicants.

"Two and two," said the psychologist.

"Four," replied the first girl promptly.

"It might be twenty-two," replied the second girl to the same key words.

The third girl thought a moment, then answered, "It might be four, and it might be twenty-two."

After the last girl had left, the psychologist turned to the boss.

"There," he said, "you have the perfect example of the efficient psychological way of hiring people. The first girl said the obvious thing. The second was suspicious. The third was cagey and wasn't going to get caught. Which do you prefer?"

There wasn't a moment's hesitation. The boss said promptly, "I'll take the blonde with the blue eyes."

—*Right Hand*

✤ ✤ ✤

THOUGHTFULNESS

Many years ago, Dwight Morrow, father of Anne Lindbergh, told a group of friends that Calvin Coolidge had real presidential possibilities. They unanimously disagreed—said he was too quiet, lacked color and political personality. "No one would like him," declared one sage.

But up piped little Anne, then aged six, "I like Mr. Coolidge." She displayed a finger with a bit of adhesive tape on it. "He was the only one who asked me about my sore finger."

Mr. Morrow nodded. "There's your answer," he said.

—Xavier Cugat.

✣ ✣ ✣

THRIFT

Among the passengers having their baggage examined in the customs of a Mexican entry port was a pretty, red-headed American girl. She was on her way to meet the family of the Mexican lad to whom she was engaged, and was also to visit American friends who had a large family of small children. American shoes are expensive in Mexico, so her friends had asked her to bring down assorted footgear for the children.

The Mexican official lined up the shoes on the top of her trunk and was writing out a bill of duty on them. She was protesting that before paying the duty she would throw the shoes into the sea. He was politely explaining the law. Neither understood a word of what the other was saying.

The whole good-neighbor policy seemed at stake, so I offered my services as interpreter. The customs official explained gravely that he was pained to inconvenience the charming young lady, but that her papers showed she was unmarried, and hence the shoes could not be her personal effects. I hastened to explain that yes, the young lady was unmarried—but she was coming to Mexico to get married.

Beaming at her, without a second's hesitation he tore up the bill, bowed and said: "You Americans, yes, you Americans are a *very* practical people."

—Carleton Beals, *Reader's Digest*.

✣ ✣ ✣

A well-to-do man was asked the secret of his success. "Surely," said the questioner, "you must have been tempted to indulge in extravagance."

"Oh, yes," agreed the opulent one. "But a long time ago I worked out a four-question formula that has saved me a lot of money. First, before I buy, I ask myself, 'Do you really want it?' Usually I can answer 'Yes!' to that one. Then I ask, 'But do you need it?' That cuts short a good many proposed purchases. The next question is, 'Can you afford it?' That's a real stopper! And finally I ask, 'But can't you get along without it?' The few items that survive after that are pretty essential!"

✤ ✤ ✤

Frugality is a common enough trait among the mountain men, but this Kentucky farmer from the north fork of the Licking ran up a new record. When he died, he was—by his own careful accounting—more than $1200 in debt to his desires. For nearly 20 years he had kept a strict ledger record of every penny saved by nonindulgence.

Most of the notations in this Spartan saga were for small sums:

To not chewing tobacco, Aug. 4–11 ....$ .10
To not eating can peaches, April 22 .... .15
To doing without fur earmuffs, Nov. 19 .... .35

But apparently a severe sacrifice was hidden behind one cryptic notation which coincided with fall crop payment time:

To not going to see that girl at West Liberty, Feb. 9. . . .

Beneath he had written and underlined:

. . . *no telling how much!*

—Stewart Sterling.

✤ ✤ ✤

The elderly Pennsylvania Dutch farmer came out of the hardware store, dumped several packages on the seat of his car, and then scrutinized the parking meter.

There were 15 minutes left.

Taking a newspaper from the back pocket of his overalls, he leaned on the meter and began to read. Alternately reading and peeking down at the dial, he stayed there until the red indicator showed that his hour was up. At once he tucked the paper under his arm, got into the car and drove off, on his face the contented look of the thrifty man who has had his full nickel's worth.

—Mrs. Joseph Bellinfante.

Jay Gould and Jim Fisk, freebooters of finance of an earlier day, were involved in many business deals together but were never particularly friendly. A clergyman once remonstrated with Fisk for some of his acid remarks about Gould. "Mr. Gould has his good points, you must admit," the clergyman insisted. "He keeps the Sabbath, for one."

"I've no doubt," agreed Fisk. "Gould keeps everything he gets his hands on."

—*Property.*

✣ ✣ ✣

TIME

I must have been about 14 then, and I dismissed the incident with the easy carelessness of youth. But the words Carl Walter spoke that day came back to me years later, and ever since have been of inestimable value to me.

Carl Walter was my piano teacher. During one of my lessons he asked how much practicing I was doing. I said three or four hours a day.

"Do you practice in long stretches, an hour at a time?"

"I try to."

"Well, don't!" he exclaimed. "When you grow up, time won't come in long stretches. Practice in minutes, whenever you can find them—five or ten before school, after lunch, between chores. Spread the practice through the day, and piano-playing will become a part of your life."

When I was teaching at Columbia, I wanted to write, but recitations, theme-reading and committee meetings filled my days and evenings. For two years I got practically nothing down on paper, and my excuse was that I had no time. Then I recalled what Carl Walter had said. During the next week I conducted an experiment. Whenever I had five unoccupied minutes, I sat down and wrote a hundred words or so. To my astonishment, at the end of the week I had a sizable manuscript ready for revision.

Carl Walter has had a tremendous influence on my life. To him I owe the discovery that even very short periods of time add up to all the useful hours I need, if I plunge in without delay.

—John Erskine.

✤ ✤ ✤

The American couple were doing the Louvre on a Cook's tour.

"What time is it?" asked the wife.

"What's the name of that painting?" was the answer.

The woman approached the painting and peered closely at the title. "Mona Lisa," she replied.

Her husband scanned his itinerary book.

"Then it's quarter past two if we're on time."

—*Christian Science Monitor.*

✤ ✤ ✤

The animals were complaining that humans were always taking things away from them. "They take my milk," griped the cow. "They take eggs from me," said the hen. "From me they get bacon and other meat," commented the hog. "They hunt me for the sake of my oil," mourned the whale.

And so on. Then the snail smiled. "I have something they would like to have—more than anything else. Something they would certainly take away from me if they could. You see, I have *time!*"

—*Sonenschein,* Bielefeld (Droke House Translation).

✤ ✤ ✤

"Every day you wait, you lose," says a man of life's experiences. "All my life I have been planning and hoping and thinking and dreaming and loitering and waiting. All my life I have been getting ready to do something worth while. I have been waiting for the summer, and waiting for the fall; I've been waiting for the winter and waiting for the spring—waiting, and dawdling and dreaming—until the day is almost spent."

—*Evans Echoes.*

✤ ✤ ✤

Two men once lost their lives in this manner: One of them became angry at the other, and, removing a pendulum from a big clock, used it as a weapon with which he beat the life out of his companion. The murderer took poison and so the two passed on. A philosopher commenting on the tragedy said: "What a shame to make violent use of that pendulum! Give it time, and it would have killed both men peacefully and decently."

—*Present Truth Messenger.*

✤ ✤ ✤

A child was overheard meditating aloud: "At Grandmamma's there isn't any We-don't-have-time-to-do-that . . . Grandmamma doesn't have a watch on her arm. . . . At Grandmamma's I feel good."

In the child's world, time is not measured grudgingly. Time is *now*. Time is being.

—LUCY NULTON, *Your Child's World.*

✤ ✤ ✤

The most natural character I know hasn't looked at a clock for 30 years. He says that all really important events such as eating, sleeping and making love, don't need to be jogged by watches. He hasn't any calendar either. Yet for 25 years he has written a marvelous quarterly full of timely comment on men and events. When the sap begins to run, he knows it's time for his spring number. When the year's last aster feels the year's first frost, he puts his autumn issue to bed. He figures that a week one way or the other won't make much difference. "How long did you work today?" I once asked him. "Just long enough to write a sonnet," he replied. Dawn is his alarm clock; twilight his supper hour. At 72, his mainspring seems scarcely to be worn at all.

—HENRY MORTON ROBINSON, *Reader's Digest.*

✤ ✤ ✤

Will Rogers, the practical philosopher, was once asked by a discouraged friend, "If you had but forty-eight hours to live, how would you spend them?"

The indomitable cow-puncher replied quietly, "One at a time."

✤ ✤ ✤

A fellow I really admired was Houdini. I once saw him put time to its maximum advantage. He jumped out of an airplane, heavily handcuffed, and had to get out of the shackles before he could pull the string of his parachute. He figured he had only 28 seconds in which to get loose. I bet he didn't waste any of that time in starry-eyed gazing at the scenery. If I were a moralist, I'd advise everyone to use his time as completely as Houdini must have used it after stepping out of that airplane.

—Christopher Morley.

✤ ✤ ✤

I don't like the jittery little modern clocks. There was something restful about the leisurely swing of the pendulums in those old clocks. We had one at home with a moon and all the planets circling slowly in their celestial orbits. Every time you looked at it, you got a cosmic feeling as well as the time of day.

—Margaret Fishback.

✤ ✤ ✤

TOLERANCE

The Rev. Dr. Wadham, in my play, *The Fool,* barred discussion of labor conditions in his parish, but was passionately concerned with eucharistic candles; very few of his cloth were shocked by that, but nearly 700 of them wrote me complaining that my rector-hero, Gilchrist, smoked a pipe!

Arthur Garfield Hays recently showed me a collection of denominational pamphlets opposing even very moderate drinking, as well as smoking, dancing, card-playing, theaters, movies and "every Sabbath sport but passing the plate." "Their chief effect," he said, "is to persuade the average man that religion is a system of trivial taboos, having nothing whatever to do with him." You can tell Mr. and Mrs. John Q. Citizen that it is important to be decent and honest; you can't tell them it's wrong to go swimming on Sunday. They know it doesn't matter to God whether they swim or not; they don't stop swimming, they stop going to church.

—Channing Pollock in *The American Mercury.*

✤ ✤ ✤

One summer evening my father caught me tearing down the street after another child screaming, "Wop, dirty wop!"

He stopped me short, and said, "Young lady, just *who* do you think *you* are?"

He took me into the house, sat me down at a desk and gave me a sheet of paper. He said, "Now, I want you to write down every way in which you are different or better than the little Italian girl."

Ah, that was easy. She was Italian, a "wop"—but I was of French descent, a "frog." Besides, we were both really Americans. I'd better not put that down. Well, she was dirty! I looked at my own grimy hands and dirt-stained dress. I'd better skip that part. I was in the fifth grade, and she was only in the fourth! Hmmm, but I was ten and she was only eight. I was blonde—but she had curly hair.

Dinnertime rolled around, and my paper was still blank. I took it slowly to my father. He smiled and said, "That's a good paper. Now until you can create a wonderful human soul, as God can, don't presume to criticize anyone because God chose to have him born a member of *any one* of His nations or races. Remember this paper."

And I always have.

—SYLVIA VAUGHN.

✤ ✤ ✤

TOLERANCE—Intolerance

"I have heard frequent use," said Lord Sandwich, in a debate on the Test Laws, "of the words 'orthodoxy' and 'heterodoxy'; but I confess myself at a loss to know precisely what they mean."

"Orthodoxy, my lord," said Bishop Warburton, in a whisper, "orthodoxy is my doxy—heterodoxy is another man's doxy."

✤ ✤ ✤

TRADITION

An elderly Vermont farmer, reminiscing about his boyhood when he used to work with his grandfather, remembered that in one of the hayfields there were some mounds. They were a bother. The mowing machine could not be used on them. His grandfather always mowed them by hand with a scythe. Once the little boy asked the old man, "What are these mounds?" His grandfather said, "Indians were buried here, long before the white settlers ever came into Vermont." The child suggested with practical good sense, "Why don't you just smooth them out? 'Twould make haying so much easier." The old Vermonter said equably, "Oh, I guess not. They've lain there a long time. We'd better leave 'em quiet a while longer."

He who had been a little boy, was now very old. To him came one day an archaeologist who told him that because of the great age of the burial mounds, there might be artifacts in them for which museums and collectors would pay high prices. He made the old farmer a proposition: if he could have permission from the owner of the land to dig up the graves, he would share, half and half, any money which came in.

The old farmer delivered no self-righteous rebuke about treating dead Indians less honorably than dead white people. He picked up his grandfather's phrase from seventy years ago and said quietly, "No, they've lain there a long time, I guess we'd better leave 'em quiet a while longer."

—Dorothy Canfield Fisher, *Vermont Tradition* (Little, Brown).

✤ ✤ ✤

TREES

In Athens, Georgia, stands a tall white oak tree which has the distinction of belonging quasi-legally to itself. The ground on which the tree stands was once owned by William H. Jackson, father of the Chief Justice of the Supreme Court, James Jackson. The old man was so fond of the tree that he wrote a deed conveying to it full possession of itself and the land into which its roots were thrust.

In Kentucky a deed grants thirty-six square feet of land to a sycamore tree "for and in consideration of its shade, coolness and inspiration."

—*Property.*

✤ ✤ ✤

TRIBUTE

When Helen Hayes was thrilling theatergoers as Mary of Scotland, a boy waited nightly outside the stage door. Miss

Hayes noticed him there night after night, but he never tried to speak to her. Then one evening he pressed forward, put a little box in her hand, and hurried away. Miss Hayes opened the box. A tiny medal lay inside. On the gold-washed surface was the inscription: "Scholarship medal. Public School No. 28, 1933."

—JUNE PROVINES' *Notebook.*

✤ ✤ ✤

TRIFLES

Pascal calls attention to the way in which a little thing may have great consequences, saying that causes so trivial that they can scarcely be recognized move all mankind. "The nose of Cleopatra—if it had been shorter, the history of the world would have been changed."

If Mark Anthony had not been enslaved by Cleopatra's beauty, he might not have lost the battle of Actium and might have become the founder of the Roman Empire.

Perhaps the most whimsical suggestion of all is to the effect that the stubborn resistance of the British army was due to the prevalence of spinsterhood in Great Britain. The explanation of this paradox is to be found in this sequence: The British soldier is nourished on beef, and the quality of the beef is due to an abundance of clover, which needs to be fertilized by bees. But bees cannot multiply and live unless they are protected against the field mice. The field mice can be kept down only if there are cats enough to catch them and cats are the favorites of the frequent old maids in England. These lonely virgins keep pets who prevent the mice from destroying the bees, so clover flourishes luxuriantly and the cattle wax fat to supply the soldiers of the queen with their strengthening rations.

—BRANDER MATTHEWS, in *Scribner's Magazine.*

✤ ✤ ✤

TROUBLE

A woman with a house full of children was once asked whether such a large brood was not the cause of a great deal of trouble.

"No," she replied thoughtfully. "No, I wouldn't say that. Sometimes they are a bother, but never a trouble. The way I look at it, trouble's on the heart, but bother is only on the hands."

✤ ✤ ✤

Most of the troubles we worry about never happen at all. They are like the trouble of the bassoon-player in an orchestra directed by Toscanini. One night, just as a concert was to begin, the bassoon-player came to the director in a panic. His instrument was out of order; he couldn't make it reach E-flat. The wise old director looked at him in total silence, thinking hard. Then he laughed, slapped the musician on the shoulder and said, "Never mind. The note E-flat doesn't appear in the music you'll play tonight."

—*Tarbell's Teachers' Guide* (Revell).

✤ ✤ ✤

One rainy summer my neighbor Clarence was having difficulty plowing a field on his Oklahoma farm. Finally his tractor became so deeply mired that Clarence had to go back to the barn for fence posts, a chain and spade. A passer-by, seeing him struggling to extricate the heavy tractor, called out, "You having a little trouble, Clarence?"

"No. No trouble at all," Clarence cheerfully replied. "What I call trouble is somethin' I cain't fix."

—Guy Harp.

✤ ✤ ✤

Once a hunter met a lion near the hungry critter's lair, and the way that lion mauled him was decidedly unfair; but the hunter never whimpered when the surgeons, with their thread, sewed up forty-seven gashes in his mutilated head; and he showed the scars in triumph, and they gave him pleasant fame, and he always blessed the lion that had camped upon his frame. Once that hunter, absent minded, sat upon a hill of ants, and about a million bit him, and you should have seen him dance! And he used up lots of language of a deep magenta tint, and apostrophized the insects in a style unfit to print. And it's thus with worldly troubles; when the big ones come along, we serenely go to meet them, feeling valiant, bold and strong, but the weary little worries with their poisoned stings and smarts, put the lid upon our courage, make us gray, and break our hearts.

—Walt Mason, *Walt Mason, His Book* (Barse & Hopkins).

✣ ✣ ✣

An old farmer had plowed around a rock in one of his fields for many years. He had grown very morbid over it, for it had caused him to break a cultivator and several plows, besides losing a lot of valuable land around it.

One day he became angered at the trouble it had given him and he made up his mind that he would dig it up and be done with it. When he put his crowbar under it, he discovered that it was less than a foot thick and that he could loosen it with comparatively little effort and carry it away in his wagon. He smiled to think how that particular rock had haunted him through so many wasted years before he determined to do something about it.

✣ ✣ ✣

TRUST

Pop Butterman was well liked in our village, yet people said of him: "Pop is smart all right, if only he'd do something!" When reproached for not fishing or working at the many other trades he knew, Pop invariably replied that he was too busy.

This was the exact truth, as I found out after my dog died. I had loved that dog dearly and yet through my own careless fault it had met a horrible death. I was in an agony of remorse when Pop appeared, bringing his own dog Jacko, an animal he adored. "I want you to have him," was all Pop said. But his eyes told me the rest. He was trusting me with something he knew I felt unworthy ever to possess again. It was the sort of faith I needed badly. And I found out later that Pop had rejected a paid fishing trip in order to bring me Jacko without delay. He had been "too busy" to work.

—Nina Wilcox Putnam.

During the first evacuation of children from bomb-torn areas in London, a train packed with children was leaving the city, taking them into the safer areas of the countryside. One little girl began to cry. She was afraid because she didn't know where she was going. Her little brother, brushing aside his own tears, said consolingly as he put his arm around her, "Sister, I don't know where we're going either, but the King knows."

—W. DALE OLDHAM, *Gospel Trumpet.*

✣ ✣ ✣

TRUSTFULNESS

A banker in a small southwestern town was visited one day by an old Navajo who had a large balance on deposit. Behind him trailed his interpreter. Understanding Indians, the banker offered them chairs and cigarettes. There was thoughtful smoking for 15 minutes, then the interpreter spoke. "He say family all sick, sheep all dying, terrible hard luck, need money."

The banker had all the Navajo's money brought out in $5 bills and stacked on the table. More cigarettes were lit and the three men settled back and stared at the stacks of money for another quarter hour. Finally the old Indian spoke to his interpreter. "He say family all well now," the interpreter translated. "Sheep all right, everything fine." And with superb dignity the two Indians stalked out.

—MRS. P. M. PRATE, *Reader's Digest.*

✣ ✣ ✣

A burglar, needing money to pay his income tax, decided to rob a safe in one of his town's retail stores. He broke in and found the safe without trouble, but was brought up short by a sign reading: "Please don't use dynamite on this beautiful safe. It's not locked. Just turn knob."

Puzzled, the burglar followed directions. Instantly, a heavy sandbag fell on him, alarm bells started ringing, and the entire area was floodlighted. As police dragged him away, he muttered, "It's enough to shake your faith in human nature."

—*Drovers' Telegram.*

A county sheriff in Maine was suspected of undue leniency toward his prisoners in the county jail, but definite proof was lacking. Then one summer evening a fellow townsman passed the jail and noticed six or seven of the inmates, neatly dressed, coming out of the jail. In the doorway stood the sheriff, watching their departure.

The curious citizen stepped behind a tree and heard the sheriff say to the prisoners, "Now you fellers be back here by 9:30, or by thunder, you'll be locked out!"

—Edith C. Weren.

✤ ✤ ✤

An airport story tells of an Army flier going through the milky haze of a cloud who caught up with a civilian ship, groping along. The lieutenant turned upside down and overtook the other in that position. The civilian, distrustful of his impression that the earth was beneath him, promptly turned upside down too.

—Wolfgang Langewiesche, in *Harper's Magazine.*

✤ ✤ ✤

TRUTH

A lawyer makes his most telling impression during cross-examination. To bully even a recalcitrant witness is dangerous, however, because the jury's sympathies may swing to the underdog. Whenever Max Steuer, a well-known lawyer, suspected a witness was lying he would become friendly and sympathetic, luring the perjurer to his doom.

A superb example of this occurred during the Triangle Shirtwaist trial. A New York factory had burned; the owners, defended by Steuer, were accused of causing the death of 100 girls by ordering that a certain exit be kept locked. As a girl survivor told her harrowing story, the jurors wept; a verdict of guilty seemed inevitable.

Steuer believed that the girl was telling a cooked-up tale but in cross-examining her he was gentle as a father. "Now Katie," he said, "just tell your story again."

The tale was repeated word for word. Then Steuer said kindly: "Katie, in order to clear up one or two points, please tell your story once more."

After the third recital, Steuer asked: "Katie, haven't you forgotten a word?"

Katie thought intently. "Yes sir, I forgot one word."

"Well, tell the story again and put that word in."

Katie obliged. The jury, convinced that the girl had been coached by the prosecution until she had learned her story by heart, ignored her testimony, and exonerated Steuer's clients.

—HENRY MORTON ROBINSON, in *Your Life.*

✣ ✣ ✣

The captain wrote in the ship's log: "First mate was drunk today."

After sobering up, the mate went to the captain and pleaded with him to strike out the record.

"It was the first time in my life I've been drunk," he pleaded, "and I promise never to do it again."

"In this log we write only the truth," stormed the skipper.

Next day it was the mate's turn to keep the log, and in it he wrote: "Captain was sober today."

—*Argonaut.*

✣ ✣ ✣

I was as much of a nuisance as any small boy and a neighbor asked my mother once, "Do you ever believe anything that boy says?"

"He is the wellspring of truth," my mother replied, "but you can't bring up the whole well with one bucket. I know his average, so he never deceives me. I discount him 90 percent for embroidery and what is left is perfect and priceless truth, without a flaw."

—MARK TWAIN.

✣ ✣ ✣

In Noel Coward's drama, *Blithe Spirit,* Charles is word-sparring with his second wife Ruth about the things that make life worth while when Ruth retorts, "You know, that's the kind of observation that shocks people." To which Charles answers, "It's discouraging to think how many people are shocked by honesty and how few by deceit."

Is it because the truth hurts, or because we don't like the truth and are content to live by falsehood?

—*Christian Herald.*

⁂

All through Hinduism there is emphasis on the idea that the seeker for truth will find it nearer than he thinks, more likely within himself than outside. Here is a typical parable:

A man awoke at midnight and wanted a smoke. He went to a neighbor's, knocked on the door and asked for a light. "Bah!" scoffed the neighbor. "You have taken all the trouble to come over here and awaken me to get a light, when in your own hand you hold a lighted lantern!"

—CHARLES FRANCIS POTTER, *The Faiths Men Live By* (Prentice-Hall).

⁂

A boy was a witness in court, and the lawyer said: "Did anyone tell you what to say in court?"

"Yes, sir."

"I thought so. Who was it?"

"My father, sir."

"And what did he tell you?"

"He said the lawyers would try to get me all tangled up, but if I stuck to the truth, I would be all right."

—*The Cash Year.*

⁂

Every great scientific truth goes through three stages. First people say it conflicts with the Bible. Next, they say it has been discovered before. Lastly, they say they have always believed it.

—LOUIS AGASSIZ.

⁂

Of all the cowards, of all the wobbly pussyfooters, the man who is afraid of his own record is the worst. The thing that should govern a man is not what he has said, but the truth as he sees it. Consistency is a paste jewel.

—WILLIAM ALLEN WHITE.

"One day," said Li Yung Ku, my wise young Tibetan teacher, "when I was about five, I told my grandfather a lie. It was not a very black lie. My grandfather asked our gardener to bring a long ladder and place it against the front of the house so that it reached the roof. When the ladder was firmly in place he said to the gardener: 'Our boy has taken to leaping from house-tops. The ladder is for him to use when he so desires.' I knew at once what this meant, for one of the proverbs in our district was: 'A lie is a leap from a house-top.'

"I brooded in silence. It was awkward to have the ladder before the front door. I began to fear that it would be there forever if I did not do something. I found my grandfather reading a book and I went quietly up to him and buried my face in his lap. 'Grandpa,' I said, 'we do not need the ladder any more.' He seemed very happy. He called the gardener and said to him: 'Take the ladder away at once. Our boy does not leap from house-tops.' I will never forget that incident."

—Manuel Komroff, *Reader's Digest*.

✤ ✤ ✤

Even a known liar is to be believed if he is sufficiently corroborated:

If six of the greatest liars in the world were to be placed in six separate cells, so that it would be impossible for them to communicate with one another, and yet each could view the sky through an aperture in the roof of his cell; and if, as a further supposition, a keeper would daily serve the liars with food:

Now, our hypothetical keeper goes to the cell of Liar No. 1 and says, "Good morning, Liar No. 1. How are you?"

Liar No. 1 answers: "Not so well, but I did see the most beautiful bird. Oh, the rarest kind of bird, through the opening on the roof this morning."

Of course, he being one of the greatest liars of the world, the keeper pays no attention, but proceeds to the cell of Liar No. 2.

"Good morning, Liar No. 2, and how have you been?"

"So-so—but I did see a most beautiful bird this morning. Oh, it was the rarest kind of bird!"

The keeper makes no comment, but begins to wonder if there

is anything to this bird story. So he goes on to the cell of Liar No. 3.

"Good morning, Liar No. 3. How are you?"

"Oh, I am very well, and I did see a beautiful bird this morning. It had the rarest kind of plumage."

By this time our keeper is becoming credulous and after hearing the same narrative from the remaining three liars, he is convinced that a rare bird of magnificent plumage had flown over the cells of the six liars, and that even from a known liar, if there is sufficient corroboration, we can get at the truth.

—MARK GREEN, *Illustrations for Argumentation.*

✤ ✤ ✤

A young man leaving the penal institution where he had served his term heard these parting words from the warden: "I am not going to preach you a long sermon, just one thing I would recommend you to do—never tell another lie in your life."

The young man went home, looked for a job everywhere but was turned down in each case because of his prison record. Then one day he answered an employment ad, presenting the certificates he had. After reading them the gentleman asked him: "Where have you been the last three years? You don't have any references to show what you have done." "Well," said the young man, "I have been in the penitentiary." "And why do you tell me that so bluntly?" asked the gentleman. The youth eyed him calmly and said, "Because I promised the warden never to tell another lie in my life."

"The job is yours," said his future boss.

—*Capper's Weekly.*

✤ ✤ ✤

All Maine people are natural-born liars, which is not at all so hideous a distinction as being a trained one. My wife hadn't got used to this when Henry Jorgen came up to brook solace with me over the continued wet weather. Instead of commenting that we'd had enough rain for anyone with normal desires, Henry, who lives 20 miles from the ocean, said, "Got a sea serpent in my pasture."

My wife was just about to put in a doubting remark, but I knew Henry was merely emphasizing his displeasure at the weather, so I beat her to it and said, "A big one?"

"Not awful big," said Henry. "But pretty-colored."

This method of making a basic fact memorable has nothing to do with injunctions against false witness. Henry, and people like him, has never been known to utter an untruth. He tells good wholesome lies because it's the most artistic way he knows of to tell the truth.

—JOHN GOULD, in *Farmer Takes a Wife* (Wm. Morrow & Co.).

✤ ✤ ✤

But (Daniel) standing in the midst of them said: "Are ye such fools, ye sons of Israel, that without examination or knowledge of the truth ye have condemned a daughter of Israel?" Then Daniel said unto them, "Put those two aside, one far from the other, and I will examine them."

So, when they were put asunder, one from another, he called one of them and said unto him: "Now, then if thou hast seen her, tell me, under what tree sawest thou them companying together?" who answered, "Under a mastick tree." And Daniel said, "Very well; thou hast lied against thine own head." So he put him aside and commanded to bring the other, and said unto him, "Now, therefore, tell me under what tree didst thou take them companying together?" who answered "Under an holm tree." Then Daniel said unto him, "Well, thou hast also lied against thine own head."

With that, all the assembly cried out with a loud voice, and praised God who saveth them that trust Him. And they arose against the two elders, for Daniel had convicted them of false witness, by their own mouth. From that day forth was Daniel held in great reputation in the sight of the people.

—*Susanna and The Elders* (Apocryhpa).

✤ ✤ ✤

It is a prudent provision which specifies that a witness in court of justice shall tell "the truth, the whole truth, and nothing but the truth."

Sometimes a limited segment of truth can present a badly

distorted picture. Merle Thorpe once told of such an instance:

An editor of a Cleveland newspaper sent a reporter to interview Commodore Vanderbilt, the railroad magnate, one day at the turn of the century. But the reporter got into a poker game and didn't get around to call on Vanderbilt until long after midnight. He threw gravel on the window of the Commodore's private car. Vanderbilt came out in his nightshirt and asked what was wanted.

"I want an interview with you," said the reporter.

"I can't talk to you now," said the financier.

"The public demands that you talk to me?" insisted the reporter.

Whereupon Commodore Vanderbilt said (and under the circumstances you must agree he had some provocation) "The public be damned at three o'clock in the morning!"

The reporter, telling only a segment of the truth, declared that Commodore Vanderbilt had said, "The public be damned!" So it was heralded throughout the United States that the leader of one of our great utilities had thus expressed his scorn for the sovereign people. For nearly half a century that phrase, quoted out of context, has brought suspicion, distrust and reprisal on our public utilities!

✤ ✤ ✤

UNDERSTANDING

When London's Bank of England built an air-raid shelter underground, to protect its staff during World War II, its A.R.P. wardens sent a health questionnaire to employes to find out if they could withstand prolonged imprisonment in the narrow, crowded shelter. One question was: "Do you suffer from claustrophobia?"

To their amazement, 95 percent of the women employes answered, "Yes." Calling in the chief of the women's division, the A.R.P. organizers asked her if she had explained to the girls exactly what "claustrophobia" meant. "Oh yes," said she. "I told them it meant being afraid of confinement."

—*Time.*

UNITY

It was visitors' day in a large state hospital. A social service worker was being shown around the asylum and his heart ached at the plight of these poor people. In one ward, however, his compassion was mixed with fear. About one hundred husky, wild-eyed inmates stared menacingly at the visitors, while only two rather inoffensive-looking guards stood by seemingly unaware of the potential danger. The visitor asked his guide cautiously:

"Do you think two guards are enough to hold these fellows in check if they all ganged up against them?"

The guide grinned good-naturedly, then chuckled: "Why, there's no danger of that. Don't you realize that lunatics never unite?"

—MAEANNA CHESTERTON-MANGLE.

✤ ✤ ✤

A crusty old sailor took out a visitor for a row in his boat. The unwieldy landsman fell overboard. The ancient mariner grabbed him by the hair, but his wig came off, and he sank. Rising again, he called, "Save me! Save me!" And this time the old salt caught him by the arm, but it was an artificial one, and came off. For the third time the man rose and screamed for help. The old sailor seized him by his clothes and said, "How can I save you, if you won't stick together?"

—*United Church Observer.*

✤ ✤ ✤

The scene was a crowded bus in New York. The driver, harassed by passengers jammed in the front of the bus, alternated between requesting and ordering his riders to move to the rear, all to no avail. Finally, in desperation, he drew up to the curb in front of the United Nations, stopped the bus, and stood up. Pointing dramatically to the towering glass building that houses the U. N., he said, "If we can't get together on this bus, how can we expect those fellows in there to get together and help keep us out of war?" Whereupon the crowd moved to the rear and the bus went on.

—*National Parent-Teacher.*

USEFULNESS

There was a salt-marsh that bounded part of the mill-pond, on the edge of which we used to stand to fish for minnows. By much trampling, we had made it a mere quagmire. My proposal was to build a wharf there fit to stand upon, and I showed my comrades a large heap of stones which were intended for a new house, and which would suit our purpose. Accordingly, in the evening, when the workmen were gone, I assembled a number of my play-fellows, and working diligently, we brought the stones all away and built our little wharf. The next morning the workmen were surprised at missing the stones, which were found in our wharf. Inquiry was made after the removers; we were discovered and complained of; several of us were corrected by our fathers; and, though I pleaded the usefulness of the work, mine convinced me that nothing was useful which was not honest.

—Carl Van Doren, "Benjamin Franklin's Autobiographical Writings," (The Viking Press).

✣ ✣ ✣

Do you know how to gather up fragments of time lest they perish? One of the Lamoignons had a wife who always kept him waiting a few minutes before dinner. After a time it occurred to him that eight or ten lines could be written during this interval, and he had paper and ink laid in a convenient place for that purpose. In time—for years are short but minutes are long—several volumes of spiritual meditations were the result.

—Ernest Dimnet, in *The Art of Thinking* (Simon & Schuster).

✣ ✣ ✣

VALUE

Poets have always done well by the wind—and in general, I'm in favor of more poetry and less wind.

Long ago Jim Coombs of Carter's Corner was becalmed with his sailing vessel down around the Solomons, and the crew sat around for two weeks without a breath stirring. About that time, Jim fished in his pocket and drew out a silver shilling. He tossed it overboard with a flourish and called at the sky, "Give us a shillin's worth of wind!" Almost immediately Jim's ship was in the middle of the worst hurricane he ever saw. When the storm abated, Jim stood on deck amid the wreckage and commented, "If I'd a-knowed wind was so cheap, I'd not a-bought so much."

—JOHN GOULD, in *Farmer Takes a Wife* (Wm. Morrow & Co.).

✣ ✣ ✣

I was just six when I asked my parents, immigrants from Rumania, if I wasn't big enough to sell papers as my two older brothers were doing. Mother consented and with ten cents in "capital" clutched in my hand I ran to the nearby newspaper circulation office and bought my first stock in trade.

By dinnertime, five pennies' profit in addition to my original investment jingled in my pockets as I strode manfully and rather proudly into the house. My whole family gathered round as I spread my pennies on the table and waited for the applause.

"Huh," scoffed one of my sisters with the cruelty of the very young, "all afternoon and only a nickel."

My spirits slumped. The pennies jingled not nearly so merrily as Mother wordlessly scooped them into her apron pocket. Still silent, she went to a nearby grocery and returned with a large loaf of bread (five cents the loaf at pre-World War I prices). She sliced it and passed it around. Then she turned to me.

"Your nickel bought this big loaf of bread," she said. "Today you have helped feed the whole family."

No one said a word. My feeling of pride in my accomplishment returned, and I don't think I ever munched a better-tasting piece of bread.

—IRVING GREENE, *Reader's Digest*.

✣ ✣ ✣

Dr. Oliver Wendell Holmes was, in stature, a rather small man, but there was nothing diminutive about his spirit. One time, when he was present at a gathering of unusually tall men, he was asked, as a joke, if he didn't feel somewhat small and insignificant in the company of such big, strapping fellows.

"Indeed I do," replied Dr. Holmes tartly. "I feel like a dime among a collection of pennies!"

✣ ✣ ✣

On the marketplace in the city of Taiz in Yemen the Arabian desert king Achmed had his two brothers beheaded, saying that they were plotting against him. According to the story, only one reporter was allowed to interview him after the deed, and that one almost took his own life in his hands by reminding him that the act hardly corresponded with 20th century ideals!

Replied Achmed: "Finest flower of civilization, it is a matter of these ideals! If my brothers had been plotting against me about the throne, I would perhaps have been satisfied with a lesser punishment, such as cutting off their hands. But they were plotting about something else—about oil!"

—*Weltbild,* Munich.

✣ ✣ ✣

Some thirty or more years ago Roger Babson, the noted economist, was on a trip to South America and in the course of his journey was the guest of the President of Argentina. It was a pleasant association, and on the evening before his departure, Mr. Babson relates, his host was commenting on the fact that while his country was almost as rich in natural resources and potential productiveness as was the United States, they were so far behind in every respect—economically, culturally, educationally, and religiously.

"You know, Mr. Babson," said the thoughtful Argentine president, "I think I know the reason." And after a moment he continued, "when the early settlers came to settle on your shores, they came to build homes where they might be free to worship God. But when our land was settled, it was settled by adventurers whose only thought was to gain the riches which were here."

—CARL S. LEDBETTER, *Link.*

✣ ✣ ✣

VANITY

The resourcefulness of the brilliant English barrister, Sir Edward Marshall Hall, was revealed in his defense of a libel suit brought against Lord Beaverbrook by Lady Terrington. Claiming that her reputation had suffered severely from a statement made about her clothes in Beaverbrook's *Daily Express,* she asked exorbitant damages.

Sir Edward timed the case so that its concluding phase should fall on Armistice Day, and arranged that the two minutes of national silence at 11 A.M. would interrupt his summation to the jury. As the hour struck, his voice was raised high in impassioned argument, but he broke off dramatically. Everybody rose. Hall stood transfigured; from a contentious barrister, he became a somber statue of mourning. After the two minutes of silence, Sir Edward resumed solemnly.

"Members of the jury," he said, "we have just commemorated our greatest national sacrifice. We have all suffered grievous losses from the war. And now"—Hall wheeled on the plaintiff —"we turn from the painful remembrance of our heroic sacrifices to the trifling grievances of this lady." Lady Terrington's vanity, set against an epic period of English history, could not stand the test. She did not get a farthing.

—HENRY MORTON ROBINSON, in *Your Life.*

✤ ✤ ✤

VARIETY

We thought we'd heard all the selling arguments there are in favor of that indispensible volume, the dictionary. But eleven-year-old Richard Earnhart, who won the National Spelling Bee some years ago, turned up with a new one:

"I enjoy reading the Dictionary," said he, "because it changes the subject so often."

—*Counter Points.*

✤ ✤ ✤

VIEWPOINT

A four-year-old once asked me: "Don't sleeves get tired of arms sometimes?" Funny—but significant too. Become aware of yourself, of the way you button your coat, of how your feet feel inside your shoes.

Each day you pass through a door to a place of work. The child would notice the doorknob, however many times he went through it, its slipperiness, shape and color, the click of its opening. He would notice that the flaps of Mr. Smith's pockets were half in, half out, not critically but because they reminded him of the ears of some animal.

Joseph Conrad had a character who was always stepping back out of the sweat of the moment to exclaim to himself, "What an adventure! What an adventure!" This is precisely the point of view. Everything can be adventure if we make the effort to see it that way.

—GEORGE KENT, in *Your Life.*

✣ ✣ ✣

Last year I visited an isolated mission station maintained by the Baptist Church for the benefit of the fishermen, trappers and moss-gatherers living in the great Atchafalaya Swamp of Louisiana. While I was there, a shrimp lugger laden with both passengers and produce glided past. The wife of the head of the mission looked after it with joyous eyes, and then turned to me.

"That lugger will go on down the bayou to Plaquemine," she said, "and if they're a mind to, the passengers can get on a river steamer there that'll take them straight to New Orleans. At New Orleans they can get a bigger steamer that'll take them across the Gulf; they can go to Mexico and South America; and then they can go on and on. *Why, you can go anywhere on earth from a bayou!*"

—FRANCES PARKINSON KEYES.

✣ ✣ ✣

A well-to-do Frenchman, meeting an old friend on the street, and noticing that he was worried-looking, remarked, sympathetically, "I'm afraid things are not going well with you, Francois. May I help you in any way?"

"Yes," replied the friend, "everything goes wrong with me and my wife and children. I need money very badly."

"I'm so sorry," replied the wealthy man. "Here are 50 francs, if that will help you."

About a year later they met again and Francois was still out of luck. Again his friend gave him money, this time 100 francs.

And some months later the same thing occurred and Francois was given 500 francs.

Then one day Francois accosted his well-to-do friend with the familiar tale of woe, and the friend gave him 25 francs, whereupon the degenerate complained, "Evidently things are not going well with you either. At first you gave me 50 francs, and then up to 500 francs, but now you give me a mere 25 francs!"

"Yes," replied the other apologetically. "You see, my children are old enough to go to school, and that is costing me a lot of money."

"Ah, I see," said Francois bitterly. "You are educating your children at my expense!"

—COL. EDWARD DAVIS, *Sunshine Magazine.*

✤ ✤ ✤

A small boy was given a new baseball with the admonition: "Now you can practice and some day maybe you'll be a world-famous pitcher at $50,000 a year!"

"Oh, no," said the boy positively, "not me!"

"You wouldn't want to?" asked the giver in surprise.

"Nope," said the boy, and then added with great dignity, "I play second base."

—CLAIRE MACMURRAY, *Cleveland Plain Dealer.*

✤ ✤ ✤

"Yours must be a dog's life," someone said to a traffic officer at a busy intersection. "It would be if I were a dog," replied the policeman. "But I'm not a dog. I am a saver of lives. Already today I have saved three lives right here at this corner. How many have you saved?"

—DR. ROY L. SMITH.

✤ ✤ ✤

It might shake some of us out of our complacency to reflect that, in the estimation of the majority of men, we Christians are outcasts from the divine presence. To the orthodox Jew, we are *goyim,* heathen. To the Mohammedan, we are infidels, to be barely tolerated because the Koran so commands. To the conservative Chinese, we are foreign devils. To the Hindu, we are people forever excluded from the light.

—*The Presbyterian Tribune.*

There is a story of two knights who quarreled over the metal composing a shield. The shield was silver within and gold without. Each could see one side only, and did not realize that the other side was of a differing metal.

—MARK GREEN, *Illustrations for Argumentation.*

✣ ✣ ✣

Man is inclined, when in the wrong, to lay the blame on someone else. He is like the small boy who was standing on the cat's tail. The mother, hearing the terrible outburst, called from an adjoining room, "Tommy, stop pulling that cat's tail!"

Tommy yelled back, "I'm not pulling the cat's tail. I'm only standing on it. He's the one that's doing the pulling."

✣ ✣ ✣

VIRTUE

The Chinese coat customarily has five buttons, each representative of one of the virtues taught by Confucius. The virtues are humanity, justice, order, prudence and rectitude. If the Five Virtues could triumph, the woes which have so long bedeviled our weary world would be relegated to permanent, unmourned exile.

—*Property.*

✣ ✣ ✣

VISION

I have never forgotten the words of an old mountaineer from the Ozarks whom I met once when I was very young.

"Son," he said, "it's might hilly country where I come from. A man's got to keep on climbin' to git anywheres, and mighty ta'ared he gits at it, too. Sometimes, when I git to a level spot, I jest set down and do a piece of still-sottin'. Mighty good fer a person, still-sottin' is. You see a lot o' things you never see otherwheres."

—TED BLANDING, *Toastmaster.*

✣ ✣ ✣

On his deathbed, Governor Hogg of Texas requested that no monument of stone or marble be placed at his grave: that instead there by planted "at my head a pecan tree and at my feet an old-fashioned walnut. And when these trees shall bear, let the pecans and walnuts be given out among the Plains people of Texas so that they may plant them and make Texas a land of trees."

His wishes have been carried out. The first nuts were saved in 1926 and planted in nursery rows, and the same thing has been done each year since. As soon as the saplings are large enough to transplant they are distributed to schools and the county boards.

—*Famous Trees* (U. S. Dept. of Agriculture).

✣ ✣ ✣

When my 18-year-old brother went to an Army camp in Virginia, he had never seen a hill, for in the flat Gulf Coastal region of Texas where we live the horizon forms a perfect circle. So when he came home for his first furlough, one of the questions my father asked was: "Well, son, how do you like all those hills up there? Did they tire out your legs?"

"Well," said Russell thoughtfully, "I don't like the hills, but not because they bother my legs. I just kind of like to see where I'm goin'."

—Carol Avant Stageberg, "Life in These United States."

✣ ✣ ✣

Michael Faraday, the great physicist, took a bit of steel and wire, and with infinite pains created a little toylike instrument. This he demonstrated to a group of men and women. A lady in the audience asked, "What is the good of this toy?"

"Madam," Faraday responded, "of what good is a new-born baby?"

The little instrument which Faraday had created is the very heart of the great commercial world of dynamos today.

✣ ✣ ✣

In the seventeenth century, a committee of the Massachusetts Bay Colony, appointed to investigate the agricultural possibilities of the country, reported that there was little cultivable land west of Newton, Massachusetts.

In a later century, Senator Benton, in an eloquent speech in

Congress, proved conclusively that there could never be any successful settlements beyond the Rocky Mountains.

Even our universities have failed to see their future large enough. In 1820, the regents of Indiana University, having spent $2400 on a building to house the entire universtiy, apologized for their extravagance. "We are aware," they admitted, "that the plan proposed may be opposed on account of its magnitude."

—WILLIAM T. FOSTER.

✤ ✤ ✤

The story is told of Michelangelo that he had the ability to hear a voice in great blocks of stone. He would lean over a block of stone and listen, then following the voice which he seemed to hear from within, he would carve a thing of beauty fit to take its place in the great cathedrals of his day.

—JESSE A. ARNUP, *The Upper Room.*

✤ ✤ ✤

WAR

It cost 75 cents to kill a man in Caesar's time. The price rose to about $3000 during the Napoleonic wars; to $5000 in the American Civil War; and then to $21,000 per man in World War I. In World War II it cost the warring countries $50,000 for each man killed.

✤ ✤ ✤

An old cannibal, hearing of the Great War raging in Europe, was most curious to know how Europeans managed to eat such enormous quantities of human flesh. When told that Europeans do not eat their slain foes, he looked in shocked horror and asked what sort of barbarians we were, to kill without any real object.

—*Tit-Bits*, London.

✤ ✤ ✤

There is not a war in the world, no, nor an injustice, but you women are answerable for it; not in that you have provoked, but in that you have not hindered. Men, by their nature, are prone to fight; they will fight for any cause, or for none. It is for you to choose their cause for them, and to forbid them when there is no cause. There is no suffering, no injustice, no misery in the earth, but the guilt of it lies lastly with you. Men can bear the sight of it, but women should not be able to bear it.

—JOHN RUSKIN.

✣ ✣ ✣

WEAKNESS

In her biography the British Mrs. Asquith tells us that when she was a child she came one day upon a ragged tramp sleeping under a hedge on her father's estate. She sat down and talked with him. When she asked, "How do you decide where you want to go each day?" the wanderer replied, "Oh, I always go with the wind at my back."

✣ ✣ ✣

WEALTH

After Cyrus had conquired an empire larger than the United States, he sat himself down to rule, and was so lavish with gifts that Croesus, his captive and adviser, who once had been the richest monarch in the world, criticized him.

"It will bring you to beggary," Croesus warned.

"How much wealth, Croesus, do you suppose I could have amassed had I collected it as you advise?"

Croesus suggested a staggering sum. Cyrus than sent word to his friends and subordinate rulers that he needed money and asked each of them to write down the amount he would be able to contribute. Croesus was instructed to open the answering messages, and he found they pledged a total vastly greater than the amount he had suggested.

Then the great Cyrus said: "Croesus, there is something the gods have implanted in our souls, and there they have made us all beggars alike, something I can never overcome. I, like all the rest, am insatiate of riches; only in one respect I fancy I am different. Most men, when they have more wealth than they require, bury some of it underground and let it rot, and some they count and measure and guard, and give themselves a world of trouble, and yet for all their wealth they cannot eat more than they have stomach for, or they would burst. Nor can they wear more clothing than they can carry—they would die of suffocation. Consequently, their extra wealth means nothing but extra work. For my part, I serve the gods, and I stretch out my hands for more and more, but when I have taken what is beyond my own requirements, I piece out the wants of my friends, and so, helping my fellows, I purchase their love and good will, and out of these I garner security and renown, fruits that can never rot, rich meats that can work no mischief."

—JAMES B. COLLINS, *Good Business.*

✤ ✤ ✤

When someone asked J. P. Morgan, "When has a man made enough to be happy?" Morgan replied, with a faintly cynical smile, "When he has made the *next* million!"

✤ ✤ ✤

When Dwight L. Moody was about to start a series of evangelistic meetings in London, a nobleman said to him, "Sir, I hope that you will be able to do something for the miserable poor in London." Moody replied, "I hope so, my Lord. I hope also that I shall be able to do something for the miserable rich."

✤ ✤ ✤

WEATHER

The local weatherman was so often wrong in his predictions that he became the laughing stock of the community. He put up with the teasing for as long as he could possibly stand it. Then he requested a transfer to another station.

"Why," wrote headquarters, on receiving his request, "do you wish to be transferred?"

"Because," the forecaster wrote back, "the climate here doesn't agree with me."

✤ ✤ ✤

Summer was skipped entirely in 1816—"Eighteen-Hundred-and-Froze-to-Death," shivering Yankees dubbed it. There was frost or snow every month of the year as far south as the Ohio and Potomac Rivers; even in Norfolk, Virginia, ice was reported on the 16th of May.

Farmers wore overcoats, mittens and ear muffs to do their spring planting. A freeze in June, with six inches of snow blanketing New England, killed many lambs, all the vegetables and thousands of birds; there were five inches of snow in Pennsylvania.

Yet on June 23, Massachusetts sweltered in a three-day torrid spell, with temperatures to 101. By July 4 New Englanders again wore overcoats. Cold in August killed the New England corn. Dearth of corn meant a pork shortage, so salt mackerel became standard diet and 1816 acquired another name, "Mackerel Year." A brief spell of good weather in September, and it was winter again—or still. October brought 12 inches of snow in Massachusetts.

Scientists have since surmised that dust from the great volcanic explosions of 1815 in the Dutch East Indies had cut off the sun's rays.

But weather may make history. Discouragement and destitution caused by the "Year without a Summer" contributed materially to the great migration from New England in 1817 that established the Middle West.

—*Baltimore Sun.*

✤ ✤ ✤

A world-wide firm had branches everywhere, including one in the Sahara Desert. One day the manager received a letter from the Sahara branch, complaining that the employees were out of water.

He brought the complaint to the attention of the president of the company. That distinguished individual passed it off with a shrug. "Oh, those Sahara people are always complaining that they are out of water."

"Well," said the manager, "somehow I think they mean it this time. You see, the stamp is attached to the letter with a pin."

✤ ✤ ✤

WISDOM

A stooped old man and a brisk young man chanced to meet one day. The young man said to the older one, in his usual braggart way:

"Why don't you walk up straight like me? That's no way to grow old. It's all a form of habit—at least, that's what I'm told."

The old man gave him a knowing look, and said:

"My dear young friend, have you ever examined your fine wheat field, and noticed the heads that bend? If not, just look them over close, as the harvest time draws nigh. You'll find the heads that are quite empty are standing tall and high, but the heads that count in the harvest time are filled, and bending low, awaiting the reaper's bright sickle—their time is short, you know."

And as the young man passed on by, he slowly bowed his head. No doubt he pondered many a day on the things the old man said.

—*Old English tale.*

✤ ✤ ✤

WORK

One day Mr. Christoff was breaking a team of huge work horses to harness. Grandfather saw him come in from the field at noon with the two horses blowing like steam engines, dripping lather, and completely done out for the day. Like all unbroken horses, they were pulling unevenly and fighting the bit.

"Say," Grandfather hailed his neighbor, "that team looks pretty well tuckered out. Think they'll amount to anything?"

Mr. Christoff smiled ruefully and pushed his old hat back on his head. "Squire and Prince are just like people," he replied. "It is not doing the work that wears them out. It is fighting the work. When they learn to be willing, they make fine team."

—ROBERT KIRKENDALL, *Weekly Unity.*

✤ ✤ ✤

One of the world's greatest paintings is *The Angelus* by Millet. The word "angelus" means a prayer, and that picture is of two people praying in the field. On the horizon is the church steeple, and we presume the bell is ringing to call people to prayer.

To understand the true significance of the picture, however, you must study where the rays of the afternoon sun fall. They are not on the bowed heads of the man and woman, neither do the rays fall on the church steeple. They fall on the wheelbarrow and the common tools. It is the artist's tribute to the dignity of work.

—Dr. Charles L. Allen, of Atlanta, Georgia.

✤ ✤ ✤

A country in Europe isn't doing as well as its harder-working, more self-denying neighbor, Germany. A woman in that country, jealous of the Germans' prosperity and her own country's lack of it, declared, "We'd be all right if the Germans would only sleep later in the morning."

But she was wrong. Even borders, treaties, foreign aid, and International plans cannot change for long the rule that the more you produce, the more you will have; the less you produce, the less you will have, whether you are a nation, an industry, or an individual worker at a machine.

—Statement by Warner & Swasey, Cleveland.

✤ ✤ ✤

After a busy life, an old-time Yankee died. The first thing he knew, a butler in another world was showing him a palatial guest room, saying: "This, sir, is your suite. The only rule here is: You ring and I bring. Just press the button and I will provide whatever your heart desires."

About a month later, the Yankee sat in his easy chair surrounded by cigars, decanters, shotguns, fishing rods, radio, and all else that a man could wish. But there was fire in his eye. He jabbed the buzzer. The butler appeared.

"Here, you! I want something to do. I want WORK."

"Sorry, sir, but work is the only thing we do not provide here."

"What! If I can't have work, I would just as soon be in hell."

"But, sir," replied the butler, "where did you think you were?"

—Alex F. Osborn.

✤ ✤ ✤

When I was a child, my small brothers were expected to keep the vegetable garden weeded. Of course they hated the job, put it off as long as possible and usually had to spend their precious Saturdays doing it. An uncle who came to visit us sauntered into the garden and saw the boys scowlingly at work.

"Do you boys know why you are pulling those weeds?" he asked. "It's because they're robbers, stealing nourishment that belongs to the vegetables. Do you know how to get the best of them and still have plenty of time to play? Just divide the garden into six little farms—three apiece. (With sticks he marked off six plots.) Now each of you clear just one little farm every second weekday afternoon. It won't take long; you'll have your Saturdays and Sundays free; what's more you'll have the whole garden so neat that you'll be proud of it."

The rest of the summer it really was a picture garden, and the boys wondered why weeding had seemed such drudgery before.

My uncle taught the boys three lessons about how to tackle a hard job that stayed with them all their lives:

1. Picture the reason for doing a thing, and hold it before your eyes.
2. Visualize the job completed.
3. Break it into manageable pieces and tackle one piece at a time.

—Corinne Updegraff Wells, *Reader's Digest.*

✤ ✤ ✤

George Bernard Shaw once visited sculptor Jacob Epstein in the latter's studio. As they chatted, Shaw noticed a huge block of stone in a corner of the room.

"What is that for?" he asked.

"I don't know yet," said Epstein. "I'm still making plans."

"You mean you plan your work?" exclaimed Shaw. "You, an artist? Why, I change my mind several times a day!"

"That's all right with a four-ounce manuscript," replied Epstein, "but not with a four-ton block."

—*Milwaukee Journal.*

✤ ✤ ✤

A man in his late sixties applied for a job doing heavy manual work. The boss was short of men so he decided to give the old timer a chance. A few days later the boss summoned the new man to his office.

"The foreman tells me," he said cordially, "that you are the hardest working man in the crew. He says you work right through the lunch hour. Now I'd like to . . ."

"Excuse me," the new man broke in, "it's nice to hear this, but I must get back to work. You see, I was a loafer for sixty-five years—and now I've retired."

—*Troy* (N. Y.) *Times-Record.*

✤ ✤ ✤

There's the farmer who was asked what time he went to work in the morning.

"Son," he replied to the interrogator, "I don't go to work in the morning. I'm surrounded with it when I get up!"

✤ ✤ ✤

A playful executive at Northrup Aircraft posted this bulletin:

"To all Employees: Due to increased competition and a keen desire to remain in business, we find it necessary to institute a new policy. Effective immediately, we are asking that somewhere between starting and quitting time and without infringing too much on the time devoted to lunch period, coffee breaks, rest period, story telling, ticket selling, golfing, auto racing, vacation planning and rehashing of yesterday's tv programs that each employee try to find some time that can be set aside and be known as *The Work Break.*

"To some, this may seem to be a radical innovation, but we honestly believe the idea has great possibilities. It can conceivably be an aid to steady employment, and it might also be a means of assuring regular paychecks. *The Management."*

—Matt Weinstock, *Los Angeles Daily News.*

✤ ✤ ✤

Mrs. Jones had raised nine children on a Michigan farm, fed them and the farm hands, done all her housework and helped with outdoor chores. She'd never been ill a day in her life. A doctor asked her secret.

"I constantly see young women," he said, "who have only one or two children and whose homes are full of gadgets to lighten work, but who suffer from nervous exhaustion or psychosomatic aches and pains. How is it that you managed through all these years never to have a nervous breakdown?"

"You know, doctor," said the hard-working woman wistfully, "I've always wanted to have a nervous breakdown. But every time I was about to get around to it, it was time to fix somebody a meal."

—*Capper's Weekly.*

✤ ✤ ✤

There's a tale of an old man with two lazy sons. Nothing he could do would make them work. Before he died he confided to them that there was a crock of gold buried in one of the fields. " 'Tis no more than a foot and a half below the sod," he said. "Dig and you'll surely find it."

After the old man died, the sons began digging, in deep furrows, for they were afraid to miss the treasure. When they came to the last sod they hadn't found it. And their fine grass field ruined! "There's nothing we can do," said one, "only sow a few oats." So they sowed oats, and the money they made was worth more than any crock of gold. And that's how they learnt what comes of work.

—ROBERT GIBBINGS, *Lovely is the Lee* (Dutton).

✤ ✤ ✤

The laziest man I ever met had, in his youth, been a promising lawyer in a Maine village. But for almost 30 years now he had lived on occasional odd jobs. His chief pursuit had been sitting in front of the general store in summer and by the potbellied stove in winter, spinning yarns with passersby and customers. One day I asked him how he happened to drop his law career.

"Well," he said, "seemed the harder I worked the more I had to do. If I kept up that way I figured I'd finish with more not done than I had done, so I just quit while I was still ahead."

—JEFFERY S. THOMAS, in "Life in These United States."

✤ ✤ ✤

In a trim bungalow near Manhattan lived a rising young novelist and his wife, presided over by a Scandinavian servant whom everyone described as a gem. This paragon one day approached her mistress in tears and announced: "I must leave on the first of the month."

"But why?" demanded the housewife. "I thought you were perfectly happy here." It wasn't that, sobbed the maid; she had met a handsome soldier a few months before, and now—and now— "Don't do any thing until I've consulted my husband," said the wife. She was back from his study in a trice. "We have decided that you must stay," she announced. "We will adopt your baby."

In due course, a son appeared upon the scene, the author adopted him legally, and all was serene for another year, when the maid again announced she was leaving. This time she had met a sailor. The author and his wife went into another huddle, and the maid was told, "It is unfair to bring up a child alone. We will adopt your second baby."

The second baby was a darling little girl, and the bungalow resounded with happy laughter. Then the blow fell. The maid resigned again. "Don't tell me," gasped the wife, "that this time you met a Marine."

"It's not that at all, ma'am," said the servant with dignity. "I'm resigning because I simply cannot work for such a big family."

—BENNETT CERF, in *The Saturday Review.*

✣ ✣ ✣

Asked who had had the greatest influence on his life, Dr. Tyndall, the renowned scientist, credited an old man who had been his servant for many years. Every morning the old man would knock on the scientist's bedroom door and say, "It is seven o'clock, sir. Get up! You have great work to do today!"

—*Wall Street Journal.*

✣ ✣ ✣

The most destructive earthquake that ever occurred in these United States hit San Francisco with a terrific rumble on April 18, 1906. John Barrymore, originally reported missing, persuaded a newspaperman to include a message to his sister, Ethel, in a press wire to New York. John wrote imaginatively that he had been thrown out of bed by the earthquake, and had wandered half-conscious into the street, where a soldier had thrust a shovel into his hands and forced him to work for 24 hours in the ruins.

Ethel Barrymore read this dramatic bit of fiction to John Drew, her uncle, and asked if he believed it. He replied: "Every word. It took an act of God to get him out of bed and the U. S. Army to put him to work."

—Jo CHAMBERLIN, in *The Baltimore Sun.*

✣ ✣ ✣

Some years ago I was spending the summer in a part of Maryland not noted for the fertility of its soil. I stood watching an old patriarch laboring with his son and two granddaughters in a cabbage patch. It was hard to find the young plants among the rocks. I should have known better than to address the proud old Scot as I did:

"Tell me, what *can* you raise in these rocky hills?"

With a withering look at me he straightened. Slowly he wiped the back of one gnarled, sweated fist across the firm lips, and then he spat the answer:

"Men!"

—MURRAY L. WAGNER.

✣ ✣ ✣

Driving through Georgia, I was stopped in the middle of the road by a litter of pigs oozing through a gaping hole in a fence. A farmer sat on the bank nonchalantly watching. Exasperated with the delay, I asked him, "Why don't you repair that fence so your pigs will stay off the road?"

"Oh, 'tain't no use, mister," he answered deliberately. "In a few weeks the pigs will be so big they won't be able to git through that hole."

—W. B. WYNNE.

✣ ✣ ✣

An elderly southern gentleman of my acquaintance, long a widower, returned to his home with a bride 30 years his junior. His butler, who had been in the family many years, greeted the new mistress with what the bridegroom fancied was a lack of enthusiasm.

The next day my friend said, "Joseph, I'm depending on you to do everything you can to make my wife happy. Why are you so gloomy?"

"Well, sir," replied Joseph, looking with melancholy devotion at his master's well-lined face, "the new madam is a right pretty young lady, and I'll do my best. But it always makes me sorrowful to see a man begin a day's work in the afternoon."

—HARRY ROGERS PRATT.

✣ ✣ ✣

WORRY

When Sir William Osler was a young man in medical school at McGill University in Montreal, his talent for his chosen profession was exceeded only by his bent for worrying. He worried about his abilities. He worried about the obstacles which destiny seemed, with incredible cunning, to place between him and his career. With the abundant vitality of all young folk, Osler met the encroaching responsibilities of manhood head-on, wearily assuming that there was no burden not meant especially for his shoulders, no problem in all the world which was not invented specifically to make him lie awake nights, worrying.

It came to an end when Osler chanced to read a few simple words from the pen of Thomas Carlyle—words which made him a towering figure in the advance of medical knowledge to the day of his death in 1919.

"Our main business in life is to see not what lies dimly at a distance, but to do what lies clearly at hand."

—Property.

✣ ✣ ✣

It was a fine old bishop who, years ago, worrying his heart over what seemed to him the evils of a doomed world, tossing on his bed at midnight, thought he heard the Lord say, "Go to sleep, Bishop. I'll sit up the rest of the night."

—The Arkansas Methodist.

✣ ✣ ✣

"Fine crops," the visitor to Maine complimented a Down Easter. "You'll have nothing to worry about this year."

The farmer meditated a minute, then replied, "Well, you know, son, crops like these are pesky hard on the soil."

—*Family Herald and Weekly Star.*

✤ ✤ ✤

The young man had come to his father, weighed down with worry. "Leave your worries alone, son," the father advised, "and they will disappear. Let me illustrate with a story.

"Once there was a contented bee with never a care in the world. It entered a primrose in quest of nectar when a hungry horse cropped the blossom and the bee.

"In the darkness of the stomach the bee was worried and frightened. It decided to sting the stomach wall in an effort to escape. While searching for a good spot to drive the stinger the warmth and darkness of the stomach lulled it to sleep."

A smile appeared on the wise old face in contrast to the blank look on the son's features. "Do you know what happened when the worried bee woke up, son?"

With an irritated shrug of the shoulders, the son indicated that he didn't.

"Well, son, when the bee woke up, the horse was gone!"

—JOHN KRILL, *Magazine Digest.*

✤ ✤ ✤

Mrs. Silas Bennet was a philosopher. "I've raised four girls and three boys, expectin' everytime they'd be twins and red-headed like their Grandpa Bennet and yet they ain't.

"And I've worried considerable over small-pox breakin' out in my big family. So fer, 'taint.

"Last summer, I was real melancholic, fearin' I'd get an appendix. But I guess I ain't.

"And through it all, it never once't occurred to me that I'd be the one to fall through them rotten old meetin' house steps and break my legs in two places; but I be."

—*Sunday.*

✤ ✤ ✤

The late Fred Fuller Shedd had a gift for stating an old truth in a new and picturesque way. While addressing a college graduating class once, he asked, "How many of you have ever sawed wood? Let's see your hands." Most of them had. Then he inquired, "How many of you have ever sawed *sawdust?*" No hands went up.

"Of course, you can't saw sawdust!" Mr. Shedd exclaimed. "It's already sawed! And it's the same with the past. When you start worrying about things that are over and done with, you're merely trying to saw sawdust."

—DALE CARNEGIE, *Your Life.*

✤ ✤ ✤

A widow who had raised six children of her own, and adopted an even larger motherless brood, was asked how she had managed, on a limited income.

"It has been very simple," said the widow. "You see, I am in a partnership. One day, a long time ago, I said to the Lord, 'Lord, I'll do the work and You do the worrying.' I haven't had a worry since."

—HERB SHELDON.

✤ ✤ ✤

When I was a small boy in Denmark, studying geography, I was astounded one day to learn that there is enough water surrounding this earth to cover the whole sphere two miles deep. That thought was frightening to me—as I imagine the atom bomb must be to today's young people.

But as I grew older I realized that I didn't have to worry. I began to have faith that the world and man would survive. Our task each day is to do the best we can where we are, and let the earth take care of itself.

—JEAN HERSHOLT, in *You.*

✤ ✤ ✤

As a youngster I was so conscientious that I made myself miserable over minor tragedies of childhood. Early one fall, when we had had an exceptionally heavy snowstorm, my father took me for a drive. "Notice these elms," he said. "The branches are so badly broken that the trees may die. But look at the evergreens—undamaged by the snow.

"There are just two kinds of trees in the world: the stubborn and the wise. An elm holds its branches rigid, and trouble piles on until its limbs finally break, disfiguring the tree or killing it. But when an evergreen is loaded with more weight than it can hold, it simply relaxes, lowers its branches and lets the burden slip away. The next morning the evergreen is unharmed. Be a pine tree, daughter. Bear what you can, then let the rest of the load slide off."

That analogy, remembered in the midst of later troubles, saved me from becoming one of the world's gloomiest neurotics.

—FREDDA DUDLEY.

✣ ✣ ✣

A grandfather clock had just been finished. The clock, being in a rather philosophical mood, got to thinking about how many times it would tick if it lived for ten years. Realizing that it would tick twice every second, the clock knew it would tick 120 times every minute. In the course of an hour it would tick 7,200 times, while in the course of a day it would tick 172,800 times. Then it projected its thinking further in the future and knew that in a year it would tick 63,072,000 times. When it got to that high figure, it gave up with nervous exhaustion. But after twenty-five years it was still ticking the time away and was well on its way toward becoming a great-grandfather clock.